# Man Walks into a BAR

# Man walks into a BAR

## OVER 5,000 OF THE MOST HILARIOUS JOKES, FUNNIEST INSULTS, AND GUT-BUSTING ONE-LINERS

Stephen Arnott and Mike Haskins

ULYSSES PRESS

Published in the United States by:
ULYSSES PRESS
PO Box 3440
Berkeley, CA 94703
www.ulyssespress.com

First published in the United Kingdom in 2004 by Ebury Press,
an imprint of Ebury Publishing, Random House

ISBN: 978-1-64604-364-4
Library of Congress Control Number: 2022932767
Printed in the United States by Kingery Printing Company

30 29 28 27 26 25 24 23 22 21 20 19

Cover design: what!design @ whatweb.com
Cover illustration: John M. Duggan
Proofreader: Joyce Wu
Production: Yesenia Garcia-Lopez

# CONTENTS

"I thought today I'd start by singing one of Irving Berlin's songs. But then I thought why should I? He never sings any of mine."

*Spike Milligan*

# ACCIDENTS

✳ A doctor examines a cowboy with back problems and asks if he's had any recent accidents. "Nope," replies the cowboy. "That's odd," says the doctor, "I thought a cowboy's job was pretty dangerous." "It sure is," replies the cowboy. "Last week I was kicked by a mule, thrown by a mustang and bit by a snake." "And you don't call those accidents?" asks the doctor. "No, sir," replies the cowboy, "those varmints done it on purpose."

✳ A man goes into a bar and admires the stuffed lion's head mounted on the wall. "What a great trophy," says the man to the bartender. "I wouldn't call it great," replies the bartender. "That damn lion killed my wife." "My God," says the man, "were you on safari?" "No," replies the bartender. "It fell on her head."

✳ A man is laying carpet in an old lady's home. When he's finished, he looks around for his pack of cigarettes, but as he does so, he notices a lump in the middle of the carpet. "Damn it," he says to himself. "I must have dropped my cigarettes on the floor and carpeted over them. I know, I'll whack the pack with my hammer and flatten it out." So he gets out his hammer and beats the bump flat. Just at that moment the old lady walks in with his cigarettes in her hand. "Here," she says. "You must have left these in the kitchen. Now if only I could find my pet gerbil..."

✳ A man walked into a bar and went "Aaaagh!" It was an iron bar.

✳ A young man is trying out his new sports car on a quiet country lane. There's no traffic, so he risks taking it up to 70 mph, then 80, and then 90. He turns a corner and sees two farmers standing in the middle of the road chatting. The man wrenches the wheel sideways, the car shoots up an embankment, flies into the air, and crashes in the middle of an adjacent field. One of the farmers turns to the other and says, "That was lucky. I reckon we got out of that field in the nick o' time."

✳ Did you hear about the guy who lost his left arm and left leg in a car accident? He's all right now.

✳ Did you hear about the man who fell into the lens-grinding machine? He made a spectacle of himself.

✳ Harry heard that most accidents happen within two miles of home, so he moved.

✳ I lost my left hand in an accident a few years ago. It drives my girlfriend crazy. She's a palm reader and wants to know what happens next.

✳ Ten percent of all accidents on the road are caused by people who have been drinking. So ninety percent of accidents are due to people who are stone-cold sober.

❋ A woman and her boyfriend have just left a wild party and are speeding down a country lane in a sports car. The woman wants some fun and strips off her dress so she can flash passers-by. Unfortunately the man gets distracted and crashes the car. The naked woman is thrown clear, but her boyfriend is trapped in the wreckage. The only cover the woman can find is one of her boyfriend's shoes, so she holds it over her crotch and runs to a nearby garage. She sees a mechanic and shouts, "Help! Help! My boyfriend's stuck!" The mechanic looks at the shoe and says, "You're going to need a doctor, miss, he's too far in."

❋ Alabama's worst air disaster occurred early this morning when a small two-seater Cessna plane crashed into a cemetery. Search and rescue workers have recovered 1,826 bodies so far and expect that number to climb as digging continues.

❋ There's a terrible accident at a railway crossing when a train smashes into a car. No one is killed, but the car's driver takes the train company to court. At the trial, the railway engineer insists that he'd given the driver ample warning by waving his lantern back and forth for nearly a minute. The court believes his story and the suit is dismissed. "Congratulations," says the defense lawyer to the engineer. "You did superbly under cross-examination." "Thanks," replies the engineer. "But the prosecuting attorney sure had me worried." "How's that?" asks the lawyer. The engineer replies, "At one point I was afraid he was going to ask if that damned lantern was lit!"

# ACCOUNTANTS

❋ A convention to prove that accountants aren't stupid is set up in a massive stadium. Accountants from all over the world watch as the emcee calls up the first volunteer and asks him, "What is fifteen plus fifteen?" After 20 seconds the volunteer says, "Eighteen." Everyone is a little disappointed, but the accountants start yelling, "Give him another chance! Give him another chance!" The emcee says, "Well I guess we can give him another chance. What is five plus five?" After 30 seconds the volunteer says, "Ninety?" Everyone is crestfallen, but the accountants again start yelling, "Give him another chance! Give him another chance!" The emcee says, "Okay! One last chance. What is two plus two?" The accountant closes his eyes and after a whole minute eventually says, "Four." The accountants start yelling, "Give him another chance! Give him another chance!"

❋ A company director is interviewing candidates for an important position and decides to select the individual who can answer the question "How much is two plus two?" The first candidate is an engineer. He pulls out a slide-rule and shows that the answer is four. The second candidate is a lawyer. He states that, in the case of *Jones v. R.*, two plus two was proven to be four. The final candidate is an accountant. When asked what two plus two equals, the accountant slips out of his chair, checks to see if anyone is listening at the door, then whispers, "Did you have a particular number in mind?"

✳ A guy in a bar leans over to the man next to him and says, "Want to hear an accountant joke?" The man replies, "Well, before you tell that joke, you should know that I'm 6 feet tall, 200 pounds, and I'm an accountant. And the guy sitting next to me is 6 foot 2 inches tall, 225 pounds, and he's an accountant too. Now, do you still want to tell that joke?" The first guy says, "God, no. Not if I'll have to explain it twice."

✳ A patient is at her doctor's office after undergoing a physical examination. The doctor says, "I have some very grave news. You have only six months to live." "What can I do?" cries the patient. The doctor replies, "Marry an accountant." "Will that make my life longer?" asks the patient. "No," says the doctor. "But it will seem longer."

✳ An accountant goes into a pet store to buy a parrot. The store owner shows him three identical parrots on a perch. "The parrot on the left costs $500," says the owner. "Why does that parrot cost so much?" asks the accountant. "It knows how to do complex audits," says the store owner. "How much does the middle parrot cost?" asks the accountant. "That one costs $1,000," replies the owner. "It can do everything the first one can, plus it knows how to prepare financial forecasts." The accountant asks about the third parrot. It costs $4,000. "So what can that one do?" he asks. "To be honest," says the store owner, "I've never seen him do anything. But the other two call him Senior Partner."

✳ An accountant is walking down the street when he comes across a bum. "Spare some loose change?" asks the bum. "And why should I do that?" asks the accountant. "Because I'm broke. Haven't got a penny to my name and nothing to eat," says the bum. "I see," says the accountant. "And how does this compare to the same quarter last year?"

✳ How do accountants liven up their office parties? They invite an undertaker.

✳ Two accountants are in a bar when armed robbers burst in. The robbers line the customers up against a wall and proceed to take their wallets, watches, etc. The first accountant slips something in the second accountant's hand and whispers, "Here's that $50 I owe you."

✳ Two accountants go to the cemetery to pay their respects at the grave of a colleague. However, they search and search and can't find his tombstone anywhere. Eventually one turns to the other and says, "Perhaps he put it in the name of his last wife?"

✳ What is the difference between a tragedy and a catastrophe? A tragedy is a shipful of accountants going down in a storm. A catastrophe is when they can all swim!

✳ You know he's a really good tax accountant when he's got a loophole named after him.

✳ He was an extrovert accountant—he'd look at your shoes while he was talking to you rather than his own.

# ADVERTISING AND MARKETING

✳ There's a fine line between marketing and grand theft.

✳ A fried chicken magnate visits the Pope and tells him that he'll make a donation of two hundred and fifty million dollars if the Pope changes the Lord's Prayer from "Give us this day our daily bread" to "Give us this day our daily chicken." The Pope refuses, so the magnate raises the offer to three hundred million. The Pope still refuses, so the offer is raised to four hundred million, at which the Pope caves in and accepts. The Pope calls his cardinals together to tell them what's happened. "I've got some good news and some bad news," he says. "The good news is that we've just made four hundred million dollars. The bad news is we just lost the Wonder Bread account."

✳ I saw a subliminal ad on TV for a new deodorant—but it only keeps you dry for a second.

✳ There was an awards ceremony for commercials on TV last week. I fast-forwarded through the whole thing.

✳ When something is "new and improved"—which is it? If it's new, then there has never been anything before it. If it's an improvement, then there must have been something before it.

✳ The owner of a hardware store is dismayed when a huge new hardware store opens up next door, erecting a large sign saying "Best Deals." He's even more horrified when another huge hardware store opens up on the other side of his store, putting up an even larger sign saying "Lowest Prices." The shopkeeper is panicked then has a bright idea. He puts a large sign over his own store saying "Main Entrance."

✳ Advertising—the art of making whole lies out of half-truths.

✳ "Not one man in a beer commercial has a beer belly." *Rita Rudner*

# AGE: MIDDLE

✳ "Middle age is when your age starts to show around your middle." *Bob Hope*

✳ "She said she was approaching forty—I couldn't help wondering from what direction." *Bob Hope*

✳ After forty-five your "get up and go" gets up and goes.

✳ Maybe it's true that life begins at forty. But everything else starts to wear out, fall out, or spread out.

✳ The good news about being middle-aged is that the glass is still half-full. The bad news is that pretty soon your teeth will be floating in it.

✳ Harry has invented a bra for middle-aged women. He calls it the "sheep dog" because it rounds them up and points them in the right direction.

✳ She's not pushing forty—she's clinging on to it for dear life.

✳ The thing about being a middle-aged woman is that when you go for a mammogram, you realize it's the only time someone's ever going to ask you to appear topless in a film.

✳ Middle age is when broadness of the mind and narrowness of the waist change places.

✳ Middle age is when you choose a cereal because of its fiber content, not the free toy.

✳ Thirty is a nice age for a woman, especially if she happens to be forty.

✳ Once over the hill, you pick up speed.

✳ What's the difference between a clown and a man having a midlife crisis? The clown knows he's wearing ludicrous clothes.

✳ Middle age is when women stop worrying about being pregnant, and men start worrying they look like they are.

✳ Life not only begins at forty, it begins to show.

✳ In our twenties we don't care what the world thinks of us. In our thirties we worry about what the world thinks of us. In our forties we realize that nobody actually gives a damn about us.

# AGE: OLD

✳ "Everything that goes up must come down. But there comes a time when not everything that's down can come up." *George Burns*

✳ "How young can you die of old age?" *Steven Wright*

✳ "If you live to the age of a hundred, you have it made because very few people die past the age of a hundred." *George Burns*

✳ "I'm so old they've canceled my blood type." *Bob Hope*

✳ "In my lifetime I saw the Berlin Wall come and I saw it go. George Burns can say the same thing about the Ice Age." *Bob Hope*

✳ "I've got to watch myself these days. It's too exciting watching anyone else." *Bob Hope*

✳ A woman congratulates her aging father—"I'm so proud of you. I noticed that when you sneeze, you've finally learned to put your hand in front of your mouth!" "Of course I have," says the old man. "How the hell else can I catch my teeth?"

✳ "Middle age is when you go to bed at night and hope you feel better in the morning. Old age is when you go to bed at night and hope you wake up in the morning." *Groucho Marx*

✳ Age is a very high price to pay for maturity.

✳ "Three things happen when you get to my age. First your memory starts to go, and I've forgotten the other two." *Denis Healey*

✳ A doctor in an old people's home is discussing an elderly resident with one of the orderlies. "I'm worried about Mr. Jones," says the doctor. "He claims that when he goes to the bathroom God switches on the light for him, then switches it off again when he's finished. Do you think he's going senile?" "Nah," says the orderly. "He's just been peeing in the fridge again."

✳ "Nice to be here? At my age it's nice to be anywhere." *George Burns*

✳ A group of retirees is on a bus trip to the seaside when one of the old ladies comes up to the driver and complains she's been molested. The driver thinks she must be senile and tells her to sit down. Ten minutes later a second old woman totters to the front and makes the same complaint. He tells her to sit down too. Ten minutes later a third old lady screams she's been molested. The driver decides to investigate. He stops and walks to the back of the bus where he finds an old man on his hands and knees. "What are you doing down there?" asks the driver. "Looking for my toupee," says the old man. "Three times I thought I'd found it, but when I grabbed it, it ran away."

✳ A husband and wife wake up one morning. The husband leans over to kiss his wife on the cheek, but she says, "Don't touch me! I'm dead!" "What on earth are you talking about?" says the husband. "We're both lying here talking." The wife replies, "I know. But I'm definitely dead." "You can't be dead," replies her husband. "What in the world makes you think you're dead?" His wife replies, "I must be dead. I woke up this morning and nothing hurts!"

✳ A man in his nineties is watching a group of teenage girls. He turns to his friend and says, "I wish I were 20 years older." "Don't you mean 20 years younger?" "No, 20 years older. That way I wouldn't give a damn one way or another."

✳ Even though I'm old, I've definitely still got it. Trouble is, nobody wants it.

✳ An aging playboy visits his doctor after a lifetime of wine, women, and song. "Well," says the doctor. "The good news is you don't have to give up singing."

✳ A widower and a widow have been friends for years, and one day the widower decides it's time to pop the question. He takes the widow to dinner and finally gathers up the courage to say, "Will you marry me?" The widow answers, "Yes. Yes, I will." The meal ends and they go to their respective homes. The next morning the widower has a problem, he knew he asked the question, but did she say yes, or no? With trepidation, he calls her on the phone. "This is kind of embarrassing," he says. "But when I asked if you would marry me, what did you say?" The widow answers, "Why, I said, 'Yes, yes I will' and I meant it with all my heart." She continues, "I'm so glad you called, because I couldn't remember who'd asked me."

✳ An elderly couple are in a romantic mood. While sitting on their loveseat, the old lady says, "I remember when you used to kiss me every chance you had." The old man leans over and gives her a peck on the cheek. Then she says, "I remember when you used to hold my hand all the time." The old man reaches over and places his hand on hers. The old lady continues, "I can also remember when you used to nibble on my neck." The old man sighs, stands up, and starts to shuffle out of the room. "Where are you going?" asks the old lady. "To find my teeth," says the old man.

✳ A real estate agent is trying to sell a very old man a new home. "It would be a marvelous investment," says the agent. "You've got to be joking," says the old man. "At my age, I don't even buy green bananas."

✳ An old couple regularly attend church, and the pastor is impressed by how harmonious they seem. One day after church, the pastor approaches them to express his admiration. "I find it so inspirational to see how deeply in love you are," he says. "Even after all these years you still hold hands all through the service." The old woman replies, "That's not love, Pastor, I'm just keeping him from cracking his damn knuckles."

✳ An old man and an old woman are talking in an old folks' home. The man says, "I'm so old, I forgot how old I am." "I'll tell you how old you are," says the old woman. "Take off your clothes and bend over." The man does so, and the woman says, "You're seventy-four." The man is astonished. "How can you tell?" he asks. The woman replies, "You told me yesterday."

✳ Andy Williams goes to an old peoples' home to host a sing-a-long but is surprised to discover that none of the residents recognize him. Puzzled, he takes an old lady aside and says, "Excuse me, but do you have any idea who I am?" "Sorry dear," says the old lady. "But you ask one of the nurses, they'll tell you."

✳ An old man hobbles up to an ice cream van and orders a cone. "Crushed nuts, grandpa?" asks the salesman. "No," replies the old man. "Rheumatism."

✳ An old man says to his wife, "You know, I think it's time for us to have another baby." "Are you crazy?" says his wife. "Well, just think," he says. "I used to complain about having to get up at two o'clock in the morning to feed the baby, but these days I get up about that time anyway!"

✳ At the age of ninety-three, Mildred was distraught to be left a widow. She decided to end it all and join her husband in death. To make sure she did the job properly, she called her doctor and asked exactly where the human heart is located. She was told that the heart is just below the left breast. Hearing this she took her husband's revolver, placed it in the right spot, and fired. Half an hour later she was admitted to the hospital with a gunshot wound—to her left knee.

✳ Boy, to father: "Daddy, why does Grandma spend so much time reading the Bible?" Father: "Shhh, son. She's cramming for her finals."

✳ By the time a man is old enough to read a woman like a book, he's too old to start a library.

✳ Definition of old age in men: chasing after women, then forgetting why when they're caught.

✳ Eighty-year-old Bessie bursts into the recreation room of the men's retirement home. She holds her clenched fist in the air and says, "Anyone who can guess what's in my hand can make wild passionate love to me all night!" An elderly gentleman at the rear calls out, "An elephant?" Bessie thinks for a moment then replies, "Close enough!"

✳ It's a windy day and a little old lady is in the street holding on to her hat with both hands. A gust blows her skirts up revealing she has no underwear and she's arrested for indecent exposure. The judge says, "Madam, you should be ashamed of yourself, letting your skirt blow around, while you tried to save your hat." The old lady replies, "Why shouldn't I? Everything under my skirt is eighty years old—that hat was brand new!"

✳ I went to a school reunion the other day; sadly all my friends had become so fat and old no one could recognize me.

✳ Remember that age and treachery will always triumph over youth and ability.

✳ The older you get, the longer it takes you to get over a good time.

✳ The reason grandchildren and grandparents get along so well is because they have a common enemy.

✳ Three old ladies are discussing the problems of old age. One says, "Sometimes I find myself with a loaf of bread in my hand and can't remember whether I need to put it away or start making a sandwich." The second lady says, "Sometimes I find myself on the stair landing and can't remember whether I was going up or down." The third one says, "Well, my memory is perfect—knock on wood." She raps her knuckles on the wooden table, then says, "Just wait till I answer the door."

✳ Two elderly people who have been courting for years finally decide to get married. They go for a stroll to discuss the wedding plans and go into a drugstore. The old man goes up to the sales clerk and says, "Do you sell heart medication?" "Of course we do," says the clerk. "How about medicine for circulation?" asks the old man. The clerk replies, "All kinds." The old man continues, "How about medicine for rheumatism?" "We have that too," says the assistant. "How about Viagra?" asks the old man. "We do stock that," replies the clerk. "Got any medicine for the memory?" says the old man. The clerk replies, "Yes, we have a large selection of drugs to improve your mental faculties." "Okay," says the old man. "So what about vitamins and sleeping pills?" "Got lots," replies the clerk. "Perfect!" says the old man. "In that case we'd like to register here for our wedding gifts."

✳ Two old ladies are playing a game of cards. One lady looks up at the other and says, "We've known each other for so many years, but for the life of me, I just can't bring your name to mind. What was it again, dear?" There's silence for a few seconds, then the other lady replies, "How soon do you need to know?"

✳ Two old men are sitting in an old people's home when one of the female residents runs past completely naked. "What was that she was wearing?" asks the first. "Don't know," replies the second. "But it sure needed ironing."

✳ She was so old a fireman had to be in attendance every time she lit her birthday candles.

✳ A man buys his grandfather the services of a call girl on his ninetieth birthday. The girl arrives and says, "Hi. I'm here to give you super sex." "Oh thank you," replies the old man. "I'll have the soup please."

✳ A man visits his aunt in a nursing home. It turns out that she's taking a nap, so he sits by her bed, flips through a few magazines and munches on some peanuts in a bowl. Eventually the aunt wakes up, and her nephew notices he's finished the entire bowl of nuts. "I'm sorry, auntie, I've eaten all of your peanuts!" he says. "That's okay, dear," replies the aunt. "I don't really like them that much, not after I've sucked the chocolate off."

✳ A priest is visiting Old John on his ninety-fourth birthday. "John, to what do you attribute your marvelous age?" asks the priest. "Well," says Old John. "I reckon it's 'cuz I never touched a woman or a drop of drink in my whole life." Suddenly there's a crash and a scream from upstairs. "What was that?" asks the priest. Old John replies, "Oh that's Dad. He got wasted again and chased the au pair into the bedroom."

✳ An elderly man lies dying in his bed. In death's agony, he suddenly smells the aroma of his favorite chocolate chip cookies wafting up the stairs. He gathers his remaining strength, lifts himself from the bed, and slowly makes his way out of the bedroom. With labored breaths, he staggers down the stairs into the hall and gazes into the kitchen. Here, spread out upon racks on the kitchen table and counters are literally hundreds of his favorite chocolate chip cookies—a final act of love from his devoted wife, seeing to it that he leaves this world a happy man. Mustering one great final effort, the old man throws himself toward the table and lands on his knees. He reaches out a withered hand toward a tray of cookies—when "Whack!" it's suddenly struck with a spatula. "You stay out of those," says his wife. "Them's for the funeral."

✳ Be nice to your kids. They'll be choosing your nursing home.

✳ The older you get, the better you realize you were.

✳ Visitor, to old man: "Have you lived here all your life?" Old man: "I don't know; I haven't died yet."

✳ What happened when the old lady streaked through the flower show? She won first prize for Best Dried Arrangement.

✳ What's pink, smells of pee, and goes in, out, in, out? Granny doing the hokey-pokey.

✳ What's pink, wrinkly, and hangs out your pants? Your mother.

✳ She's so old she has Jesus's beeper number!

✳ Bert and Ethel got married yesterday. He's ninety-eight and she's eighty-seven. The guests didn't throw confetti; they threw vitamin pills.

✳ "I can remember when the air was clean and sex was dirty." *George Burns*

# AGE: YOU KNOW YOU'RE GETTING OLD WHEN...

✳ ...the end of your tie doesn't come anywhere near the top of your pants.

✳ ...the four-letter word for something two people can do together in bed is "read."

✳ ...the names in your little black book are mostly doctors.

✳ ...the candles cost more than the cake.

✳ ...you and your teeth no longer sleep together.

✳ ...you get the same sensation from a rocking chair that you used to get from a roller coaster.

✳ ...you can live without sex, but not without glasses.

✳ ...you have a party, and the neighbors don't even realize it.

✳ ...your back goes out more than you do.

✳ ...your ears are hairier than your head.

✳ ...you're asleep, but others worry that you're dead.

✳ ...you can't tell the difference between a heart attack and an orgasm.

✳ ...you sink your teeth into a steak—and they stay there.

✳ ...work is a lot less fun, and fun is a lot more work.

✳ ...the gleam in your eye is the sun hitting your bifocals.

✳ ...you start having dry dreams and wet farts.

# APATHY

✳ "Some mornings, it's just not worth chewing through the leather straps."
*Emo Phillips*

✳ Well, today was a total waste of makeup.

✳ What's the difference between ignorance and apathy? I don't know and I don't care.

# APPEARANCE

✳ A man says to his friend, "I hear your wife has a complexion like a peach." "She certainly has," says the friend. "She's all yellow and fuzzy."

✳ "How would you like to feel the way she looks?" *Groucho Marx*

✳ A man at the bar gave me a nasty look, I said, "Thanks, but I've got one already."

✳ Don't you love nature, despite what it did to you?

✳ A woman says to her husband, "Our neighbor says I've got the skin of an eighteen-year-old girl." "Yeah?" says the husband. "Well give it back. You're getting it all wrinkled."

✳ Boy, to friend: "What do you first notice in a girl?" Friend: "It depends which way she's facing."

✳ Christine has such beautiful eyes; the trouble is they're so lovely, they spend all their time looking at each other.

✳ Girl, to boyfriend: "Do you think I'm vain?" Boyfriend: "No. Why do you ask?" Girl: "Because girls as good-looking as me usually are."

✳ Is that your nose, or are you eating a banana?

✳ She was a nice girl, but her legs were very thin. In fact, the last time I saw a pair of legs like hers, someone had tied a message to one of them.

✳ The invisible man married an invisible woman. Their kids were nothing to look at.

✳ Time is a great healer, but a lousy beautician.

﹡ Why do more women pay attention to their appearance than to improving their minds? Most men are stupid, but few are blind.

﹡ Your teeth are like stars—they come out at night.

﹡ You're dark and handsome. When it's dark, you're handsome.

﹡ I think Tom was born upside down. His nose runs, and his feet smell.

﹡ Whatever kind of look you were going for, you missed.

﹡ I have the body of a god—Buddha.

# ARCHAEOLOGY

﹡ One man says to another, "Did you hear the joke about the archaeologist who had two skulls of Cleopatra, one as a young girl, and the other as a grown woman?" "No," says his friend. "Let's hear it then."

﹡ Some tourists in the Natural History Museum are looking at the dinosaur bones. One of them says to the guard, "Can you tell me how old these bones are?" "Three million and four years and six months," says the guard. "Good heavens," says the tourist. "How do you work out the age so precisely?" "Well," the guard answers, "they were three million years old when I first started working here. And that was about four and a half years ago."

﹡ Why was the archaeologist upset? His job was in ruins!

# ARGUMENTS

﹡ "I am not arguing with you—I am telling you." *James McNeill Whistler*

﹡ A woman has the last word in any argument—anything a man says after that is the beginning of a new argument.

﹡ For my anniversary, my wife let me do something I'd always dreamed of doing. She let me win an argument.

﹡ Never argue with an idiot—they drag you down to their level then beat you with experience.

✳ Ray has just reached his 110th birthday. A reporter comes to his birthday party and says, "Excuse me, sir, but how did you come to be so old?" Ray replies, "It's easy. The secret is never to argue with anyone." The reporter is not impressed. "That's insane!" he says. "It has to be something else—diet, meditation, or 'something.' Just not arguing won't keep you alive for 110 years!" Ray looks at the reporter and says, "Y'know, maybe you're right."

✳ She decided to bury the hatchet—between his shoulder blades.

✳ "I can't take it anymore," says a man to his friend. "It's my wife. Every time we have an argument, she gets historical!" "Don't you mean 'hysterical'?" says his friend. "No, I mean historical," replies the man. "Every argument we have, she'll go, 'I still remember that time when you...'"

✳ She was so angry with him she threw his clothes out of the window. Unfortunately he was wearing them at the time.

✳ After having a fight with his wife, a husband tries to make peace. "Why don't you meet me halfway?" he says. "I'll admit you're wrong if you admit I'm right."

# ART AND LITERATURE

✳ "From the moment I picked up your book until I laid it down, I was convulsed with laughter—someday I intend reading it." *Groucho Marx*

✳ "Hitler! There was a painter! He could paint an entire apartment in one afternoon. Two coats!" *Mel Brooks (The Producers)*

✳ "I'm writing a book. I've got the page numbers done, so now I just have to fill in the rest." *Steven Wright*

✳ A man finds an old violin and an oil painting in his attic and takes them to be valued. "You know what you've got here," says the antiques dealer. "A Stradivarius and a Rembrandt." "Wow!" says the man. "So they must be worth millions." "Unfortunately not," replies the dealer. "Rembrandt made the violin and Stradivarius painted the picture."

✳ A chicken runs into a library, goes to the main desk and says, "Book, bok, bok, boook." The librarian hands the chicken a book and it tucks it under its wing and runs out. A while later, the chicken runs back in, throws the book on the desk and says, "Book, bok, bok, bok, boook." Again the librarian gives it a book, and the chicken runs out with it. A few minutes later the chicken is back, and returns the book saying, "Boook, book, bok, bok, boook." The librarian gives the chicken a third book, but this time follows it as it runs out. The chicken runs down the street, through a park, and down to the river where a frog is sitting on the bank. The chicken holds up the book to the frog, saying, "Book, bok, bok, boook." The frog replies, "Read-it, read-it, read-it…"

❋ A critic is a legless man who teaches running.

❋ A man is on an operating table having his legs sawed off at the knee by a surgeon. "Of course," says the surgeon to the man, "this doesn't necessarily mean you'll be able to paint like Toulouse-Lautrec."

❋ A writer dies and Saint Peter offers him the choice of Hell or Heaven. To see what he has in store, Saint Peter takes him to Hell where rows of writers are chained to their desks being whipped by demons in a steaming dungeon. However, when they get to Heaven the writer is astonished to see that nothing has changed—rows of writers are chained to their desks in a steaming dungeon being whipped. "Hey!" says the writer, "this is just as bad as Hell!" "No, it's not," replies Saint Peter. "Up here you get published."

❋ A young man professed a desire to become a great writer. When asked to define "great," he said, "I want to write stuff that the whole world will read, stuff that people will react to on a truly emotional level, stuff that will make them scream, cry, howl in pain and anger!" He now works for Microsoft writing error messages.

❋ Always try to read stuff that will make you look good if you die in the middle of it.

❋ Artist, to critic: "So what's your opinion of my painting?" Critic: "It's worthless." Artist: "I know, but I'd like to hear it anyway."

❋ Dick is introduced to an author at a party. "My last book was incredibly difficult," the author says. "It took me over six years to complete." "I can sympathize," replies Dick. "I'm a slow reader myself."

❋ Of course Vincent Van Gogh was notoriously vague. Whatever you said to him just went in one ear—and straight out the same ear.

❋ "I read part of the book all the way through." *Samuel Goldwyn*

❋ She asked a famous artist if he would paint her in the nude. He said that was fine, but he'd have to keep his socks on otherwise he'd have nowhere to put his brushes.

❋ The pen is mightier than the sword, but only if the sword is quite small and the pen is really, really sharp.

❋ A man walks into a book shop and says, "Can I have a book by Shakespeare?" "Of course, sir," says the salesman. "Which one?" The man replies, "William."

✳ Tom, to Dick: "That's a great collection of books you've got there. But why are they on the floor? You should put up some shelves." Dick: "I would, but no one wants to lend me shelves."

✳ A woman goes into an art gallery and sees two still-life pictures. Both are of a table laid for lunch with a glass of wine, a basket of bread rolls and a plate of sliced ham. However, one picture is selling for $75 and the other for $100. Curious, she goes to the gallery owner and asks him what the difference is between the two pictures. The owner points at the $100 painting and says, "You get more ham with that one."

✳ A writer sends his manuscript to a publisher with a note saying "None of the characters in this story bear any resemblance to any person living or dead." The publisher sends back the book with a note saying "That's what's wrong with it."

✳ Harry took up writing as a profession and sold loads of stuff—his TV, his stereo, his furniture, his car…

# ART AND LITERATURE: FUNNY BOOKS

*A Young Man's Guide to Dating*—by Caeser Titly

*Bank Robbery*—by Xavier Muny

*Carpet Laying*—by Walter Wall

*Challenging Uncertainty*—by R. U. Shaw

*Costume Jewelry*—by Fay Kerings

*Dating Period Furniture*—by Anne Teak

*Dealing with Alcoholism*—by Carrie M. Holme

*Drop Your Shorts*—by Lucy Lastic

*Eating Cheap*—by Roland Marge

*Entertaining with Friends*—by Maude de Merryer

*Fun at the Fairground*—by Felix Ited

*Growing Vegetables*—by Tom R. Tow

*I Was a Failed Lion Tamer*—by Claude Bottom

*Improve Your Memory*—by Ivor Gott

*Keeping Caged Birds* — by Ken Airey

*Know Your Letters* — by Alf A. Bet

*Living With Large Families* — by Bertha Twins

*My Favorite Sandwich* — by Hammond Tonge

*My Political Memoirs* — by Liza Lott

*Reading Problems* — by Liz Dexia

*Sailing for Beginners* — by Abal C. Man

*She Stoops to Conquer* — by Eileen Dover

*Simple Tattoos* — by Marcus Alover

*The Big Book of Polish Jokes* — by Dai Laffin

*The Expectant Bride* — by Marius Ina Hurrie

*The Library Thieves* — by M. T. Shelves

*The Runaway Bull* — by Gay Topen

*The Stripper* — by Eva Drawsof

*The Typical Scot* — by Titus Canbee

*The World of Hairdressing* — by Aaron Floor

# ART AND LITERATURE: MUSEUMS AND GALLERIES

✳ "I went to the museum where they had all the heads and arms from the statues that are in all the other museums." *Steven Wright*

✳ "One time I went to an art gallery where all the work had been done by children. They had all the paintings up on refrigerators." *Steven Wright*

✳ An artist asks the gallery owner if there has been any interest in his paintings. "I have good news and bad news," the owner replies. "The good news is that a gentleman inquired about your work and wondered if it would appreciate in value after your death. When I told him it would, he bought all fifteen of your paintings." "That's wonderful," the artist exclaims. "What's the bad news?" The owner replies, "The guy was your doctor…"

✳ I was surprised to see they had a picture of me in the National Portrait Gallery—then I realized it was a mirror.

✳ A man goes to an art gallery and sees a painting that is a violent incoherent swirl of clashing colors. The artist happens to be in the gallery, so the man asks him where he got the idea for the painting. "I had no idea," replies the artist. "I merely painted to expel what was inside of me." "Really?" replies the man. "Well, next time try some indigestion pills."

# ART AND LITERATURE: WORLD'S SHORTEST BOOKS

*A Guide to French Hospitality*

*Amelia Earhart's Guide to the Pacific*

*Career Opportunities for History Majors*

*Different Ways to Spell Bob*

*Everything Men Know About Women*

*Everything Women Know About Men*

*Staple Your Way to Success*

*The Amish Phone Directory*

*The Australian Book of Foreplay*

*The Big Book of Tasty Bile Recipes*

*The Book of French Military Victories*

*The Engineers' Guide to Fashion*

*The Lawyers Code of Ethics*

*The Ronald Reagan Memoirs*

*The Very Best of German Humor*

*Things I Can't Afford by Bill Gates*

*Zagat's Guide to Cities Without a Starbucks*

# ASTROLOGY

✳ "I don't believe in astrology. I'm a Sagittarius and we're skeptical." *Arthur C. Clarke*

✳ He had to fill in a form. At the bottom where it said "Sign," he wrote "Pisces."

✳ A husband and wife are arguing. "We're just not compatible," says the wife. "I'm a Virgo, and you're a buffoon."

# AUDIENCES

✳ If all the world's a stage, where does the audience sit?

✳ The number of people watching you is directly proportional to the stupidity of your action.

✳ What is forty feet long, has eight teeth, and smells of pee? The front row at a Rolling Stones concert.

✳ What has 180 legs and no pubic hair? The front row of a Justin Timberlake concert.

# BATS

✳ A vampire bat comes flapping into its cave covered in fresh blood. All the other bats smell the blood and begin hassling him about where he got it. "Okay, follow me," he says and flies out of the cave with hundreds of bats behind him. Down through a valley they go, across a river and into a forest. Finally he slows down and all the other bats excitedly mill around him. "Now, do you see that tree over there?" he asks. "Yes, yes, yes!" scream the bats. "Good!" says the first bat, "because I didn't!"

# BATTLE OF THE SEXES

✳ Men and women should put their differences behind them—which is either physically impossible or very uncomfortable.

✳ "What would men be without women? Scarce, sir. Mighty scarce." *Mark Twain*

✳ Few women admit their age; few men act it.

✳ It's women's fault that men lie to them—they ask too many questions.

✳ Men are from Earth, women are from Earth. Deal with it.

✳ Nobody will ever win the battle of the sexes. There's too much fraternizing with the enemy.

✳ The Five Secrets to a Great Relationship: 1. It's important to find a man who works around the house, occasionally cooks and cleans, and has a job. 2. It is important to find a man who makes you laugh. 3. It is important to find a man who is dependable, respectful, and doesn't lie. 4. It is important to find a man who's good in bed and who loves to have sex with you. 5. It is important that these four men never meet.

✳ To be happy with a man, you must understand him a lot and love him a little. To be happy with a woman, you must love her a lot and not try to understand her at all.

✳ What's the difference between men and women? A woman wants one man to satisfy her every need. A man wants every woman to satisfy his one need.

✳ Why are women called "birds"? Because they tend to pick up worms.

✳ "Men like cars, women like clothes. Women only like cars because they take them to clothes." *Rita Rudner*

✳ Never tell a woman you're unworthy of her love. She knows.

✳ "If you think women are the weaker sex, try pulling the blankets back to your side." *Stuart Turner*

✳ There are two theories of arguing with women. Neither one works.

✳ If all men are the same, why does it take a woman so long to pick one?

# BATTLE OF THE SEXES: MEN

✳ "Don't try to teach men how to do anything in public. They can learn in private; in public they have to know." *Rita Rudner*

✳ "Give a man a free hand, and he'll try to put it all over you." *Mae West*

✳ "Men are those creatures with two legs and eight hands." *Jayne Mansfield*

✳ "Men do cry, but only when assembling furniture from Ikea." *Rita Rudner*

✳ A couple are lying in bed. The man says, "I'm going to make you the happiest woman in the world." The woman replies, "I'll miss you."

✳ All men are animals. Some just make better pets.

✳ Give a man an inch and he thinks he's a ruler. Give him 12 inches and he is a ruler.

✳ How can you tell if a man is sexually aroused? He's breathing.

✳ How do men define a "50-50" relationship? We cook—they eat. We clean—they dirty. We iron—they wrinkle.

✳ How do men sort their laundry? "Filthy" and "Filthy but Wearable."

✳ How do you get a man to stop biting his nails? Make him wear shoes.

✳ How do you scare a man? Sneak up behind him and start throwing rice.

✳ How does a man show he's planning for the future? He buys two cases of beer instead of one.

✳ How does a woman know her man is cheating on her? He starts bathing twice a week.

✳ How many men does it take to tile a bathroom? Two. If you slice them very thinly.

✳ Man: "I don't know why you wear a bra—you've got nothing to put in it." Woman: "You wear underwear, don't you?"

✳ Man, to woman: "Feel like a quickie?" Woman: "As opposed to what?"

✳ Men are proof of reincarnation—you can't get that dumb in just one lifetime.

✳ Men read maps better than women do because only men can understand the concept of an inch equaling a hundred miles.

✳ Once upon a time a female brain cell happened to end up in a man's head. The cell looked around nervously, but the place appeared deserted. "Hello?" she shouted, but there was no answer. "Is there anyone here?" she cried a little louder. Still no answer. Now the female brain cell started to feel scared and yelled, "Hello, is anyone there?" Then she heard a faint voice from far, far away. "Hello! We're all down here...!"

✳ Only a man would buy a $500 car and put a $4,000 stereo in it.

✳ Research shows most men sleep on the right side of the bed. Even when they're asleep they have to be right.

✳ Scientists have just discovered something that can do the work of five men—a woman.

✳ There are a lot of words you can use to describe men; strong, caring, loving—they'd be wrong, but you could still use them.

✳ What did God say after creating man? "I'm sure I can do better than that."

✳ What did God say after She made Eve? "Practice makes perfect."

✳ What do most men consider a gourmet restaurant? Any place without a drive-up window.

✳ What do you call a handcuffed man? Trustworthy.

✳ What do you call a man with 99 percent of his brain missing? Castrated.

✳ What do you call a man with half a brain? Gifted.

✳ What do you call an intelligent, good-looking, sensitive man? A rumor.

✳ What do you do with a bachelor who thinks he's God's gift to women? Exchange him.

✳ What do you instantly know about a well-dressed man? His wife is good at picking out clothes.

✳ What does it mean when a man is in your bed gasping for breath and calling your name? You didn't hold the pillow down long enough.

✳ What has eight arms and an IQ of 60? Four guys watching a football game.

✳ What makes a man think about a candlelit dinner? A power failure.

✳ What should a woman do if she saw her ex-husband rolling around in pain on the ground? Shoot him again.

✳ What's a man's definition of a romantic evening? Sex.

✳ What should you give a man who has everything? A woman to show him how to work it.

✳ What's a man's idea of doing housework? Lifting his legs so you can vacuum.

✳ What's a man's idea of foreplay? Half an hour of begging.

✳ What's the difference between a golf ball and a G-spot? A man will spend twenty or thirty minutes looking for a golf ball.

✳ What's the difference between a man and a condom? Condoms have changed. They're no longer thick and insensitive.

✳ What's the difference between government bonds and men? Bonds mature.

✳ What's the difference between a man and Bigfoot? One is covered with matted hair and smells awful. The other has big feet.

✳ What's the difference between a man and childbirth? One can be terribly painful and sometimes almost unbearable while the other is just having a baby.

✳ What's the difference between a new husband and a new dog? A dog is always happy to see you and only takes a month to train.

✳ What's the difference between a sofa and a man watching football? The sofa doesn't keep asking for beer.

✳ What's the one thing that all men at singles bars have in common? They're married.

✳ What's the one thing that keeps most men out of college? High school.

✳ What's the quickest way to a man's heart? Straight through the ribcage.

✳ What's the smartest thing a man can say? "My wife says…"

✳ Why are all "dumb blonde" jokes one-liners? So men can understand them.

✳ Why can't men get mad cow disease? Because they're all pigs.

✳ Why didn't the husband change the baby for a week? Because the instructions on the diapers said "18–40 lb."

✳ Why do men buy electric lawnmowers? So they can find their way back to the house.

✳ Why do men chase women they have no intention of marrying? For the same reason dogs chase cars they have no intention of driving.

✳ Why do men die before women? Who cares?

✳ Why do men like smart women? Opposites attract.

✳ Why is food better than men? Because you don't have to wait an hour for seconds.

✳ Why do men snore when they lie on their backs? Because their balls fall over their butts and they vapor-lock.

✳ Why do men whistle when they're sitting on the toilet? Because it helps them remember which end they need to wipe.

✳ Why is a man like a moped? They're both fun to ride until your friends see you with one.

✳ Why is it difficult to find men who are sensitive, caring, and good-looking? They already have boyfriends.

✳ Why is psychoanalysis quicker for men than for women? When it's time to go back to childhood, he's already there.

✳ Why is sleeping with a man like a soap opera? Just when it's getting interesting, they're finished until next time.

✳ Why would men like to vote for a female president? Because they think they'd only have to pay her half as much.

✳ Why would women be better off if men treated them like cars? At least they'd get a little attention every six months or 50,000 miles, whichever came first.

✳ "Men are self-confident because they grow up identifying with superheroes. Women have bad self-images because they grow up identifying with Barbie." *Rita Rudner*

✳ Grow your own dope—plant a man.

✳ How do you keep a man from reading your e-mail? Rename the mail folder "Instruction Manuals."

✳ Husband, to wife: "Why can't I tell when you have an orgasm?" Wife: "Because you're never at home when it happens."

✳ What's easier to make, a snowman or a snowwoman? A snowwoman. With a snowman you have to hollow out the head and pack all that extra snow into balls to make its testicles.

✳ Men are all the same—they just have different faces so you can tell them apart.

✳ The one thing my husband is good for, he's not good at!

✳ What do a clitoris, an anniversary, and a toilet have in common? Men always miss them.

✳ What do you call a man who's just had sex? Anything you like—he's asleep.

✳ What is a man? A life-support machine for a penis.

✳ What's the best way to kill a man? Put a naked person and a six-pack in front of him. Then tell him to pick only one.

✳ What's the difference between a single forty-year-old woman and a single forty-year-old man? The forty-year-old woman thinks of having children. The forty-year-old man thinks about dating them.

✳ When do you care for a man's company? When he owns it.

✳ Why do doctors slap babies' butts when they're born? To knock the penises off the smart ones.

✳ Why do men become smarter during sex? Because they are plugged into a genius.

✳ Why do men have a hole in their penis? So oxygen can get to their brain!

✳ Why do men like frozen microwave dinners so much? They like being able to both eat and make love in under five minutes.

✳ Why do so many women fake orgasm? Because so many men fake foreplay.

✳ Why does it take 100 million sperms to fertilize one egg? Because not one will stop and ask for directions.

✳ Why don't women have men's brains? Because they don't have penises to keep them in.

✳ Why is Colonel Sanders like the typical male? All he's concerned with is legs, breasts, and thighs.

✳ Women might be able to fake orgasms. But men can fake whole relationships.

✳ Women's faults are many. Men only have two faults: everything they say and everything they do.

✳ How can you tell the difference between men's real gifts and their guilt gifts? Guilt gifts are nicer.

✳ Behind every successful man stands a surprised mother-in-law.

# BATTLE OF THE SEXES: MEN (SIMILES)

✳ Men are like animals—messy, insensitive, and potentially violent—but they make great pets.

✳ Men are like bank accounts—without a lot of money, they don't generate much interest.

✳ Men are like bike helmets—handy in an emergency, but otherwise they just look silly.

✳ Men are like blenders—you need one, but you're never quite sure why.

✳ Men are like high heels—they're easy to walk on once you get the hang of it.

✳ Men are like horoscopes—they always tell you what to do, and they are always wrong.

✳ Men are like lawnmowers—hard to get started, they emit noxious odors, and half the time they don't work.

✳ Men are like mascara—they usually run at the first sign of emotion.

✳ Men are like miniskirts—if you're not careful, they'll creep up your legs.

✳ Men are like parking places—all the good ones are taken, and the rest are handicapped.

✳ Men are like popcorn—they satisfy you, but only for a little while.

✳ Men's brains are like the prison system—not enough cells.

✳ Men are like lava lamps—fun to look at, but not all that bright.

✳ Men are like linoleum—lay them right once and you can walk all over them for the next 20 years.

✳ Men are like pantyhose—they either cling, run, or don't fit right in the crotch!

✳ Men are like public toilets—all the good ones are engaged and the only ones left are full of crap.

✳ Men are like women—both of them distrust men.

# BATTLE OF THE SEXES: WOMEN

✳ "I know I'm not gonna understand women. I will never understand how you can take boiling-hot wax, pour it on to your upper thigh, rip the hair out by the root—and still be afraid of a spider." *Jerry Seinfeld*

✳ "That woman speaks eighteen languages and can't say 'no' in any of them." *Dorothy Parker*

✳ "Women: You can't live with them, and you can't get them to dress up in a skimpy Nazi costume and beat you with a warm squash." *Emo Phillips*

✳ Men wake up as good-looking as they went to bed. Women somehow deteriorate during the night.

✳ Adam asks God for a mate. God replies, "You shall have the best of all companions— woman. She will be beautiful, and intelligent, and good-natured. She will cook for you, clean for you, and take care of your every need without complaint. Your life will be one of undiluted pleasure." "Sounds good," says Adam. "What do I have to do to get her?" God replies, "You must give up an arm, a leg, a kidney, a rib, and your left eye." Adam thinks for a second, then says, "And what do I get for just a rib?"

✳ An airplane is about to crash. A female passenger jumps up and shouts, "If I'm going to die, I want to die feeling like a woman." She strips off her clothes and says, "Is there someone on this plane who's man enough to make me feel like a woman?" A male passenger shouts, "Yes, me!" He stands up, tears off his shirt, and says, "Here, iron this!"

✳ In the beginning, God created the earth and rested. Then God created man and rested. Then God created woman. Since then, neither God nor man has rested.

✳ "Men don't feel the urge to get married as quickly as women because their clothes all button and zip in the front. Women's dresses usually button and zip in the back. We need men emotionally and sexually, but we also need men to help us get dressed." *Rita Rudner*

✳ "Intuition: the strange instinct that tells a woman she's right, whether she is or not." *Oscar Wilde*

✳ I haven't spoken to my wife for 18 months—I don't like to interrupt her.

✳ In an average day a man speaks 35,000 words and a woman speaks 30,000. Unfortunately, by the time I get home, I've done my 35,000, and she hasn't even started on her 30,000.

✳ My son must get his brains from his mother—I still have mine.

✳ The geography of a woman: between the ages of fifteen and eighteen, a woman is like China. Developing fast with a lot of potential, but as yet still not free or open. Between the ages of eighteen and twenty-one, a woman is like Africa. She's half discovered, half wild, and naturally beautiful. Between the ages of twenty-one and thirty, a woman is like America. Completely discovered, very well developed, and open to trade, especially with countries with cash or cars. Between the ages of thirty and forty, she's like India. Very hot, relaxed, and convinced of its own beauty. Between the ages of forty and fifty, she's like Iraq. She lost the war and is haunted by past mistakes. Massive reconstruction is now necessary. Between the ages of fifty and sixty, she's like Canada. Very wide, quiet, and the borders are practically unpatrolled, but the frigid climate keeps people away. Between the ages of sixty and seventy, a woman is like Mongolia. With a glorious and all-conquering past, but alas no future. After seventy, they become Albania. Everyone knows where it is, but no one wants to go there.

✳ The three ages of woman: at twenty-five they are attractive. At thirty-five they are attentive. At forty-five they are adhesive.

✳ There are three types of women; the intelligent, the beautiful, and the majority.

✳ Two men are admiring a famous actress. "Still," says one. "If you take away her beautiful hair, her fantastic breasts, her eyes, her perfect features, and her stunning figure—what are you left with?" The other replies, "My wife."

✳ What is love? The delusion that one woman differs from another.

✳ What's the difference between a battery and a woman? A battery has a positive side.

✳ Two girlfriends are on vacation when they see a five-story store advertising men for sale. They go in and see a first-floor sign that reads "All the men on this floor are short and ugly." The women decide to take the elevator to the next floor. There the sign reads "All the men here are short and handsome." This isn't good enough, so the women continue up. On the third floor the sign reads "All the men here are tall and ugly." The women want to do better so they keep going. On the fourth floor the sign reads "All the men here are tall and handsome." The women get excited but decide to see what's on the fifth floor. There they find a sign that reads, "No men here. This floor was built to prove there's no way to please a woman."

✳ What's the difference between PMS and BSE? One's mad cow disease and the other is an agricultural problem.

✳ Why are middle-aged women like MTV? They get turned on about once a month, and you've had enough after about fifteen minutes.

✳ Why did God create Adam first? So he'd have a chance to talk before Eve came along.

✳ Why did God create man before woman? He didn't want any advice.

✳ Why do men die before their wives? They want to.

✳ Why do women close their eyes while they are having sex? They can't stand to see a man having a good time.

✳ Why do women live longer than men? Because they don't have wives.

✳ Women like silent men—they think they're listening.

✳ A psychiatrist and a friend are sitting in a restaurant. The psychiatrist points at one of the other diners. "See that man over there. He claims to understand women." "Is he a colleague of yours?" asks the friend. "No," replies the psychiatrist. "He's one of my patients."

✳ Many women believe that a man's ultimate fantasy is to have two women at once. This is true, but one woman is cooking, and the other is cleaning.

✳ Why do men fart more than women? Because women won't shut up long enough to build up sufficient pressure.

✳ Three words women hate to hear when having sex? "Honey, I'm home!"

✳ Why can only 30 percent of women get into heaven? Because if it were more, it would be hell.

✳ Why do women have orgasms? It gives them an extra reason to moan.

✳ Why do women have tits? So men will talk to them.

✳ Yesterday scientists revealed that beer contains small traces of female hormones. To prove their theory, the scientist fed one hundred men twelve pints of beer each and observed that all the men gained weight, talked excessively without making sense, became emotional, couldn't drive, couldn't think, and refused to apologize when wrong.

✳ How do you fix a woman's watch? No need. There's a clock on the oven.

✳ How many men does it take to fix a vacuum cleaner? Why the hell should we fix it? We don't use the damn thing.

✳ How many men does it take to open a can of beer? None, it should be open when she brings it to you.

✳ How many women does it take to change a light bulb? None, they just sit in the dark and bitch.

✳ If a motorcyclist runs into a woman, who's to blame? The motorcyclist—he shouldn't have been riding in the kitchen.

✳ If you go to bed nine hours before you have to wake up, and your wife wants to have two hours of sex, how much sleep will you get? Eight hours, fifty-nine minutes—who cares what she wants!

✳ What do you do if your boiler explodes? Buy her some flowers.

✳ What's the one thing worse than a male chauvinist? A woman who won't do as she's told.

✳ Why do women have smaller feet than men? So they can stand closer to the stove.

✳ Why does the bride always wear white? Because it's always a good idea to have the dishwasher match the stove and refrigerator.

✳ Why shouldn't you pick up women in laundromats? Because if she can't even afford a washing machine, how the hell is she going to keep you in beer?

# BEARS

✳ A Canadian park ranger is giving some hikers a warning about bears: "Brown bears are usually harmless. They avoid contact with humans, so we suggest you attach small bells to your backpacks and give the bears time to get out of your way. However, grizzly bears are extremely dangerous. If you see any grizzly-bear droppings leave the area immediately." "So how do we know if they're grizzly-bear droppings?" asks one of the hikers. "It's easy," replies the ranger. "They're full of small bells."

✳ Two men go out for a walk in the forest when they see a bear. The first takes off his backpack, takes out a pair of Nikes, and puts them on. The other looks at him and says, "That's pretty stupid. You can't outrun a bear!" "That's true," says his friend. "But then again, I only need to outrun you."

✳ Why are bears large, brown, and hairy? Because if they were small, round, and white they'd be eggs.

✳ Why do polar bears have fur coats? Because they would look silly in parkas.

# BEAUTY TREATMENT

✳ "Gosh. You look nice," he said. "It must have taken you ages."

✳ Beauty comes from within. From within bottles, jars, tubes, compacts…

✳ Every night my wife puts a mudpack on her face and curlers in her hair. It doesn't help though. I can still tell it's her.

✳ Jill hears that milk baths will make her beautiful, so she leaves a note for her milkman asking for 15 gallons of milk. When the milkman reads the note, he thinks there must be a mistake so he knocks on the door. Jill answers and the milkman says, "I found your note to leave 15 gallons of milk. Did you mean 1.5 gallons?" Jill replies, "No. I want 15 gallons. I'm going to fill my bathtub with milk." "Pasteurized?" asks the milkman. "No," says Jill. "Just up to my boobs."

✳ Modern women put on wigs, fake eyelashes, false fingernails, sixteen pounds of assorted makeup/shadows/blushes/creams, push-up bras, various pads, have plastic surgery, then complain they cannot find a "real" man.

✳ My wife is as beautiful today as the day I married her—it just takes her fifteen minutes longer each morning to get there.

✳ My wife tried a mudpack to make herself more attractive. It worked for a while, but then it fell off.

✳ A small boy is watching his big sister put cold cream on her face. "Why are you doing that?" he asks. "To make myself more attractive," replies his sister. The small boy comments as she wipes it off, "Didn't work, did it?"

✳ How do you make six pounds of fat look attractive? Put a nipple in the middle of it.

✳ Some wives get their good looks from their mothers. Mine gets hers from the pharmacist.

# BEDS

✳ Do you want to hear the joke about the bed? Well you can't, it hasn't been made yet.

# BIRDS

✳ A chicken and an egg are lying in bed next to each other. The chicken is smoking a cigarette and the egg is looking annoyed. "Well," says the egg, "I guess that answers that question!"

✳ A couple of parrots are sitting on a perch. One says to the other, "Can you smell fish?"

✳ A man buys a parakeet but is disappointed when it doesn't speak. He goes back to the pet shop, where the owner suggests getting the parakeet a mirror to play with. This doesn't make the parakeet any more talkative, so the pet shop owner next suggests buying it a cuttlefish bone. The bone has no effect either, so the owner suggests the man buys the parakeet a bell and a ladder. Finally, the man returns to the pet shop and announces he's had success. "The parakeet looked in the mirror," says the man. "It pecked at the cuttlefish, climbed the ladder, rang the bell, then said a few words, and fell dead off its perch." "Oh dear," said the pet shop owner, "What did it say?" The man replies, "It said, 'Hasn't that shop got any damn bird seed?'"

✴ A Frenchman with a parrot perched on his shoulder walks into a bar. The bartender says, "Wow, that's really lovely. Where did you get him?" "In France," replies the parrot. "They've got millions of 'em."

✴ A man goes into a pet shop and sees a duck tap-dancing on an upturned flowerpot. The man buys the duck for a five spot and takes it home. The next day he calls the pet shop to complain. "This duck has been sitting on my kitchen table for hours," says the man. "It hasn't danced a single step." The pet shop owner replies, "Did you remember to light the candle under the flowerpot?"

✴ A man goes to an auction and bids for a parrot. The man starts the bidding at $10 then another bidder goes to $20. The man bids to $40 and the other bidder raises it to $60. The man is running out of cash but puts in a final bid of $70 and wins the parrot. "For all that money I hope the damn parrot can talk," says the man to the auctioneer. The auctioneer replies, "Of course it can. Who d'you think you were bidding against?"

✴ A woman buys a beautiful parrot, but the only phrase it knows is "Who is it?" She takes the parrot home but soon realizes that the bird's color clashes with her living-room decor, so she calls a decorator to create a new color scheme. However, by the time the decorator turns up, the woman has gone out shopping. The decorator knocks on the door and the parrot says, "Who is it?" The man says, "It's the decorator." The parrot says, "Who is it?" The man repeats, "It's the decorator." The parrot says, "Who is it?" The man yells, "It's the decorator!" The parrot says, "Who is it?" The man screams, "I said, it's the decorator…!" The decorator gets so mad he pops a blood vessel and dies on the spot. The woman comes home and finds a dead man lying on her front porch. She says, "Oh my goodness! Who is it?" The parrot replies, "It's the decorator!"

✴ A woman walks past a pet shop every day and every day she is abused by a parrot in the window. "Hey, ugly! Put a bag over your head!" shouts the parrot, or "Hey, lard-ass! Lose some weight, why don't you!" Eventually the woman has enough and threatens to sue the pet shop owner if the parrot continues to harass her. In turn the pet shop owner threatens to wring the parrot's neck if it doesn't behave. The next day the woman walks past the shop and the parrot shouts, "Hey, lady!" "Yes?" shouts back the woman, "What is it?" The parrot glares at her and hisses, "You know!"

✴ Each evening, bird lover Tom stood in his backyard, hooting like an owl and, one night, an owl finally called back to him. For a year, the man and his feathered friend hooted back and forth. He even kept a log of their "conversations." Just as he thought he was on the verge of a breakthrough in interspecies communication, his wife had a chat with her next-door neighbor. "My husband spends his nights calling out to owls," she said. "That's odd," the neighbor replied. "So does mine."

✳ In his spare time, my granddad races pigeons. I don't know why, he never beats them.

✳ Mrs. Evans can't tell which of her two parakeets is the male, so a friend suggests waiting till they are "doing the business" then putting a collar on the bird on top. The idea works and the male parakeet is collared. A few days later, the priest comes over for tea. The parakeet eyes him and says, "Caught you too did they, pal?"

✳ Tim goes into a pet shop and asks for a big bag of bird seed. "How many birds have you got?" asks the shopkeeper. "None," replies Tim. "I was hoping to grow some."

✳ Two men are walking down the street. One says to the other, "Oh dear! Look at that dead bird." His friend looks up in the sky and says, "Where?"

✳ What do you call a duck that's been dead for a week? A humming bird.

✳ What d'you call a woodpecker with no beak? A headbanger.

✳ When your pet bird sees you reading the newspaper, does he wonder why you're sitting there, staring at carpeting?

✳ Which side of the chicken has the most feathers? The outside.

✳ Why do birds fly south in the winter? Because it's too far to walk.

✳ Why do chicken coops have two doors? Because if it had four doors it'd be a chicken sedan.

✳ Why do owls avoid making love in a storm? Because it's too wet to woo.

✳ Why does a flamingo lift up one leg? Because if it lifted up both it would fall over.

✳ Why was the parrot wearing a raincoat? So it would be poly-unsaturated.

✳ A man buys a parrot but discovers too late that it is extremely foul mouthed and bad tempered. The bird keeps shouting obscenities at the man, who is forced to lock it in his garden shed to try to shut it up. This doesn't work, and he can still hear the filthy-mouthed bird from the house. In desperation, the man retrieves the parrot and shuts it in a cupboard, but the bird still keeps screaming at him, and now the neighbors are starting to complain about the noise. As a last resort, the man shoves the parrot into the fridge. Miraculously the parrot suddenly shuts up, so the man takes the bird out of the fridge and puts it back on its perch. The parrot then apologizes for its appalling behavior and asks to be forgiven. "That's okay," says the man. "As long as you don't do it again." "I won't," says the parrot, casting a nervous eye at the fridge. "By the way...what did the chicken do?"

✳ A man suspects his wife of cheating on him, so he decides to buy a parrot that will tell him what she's up to when he's away. The man goes into a pet shop but is told that the only talking parrot they have is legless. "How does he stay on his perch without legs?" asks the man. "He's got a really long penis," says the shop keeper. "He wraps it around the perch." The man decides to buy the parrot and takes it home. In the following weeks he comes home every day and asks the parrot if his wife has been cheating on him. Every day he gets the same answer, "Nothing doing." This goes on for weeks, until one day the man comes home and finds the parrot lying on the floor. "What happened?" asks the man. "A lot," replies the parrot. "First your best friend came over. Then your wife made him breakfast. Then they started kissing. Then your wife took off her blouse. Then your wife took off her skirt. Then your wife took off her underwear." "And what happened then?" asks the man. "And then I fell off my perch," says the parrot.

✳ A religious woman inherits two female parrots that have been trained to say one phrase over and over again—"I'm a whore, I'm a whore…" She asks her minister if she should give up her foul-mouthed birds, but the minister has a solution. "I have two well-behaved male parrots who sit in their cages and pray all day long," he says. "Perhaps if we put your birds in with mine, your birds will see the error of their ways and become more pious." The next day the woman takes her parrots to the minister's house and puts them in with the praying parrots. After a few seconds the female parrots start saying "I'm a whore, I'm a whore…" One of the male parrots turns to the other and shouts, "See! I told you this praying would work!"

✳ Harry pins a warning sign to his front door saying "Beware of the parakeet." A passerby sees this and says, "Excuse me, but I didn't know parakeets could be dangerous." "They're not," says John. "But this one can whistle for the Rottweiler."

✳ What's a polygon? A dead parrot!

✳ Why do seagulls fly over the sea? Because if they flew over the bay, they'd be bagels.

✳ A priest visits a little old lady who has just moved into his parish and finds she has a parrot with blue ribbons tied to both legs. "And what are these ribbons for?" asks the priest. "Well," says the old lady, "If I pull the left ribbon, he sings, 'Abide With Me' and if I pull on the right ribbon, he sings 'All Things Bright and Beautiful.'" "And what happens if you pull both ribbons at the same time?" inquires the priest. "I fall off the stupid perch!" says the parrot.

✳ A man in a passenger jet finds himself sitting next to a parrot. The man calls over a flight attendant and asks for a coffee. The parrot screeches, "And while you're there, get me gin and tonic, you fat cow!" A few moments later the flight attendant returns with the parrot's drink. Again the man asks for a coffee. The parrot screeches, "And while you're at it, get me some peanuts, you stupid old tramp." The flight attendant hurries away and comes back with the parrot's peanuts. The man asks where his coffee is, but the parrot screeches, "Now get me a glass of water, you old hag!" The flight attendant quickly brings the parrot a glass of water. By now the man is annoyed at not getting his coffee after asking three times, so he decides to act like the parrot, "Listen, you moron!" he shouts. "Get me some damn coffee pronto!" The flight attendant has had enough. She calls over two flight attendants, and the man and the parrot are thrown out of the plane. As the man and the parrot plummet toward the ground, the parrot says, "Well, you've certainly got a lot of guts for someone who can't fly."

✳ My wife has Parrot's Disease—she repeats everything she hears.

✳ A chicken crossing the road is poultry in motion.

✳ Why are woodpeckers smarter than chickens? Ever heard of a Kentucky Fried Woodpecker?

✳ An old lady buys a parrot, but it refuses to say a word. Three years pass and the parrot remains silent until, one day, the old lady gives it an apple. "Oh my God!" shouts the parrot. "There's a damn maggot in it!" "Good heavens," says the old lady. "All these years without speaking. Why have you started now?" "Well," replies the parrot. "Until today the food has been pretty good."

# BIRTH

✳ "I must confess, I was born at a very early age." *Groucho Marx*

✳ "I was born by cesarean. You can't usually tell, but whenever I leave my house I go out by the window." *Steven Wright*

✳ A boy is given some homework on childbirth. He goes to his mother and says, "How was I born?" "Well, honey," says the embarrassed mother, "the stork brought you to us." "Oh," says the boy. "And how did you and Daddy get born?" "Oh, the stork brought us too," says the mother. "Well how were Grandpa and Grandma born?" the boy persists. "Well darling, the stork brought them too!" says the frustrated mother. A few days later the boy hands in his homework with the following opening sentence, "This report has been very difficult to write due to the fact that there hasn't been a natural childbirth in my family for three generations."

✳ A Catholic couple, trying for a baby, ask their priest to pray for them. "I'm going to Rome for a few months," says the priest, "while I'm there I'll light a candle for you at the altar of Saint Peter." The priest comes back nine months later and finds the women has given birth to quintuplets. "Praise be to God," says the priest, "but where has your husband gone? I heard he left the country." "So he did, Father," says the woman. "He flew to Rome to blow your damn candle out."

✳ A Catholic woman has had six children in five years and is tired of being pregnant. She goes to a priest who advises her to spend every night sleeping in a chair with her feet in a 10-gallon bucket of water. The woman is puzzled by this advice but agrees to follow it. Three months later the woman comes back and tells the priest that she's pregnant again. "And did you do as I suggested?" asks the priest. "Yes and no," replies the woman. "I put my feet in water, but I couldn't find a 10-gallon bucket. I put them in two 5-gallon buckets instead."

✳ A little girl says to her mommy, "Mommy, you're getting really fat!" "Yes," replies mommy. "But remember, Mommy has a baby growing in her tummy." "I know that," says the little girl. "But what's growing in your ass?"

✳ A guy phones the local hospital and yells, "You've gotta send help! My wife's in labor!" The nurse says, "Calm down. Is this her first child?" He replies, "No! This is her husband!"

✳ I was born two days premature, which means, all my life, I've been able to send mail second class and it gets there the same time as if I'd gone to full term and sent it first class.

✳ Jane has a baby each year because she doesn't want the youngest one to get spoiled.

✳ My father died during childbirth. He was run over by the ambulance carrying my mother to the hospital.

✳ She was a very busy woman. In fact, she was too busy to attend the birth of her child.

✳ We are born naked, wet, and hungry. Then things get worse.

✳ When I was born, the doctor came out to the waiting room and said to my father, "I'm very sorry. We did everything we could. But he pulled through." *Rodney Dangerfield*

✳ A couple go to their first prenatal class. The husband is told to wear a bag of sand so he has an idea of what it feels like to be pregnant. The husband stands up saying, "This doesn't feel so bad." The instructor then drops a pen and asks the husband to pick it up. "You want me to pick up the pen as if I were pregnant, the way my wife would do it?" asks the husband. "Exactly," replies the instructor. The husband turns to his wife and says, "Honey, pick up that pen for me."

✳ Somewhere in the world a woman gives birth to a child every minute. We have to find this woman and stop her.

✳ How could two people as beautiful as you have such an ugly baby?

# BIRTHDAYS

* Harry shows Tom a beautiful diamond ring he's bought for his girlfriend's birthday. "I thought she wanted a four-wheel drive," says Tom. "She did," replies Harry. "But where am I going to find a fake Land Rover?"

* "I noticed your first couple of birthdays in life and your last couple of birthdays in life are very similar. In both cases, you don't really even know it's your birthday. People have to say, "These are your friends. They've come to help you celebrate your birthday." And you need a little help with the cake blow, in both cases." *Jerry Seinfeld*

* "When's your birthday?" "Ninth of December." "Which year?" "Every year."

* David's wife is mad at him because he forgot her birthday. David saves his skin. "Sweetheart," he says. "How do you expect me to remember your birthday when you never look any older?"

* Every morning a man passes a house in his street and every morning he sees a woman in her front garden beating her husband over the head with a French loaf. This goes on for months, until one morning, he passes the house and sees the woman is beating her husband with a large éclair. Later that day he meets the woman in the street. "Aren't you the woman who beats her husband with a French loaf?" asks the man. "Only, today, I could have sworn you were hitting him with a big cake." "Oh, I was," replies the woman. "Today is his birthday."

* The most effective way to remember your wife's birthday is to forget it once.

* Darth Vader, to Luke Skywalker: "I know what you're getting for your birthday, Luke. I have felt your presents."

* Happy Birthday! You look great for your age. Almost lifelike!

* Your friends and I wanted to do something special for your birthday—so we're having you put to sleep.

# BOREDOM

* "When I bore people at a party, they think it's their fault." *Henry Kissinger*

* Harry has a very boring hobby—he just sits in the corner and collects dust.

* He's so boring, people throw parties just to not invite him.

✳ You're so boring, if you threw a boomerang, it wouldn't come back to you.

✳ How do you tell if a girl has been to a boring party? She comes home with the same amount of lipstick she went out with.

# BRAINS

✳ "I used to think that the brain was the greatest organ in the human body, then I realized, 'Hey! Look what's telling me that!'" *Emo Phillips*

✳ "The brain—that's my second favorite organ." *Woody Allen*

✳ "The brain is a wonderful organ; it starts working the moment you get up in the morning and doesn't stop until you get to work." *Steven Wright*

# BREASTS

✳ "Who ever thought up the word 'mammogram'? Every time I hear it, I think I'm supposed to put my breast in an envelope and send it to someone." *Jan King*

✳ A flat-chested woman goes out shopping for a new bra. She goes into shop after shop asking if they have a size 28A, but she can't find one anywhere. Eventually she tries her luck in a small lingerie shop run by an old deaf lady. "Have you got anything in size 28A?" asks the woman. "What was that, dear?" says the old lady. The woman lifts up her T-shirt exposing her breasts and says, "Have you got anything for these?" The old lady peers at the woman's boobs and says, "No, dear. Have you tried Clearasil?"

✳ What did the bra say to the hat? You go on ahead, and I'll give these two a lift.

✳ What happened to the large-breasted streaker at the pop concert? She was thrown out by the bouncers.

✳ Why do men find it hard to make eye contact? Breasts don't have eyes.

✳ "Genetic scientists say that one day it will be possible to grow new body parts, like new breasts and new hands. It's going to be a huge moneymaker, because you know that as soon as women grow another breast, men will want another hand." *Jay Leno*

✳ A woman suggests to her husband that she have surgery to make her breasts bigger. Her husband suggests she rub toilet paper between them as an alternative. "How would that make my breasts bigger?" she asks. "I don't know," he replies. "But it sure worked for your backside."

* How is the Wonderbra like a cattle drive? They both round 'em up and move 'em out.

* In the beginning God created Eve, and she had three breasts. After a month in the garden, God comes to visit Eve. "How're things, Eve?" he asks. "It is all so beautiful," she replies. "Everything is wonderful, but I just have this one problem. It's these three breasts. The middle one pushes the other two out, and I'm constantly knocking them with my arms. They're a real pain." "That's a fair point," replies God, "I'll fix that right away!" So, God reaches down and removes the middle breast, tossing it into the bushes. Another month passes, and God once again visits Eve in the garden. "Well, Eve, how's my favorite creation?" he asks. "Just fantastic," she replies, "but for one small oversight on your part. All the animals have a mate, except me." God thinks for a moment. "You know, Eve, you're right! You do need a mate and I will immediately create Man from a part of you! Now, let's see…where did I put that useless tit?"

* I'm going to tell you a joke that's so funny, you'll laugh your tits off. Oops, you've already heard it.

* What do electric train sets and women's breasts have in common? They're both intended for children, but it's fathers who play with them.

* What does a seventy-five-year-old woman have between her breasts that a twenty-five-year-old doesn't? Her navel.

* Why is the space between a women's breasts and her hips called a waist? Because you could fit another pair of breasts there.

* Why is the Wonderbra called a Wonderbra? Because when she takes it off, you wonder where her tits went.

* "In the last couple of weeks I have seen the ads for the Wonderbra. Is that really a problem in this country? Men not paying enough attention to women's breasts?" *Jay Leno*

# BREASTS: BREAST-FEEDING

* "I had a traumatic childhood. I was breast-fed from falsies." *Woody Allen*

* "I was such an ugly baby. My mother never breast-fed me. She told me she only liked me as a friend." *Rodney Dangerfield*

✳ A woman comes home with her blouse open and her right breast hanging out. "What happened?" asks her husband. "Oh my goodness," says the woman. "I've left the baby on the bus!"

✳ I had a nightmare last night. I dreamed Dolly Parton was my mother, and I was a bottle baby.

✳ A young woman takes a baby to the doctor's office. "Baby seems to be ill," she says. "Instead of gaining weight, he lost three ounces this week." The doctor examines the baby, then says to the woman, "Is he breast-fed, or on the bottle?" "Breast-fed," she replies. "Let's take a look," says the doctor. "Strip down to your waist." She does so and the doctor squeezes both breasts, massages them and pinches both nipples. Eventually he says, "No wonder this baby is hungry, you don't have any milk." "Of course I don't," says the woman. "I'm his aunt."

✳ She didn't like to breast-feed her children. She said it hurt when she boiled her nipples.

# BRUNETTES

✳ What do you call a good-looking man with a brunette? A hostage.

✳ Why are brunettes so proud of their hair? It matches their mustache.

# BUMS

✳ A bum says to me, "Can I have $500 for a cup of coffee?" I say, "Coffee only costs a dollar!" He says, "Yeah, but I want to drink it in Brazil!"

✳ A bum says to me, "Give me $10 till pay day." I say, "When's pay day?" He says, "I don't know, you're the one who's working!"

✳ A bum walks into a country bar and orders a pint of beer. The owner pours him one, but the bum changes his mind and asks for a plowman's lunch instead. The landlord gives him a plowman's but when the time comes to pay, the bum says he doesn't owe anything—the plowman's had been given in exchange for a pint of beer that he never received. The landlord is pissed at being had, but decides to make the best of it. "Here," he says, taking $10 out of his pocket. "Take this ten and play the same trick in the Red Lion over the road." "Well, I would," says the bum. "But the owner of the Red Lion paid me a ten to play the trick on you."

✳ Little Johnny is out walking with his father when a bum comes up and says, "Can you help, sir? I haven't had a bite all day." So Johnny bites him.

# BUTCHERS

✳ A butcher backed into the bacon slicer and got a little behind in his orders.

✳ A man walks into a butcher's and says, "Have you got a sheep's head?" The butcher replies, "No, it's just the way I brush my hair."

✳ Our local butcher is selling meat on credit—but you have to take out a joint account.

# CANNIBALS

✳ Did you hear about the cannibal who passed his mother in the woods?

✳ Did you hear about the cannibal who went on a diet? He only ate midgets.

✳ Hannibal Lecter is seeing someone new, but she hates talking to him when he's nauseous—he keeps bringing up old girlfriends.

✳ Hear about the cannibal who ate his mother-in-law? She still didn't agree with him.

✳ I like kids, but I don't think I could eat a whole one.

✳ Some cannibals get a job in a big corporation on the condition that they don't eat any of the other staff. Things go very well until their boss calls them into his office one day and gives them some bad news—a janitor is missing in mysterious circumstances, and the cannibals are under suspicion. The cannibals get together after work. Their leader says, "Which of you idiots had the janitor?" One of the cannibals raises his hand. "You idiot! For weeks we've been feasting on team leaders, project managers, and human resources staff, then you go and eat someone they'll actually miss!"

✳ Two cannibals are relaxing after a big meal. One turns to the other and says, "Y'know, that missionary we had has given me terrible indigestion." The other replies, "You know what they say, you can't keep a good man down."

✳ Two cannibals are eating a clown. One says to the other, "Does this taste funny to you?"

✳ Two cannibals are having dinner. "Your wife makes a great roast," says one. "I know," says the other. "But I'm going to miss her."

✳ Two cannibals, a father and son, walk into the jungle to look for something to eat. Before long they come across a little old man. The son says, "Dad, how about him?" "No," says the father. "There's not enough meat on him. We'll wait." A little while later, along comes a really fat woman. The son says, "Hey, Dad, how about her?" "No," says the father. "We'd die of a heart attack if we ate her. We'll wait." An hour later an absolutely gorgeous woman walks by. The son says, "There's nothing wrong with this one, Dad. Let's eat her." "No we won't," says the father. "Why not?" asks the son. "Because," says the father, "we're going to take her home and eat your mother."

✳ Why do cannibals like Jehovah's Witnesses? They're free delivery.

✳ What's the most important thing to do if you're captured by cannibals? Keep calm and try not to get in a stew.

✳ Why aren't cannibals popular at weddings? They insist on toasting the bride and groom.

✳ Why was the cannibal student expelled from school? He kept buttering up his teacher.

✳ A newspaper man is captured by cannibals. "What was your job?" asks the chief cannibal. "I was a sub-editor," replies the man. "Well look forward to a promotion," replies the cannibal. "You're about to become an editor-in-chief."

✳ Small cannibal: "I hate my teacher." Mother cannibal: "Well, just eat your chips then."

✳ What did the cannibal at the house party have for breakfast? Buttered host.

✳ Why did the cannibal become a policeman? So he could grill suspects.

# CARS AND DRIVING

✳ "I have a rented car, which is a flat rate 12 cents a mile. In an effort to cut down on the mileage charge, I back up every place." *Woody Allen*

✳ A man has been driving all night. He decides to stop in the next town for a few hours and get some sleep. As luck would have it, he pulls up by a park frequented by early morning joggers. No sooner has he settled back to get some shut-eye when a jogger starts knocking on his window. "Excuse me, sir," says the jogger. "Do you have the time?" The man looks at his car clock and says, "8:15." The jogger says his thanks and leaves. The man settles back again, but just as he's dozing off, there's another jogger knocking on the window. "Excuse me, sir. Do you have the time?" asks the jogger. "8:25!" snaps the man. To prevent any more interruptions, the man writes a note saying

"I do not know the time!" and sticks it to his window. He settles back but is disturbed by yet another jogger knocking on the window. "Excuse me, sir," says the jogger. "It's 8:35."

✳ "I replaced the headlights in my car with strobe lights, so it looks like I'm the only one moving." *Steven Wright*

✳ "If you're in a car with a man and he stops and asks for directions, listen carefully because he won't, and it will be your fault if you get lost." *Rita Rudner*

✳ A car jumper cable walks into a bar. The bartender says, "I'll serve you, but don't start anything."

✳ "My wife isn't very bright. The other day she was at the store, and just as she was heading for our car, someone stole it! I said, 'Did you see the guy who did it?' She said, 'No, but I got the license plate.'" *Rodney Dangerfield*

✳ "One time a cop pulled me over for running a stop sign. He said, 'Didn't you see the stop sign?' I said, 'Yeah, but I don't believe everything I read.'" *Steven Wright*

✳ A constipated elephant traveling up the roadway has shed its load. Drivers are advised to treat it as a mini-roundabout.

✳ A man comes home from work and is greeted by his wife. She tells him she has good news and bad news about their car. The man says, "Okay, so give me the good news." His wife replies, "The good news is, the air bag works…"

✳ A defendant is in front of a judge on a speeding charge. "I understand you were doing 60 in a 30-mile-per-hour-zone," says the judge. "That's a lie," replies the defendant. "I wasn't doing 30. I wasn't even doing 10 in fact…" "Hold it," says the judge. "I'm going to fine you $50 before you back into something."

✳ A driver pulls up by a traffic cop. "If I park on these double yellow lines and run across the road to mail a letter, will you give me a ticket?" asks the driver. "Of course I will," replies the cop. "But these other cars are parked on double yellow lines," argues the driver. "I know," replies the warden. "But they didn't ask me to give them a ticket."

✳ A farmer living by a country road is increasingly concerned by speeding traffic. Worried that he and his livestock are in danger, he calls the police and asks them to put up a sign. They put up a "slow" sign, but it has no effect. They try putting up a "pedestrian crossing" sign, but that has no effect either. Finally they try erecting a "children at play" sign, but the traffic still keeps whizzing past. Eventually the farmer asks if he can put up his own sign, and the police agree. A few days later a policeman stops by to see how things are going. He's amazed to see the traffic moving at a snail's pace, then he notices the farmer's home-made sign by the roadside. It reads "Nudist Colony."

* A juggler, driving to his next performance, is stopped by the police. "What are these matches and lighter fluid doing in your car?" asks the cop. "I juggle flaming torches in my act," replies the juggler. "Oh yeah?" says the doubtful cop. "Let's see you do it." The juggler starts juggling the blazing torches masterfully. A couple driving by slows down to watch. "Wow," says the driver to his wife. "I'm glad I quit drinking. Look at the test they're giving now!"

* A man gets lost and walks into a village store for directions. "Can you tell me the quickest way to Lincoln?" he asks. The clerk says, "Are you walking or driving?" The man replies, "I'm driving." "Oh good," says the clerk. "Because that's definitely the quickest way."

* A man is out on the interstate having an evening drive in his sports car. He decides to open her up and the needle jumps to 120 mph. Suddenly he sees a flashing red and blue light behind him. He thinks about outrunning the cops, accelerates for a few seconds, then comes to his senses and pulls over. The officer comes over to check his license. "I've had a tough shift," says the officer. "And this is my last traffic stop. I don't feel like more paperwork, so if you can give me an excuse for your driving that I haven't heard before you can go!" "Uh, last week my wife ran off with a cop," says the man. "And when I saw your car I was afraid he was trying to give her back!" "Have a nice night," says the officer."

* A man is taking his son to school when he inadvertently makes an illegal turn at the lights. "Uh-oh, I just made an illegal turn!" the man says. "It's okay, Dad," replies his son. "The police car behind us did the same thing!"

* A driver stops at a river crossing and asks an old hillbilly sitting nearby how deep the water is. "Couple of inches," replies the hillbilly. The driver drives into the ford and disappears in a seething mass of bubbles. "That's funny," said the hillbilly. "It only goes halfway up on them ducks."

* A police officer pulls a woman over. "Is there a problem, Officer?" she asks. "Ma'am, you were speeding. Could I see your license?" "I'm sorry," says the woman. "I don't have one. I lost it four times for drunk driving." "Okay," says the officer. "Can I see your vehicle registration?" "Nope," says the woman. "Can't do that either. I stole this car, killed the owner, and put his remains in the trunk." The horrified officer calls for back-up and within minutes, five police cars circle the woman. A police chief slowly approaches, clasping a gun. "Ma'am," he says, "open the back of the car please." She does so, but the back of the car is empty. "Is this your car, ma'am?" asks the chief. "Yes," says the woman. "Here are the registration papers." The chief is confused. "The officer claimed you don't have a driver's license." The woman digs into her handbag and pulls out the license. "Ma'am, this is a puzzle," says the chief. "My officer told me you didn't have a license, that you stole this car, and that you'd murdered the owner." "I don't believe it!" says the woman. "Next you'll tell me the lying bastard said I was speeding too."

✳ A policeman is investigating a crash on a railway crossing. He goes up to the injured car driver and says, "Can you describe what you were doing at the time of the accident?" "Well," replies the driver. "I got to the crossing, stopped, looked both ways, and then the train hit me."

✳ A policeman watches as a car careens all over the road before crashing into a rail. He runs over to help and asks the driver what happened. "It was a nightmare," says the driver. "I swerved to miss a tree then another one swung in front of me so I swerved to avoid it when another one came into view. There were trees everywhere. I couldn't get away from them." The policeman looks in the car and says, "Those weren't trees, that was your air freshener."

✳ A rich lady is riding with her chauffeur when they get a flat tire. He gets out and starts trying to pry off the hubcap. After a few minutes of his struggling, the lady leans out of the window and says, "Would you like a screwdriver?" He replies, "We might as well. I can't get this damn wheel off."

✳ A bum knocks on the door of a large house and begs for a meal. "Tell you what," says the homeowner. "If you go around the back and paint my porch with whitewash I'll give you all the food you can eat." The bum agrees. He goes around the back, finds a can of whitewash, and a brush, and gets started. Ten minutes later the bum knocks on the door for his reward. "That was fast work," says the homeowner. "I thought it would take hours to paint that huge porch." "Oh, it wasn't so big," replies the bum. "And, by the way, it isn't a Porsche. It's a BMW."

✳ A woman is driving the wrong way up a one-way street. A cop pulls her over and says, "Where are you going?" The woman replies, "I don't know. But I must be late—everyone is coming back!"

✳ An man is taking his driving test. The instructor asks him what a yellow line means. "It means you can't park there at all," says the man. "And what does a double yellow line mean?" asks the instructor. The man says, "It means you can't park there at all... at all."

✳ An old man is out driving on the freeway when his cell phone rings. It's his wife calling. She says she's just heard a news report about a car that's driving the wrong way up the freeway. "I know," says the old man. "But it's not just one car. It's hundreds of them."

✳ And now an important announcement for drivers traveling to New York City on the I-95. The I-95 doesn't go to New York City.

✳ Every young woman should hang on to her youth. But not while he's driving.

✳ Driver, to mechanic: "Could you check the battery? I think it's flat." Mechanic: "What shape did you want it to be?"

✳ Harry and Bob are out in their car. They park, get out, and shut the doors when Harry realizes that they've locked themselves out. Bob says, "We can get a coat hanger and try to unlock the door." Harry says, "Or perhaps we could try to pry the door open." "Well, whatever we do, we'd better hurry," says Bob. "A storm's coming and the top's still down."

✳ Harry died with his boots on—sadly one was on the accelerator at the time.

✳ Harry discovers that someone has backed into his Jaguar while it's been in the parking lot. He finds a note under the windscreen. It says "Sorry about wrecking your car. The policeman watching me from over the road thinks I'm leaving you my details. But I'm not."

✳ Do you know why Turtle Wax is so expensive? Because turtles have really tiny ears.

✳ Harry is fiddling under the hood of his car. A bum walks by, stops, and looks at him. "Piston broke," explains Harry. "Ah yes," says the bum. "So am I."

✳ He got a BMW because he wanted a car he could spell.

✳ How come so many cars are named after pornographic magazines? There's the Escort, the Fiesta, the Mini Mayfair, and of course, the Fiat Big Jugs Monthly Popular Plus.

✳ Husband, to wife: "I don't believe it! You just backed the car over my bike!" Wife: "Well, you shouldn't have left it on the lawn."

✳ I asked my wife why there were so many dings on the driver's side of her Mercedes, she said the brakes must be bad on that side.

✳ I bought a second-hand car. It only had one previous owner. A little old lady who only used it on a Sunday—when she took it drag racing.

✳ I found a way to make my wife drive more carefully. I told her, if she ever got in an accident, the newspapers would print her real age.

✳ I've figured out how to avoid getting parking tickets. I've taken the windshield wipers off my car.

✳ I got pulled over by the police and failed a Breathalyzer test. I wouldn't have minded but I wasn't in a car at the time.

✳ I took my old bucket for a tuneup yesterday—the mechanic advised me to keep the oil and change the car.

✳ I was getting into my car, and this man says to me, "Can you give me a lift?" I said, "Sure. You look great. The world's your oyster. Go for it."

✳ I was out driving the other day when I came up on a Camry with a license plate reading "BOBS VW." I pulled up beside the car at the next light and said to the driver, "Hey, that's not a VW." The driver looked at me and said, "And I'm not Bob."

✳ It's said that if you line up all the cars in the world end to end, someone would be stupid enough to try and pass them.

✳ I've got a stereo system in my car. My wife at the front and her mother at the back.

✳ Man, to friend: "My brother commutes with the spirits." Friend: "Don't you mean he 'communes' with the spirits?" Man: "No, he drives a delivery truck for the distillery."

✳ Man, to robber: "Why have you painted your car green on one side and yellow on the other?" Robber: "Because I like to hear the witnesses contradict each other."

✳ Man, to taxi driver: "Can you take me to Denver?" Driver: "Sure. What part?" Man: "All of me."

✳ People don't want cheap cars, they want expensive cars that cost less.

✳ Policeman, to driver: "Have you seen the state of your rear lights?" Driver: "Screw the lights! What the hell happened to my caravan?"

✳ Policeman, to driver: "I'm arresting you for speeding. You were going at least 100 miles per hour." Driver: "That's nonsense, officer. I've only been driving ten minutes."

✳ Tom is driving down a country lane when he slows down to let another driver pass him going the other way. The other driver shouts, "Pig!" as he passes. Tom shouts back, "Bastard!" then crashes into a pig.

✳ Reporter, to racing driver: "Would you say it's very dangerous taking a corner at that speed?" Driver: "It's very dangerous taking a corner at that speed."

✳ Somebody complimented me on my driving today. They left a note on the windscreen— it said "parking fine."

✳ The garage told me they couldn't repair my brakes, so they just made my horn louder.

✳ The journey of a thousand miles begins with a broken fan belt and a flat tire.

✳ The Pope is visiting the United States and decides to take a turn at the wheel of his limo. The Pope gets in the driving seat, while his driver hops in the back, and they shoot off at 80 mph. Not surprisingly, they're pulled over by a traffic cop. The cop radios into the police station. "We've got a VIP situation here," says the cop. "I just pulled over someone who's really, really important." "Who is it?" asks the station controller. "I don't know," says the cop. "But his chauffeur is the Pope."

✳ Three weeks ago, my wife learned how to drive. Last week she learned how to aim it.

✳ Tom and Dick are driving along when Dick goes through some red lights. "Careful," says Tom. "You'll have an accident." "It's all right," says Dick. "My brother does it all the time." At the next red light, Dick again speeds through without a care in the world. "That's really dangerous," says Tom. "It's okay," replies Dick. "My brother does it all the time." The next set of lights are green, and Dick puts on the brakes. "Why are you stopping now?" asks Tom. "My brother might be coming the other way," replies Dick.

✳ Two old women, Millie and Dolly, are out driving in a large car. Both can barely see over the dashboard. As they cruise along they come to an intersection and go through a red light. Millie, in the passenger seat, thinks to herself, "I must be losing my mind, I swear we just went through a red light." After a few minutes they come to another intersection and go through another red light. Millie is almost sure that the light was red, but is concerned she might be mistaken. At the next intersection they go through another red light. Millie turns to Dolly and says, "Dolly! Did you know we just ran through three red lights in a row! You could have killed us!" Dolly looks around and says, "Oh! Am I driving?"

✳ What information is in every Geo manual? A bus timetable.

✳ What's the difference between a Geo and a golf ball? If you're lucky you can drive a golf ball more than 200 yards.

✳ Why do Geos have heated rear windows? So your hands won't get cold when you're pushing it.

✳ Why is it that when you're driving and looking for an address, you turn down the volume on the radio?

✳ A car breaks down on the hard shoulder of a freeway. The driver opens his trunk and lets out two dirty old men in raincoats. The men stand at either end of the car and start flapping their coats open and closed, exposing themselves to the passing traffic. A police car soon pulls up. "What are those two doing?" says the policeman. "Them?" replies the driver. "They're my emergency flashers."

✳ A glue tanker on the motorway has shed its load. Drivers are advised to stick to the inside lane.

✳ A man is sitting on the roadside, looking unhappy. A passerby sees his glum face and asks what the problem is. "I've locked myself out of my car," replies the man. "No problem," replies the passerby. "Let me try rubbing my rear end on the door." The driver is perplexed but decides there's no harm in letting the man try. The passerby presses his butt to the car and slowly rubs it up and down the door. Suddenly, the lock clicks open. "That's amazing!" says the driver. "How did you do it?" "Easy," replies the passerby. "I'm wearing khaki pants."

✳ A man pushes his car into the garage and tells the mechanic that the engine just died on him in the street. After a few moments of tinkering under the hood, the engine is purring again. "Great," says the driver. "How did you fix it?" "Just crap in the carburetor," replies the mechanic. "Okay," replies the man. "So how often do I have to do that?"

✳ A woman tells her husband that her car won't start. "I think there's water in the carburetor," she says. "How do you know that?" asks the husband. The wife replies, "I drove it into the canal."

✳ Driver to passenger: "Lean out the window and tell me if my indicator light is working." Passenger: "Okay... Yes... No... Yes... No... Yes... No..."

✳ He's a terrible snob. He won't ride in the same car as his chauffeur.

✳ I got my car through my work. I'm a car thief.

✳ If your wife wants to learn to drive, don't stand in her way.

✳ My car has been up and down on the garage lift so often, it's the only vehicle with a higher mileage vertically than horizontally.

✳ Stupidity is not a handicap. Park somewhere else!

✳ Tom is taking his driving test. The examiner says, "When I tap the dashboard I want you to show me what action you'd take if a child ran out in front of the car." When he taps on the dashboard, Tom screeches to a halt, winds down the window, and yells, "Get out the way, you little bastard!"

✳ What do you do if a bird craps on your car? Don't ask her out again.

✳ What's the difference between a sperm and a traffic cop? A sperm has a one in 1,000,000 chance of becoming a human being.

✳ You never really learn to swear until you learn to drive.

✳ A boy is walking along the road when a car pulls up alongside him. "If you get in my car," says the driver. "I'll give you a bag of sweets." The boy ignores him. "Okay," says the driver. "Get in my car and you can have two bags of sweets and $5." The boy ignores him. "The driver says, "Listen, if you'll just get in the car I'll give you all the sweets you want and $20." The boy turns to the driver and says, "Dad, for the last time, I'm not getting into that Geo."

* Harry is out driving with his wife. "Can't you slow down when you're turning corners?" she complains. "You're scaring the life out of me." "Do what I do," replies Harry. "Shut your eyes."

* Some people say that a man's personality is reflected by the car he drives. Well, I have no car.

* The one thing that unites all human beings, regardless of age, gender, religion, economic status, or ethnic background, is that, deep down inside, we all believe that we are above-average drivers.

* Patience is something you admire in the driver behind you and can't stand in the driver ahead of you.

* One-way streets are far safer to drive on. People only crash into you from one direction.

* Cars are almost foolproof, as long as the fool stays awake at the wheel.

* I wouldn't say my car is old, but it's insured against fire, theft, and Vikings.

# CATERPILLARS

* Two caterpillars are watching a cocoon. It bursts open to reveal a beautiful butterfly that stretches its wings and flies away. One caterpillar turns to the other and says, "You'll never get me up in one of those things."

* What did the earthworm say to the caterpillar? "Who did you have to sleep with to get that fur coat?"

# CATS

* I've never understood why women love cats. Cats are independent, they don't listen, they don't come in when you call, they like to stay out all night, and when they're home they like to be left alone and sleep. In other words, every quality that women hate in men, they love in cats.

* A man hates his wife's cat and decides to get rid of it by driving it twenty blocks from home and dumping it. As he gets back home he sees the cat walking up the driveway, so he drives the cat forty blocks away and dumps it again. When he gets back, there once again is the cat wandering up the driveway. In the end he drives the cat for miles

and miles until he's in the middle of a huge forest, where he dumps it yet again. Three hours later his wife gets a call at home. "Darling," says her husband. "Is the cat there?" "Yes," says the wife. "Why?" "Just put him on the line will you?" says the husband. "I need directions!"

✳ A man goes into a pub with a cat sitting on his head. The bartender pulls him a pint and says, "Look, I don't know if you know it, but there's a cat sitting on your head." "What of it?" asks the man. "I always wear a cat on my head on a Monday." "But today's Tuesday," replies the bartender. "Oh God. Is it?" says the man. "I must look like a real ass."

✳ A man runs over a cat. The cat's address is on its collar, so the man goes to apologize to the owner. He knocks on the door, and a little old lady answers. The man says, "I'm so sorry. I've just run over your cat. Can I replace it?" "I don't know," replies the old lady. "How are you at catching mice?"

✳ Mother to little boy: "Stop pulling the cat's tail." Boy: "I'm not. I'm just holding it. It's the cat that's doing the pulling."

✳ Cats took many thousands of years to domesticate humans.

✳ How do you know if your cat has eaten a duckling? She's got that down-in-the-mouth look.

✳ I love cats—they taste just like chicken.

✳ I love my cat. My cat does not care.

✳ Radioactive cats have eighteen half-lives.

✳ The more people I meet, the more I like my cat.

✳ Thousands of years ago, cats were worshiped as gods. Cats have never forgotten this.

✳ What do you get if you cross a cat with a gorilla? An animal that puts you out at night.

✳ What looks like half a cat? The other half.

✳ What's the difference between cats and dogs? Dogs have owners, cats have staff.

✳ A three-year-old boy goes to see a litter of kittens with his dad. Later he says to his mother, "There were two boy kittens and two girl kittens." "How did you know?" asks his mother. "Daddy picked them up and looked underneath," he replies. "I think they must have it printed on their bottoms."

✳ I had to go next door and watch my neighbor's cat while he was away. Now there's a great pile of crap and a puddle of pee on his kitchen floor. Hopefully he'll think the cat did it.

✳ My cat can talk. I asked her what two minus two was, and she said nothing.

✳ Yesterday I saw a man trying to chat up a cheetah. "Hey," I thought. "He's trying to pull a fast one."

✳ An old lady's cat gives birth to a litter of kittens. She says to the vet, "How could it have happened? She never leaves the house. How could she meet another cat?" "What about that tom sitting on the sofa?" asks the vet. "Don't be ridiculous," says the old lady. "That's her brother!"

✳ My tomcat used to stay out all night, so I took him to the vet and had him neutered. Now he still stays out all night—it turns out he likes to watch!

# CELEBRITY AND CELEBRITIES

✳ "Elvis is just a young, clean-cut American boy who does in public what everybody else does in private." *Bob Hope*

✳ "I always wanted to be somebody, but I should have been more specific." *Lily Tomlin*

✳ "If God doesn't destroy Hollywood Boulevard, he owes Sodom and Gomorrah an apology" *Jay Leno*

✳ Harry is in the VIP lounge of a transatlantic airline when he sees Donald Trump. Harry goes up to him and asks a favor. "I'm meeting an important client here in a few minutes," says Harry. "Would you mind just passing by and saying hello? It would really impress my client if he thought I knew you." Mr. Trump agrees to this harmless request and a few minutes later he spots Harry deep in conversation with his client. He walks up, taps Harry on the shoulder, and says, "Hi, Harry. How you doing?" Harry turns around and says, "Buzz off, Trump, I'm busy."

✳ "I look just like the girl next door—if you happen to live next door to an amusement park." *Dolly Parton*

✳ A celebrity is somebody who spends the first half of their life trying to become famous and the second wearing dark glasses so no one will recognize them.

✳ In a recent survey, 10,000 American men said they'd never make love to Madonna—again.

✳ Joan Collins had to go to the hospital today to attend the birth of her next husband.

✳ They broke the mold when they made Michael Jackson — each time apparently.

✳ They're giving Justin Timberlake a lifetime achievement award. If they give it to him now they're hoping he might retire early.

✳ What goes 10, 9, 8, 7, 6, 5, 4… ? Bo Derek getting older.

✳ What's the difference between Justin Timberlake and a supermarket cart? The supermarket cart has a mind of its own.

✳ Why did Mark Chapman shoot John Lennon? Yoko ducked.

✳ Why do Mike Tyson's eyes water during sex? Mace.

✳ Harry dies and goes to heaven. On his introductory tour he's shown a huge shed full of clocks. "Each clock represents a person's life," explains an angel. "If you see a clock's hands moving very quickly, it means that the person has committed some act of stupidity and so shortened their existence." "That's interesting," says Harry. "It would be fun to see a celebrity's clock. Could you point out Michael Jackson's for instance?" "I'm afraid not," replies the angel. "It's up in the office. We've been using it as a fan."

✳ How does Michael Jackson pick his nose? From a catalog.

# CENTIPEDES

✳ What goes ninety-nine-clonk, ninety-nine-clonk, ninety-nine-clonk? A centipede with a wooden leg!

✳ What has fifty legs but can't walk? Half a centipede!

✳ A guy goes to a pet store to buy an unusual pet and walks out with a centipede in a white box. Once he gets it home, the guy decides to take the centipede to his local bar and show it to his drinking buddies. He taps on the box and says, "Would you like to go to McGuire's with me and have a beer?" There's no answer from the centipede. He waits a few moments then says, "How about you and me going to a bar?" Again, there's no answer. Thinking the centipede can't hear him, the man goes right up to the box and yells, "Hey! Would you like to go to McGuire's bar and have a drink?!" A little voice comes out of the box — "I heard you the first time! I'm putting on my shoes."

# CHILDREN AND CHILDHOOD

✳ "I married your mother because I wanted children—imagine my disappointment when you came along." *Groucho Marx*

✳ "Men name their children after themselves, women don't. Have you ever met a Sally Junior?" *Rita Rudner*

✳ "My mother loved children—she would have given anything if I'd been one." *Groucho Marx*

✳ A four-year-old boy is asked to say grace before Christmas dinner. The boy thanks God for all his friends. Then he thanks God for Mommy, Daddy, brother, sister, Grandma, Grandpa, and all his aunts and uncles. Then he begins to thank God for the food. He gave thanks for the turkey, the potatoes, the cranberry sauce, and the gravy. There's a pause and the little boy looks up at his mother: "Mommy, if I thank God for the broccoli, won't he know that I'm lying?"

✳ A little girl goes to her local library to take out a book called Advice for Young Mothers. "Why do you want a book like that?" says the librarian. The little girl replies, "Because I collect moths."

✳ A little girl is pounding away on her father's computer. She tells him she's writing a story. "What's it about?" asks Dad. "I don't know," she replies. "I can't read."

✳ A little girl runs up to her mother and asks, "Mommy, where do babies come from?" "The stork, dear," replies her mother. "Mommy, who keeps bad people from robbing our house?" asks the girl. "The police, dear," answers the mother. "Mommy," says the girl, "if our house were on fire, who would save us?" "The fire department," answers the mother. "Mommy, where does food come from?" asks the girl. "Farmers, dear," says the mother. "Mommy," says the girl, "what do we need Daddy for?"

✳ A man comes home from the bar pushing a baby carriage. "You idiot!" shouts his wife, "that's not our baby!" "I know," says the husband, "but it's a nicer stroller."

✳ A mother is getting ready to go out with her small son. "Where are you going?" asks the boy's father. "I'm taking Billy to the zoo," says Mom. "Lazy bastards," says the father. "If they want him, tell them they can pick him up themselves."

✳ A salesman rings on the doorbell of a house. The door is answered by a young boy smoking a cigar, holding a glass of brandy, with a copy of *Playboy* tucked under his arm. "Say, sonny," says the salesman. "Is your mother at home?" The boy taps the ash off his cigar and says, "What the hell do you think?"

✳ A salesman sees a young boy siting on a porch and says, "Hi there, sonny. Is your mommy at home?" "She sure is," replies the boy. The salesman rings on the bell, then again, and again, but with no answer. He turns to the boy and says, "Hey, I thought you said your mommy was at home." "She is," replies the boy. "But I don't live here."

✳ A six-year-old boy and his friends are looking at his family picture album. When he gets to his parents' wedding portraits, he says, "And this is the day that Mommy came to work for us."

✳ A small boy gets separated from his father at the carnival and asks a policeman to help find him. The policeman tries to get a description. "What's your father like?" he asks. "Beer and women," replies the boy.

✳ A small boy is talking with his granddad. "Why does it rain?" he asks. Granddad replies, "To make the plants grow." The boy looks puzzled and says, "So why does it rain on the pavement?"

✳ A Sunday school teacher asks her pupils where God lives. A small girl sticks up her hand and says, "Miss. God lives in our bathroom." "In your bathroom?" says the teacher. "Why do you think he's in there?" The girl replies, "Because every morning my daddy bangs on the bathroom door and shouts, 'God, are you still in there?'"

✳ Every parent is always going on about how their baby is the most marvelous special baby in the world. It clearly can't be true—it's my baby who is the most marvelous special baby in the world.

✳ A Wichita couple have five children: Harry, Richard, Sally, Jane, and Ho Yung. Ho Yung is an unusual name for a Kansan, but the couple read that every fifth baby born in the world is Chinese.

✳ Daddy comes home with a big bag of sweets and says to the kids, "I'm going to give these to the person who never talks back to Mommy and always does what they're told. Now who's going to get them?" And the kids reply, "You are."

✳ Groucho Marx, to Mrs. Story, a quiz show contestant: "How many children do you have?" Mrs. Story: "Nineteen." Groucho: "Nineteen! Why do you have so many children? It must be a terrible responsibility and a burden." Mrs. Story: "Well, because I love my children and I think that's our purpose here on Earth, and I love my husband." Groucho: "I love my cigar, too, but I take it out of my mouth once in a while!"

✳ I was the kid next door's imaginary friend.

✳ Little Johnny comes running into the house and says, "Mommy, can little girls have babies?" "No," says his mom, "of course not." Little Johnny runs back outside and yells, "It's okay, we can play that game again!"

✳ Little Johnny goes to his mother and says, "Mommy, tomorrow I have an oral exam. One question the teacher will ask me is 'Who made you?' What should I say?" "Say God made you," replies his mother. The next day Little Johnny is asked the question but forgets what his mother said. He explains, "Teacher, until yesterday I was sure it was my father who made me. But then Mother said it was someone else—and now I can't remember the guy's name."

✳ If I want to hear the pitter patter of little feet, I'll put shoes on my cat.

✳ Little Johnny is talking to a couple of boys in the schoolyard. Each is bragging about how fast their fathers are. The first one says, "My father runs the fastest. He can fire an arrow, start to run, and get to the target before it hits!" The second one says, "You think that's fast? My father's a hunter. He can shoot his gun and be there before the bullet!" Johnny says, "You two know nothing about fast. My father's a civil servant. He stops working at five and he's home by four-thirty!"

✳ Little Johnny shouts, "Mommy! Mommy! Do you know the beautiful vase in the dining room that's been handed down from generation to generation?" "Yes," says his mother. "What about it?" Johnny replies, "Well the last generation just dropped it."

✳ Out of the mouths of babes come all manner of things. Usually puke.

✳ Until I was thirteen, I thought my name was "Shuttup."

✳ A little boy embarrasses his mother when they're out by loudly asking if he can go for a pee. His mother tells him, "Don't shout out like that. In future, if you want a pee just say 'I want a whisper' and I'll know what you mean." A few days later the boy goes into his parents' bedroom and finds his dad having a nap. "What d'you want?" asks Dad. "I want a whisper," says the little boy. "Okay," replies Dad. "Whisper in my ear."

✳ A little boy is raiding the freezer for ice cream when his mother catches him. "Put that ice cream back," she scolds. "Dinner is only an hour away." "But I'm bored," says the boy. "I've got no one to play with." "All right," says Mother. "I'll play with you for a few minutes. What do you want to do?" "I want to play Mommies and Daddies," says the boy. "But you have to sit in that chair and be mommy." Mother does so and says, "So now what? Are you going to be daddy?" "Yes," says the boy. He takes a deep breath and shouts, "Now get off your fat ass, you lazy cow, and bring me some ice cream!"

✳ A mother is putting her small son to bed in the middle of a thunderstorm. "Mommy, can I sleep with you tonight?" asks the nervous boy. "I'm sorry, darling," says Mother. "But I have to sleep with Daddy tonight." "What?" replies the boy. "Tell the big coward not to be such a baby!"

✳ A wife tells her husband to go and change their son—two hours later he comes back with a baby girl.

✳ Insanity is hereditary. You can get it from your children.

✳ Some schoolchildren have been told to write about a recent exciting event. A small boy is selected to read out his composition. "Daddy fell in the well last week…" he begins. "Gracious," said his teacher. "Is he all right now?" "He must be," replies the boy. "He stopped yelling for help yesterday."

✳ "I was raised by just my mom. See, my father died when I was eight years old. At least, that's what he told us in the letter." *Drew Carey*

✳ No matter how much you try to protect your children, they will eventually get arrested and end up in the local paper.

✳ "If your parents never had children, chances are you won't either." *Dick Cavett*

✳ Why was the new baby just like Daddy? It was bald, sleepy, and uneducated.

✳ A little boy starts handing out sweets in the playground. "What's the occasion?" asks one of his friends. "Is it your birthday?" "No," says the boy. "Last night I became a brother."

✳ I wouldn't say my mother was ashamed of me, but she used to go to parents' nights under an assumed name.

✳ A woman sees a small boy leaning against a wall smoking a cigarette and taking nips from a hip flask. "Shouldn't you be at school?" says the woman. "School?" says the boy. "You've got to be joking. I'm only four."

✳ Dad brings a business associate home for dinner. The family assemble at the table and Mom starts serving a roast. "This is just ordinary roast lamb!" complains the young son. "Yes," says his mother. "But you said you liked lamb." "I do," says the boy, "but Dad said he was bringing an idiot home for dinner."

✳ Children brighten a home—they never turn the lights off.

✳ Jane is carrying her new baby son down the street when Mary comes over to take a look. "How lovely!" she exclaims. "He looks just like his father." "Yes," says Jane. "But it's a pity he doesn't look more like my husband."

✳ Little girl to mother: "Mommy, how soon is Christmas?" Mother: "Not long. Why do you ask?" Girl: "I was wondering if it was near enough for me to start being good."

✳ A woman gets on a bus with three sets of twins. "Wow," says the driver. "Do you always have twins?" "No," says the woman. "The first two or three hundred times, we didn't get anything at all."

✳ Little Johnny comes home and says, "I'm glad you decided to call me Johnny." "Why's that?" asks his mother. Johnny replies, "Because that's what all the other kids call me."

✳ Good: Your son is finally maturing. Bad: He's having an affair with the woman next door. Ugly: So are you.

✳ Good: You give the "birds and the bees" talk to your fourteen-year-old daughter. Bad: She keeps interrupting. Ugly: With corrections.

# CHRISTMAS

✳ "Santa Claus has the right idea—visit people only once a year." *Victor Borge*

✳ One year Father Christmas is forced to have an official from the FAA check his sleigh to make sure it's airworthy. The official checks out the sleigh on the ground then sits beside Father Christmas for a test flight. Suddenly Father Christmas notices the official has a gun in his pocket. "What's that for?" he asks. "You're not a hijacker are you?" "No," replies the official. "But we have to see how you handle this craft when you lose an engine on take-off."

✳ Santa was very cross. It was Christmas Eve and nothing was going right. The elves were complaining about not getting paid overtime. The reindeer had been drinking all afternoon and the sleigh was broken. Santa was furious. "I can't believe it!" he yells. "I've got to deliver millions of presents all over the world in just a few hours—all of my reindeer are drunk, the elves are on strike, and I don't even have a Christmas tree! I sent that stupid little angel to find one hours ago! What am I going to do?" Just then, the little angel opens the front door and steps in from the snowy night, dragging a Christmas tree. "Hey fatty!" she says. "Where d'you want me to stick this?" And thus the tradition of angels atop the Christmas trees came to pass.

✳ The four stages of life—You believe in Santa Claus—You don't believe in Santa Claus—You become Santa Claus—You look like Santa Claus.

✳ The year you stop believing in Santa Claus is the year you start getting clothes for Christmas.

✳ Why doesn't Santa have any children? He only comes one a year, and that's down the chimney.

✳ Why is Santa so jolly? Because he knows where all the bad girls live.

✳ Why was Santa's little helper feeling depressed? He had low elf-esteem.

✳ What's the most popular Christmas wine? "I don't like Brussels sprouts!"

✳ What does Santa do with fat elves? He sends them to the Elf Farm.

# CIRCUMCISION

✳ A surgeon retires from his long career as a specialist in circumcision. Throughout his career he has saved hundreds of foreskins as mementos and now wishes to turn them into a souvenir. He takes his specimens to a leathersmith and asks him to make something out of them. A week later the surgeon returns, and the leathersmith presents him with a wallet. "All those foreskins and you only made me a wallet?" exclaims the surgeon. The leathersmith replies, "Yes, but if you stroke it, it becomes a briefcase."

✳ The Emperor of Japan advertises for a new bodyguard. Three swordsmen apply: one is Japanese, one is Chinese, and one is Jewish. To test him, the Emperor lets a fly loose in the room and tells the Chinese swordsman to kill it. The swordsman sweeps down his blade and chops the fly in two. The Japanese swordsman is given the same test. He swings his sword twice and manages to cut the fly into quarters before it hits the ground. The Jewish swordsman is then given a fly. He chases it around the room, swings his sword a few times, then sits down with the fly buzzing around his head. "Why have you stopped?" asks the Emperor. "The fly is still alive." "Yes," replies the Jewish swordsman. "But now it's circumcised."

✳ What happened to the short-sighted circumciser? He got the sack.

✳ When they circumcised him, they threw away the wrong bit.

# CIVIL SERVANTS

✳ Why don't civil servants stare out the window in the morning? If they did, they'd have nothing to do after lunch.

✳ An engineer, an accountant, a pharmacist, and a civil servant are comparing their pet dogs. To see which is the most intelligent, each dog shows off its best trick. The engineer's dog draws a square and a circle on a sheet of paper. The accountant's dog divides a pile of cookies into three equal parts. And the pharmacist's dog pours exactly a third of a carton of milk into a bowl. Then it's the turn of the civil servant's dog. The dog strolls over, pees over the drawing paper, eats the cookies, drinks the milk, has sex with the three other dogs, claims a back injury as a result, and applies for compensation before going on sick leave.

✳ A civil servant goes to his doctor with a sleep problem. "I get to sleep at night," says the civil servant. "And mornings are okay, but I'm having trouble dropping off in the afternoon."

# CLONING

✳ Clones are people two.

✳ Cloning is the sincerest form of flattery.

✳ John decides life will be much easier if he has a clone. He has one made and sends him to work while he stays home and relaxes. This backfires when the clone comes home and says he's been fired for making sexual advances to women in the office. John decides he has to get rid of his clone, so he takes it to the top of a tall building and pushes it off. Unfortunately, someone sees John, and he's arrested for making an obscene clone fall.

# CLOTHES AND FASHION

✳ A man with two left feet walks into a shoe shop and says, "Got any flip-flips?"

✳ A man walks into an army surplus store and asks if they have any camouflage jackets. "Yes, we do," replies the assistant. "But we can't find any of them."

✳ A shy young country boy is invited to a nightclub where all the girls are wearing extremely low-cut outfits. One of the girls comes up to him and says, "I bet you never seen anything like this before." The boy replies, "Well no, not since I was weaned."

✳ "She said, 'You're wearing two different-colored socks.' I said, 'I know, but to me they're the same because I go by thickness.'" *Steven Wright*

✳ A woman catches a train and finds herself sitting opposite a little old Scotsman wearing a kilt. "Excuse me," she says. "I hope you don't mind my asking, but I always wanted to know what a man wears under one of these things." The Scotsman replies, "I'm a man o' few words, madam. Give me yer hand…"

✳ A young woman goes to a dinner party with a head cold. Her dress hasn't got anywhere to put a tissue, so she stuffs one into each cup of her bra. During the dinner party she feels a sneeze coming on. She discreetly rummages inside her left cup, but is unable to find anything. She notices that the man next to her is watching. "Sorry," she whispers. "But I'm sure I had two when I arrived."

✳ Before short skirts came into fashion, you had to listen if you wanted to know if a girl was knock-kneed.

✳ Harry knew he could count on his wife. She always wore beads.

✳ He was wearing his Italian suit. It had spaghetti bolognese all down the front.

✳ I don't know if he bought his suit for a ridiculous price, but I could see it was for an absurd figure.

✳ Man, to friend: "How come you're only wearing one glove? Did you lose one?" Friend: "No, I found one."

✳ My uncle tried to make ready-made fur coats by crossing gorillas with minks. He managed it in the end but had to give up—the sleeves were too long.

✳ The recent fashion for gold lamé pixie boots was absolutely ridiculous. I'm so glad Granddad has stopped wearing them.

✳ "When a woman tries on clothing from her closet that feels tight, she'll assume she's gained weight. When a man tries something from his closet that feels tight, he'll assume the clothing has shrunk." *Rita Rudner*

✳ A busty girl in a tight, low-cut dress is at a party with her boyfriend. "A little crowded," she says. "Yes," he replies. "But it suits you."

✳ A teenager buys a tiny bikini and tries it on. "What do you think?" she says to her mother. "What do I think?" replies mother. "I think if I'd worn that when I was your age, you'd be five years older."

✳ It doesn't take my daughter long to get ready for a night on the town—all she has to do is put on her face and take off a few clothes.

✳ Harry is chatting with Tom. "I like your new suit," says Tom. "Thanks," says Harry. "It was a surprise present from my wife. I came home early last night and found it hanging over a chair in the bedroom."

# CLOWNS

✳ "I had an uncle who was a circus clown. When he died, all his friends went to the funeral in one car." *Steven Wright*

✳ A group of clowns rent furnished apartments in a condominium but are annoyed to discover they have not been provided with ironing boards. They go to complain to their landlord saying that all the other tenants have ironing boards except the clowns. "It's in the contract," says the landlord. "You clowns have to use your window sills. Every clown has a sill for ironing."

# CLUBS

✳ "If the bouncer gets drunk, who throws him out?" *George Carlin*

✳ "I don't care to belong to a club that accepts people like me as members." *Groucho Marx*

# CONSCIENCE

✳ A clear conscience is usually the sign of a bad memory.

✳ A conscience is what hurts when all your other parts feel so good.

✳ Why does a man have a clear conscience? Because it's unused.

# CONSTIPATION, DIARRHEA, AND INCONTINENCE

✳ A man goes to his doctor suffering from constipation. The doctor prescribes a powerful laxative but asks the man some questions so he can calculate the right dosage. "How long will it take you to get home from here?" asks the doctor. "20 minutes," replies the man. The doctor pours a dose of laxative into a glass. "And how long will it take you to get from the front door of your house to your bathroom?" asks the doctor. "I'd guess about 30 seconds," replies the man. The doctor adds a small amount of laxative to the glass. "And how long will it take you to drop your pants and sit on the toilet?" asks the doctor. "I'd say 5 seconds," answers the man. The doctor adds a tiny amount of laxative to the glass and gives it to the man. "Take that, drink it all down, and go straight home," says the doctor. The next day the doctor calls the man to see how he's feeling. "Not so good," replies the man. "Didn't the laxative work?" asks the doctor. "It worked fine," replies the man. "But it was 7 seconds early."

✳ Did you hear about the constipated accountant? He couldn't budget.

✳ Did you hear about the constipated composer? He got stuck on his last movement.

✳ Did you hear about the constipated mathematician? He worked it out with a pencil.

✳ Four out of five people say they suffer from diarrhea. So does that mean that one out of the five actually enjoys it?

✳ I go with the flow—I'm a bed-wetter.

✳ If diarrhea only runs down one leg, is it called monorrhea?

✳ A man returns from safari and tells his friend about a narrow escape he had. "I was by the water hole when a lion jumped out at me, so I ran for the tents," says the man. "It had just about caught up with me when it slipped and I managed to vault over a log. The lion jumped over the log too, but then it slipped up and landed on its back. By that time I was almost at the tents and I could see the safari guide with his gun, so I called out and he took aim. But he couldn't fire because the lion was only a few feet behind me. It bounded up at me, then it slipped again, and I had just enough time to duck into the camp before the guide shot it." "Oh my god," says this friend. "If that had happened to me, I'd have crapped myself." "I did," replies the man. "Why do you think the lion kept slipping?"

✳ A man walks into a bar and sits down next to an old drunk. He smells a foul odor, turns to the drunk and says, "Jesus! Did you crap your pants?" "Yup," replies the drunk. "Then why don't you go to the bathroom?" asks the man. The drunk replies, "Cause I ain't finished yet!"

✳ A nurse walks into a hospital waiting room and is greeted with an unmistakable stench. "Who messed their pants?" she asks. No one answers so, determined to get to the bottom of the odor, she walks around to each patient. Finally she finds the culprit, an old drunk in the corner. "Hey," she says. "How come you didn't answer when I asked who messed their pants?" "Oh," replies the drunk. "I thought you meant today."

✳ A teenager is giving an old man a lift. He pulls out into the heavy traffic so fast the tires start smoking. "Phew," says the young driver. "Can you smell that shit?!" The terrified old man replies, "I should think I can. I'm sitting in it!"

✳ Diarrhea is hereditary. It runs in your jeans.

✳ Three old men are comparing ailments. "I've got problems," says one. "Every morning at seven o'clock I get up and try to urinate, but I can never manage it." The second old man says, "You think you have problems. Every morning at eight o'clock I get up and try to move my bowels, but it never works." The third old man speaks up, "Every morning at seven o'clock I urinate and every morning at eight o'clock I defecate." "You've got no problem then," says the first man. "Yes I do," says the third man. "I don't wake up till nine."

✳ Constipation is the thief of time, but diarrhea waits for no man.

# CONTRACTORS

✳ If contractors built buildings the way lawyers write laws, the first woodpecker to come along would destroy civilization.

✳ The son of a contractor is approaching his sixth birthday and his father asks him what he'd like as a present. "What I really want is a baby brother." says the boy. "Sorry, son," says the father. "Your birthday is five days away, I can't get you a baby brother in that time." The son replies, "Can't you do what you do at work and put more men on the job?"

✳ Two men on a building site are arguing about who's the strongest. One says to the other, "I bet you a week's wages I can haul a load in this wheelbarrow that you'd never be able to lift off the ground." "Okay," says the second man. "You're on." The first man grabs the handles of the barrow and says, "All right. Hop in."

✳ Tom and Dick are building a house when Tom sees Dick going through a bag of nails. He looks at each nail in turn and some he puts into a box and others he throws into a trash can. "Why are you throwing those nails away?" asks Tom. "Because they're pointed at the wrong end," says Dick. "You idiot," replies Tom. "Those nails are for the other side of the house."

✳ Fred West is interviewed by the police. "How many people have you murdered?" asks the detective. "Fourteen," replies West. "You're a liar," replies the detective. "We've just dug up your garden and found twenty." "Be fair," replies West. "I'm a contractor. It was only an estimate."

# COSMETIC SURGERY

✳ A forty-seven-year-old man has a face lift for his birthday. On his way home from the clinic, he pops into the newsstand to buy a paper. Before leaving he says to the vendor, "I hope you don't mind my asking, but how old do you think I am?" "About thirty-five," is the reply. "I'm actually forty-seven years old," the man says, feeling really happy. Next he goes into the butcher shop and, again, before leaving he asks the same question, to which the reply is "Oh, you look about twenty-nine." This makes the man feel really good. While standing at a bus stop, he asks an old woman the same question. She replies, "I'm eighty-five years old and my eyesight is going. But when I was young there was a sure way of telling a man's age. If I put my hand down your pants and play with your wedding tackle for ten minutes, I will be able to tell your exact age." The man thinks "What the hell" and lets her slip her hand down his trousers. Ten minutes later the old lady announces, "You're forty-seven years old." Stunned, the man says, "That was incredible. How did you do that?" The old lady replies, "I was behind you in the butcher shop."

✳ A plastic surgeon is asked if he's ever been asked to do anything unusual. "No," replies the surgeon. "But I have raised a few eyebrows."

✳ A woman goes to a plastic surgeon and has a radical new treatment. The surgeon puts a small screw in the back of her head so she can turn it and tighten up her skin every time it shows signs of wrinkling. A month later she comes back very upset: "Doctor your treatment is horrible! Look at my face! The bags under my eyes are huge, and no matter how much I turn the screw they won't go away!" "They're not bags," replies the doctor, "those are your breasts. And if you keep turning that screw you're going to end up with a goatee."

✳ Female patient: "Doctor, after my bust enhancement will the scars show?" Doctor: "Well, that's rather up to you."

✳ I don't know anything about cosmetic surgery, but a good rule of thumb is, it's time to stop when you look permanently frightened.

✳ Man, to friend: "I'm sure that woman has had a face lift." Friend: "How can you tell?" Man, "Every time she crosses her legs her mouth snaps shut."

✳ She had one of those non-surgical face lifts. She was really pleased with it, but to be honest, you could see some of the tape at the sides.

✳ She's had her face lifted so often, when she raises her eyebrows, her socks go up.

✳ "She got her looks from her father—he's a plastic surgeon." *Groucho Marx*

✳ My wife went to have a face-lift last week, but when they saw what was under it they dropped it again.

# COSTUME PARTIES

✳ A man goes to a costume party with a woman draped over his shoulders and says he's come as a tortoise. "Who's that on your back?" asks the host. "That?" he says. "That's Michelle."

✳ When he met her at the costume party she said she'd come as an old witch. Unfortunately when he woke up beside her the next morning, he discovered she hadn't been wearing a costume.

✳ A man turns up at a costume party, completely naked apart from a bit of colored ribbon tied around one of his testicles. "What have you come as?" asks the host. "I'm it," says the man. "I'm the costume ball."

✳ Doris had a very imaginative costume. She stripped naked, dyed her pubic hair black, put on black gloves and shoes, and went as the five of spades.

# COWBOYS

✳ A cowboy comes out of a saloon and finds that someone has painted his horse with whitewash. He storms back inside and shouts, "Which one of you bastards whitewashed my horse?" A huge gunslinger stands up and says, "Me. Why d'you want to know?" "No reason," says the cowboy. "Just thought I'd tell you the first coat is dry."

✳ A cowboy rides into town and hitches his horse to a post. He then lifts his horse's tail and kisses its backside. An old-timer is watching and asks what's going on. "It helps my chapped lips," replies the cowboy. "Y' mean kissing a horse's ass cures 'em?" says the old timer. "It doesn't cure them," replies the cowboy. "But it stops me from licking them."

✳ A cowboy rides into town and stops at the saloon. However, when he's finished his drink, he walks out to find his horse has been stolen. The cowboy walks back into the bar, loosens his guns in their holsters and says, "I'm gonna have another beer, and if my horse ain't back outside by the time I'm finished, I'm gonna do what I dun back in Texas." The cowboy has his drink and goes out to find his horse is back where he left it. The bartender calls out after him, "Hey partner, what exactly did happen in Texas?" The cowboy says, "I had to walk home!"

✳ Roy Rogers gets a brand new pair of cowboy boots. He leaves them out on the porch of his ranch house and, in the morning, discovers they've been gnawed by a mountain lion. Roy grabs a rifle and his horse and goes out to kill the varmint. Three hours later

Roy's back with a dead mountain lion tied across his saddle. A ranch-hand goes up to him and says, "Pardon me, Roy. Is that the cat that chewed your new shoes?"

✳ Two cowboys stagger out of a zoo with their clothes in shreds. One turns to the other and says, "That lion dancing sure ain't as restful as they made out."

✳ Why are cowboy hats like hemorrhoids? Because sooner or later, every asshole gets one.

✳ Did you hear about the cowboy dressed in brown paper? He was arrested for rustling.

# COWS

✳ If a cow laughs, does milk come out of her nose?

✳ What has four legs and says "Boo?" A cow with a cold.

✳ What's the difference between a duck and a cow? They both swim, except for the cow.

✳ What's the difference between a hamster and a cow? Cows survive the branding.

✳ Where do milkshakes come from? Excited cows!

✳ Why do cows have horns? Because they'd look silly with bells on their heads.

✳ Two cows, Daisy and Dolly, are in a field. Daisy says, "I was artificially inseminated this morning." "I don't believe you," says Dolly. Daisy says, "It's true, no bull!"

# DANCING

✳ "I could dance with you until the cows come home—on second thought, I'd rather dance with the cows until you come home." *Groucho Marx*

✳ "I grew up with six brothers. That's how I learned to dance—waiting for the bathroom." *Bob Hope*

✳ "I was watching a ballet at City Center. I'm not a ballet fan at all, but they were doing the dying swan, and there was a rumor that some bookmakers had drifted into town and that they'd fixed the ballet. Apparently there was a lot of money bet on the swan to live." *Woody Allen*

✳ Ballet dancers are always dancing around on their toes. Why don't they just hire taller dancers?

✳ Did you hear about the overweight ballerina? She had to wear a three-three.

✳ Who invented break dancing? A guy trying to steal hubcaps off a moving car.

✳ Did you hear about the tap dancer who slipped and fell in the sink?

✳ "My friend Winnie spends all of his time practicing limbo. He's pretty good. He can go under a rug." *Steven Wright*

# DATING

✳ "What is a date, really, but a job interview that lasts all night? Only difference between a date and a job interview is that not many job interviews have a chance that you'll end up naked at the end of it. 'Well, Bill, the boss thinks you're the man for the position, why don't you strip down and meet some of the people you'll be working with.'" *Jerry Seinfeld*

✳ A bachelor asks a computer dating agency to find him the perfect mate. "I want a companion who is small and cute," he says. "She must love water sports and enjoy group activities." The computer says, "Marry a penguin."

✳ A college student picks up his date at her parents' home. He's scraped together every penny he has to take her to a fancy restaurant but, to his dismay, she orders everything expensive on the menu. Appetizers, lobster, champagne—everything. Finally he says, "Does your mother feed you like this at home?" "No," replies his date, "but then Mother's not looking to get laid."

✳ A girl asks her lover, "If we get engaged, will you give me a ring?" "Of course," he says. "What's your phone number?"

✳ A girl brings her boyfriend home after a night on the town. Her parents are in, so she tells him to be quiet. Unfortunately, the boyfriend is desperate to use the bathroom, but rather than send him upstairs and risk his waking the parents, she tells him to use the kitchen sink. A few minutes later he sticks his head around the corner. "Have you finished?" she whispers. "Yes," he replies. "Have you got any paper?"

✳ A young couple park in Lovers Lane. "It's very peaceful," says the girl. "Listen, you can hear the crickets." "They're not crickets," replies the boy. "They're zippers."

✳ A girl brings her boyfriend home for the first time, and her father takes him aside. "I hope you're going to respect my daughter," he says. "I want her to know the difference between right and wrong." "You've brought her up to know what's right, haven't you?" asks the boy. "Yes, I have," says the father. The boy replies, "Good. Well now I'm taking care of the other side."

✳ A kiss is an application in the top floor for a job in the basement.

✳ A lonely frog goes to a fortune teller. "You're going to meet a beautiful young girl who will want to know everything about you," says the fortune teller. The frog is thrilled. "This is great!" he croaks. "Will I meet her at a party?" "No," replies the fortune teller, "in a biology class."

✳ A man gives his girlfriend a small diamond. "You said I was getting an engagement ring," complains the girl. "This is just an unmounted stone." "Don't worry," says the man. "It'll be mounted the day after you are."

✳ A man goes into a bar and sees a beautiful woman sitting at a table. After gathering up his courage, he finally goes over to her and says, "Um, would you mind if I chatted with you for a while?" She yells back, "No! I won't sleep with you tonight!" Everyone in the bar is now staring at them, and the man slinks back to his table. After a few minutes, the woman walks over to him and apologizes. "I'm sorry if I embarrassed you," she says. "You see, I'm a graduate student in psychology, and I'm studying how people respond to embarrassing situations." The man shouts back, "What do you mean $200?"

✳ A mushroom walks into a bar. He sits next to a beautiful woman and tries to pick her up. He gives her a few cheap lines, but she says, "Get out of here, I don't want anything to do with you!" The mushroom replies, "What's the matter? I'm a fun-gi!"

✳ Harry and Tom are discussing former girlfriends. Harry says, "Y'know I once dumped a girl because she had an incurable speech impediment." "That was cruel," replies Tom. "What was her problem?" Harry replies, "She couldn't say 'yes.'"

✳ A teenage boy comes home and announces that he wants to marry the girl next door, Jane Jones. His father takes him aside and says, "I'm sorry, Son, but years ago I was having an affair with Jane's mother and I got her pregnant. You can't marry her because she's your half-sister." A month later the son comes home and announces that he wants to marry a girl up the street, Sarah Smith. Again his father confesses that he once had an affair with Mrs. Smith, and that Sarah is in fact another half-sister. A month later the son announces his engagement to Amy Armstrong, but once more his father confesses that Amy is in fact another of his daughters. The son complains to his mother. "Dad's driving me crazy," he says. "Every time I fall in love with a girl it turns out she's one of Dad's daughters." "Oh pay no attention to him," says his mother. "It's not like he's your real father."

✳ A young man takes his Chinese girlfriend on a date. After a night of drinking they go back to his place and end up in the bedroom. "What do you want to do?" asks the Chinese girl. "I'm up for anything." "Okay," replies the boyfriend. "What I'd really like is some sixty-nine." "Oh forget it!" she replies, "I'm not cooking at this time of night!"

✳ A young woman brings her boyfriend, a theology student, home to meet her parents. "Do you own a house?" asks her father. "Not yet, but God will provide," says the student. "And how do you intend to earn a living?" asks her father. "I don't know, but God will provide," replies the student. "Have you made any long-term plans?" asks her father. "No," says the student. "But I trust God will provide." Later the mother asks the father what he thought of their prospective son-in-law. "Well, he's broke and seems fairly stupid," replies the father. "But on the other hand, he thinks I'm God."

✳ A young woman is sitting in a café telling her friends her idea of the perfect mate. "The man I marry must be a shining light among company. He must be musical. Tell jokes. Sing. Entertain. And stay home at night!" The elderly waitress overhears her and says, "If that's all you want, get a TV!"

✳ Advice to single girls—don't look for a husband, look for a bachelor.

✳ Girl, to friend: "I had a terrible time last night, I had to slap my boyfriend three times." Friend: "What, to keep him in line?" Girl: "No, to keep him awake."

✳ Girl, to mother: "I've been out with dozens of boys and I haven't let one of them kiss me." Mother: "Really? And which one was that?"

✳ Girl, to mother: "My boyfriend boasts to everyone that he's going to marry the most beautiful girl in the world." Mother: "Oh that's a shame. I thought he liked you."

✳ Harry wants to get married but can't find a girl his mother approves of. To solve this dilemma a friend suggests that he look for a girl just like his mother, so he does. He finds a woman who looks like her, dresses like her, and talks like her. Then he takes her home to meet his parents. "How did it go?" asks the friend. "Terrible," says Harry. "Father hated her guts."

✳ I once met a girl who said I could fill a void in her life. It was only later I realized she'd been referring to her wardrobe.

✳ Ladies, go for younger men. You might as well—they never mature anyway.

✳ My girlfriend told me I should be more affectionate. So I got two girlfriends.

✳ On their first date, Sam asks Rosie what she'd like to do. Rosie replies, "Get weighed!" Sam finds this a curious request but takes her to the automatic scales outside the pharmacy. Then he suggests they go to the movies. After seeing the film, Sam again asks Rosie what she wants to do. "Get weighed!" says Rosie. Again Sam takes her to the pharmacy, to get weighed, then suggests they have a meal. After dinner he asks what she'd like to do now. "Get weighed!" says Rosie. Sam is exasperated by these odd requests, and after taking her to the pharmacy for another weighing, drops her home. Rosie's mother greets her at the door. "How was your date, darling?" asks her mother. "Wousy!" replies Rosie.

✳ Suitor, to man: "Sir, I want your daughter for my wife." Man: "Well, go home and tell your wife she can't have my daughter."

✳ Tom's very lonely. He goes to women's prisons and volunteers for conjugal visits.

✳ Tom confronts his girlfriend. "Who were you talking to on the phone? Is there somebody else?" "Of course not," replies his girlfriend. "Do you think I'd be hanging out with a loser like you if there were somebody else?"

✳ The date had gone well, but her kisses left something to be desired—the rest of her.

✳ Tom, to Dick: "Who was that girl I saw you with last night?" Dick: "It was someone from school." Tom: "Teacher?" Dick: "No. I didn't have to."

✳ A girl goes to her mother and says, "I've found a man just like Daddy!" Mother replies, "So what do you want from me, sympathy?"

✳ Two Broadway showgirls are dressing for a performance when one notices that her friend is no longer wearing a flashy engagement ring. "What happened, Lily?" she asks. "Is the wedding off?" "Yeah," replies Lilly. "I saw him in a bathing suit last week, and he looked so different without his wallet."

✳ What's the difference between a walrus and a fox? About seven drinks.

✳ When I was in high school, I got in trouble with my girlfriend's dad. He said, "I want my daughter back by 8:15." I said, "The middle of August? Cool!"

✳ When I'm not in a relationship, I shave one leg so it feels like I'm sleeping with a woman.

✳ When virtual reality gets cheaper than dating, humanity is doomed.

✳ Why is an engagement ring like a tourniquet to a bachelor? It stops his circulation.

✳ "A girl phoned me the other day and said, 'Come on over, there's nobody home.' I went over. Nobody was home." *Rodney Dangerfield*

✳ A man visits his girlfriend in her tenth-floor apartment. While waiting for her to get ready for an evening out, he starts playing ball with her pet dog, Fluffy. Unfortunately

Fluffy gets carried away and, when the ball accidentally flies out of the window, Fluffy follows it, plunging to the pavement. The girlfriend comes out and says, "Are you all right? You look as white as a sheet." "I'm fine," replies the man, "But, tell me, has Fluffy been showing any signs of depression?"

✳ A young woman goes to confession. "Bless me Father, for I have sinned," she says. "Last night my boyfriend made love to me seven times." "My child," replies the priest. "You must go home and suck the juice of seven lemons." "And will that absolve me?" asks the woman. "No," replies the priest. "But it might take that smug look off your face."

✳ Harry and his fiancée Daphne go to the carnival. Daphne wants to go on the ferris wheel but Harry gets vertigo, so she goes up alone. After she's been around a few times, a girder snaps in the wheel, Daphne's cart tips over, and she's thrown to the ground. Harry runs up and says, "Oh my God, darling! Are you hurt?" "What do you think?" replies Daphne. "I went around three times and you didn't wave once..."

✳ See no evil, hear no evil, date no evil.

✳ Two men are sitting in a singles club. They're talking about another man sitting at the bar. "I don't get it," complains one. "He's ugly, he has no taste in clothes, he drives a wreck of a car, yet he always manages to go home with the most beautiful women here!" "Yeah," replies the other, "He's not even a very good conversationalist. All he does is sit there and lick his eyebrows."

✳ Woman to friend: "My feelings toward him changed so I broke off the engagement." Friend: "So why are you still wearing his ring?" Woman: "Because my feelings for the ring haven't changed."

✳ What did Jack the Ripper's mother keep saying to him? "No wonder you're still single; you never go out with the same girl twice."

✳ A lot of people wonder how you know if you're really in love. Just ask yourself this one question: Would I mind being financially destroyed by this person?

✳ I almost fell in love with a psychic, but she left me before we met.

✳ You can get by on charm for about fifteen minutes. After that, you'd better have a big dick or huge boobs.

✳ You cannot make someone love you. All you can do is stalk them and hope they panic and give in.

# DEATH

* "Either he's dead or my watch has stopped." *Groucho Marx*

* "I always remember the last words of my grandfather—'A truck!'" *Emo Phillips*

* "I don't want to achieve immortality through my work. I want to achieve immortality by not dying." *Woody Allen*

* "I'll tell you what makes my blood boil—crematoriums." *Tim Vine*

* "I'm not afraid to die. I just don't want to be there when it happens." *Woody Allen*

* A doctor pulls the bedsheet over the face of one his patients. He turns to the nurse and says, "We'll look on the bright side. At least he's stable."

* "My girlfriend's weird. One day she asked me, "If you could know how and when you were going to die, would you want to know?" I said, "No." She said, "Okay, forget it." *Steven Wright*

* "What's the death rate around here?" "Same as everywhere else—one per person."

* "When I die, I'm leaving my body to science fiction." *Steven Wright*

* A doctor is speaking to his patient. "The results of your last test are conclusive," he says. "You've got six months to live." "Oh my God," says the patient. "Is there any thing I can do?" "You could try lots of mud baths," says the doctor. "And will that cure me?" asks the patient. "No," replies the doctor. "But it will help you get used to lying in dirt."

* "I'm really worried," says a nervous patient to his nurse. "Last week, I read about a man who was in the hospital because of heart trouble and he died of malaria." "Relax," replies the nurse. "This is a first-rate hospital. When we treat you for heart trouble, you die of heart trouble."

* A father is at the beach when his four-year-old son runs up, grabs his hand, and leads him to where a seagull is lying dead in the sand. "Daddy, what happened?" asks the little boy. "Well, son," says Dad. "This seagull died and he went up to Heaven." "Uh huh," says the boy. "So why did God throw him back down?"

* A flabby middle-aged woman has a near-death experience on the operating table. However, she hears the voice of God telling her not to worry, as he will give her another thirty years of life. When she recovers, the woman decides to make the most of the time left to her. She has extensive plastic surgery and takes a long exercise program to lose weight and get back into shape. After she's transformed herself, she takes up tennis

but is killed by a bolt of lightning during her first game. Standing before God the woman complains, "So what was all that about giving me another thirty years?" God does a double-take, puts on his glasses, and says, "Oh, sorry. I didn't recognize you."

✳ A little boy is in his back garden filling in a hole. A neighbor looks over the fence and asks what he's doing. "I'm burying my pet goldfish," says the little boy. "That's a big hole for a little goldfish, isn't it?" comments the neighbor. "Not really," replies the little boy. "It's inside your damn cat."

✳ Death is God's way of saying "Hey, you're not alive any more."

✳ A man goes on vacation to Jamaica. His wife is on a business trip and is planning to meet him there the next day. When the man reaches his hotel, he sends his wife a quick e-mail but mistypes the address. The next day the grieving wife of a recently dead preacher checks her e-mail, screams, and drops dead from a heart attack. Her family find a disturbing message on the screen: "Dearest Wife, Just got checked in. Everything prepared for your arrival tomorrow. Your Loving Husband. P.S. Sure is hot down here."

✳ A rich businessman goes on vacation. While he's away his butler sends him a message saying "The cat's dead." Distraught at the death of his beloved pet, the man returns home and berates the butler for being so callous. "You should break bad news gently," says the businessman. "If I'd been telling you that your cat was dead, I'd have written, 'The cat's on the roof and can't get down.' A few hours later I'd have written, 'The cat's fallen off the roof and is badly hurt.' A while later I would have sent another message saying, 'The cat has sadly passed away.'" "Very good, sir," says the butler, "I'll remember that in future." The businessman resumes his trip, books into his hotel, and finds that the butler has left another message—it reads, "Your mother is on the roof and can't get down."

✳ A woman goes for her yearly check-up and is told she only has one day to live. She rushes home, explains her condition to her husband, and says, "I want us to spend my last night having wild, crazy sex." Her husband exclaims, "Well, that's easy for you to say. You don't have to get up in the morning!"

✳ A woman is speaking to her friend: "My husband has got one foot in the grate." "Don't you mean one foot in the 'grave'?" says the friend. "No," replies the woman. "He wants to be cremated."

✳ Always go to other people's funerals, or they won't go to yours.

✳ A woman's coffin is being carried to the graveyard when it's accidentally knocked against a wall. The pallbearers hear a low moan from inside and the casket is thrown open to reveal that the woman is still alive. She lives for another ten years and when she dies, her body is taken to the same graveyard. As the pallbearers approach the graveyard's entrance, the woman's husband shouts out, "And this time watch out for the damn wall!"

✳ An elderly couple die in a heat-wave, but there have been so many deaths, the local undertakers can't cope. In desperation, the ambulance driver takes the two corpses to a taxidermist to see if he can help. "I'll do what I can," says the taxidermist. "But do you want them mounted?" "Nah," says the ambulance driver. "Holding hands will be fine."

✳ First man: "I follow the medical profession." Second man: "Are you a doctor?" First man: "No, I'm an undertaker."

✳ George visits his lawyer to make a will. "So what exactly do I do?" asks Harry. "Just answer a few questions then leave it all to me," says the lawyer. "Well," says George, "I'm really fond of you, but I was hoping to leave some of it to my wife."

✳ Harry believed so strongly in reincarnation, he wrote a will leaving everything to himself.

✳ Harry is walking down the road when he notices an unusual funeral procession approaching the local cemetery. A hearse is followed by a second hearse, and behind that walks a solitary man with a pitbull on a leash. Following behind the man are 200 other men walking in single file. Curious, Harry approaches the man with the dog. "I hope you don't mind my asking, but whose funeral is this?" The man replies, "Well, the first hearse is for my wife. She died after my dog attacked her. And the second hearse is for my mother-in-law. She was trying to help my wife when the dog turned on her too." A thoughtful moment of silence passes. "Any chance I could borrow your dog?" asks Harry. "Join the line," says the man.

✳ Harry's wife dies and he takes it very badly—he even collapses over her coffin at the funeral. A friend takes him aside and tries to calm him down. "Look, Harry. It's tough right now but you'll get over it. Who knows, in five or six months you might even find yourself a new girl." "Five or six months?" sobs Harry. "What am I going to do tonight?"

✳ He's not dead, he's just electroencephalographically challenged.

✳ I wouldn't be caught dead with a necrophiliac.

✳ I want to die peacefully, in my sleep, like my grandfather. Not screaming and terrified, like his passengers.

✳ If he were alive today, he'd turn in his grave.

✳ If you get fed up with elderly relatives coming up to you at weddings and saying "You'll be next," try doing the same to them at funerals.

✳ Mary gets married and has seventeen children. Her husband dies, so she remarries two weeks later and has another twelve children. Her second husband then dies, as does Mary a month later. The local priest attends her wake and looks down on her in her coffin. "Thank God," says the priest. "The two of them are together at last." "So, Father," says one of the mourners. "When you say that, are you talking about her first husband, or her second husband?" "I'm not talking about her husbands," says the priest. "I'm talking about her legs."

\* My grandmother died on her ninetieth birthday. It was a terrible shame. We were only halfway through giving her the presents at the time.

\* My grandfather worked in a whiskey distillery. One night he was working late, fell in the vat, and six hours later he drowned. It shouldn't really have taken him that long to die, but he'd got out three times to go to the toilet.

\* Only the young die good.

\* Reporter, to man: "Is it true that you found the body of a complete stranger in your back garden?" Man: "Well, no, he was a partial stranger—he had an arm and a leg missing."

\* The last funeral I went to had people in the front pew whom I wouldn't have to my funeral over my dead body.

\* The man who wrote the song "The Hokey Pokey" was buried yesterday, but they had a lot of trouble keeping his body in the casket. They'd put his left leg in…

\* Where there's a will, I want to be in it.

\* Three bodies turn up at the mortuary, all with huge smiles on their faces. The coroner calls the chief of police to tell him the causes of death. "First body: Frenchman. Died, smiling, of heart failure while making love to his mistress. Second body: Scotsman. Won a thousand dollars on the lottery. Spent it all on whiskey. Died, smiling, of alcohol poisoning. Third body: Irishman. Died, smiling, after being struck by lightning." "Why was the Irishman smiling?" asks the police chief. The coroner replies, "He thought he was having his picture taken."

\* Three friends die in a car crash and find themselves at the gates of Heaven. Before entering, they are each asked a question by Saint Peter. "When you are in your coffin and friends and family are mourning you," says the saint, "what would you like to hear them say about you?" The first friend says, "I would like to hear them say that I was a great doctor and a great family man." The second friend says, "I would like to hear that I was a wonderful husband and wonderful school teacher." The third friend says, "I would like to hear them say, 'Look! He's moving!'"

\* Tom, Dick, and Harry are building a skyscraper. Tom falls off and is killed instantly, and Harry is sent to break the news to his wife. Two hours later Harry comes back carrying a six-pack. "Where did you get the beer?" asks Dick. "Tom's wife gave it to me," replies Harry. "That's unbelievable," says Dick. "You told the lady her husband's dead, and she gave you beer?" "Not exactly," replies Harry. "When she answered the door I said to her, "You must be Tom's widow." She said, "I'm not a widow." And I said, "Wanna bet me a six-pack?"'

✳ Two men are at a friend's funeral. "Do you know if he left his wife much?" asks one. "Yes," said the other. "Almost every night."

✳ What did the corpse say when they lowered his coffin into the wrong hole? "You're making a grave mistake."

✳ What do a coffin and a condom have in common? They're both full of stiffs. Why are the stiffs different? One's coming, the other's going.

✳ Widow, to friend: "Don't talk to me about lawyers, I had so much trouble settling his estate I sometimes wished he hadn't died at all." .

✳ When her late husband's will is read out, a widow learns he's left the bulk of his fortune to another woman. Enraged, she rushes to change the inscription on her spouse's tombstone. "Sorry, lady," says the stone mason. "I inscribed 'Rest in Peace' on your orders. I can't change it now." "Okay," she replies grimly. "Just add 'Until We Meet Again.'"

✳ "I know when I'm going to die—my birth certificate has an expiration date." *Steven Wright*

✳ "My uncle Jack died the other day." "Oh dear. What of?" "I don't know, but apparently it wasn't anything serious."

✳ A little boy goes up to his granddad and says, "Granddad, can you make a sound like a frog?" "Well I suppose I could if I tried," replies Granddad. "Great!" replies the boy, "because Grandma said we can all go to Disneyland when you croak."

✳ A son is discussing funeral arrangements with his dying mother. "Would you like to be buried or cremated?" asks the son. The mother replies, "I don't know. Surprise me."

✳ Death must be the best part of life; it's always saved for last.

✳ In one Intensive Care Unit, patients always died in the same bed at 11 a.m. on a Sunday morning, regardless of their condition. This puzzled the medical staff, so a group of doctors decided to observe the bed in secret and waited for the fateful hour. Some held crosses and prayer books to ward off evil influences, while the less superstitious had video cameras to capture every moment on tape. At the eleventh hour, the door to the ward slowly opened, then a cleaner came in, disconnected the life support and plugged in a vacuum cleaner.

✳ The body-snatchers, Burke and Hare, go to a mortuary to try to claim one of the bodies. "Did your deceased relative have any distinguishing features?" asks the suspicious undertaker. "Well," says Burke. "He was a little deaf in one ear."

✳ Tom, to Dick: "My grandfather knew the exact date of his death and the exact time of day he would die." Dick: "Incredible. Was he psychic?" Tom: "No. The judge told him."

✳ Why are there fences around cemeteries? Because people are dying to get in.

✳ "They say such nice things about people at their funerals that it makes me sad to realize that I'm going to miss mine by just a few days." *Garrison Keillor*

✳ Old bankers never die—they just lose interest.

✳ Old bricklayers never die—they just throw in the trowel.

✳ A bereaved wife listens as a lawyer reads out her late husband's will. "My dear wife," reads the lawyer. "I always said I'd mention you in my will, so: Hi Beryl, I'm leaving it all to the cat."

✳ Harry died when he went to give blood the other day—he forgot to say "when."

# DEATH: AFTERLIFE

✳ A woman goes to a psychic and contacts her recently dead husband. "Are you happy?" asks the woman. "Yes," says the husband. "I'm in a field surrounded by beautiful cows." "Can you see any angels?" asks the woman. "No, but there's a prize-winning cow standing in front of me. A real stunner." "Have you seen God?" asks the woman. "No," replies the husband. "But the cows are really, really fantastic." "Why do you keep going on about cows?" shouts the woman. "Sorry," says the husband, "I forgot to mention— I'm in Wisconsin. I've come back as a bull."

✳ Psychiatrist, to patient: "How long have you believed in reincarnation?" Patient: "Ever since I was a puppy."

✳ Trying to contact her dead husband, Edna goes to a psychic who tells her that her husband is fine and looking forward to their reunion. "Is there anything he needs?" asks Edna. The psychic replies, "He says he'd love a pack of cigarettes." "Oh," says Edna. "And did he say where I should try to send them?" "No," replies the psychic. "But then again, he didn't ask for any matches."

✳ "Sex is one of the nine reasons for reincarnation. The other eight are unimportant." *George Burns*

# DEATH: AFTERLIFE (HEAVEN)

✳ In case Heaven is anything like the IRS, make sure you get a receipt every time you do a good deed.

✳ A famous Hollywood director dies and goes to Heaven. At the Pearly Gates, Saint Peter meets him and says that God would like the director to make one last movie. The director isn't enthusiastic—"I'm tired of making movies," he says, "I just want to rest." "Listen," says Saint Peter, "We've got Ludwig van Beethoven to write a new score for the movie. We've got Leonardo da Vinci to do the set designs. And we've got William Shakespeare to write the script. This could be a really good movie." "Wow," says the director. "With a team like that it could be a fantastic movie. I'll do it!" "That's great!" says Saint Peter. "There's only one hitch. God's got this girlfriend who thinks she can act..."

✳ A man dies and goes to Heaven. He stands before God and sees Jesus sitting at his right hand. However, he's surprised to see a janitor with a mop sitting at God's left hand. "Who are you?" asks the man. "I'm Cleanliness," replies the janitor.

✳ A nurse dies and is greeted in the afterlife by Saint Peter. He tells her there's a policy of allowing people to choose whether they want to spend eternity in Heaven or in Hell, and she can spend a day in each before making a decision. The nurse goes to Hell for the day, where she meets many old friends and colleagues in a sunny garden. They take her for an excellent dinner, and she even meets the Devil, who turns out to be pretty decent. The next day, she spends a day in Heaven, where she sits around on clouds, sings, and plays the harp. When Saint Peter asks what her choice is, she says, "Well, Heaven was nice, but I had a better time in Hell. So I'd like to go there please." Her wish is granted and down to Hell she goes. When she gets there she finds a desolate wasteland covered in filth and her friends, dressed in rags, collecting garbage and putting it in sacks. The Devil walks over to greet her, and the nurse says, "How could this place change so much in a day. Yesterday it was like paradise." The Devil smiles and says, "Yes, but yesterday we were recruiting—today you're staff."

✳ In Heaven, a recently deceased priest and a cab driver are shown their reward for their earthly endeavors. To the priest's disappointment he's given the keys to a small shed in a vegetable patch, while the cab driver is presented with a huge mansion in its own grounds. "What's going on?" complains the priest. "I devoted all my life to the church and all I get is a shed?" "We pay depending on performance," says Saint Peter. "When you preached, people fell asleep, but while the cab driver drove, people prayed like crazy."

✳ The Three Stooges, Larry, Curly, and Mo, die and go to Heaven. At the Pearly Gates, Saint Peter greets them and tells them that, to enter Heaven, each must answer a question. Peter turns to Larry and asks, "What is Easter?" Larry replies, "That's when kids get dressed up in Halloween costumes." "Wrong," says Peter and sends Larry to

Hell. Peter turns to Curly and asks, "What is Easter?" Curly says, "That's when the fat man comes down the chimney." "Wrong," says Peter and sends Curly to Hell. Peter then turns to Mo and asks, "What is Easter?" Mo answers, "That's when Jesus rises out of his grave." "And..." prompts Peter. "And, if he sees his shadow, there's another six weeks of winter!"

✳ Three couples die on the same day and line up at the Pearly Gates. The first couple approaches Saint Peter, who asks them their names. "We're Bill and Penny Jones," says the husband. "Sorry," says Saint Peter. "No one is allowed in with a name connected with money." The second couple approach Saint Peter, "We're Jack and Brandy O'Leary." "Sorry," says Saint Peter. "No one is allowed in with a name that refers to alcohol." The third husband whispers to his wife, "Listen, Fanny, from now we're calling you Mary."

✳ Three women die in an accident and go to Heaven. There, Saint Peter says, "We only have one rule—don't step on the ducks!" They enter Heaven, and sure enough, there are ducks everywhere. In fact, it's almost impossible not to step on a duck, and the first woman accidentally steps on one straight away. Saint Peter comes along with the ugliest man the woman has ever seen and chains them together saying, "Your punishment for stepping on a duck is to spend eternity chained to this ugly man!" The next day the second woman steps on a duck and she too is chained to an incredibly ugly man. The third woman is very, very careful with the ducks and manages to avoid stepping on any of them. One day Saint Peter comes along and chains her to an incredibly handsome man. The woman is delighted but wonders why she's been blessed. She gets on her knees and prays aloud, "Oh Lord, what have I done to deserve this bounty?" The man says, "I don't know about you, lady, but I stepped on a duck."

✳ Two priests die and go to Heaven. Unfortunately a backlog of work means that Saint Peter can't let them in right away. Rather than have them hanging around in limbo, Saint Peter tells the priests that they can return to earth for one week in any form they wish. They can be what they like and do what they like. The first priest says, "I always wanted to be an eagle soaring above the clouds." The second priest says, "Well if I can do anything, I'd like to be a stud." Saint Peter grants them their wishes, and off they go. A week later God asks Saint Peter if Heaven is ready to receive the priests. "Yes," says Saint Peter, "I've sent off angels to bring them back now." "Won't they be difficult to find?" asks God. "Shouldn't be too hard," replies Saint Peter. "The eagle's flying around the Rockies." "And what about the stud?" asks God. The priest replies, "Oh, he's on a tire in Alaska."

✳ A man approaches the Pearly Gates and seeks admittance. Saint Peter asks him if he's ever done any good deeds. "Why, yes," replies the man. "Once I saved a young lady from being attacked by a gang of Hells Angels. I ran my car over their bikes, then got out and kicked the chief biker in the crotch until he let the girl go." "Really?" says Saint Peter. "It doesn't seem to be in our records. When did this take place?" "Oh, about five minutes ago," says the man.

✻ There's a knock on the Pearly Gates. Saint Peter looks out and sees a man waiting to come in. Saint Peter goes out and is about to begin his interview when the man disappears. A short time later there's another knock. Again Saint Peter gets the door, sees the man, opens his mouth to speak, and the man disappears. Saint Peter has just gone back inside when there's yet another knock. Sure enough, the man is back standing at the Gates. "Are you playing games?" says Saint Peter. "No," replies the man. "They're trying to resuscitate me."

# DEATH: AFTERLIFE (HELL)

✻ A dead English lord and his dead butler run into each other in Hell. "My lord," the butler exclaims. "What are you doing here?" The lord sighs, "I'm here because I lied, cheated, and stole to pay the debts run up by that playboy son of mine. But you were a faithful, loyal servant. Why are you here?" The butler replies, "For fathering your playboy son."

✻ An engineer dies and is sent to Hell. He sets to work on the amenities and after a while, they've got hot and cold running water, air conditioning, and flush toilets. One day God hears about the increasing comfort levels in Hell and demands that the engineer is sent up to Heaven. "No way," says the Devil. "I like having an engineer around. I'm keeping him." God says, "Send him back up here or I'll sue." To which the Devil replies, "Oh yeah? And just where are you going to get a lawyer?"

✻ A man dies and goes to hell but is astonished when he's shown into a room full of beautiful women and huge kegs of beer. The man turns to a nearby demon and says, "You call this hell? This is my idea of heaven." The demon replies, "Not so fast, sonny. The kegs all have holes in them, and the women don't."

# DEFINITIONS

✻ "Acquaintance: a person whom we know well enough to borrow from but not well enough to lend to." *Ambrose Bierce*

✻ Abundance: a social event held in a farm building.

✻ Accountant: the sort of man who'd marry Elle Macpherson for her money.

✻ Acme: spots on the top of your head.

✻ Agrophobia: the fear of being beaten up in an open space.

✻ Alcoholic: someone who drinks as much as you do, but whom you don't like.

* Alimony: the screwing you get for the screwing you got.

* Alimony: a mistake by two people paid for by one.

* Arachnophobia: the fear of spiders wearing waterproof coats.

* Antibody: your uncle's wife.

* Aromatic: an automatic crossbow.

* Boycott: somewhere to keep male babies.

* Budget: an orderly system for living beyond your means.

* Campers: nature's way of feeding mosquitoes.

* Catastrophe: first prize at a cat show.

* Claustrophobia: the fear of Santa Claus.

* Climate: what you do with a ladder.

* Cobra: a bra for conjoined twins.

* Committee: a group of the unwilling, picked from the unfit, to do the unnecessary.

* Conference: the confusion of one man multiplied by the number present.

* Conference room: a place where everybody talks, nobody listens, and everybody disagrees later on.

* Confidence: when your wife catches you in bed with another woman and you slap her on the rear saying, "Steady, tiger! You're next!"

* Consciousness: that annoying time between naps.

* Copulate: a late police response.

* Coward: a man who thinks with his legs.

* Déjà Moo: the feeling that you've heard this bullshit before.

* Deliberate: to take back to prison.

* Diatribe: an extinct race.

* Diplomacy: the art of letting someone else get your way.

* Divorce: future tense of marriage.

* Dulcet: a boring tennis match.

* Eternity: the time between your coming and her going.

* Experience: something you don't get until just after you needed it.

* Experience: knowing all the things you shouldn't.

* Expert: someone who takes a subject you understand and makes it sound confusing.

* Factory: a set of encyclopedias.

* Faggot: a lady maggot.

* Failure: a one-armed man trying to climb a rope.

* Fine: a tax for doing wrong. Tax: a fine for doing well.

* Flashlight: a case for holding dead batteries.

* Fortune: a singing quartet.

* His: pronoun, meaning hers.

* Home: the place you stay while your car is being fixed.

* Intense: a camping vacation.

* Karaoke: Japanese for "tone deaf."

* Laugh: a smile that burst.

* Laziness: the overwhelming ambition to lead a quiet life.

* Lecture: the art of transferring information from the notes of the lecturer to the notes of the students without passing through the minds of either.

* Lobster: a tennis champion.

* Lottery: a tax on people who are bad at math.

* Macaroon: a Scottish cookie.

* Maintenance: a man's cash surrender value.

* Margin: mother's ruin.

* Marriage (as defined by men): an expensive way to get laundry done for nothing.

* MC: a man who introduces people who need no introduction.

* Middle age: when you exchange emotions for symptoms.

* Middle age: when you have a choice between two temptations and you choose the one that gets you home the earliest.

* Mistress: something between a mister and a mattress.

* Obscenity: anything that gives the judge a hard-on.

* Odious: bad poetry.

* Office: a place where you can relax after your strenuous home life.

* Optimist: someone who allows his teenage son to borrow the car. A pessimist: one who won't. A pedestrian: one who did.

* Osmosis: an early Australian prophet.

* Out of bounds: an exhausted kangaroo.

* Overture: someone who masticates too loudly.

* Oyster: a large crane.

* Palaver: a kind of sweater.

* Pandemonium: a black and white musical instrument.

* Pantry: a trouser cupboard.

* Parachute: a double-barreled shotgun.

* Peace: a period of unrest and confusion between wars.

* Pessimist: someone who burns their bridges before they get to them.

* Porcupine: a yearning for bacon.

* Portable: cheap furniture.

* Posse: a Wild West cat.

* Reality: the place the pizza delivery man comes from.

* Reoriented: sent back to China.

* Research: something that tells you a donkey has two ears.

* Rugged: the act of sitting on a mat.

* Savory: a piggy bank.

* Shamrock: imitation mineral.

* Shin: a device for finding furniture in the dark.

* Southern gentleman: the guy who gets out of the bath to pee in the sink.

* Spellbinding: the cover of a dictionary.

* Stalemate: old spouse.

* Suburbia: where they tear out the trees and then name streets after them.

* Syntax: the money collected at the church from sinners.

* Tantamount: riding a French aunt.

✳ Time: what keeps things from happening all at once.

✳ Vacation: the two weeks you have to work fifty weeks to pay for.

# DENTISTS AND DENTAL CARE

✳ A dentist is working on a female patient's teeth when he asks her if she'd mind screaming loudly. She does so then asks why. "I've got to catch a train in thirty minutes," he replies. "And my waiting room is packed."

✳ A Texan goes to the dentist. "Your teeth look fine," says the dentist. "Nothing needs doing here." "Drill anyway," says the Texan. "I feel lucky."

✳ A husband and wife enter a dentist's office. The husband says, "I want a tooth pulled. I don't want gas or Novocaine because I'm in a terrible rush. Just pull the tooth as quickly as possible." "You're a brave man," says the dentist. "Now, which tooth is it?" The husband turns to his wife and says, "Show him your tooth, dear."

✳ A patient is asking a dentist his prices. "How much for an extraction?" "Seventy dollars," replies the dentist. "Seventy bucks? For a few minutes' work," complains the patient. "I can make it last all afternoon if you like," replies the dentist.

✳ A woman drops her false teeth in the park and is unable to find them in the long grass. A passerby spots her predicament and offers her a spare set. Unfortunately the teeth are too loose, so the passerby offers her a second pair. These are too tight, so the passerby gives her a third set, which fit perfectly. "Thank you," says the woman. "I've been looking for a good dentist for ages." "I'm not a dentist," says the passerby. "I'm an undertaker."

✳ I used some of that stripy toothpaste. Now I've got striped teeth.

✳ I went to the dentist. He said, "Say, aaah." I said, "Why?" He said, "My dog's died."

✳ My dentist found a very big cavity when he examined me. In fact it was so big he sent me to a podiatrist.

✳ Man, to dentist: "Can you recommend anything for yellow teeth?" Dentist: "A brown tie?"

✳ My uncle was the best false teeth maker in town—they were so lifelike, they even ached.

✳ Three ways to keep your teeth: brush after every meal, see your dentist every few months, and keep your nose out of other people's business.

✳ I accidentally left my electric toothbrush on all night. I've never seen the bathroom look so clean.

✳ Did you hear about the man who put his false teeth in backward and ate himself?

# DICTIONARIES

✳ "The other night I was reading the dictionary—I thought it was a poem about everything." *Steven Wright*

✳ I don't know if you've heard, but apparently they've removed the word "gullible" from the *Oxford English Dictionary*.

✳ "If a word in the dictionary were misspelled, how would we know?" *Steven Wright*

# DISABILITY

✳ A doctor is explaining the idea of sensory compensation to an intern. "If a man becomes blind, his sense of hearing improves to compensate," says the doctor. "Yes, sir," says the intern. "And I've noticed that if one of a man's legs is slightly short, then the other gets slightly longer."

✳ A woman is talking with her neighbor. "Did you know the milkman has a glass eye?" "No," replies the neighbor. "How did you discover that?" "Oh," says the woman, "it just came out when we were chatting."

✳ The Godfather, accompanied by his attorney, meets with his accountant. The Godfather says to the accountant, "Where's the three million bucks you embezzled from me?" The accountant doesn't answer. The Godfather pulls out a gun and says, "If you don't tell me where it is, I'll shoot you in the head and splatter your brains against the wall!" The attorney interrupts, "Sir, the man is unable to hear or speak, but I can interpret for you." The attorney, using sign language, asks the accountant where the three million dollars is. The accountant signs back, "The money's hidden in a suitcase behind the shed in my backyard!" "Well, what did he say?" asks the Godfather. The attorney replies, "He says he doesn't think you have the guts to pull the trigger."

✳ Grandma finally figured out how to stop Grandpa from chasing after other women— she let the air out of his wheelchair tires.

✳ I tried going to the Special Olympics but I couldn't get a parking space anywhere near the place.

✳ Quasimodo comes home and finds Esmeralda holding a wok and a laundry basket. "Great," says Quasimodo. "Are you cooking Chinese tonight?" "No," says Esmerelda. "I'm ironing your shirt."

✳ A woman looking for a boyfriend takes out a personal ad in the paper. It reads "Wanted: a good lover who won't run out on me." A few days later her doorbell rings. She answers it and lying on her doormat is a man with no arms or legs. "I'm responding to your ad," he says. "You must be joking! You don't have any arms or legs!" says the woman. "I know," says the man. "But in your ad, you said you wanted a man who wouldn't run out on you." "Yes," agrees the woman. "But I also want a good lover." The man replies, "Well, how d'you think I rang the doorbell?"

✳ Harry is looking for a new assistant at work but wants to hire someone who is sensitive about his disability—he has no ears. Three men apply for the job, and Harry arranges to meet them. He calls the first man into his office and interviews him. The applicant does very well, but then Harry asks him if notices anything unusual about his appearance. Rather than be tactful and say no, the man says, "Yes. You have no ears." Harry gets upset and throws the man out. The second man is called in and, again, the interview goes very well until Harry asks the same question. Again the man says, "You have no ears." And Harry throws him out. The last man is invited in and the interview proceeds as before. Finally Harry asks the question "Do you notice anything unusual about my appearance?" The man says, "Apart from the contact lenses, no." "That's very observant," says Harry. "Not many people would notice I'm wearing contact lenses." "I didn't," replies the man. "I saw an optometrist's bill on your desk and figured you couldn't wear glasses without any ears."

✳ A man with one leg shorter than the other has a small son with a stutter. One day they're walking down the road when the son says, "D-d-dad, w-w-why n-not t-t-try w-walking w-w-with one f-f-foot in t-the g-g-g-gutter? T-t-that w-w-way p-p-p-people w-w-won't n-n-notice y-your l-l-limp." "Good idea, son," says Dad and puts his long leg in the gutter so it matches his short leg. At this point he's knocked over by a taxi. Later, in the hospital, the little boy is by his father's bedside. "Son," says Dad. "I think I know how we can fix that stutter of yours." "W-w-w-what's t-t-that, d-d-dad?" says the little boy. Dad replies, "You can keep your damn mouth shut."

# DISABILITY: BLINDNESS

❋ A blind man is at the optometrist's with his guide dog. Both are facing the eye test chart on the wall. The optometrist takes the guide dog away, replaces it with another guide dog, and asks, "Is that better or worse?"

❋ A blind man walks into a store with his guide dog. He takes the dog's leash and starts swinging the animal around his head. The storekeeper says, "May I help you, sir?" The blind man replies, "No thanks. I'm just looking."

❋ Stevie Wonder and Tiger Woods get talking in a bar. Tiger is surprised to discover that Stevie can play golf. "How can you play golf blind?" asks Tiger. Stevie says, "I get my caddy to stand in the middle of the fairway. Then he calls to me and I play the ball toward the sound of his voice." "That's fantastic," says Tiger. "So what's your handicap?" "Actually I'm a scratch golfer," says Stevie. "Incredible," says Tiger. "We should play a round sometime." "I'd like that," says Stevie. "But I should warn you, I usually play for $10,000 a hole." "Suits me," says Tiger. "When do you want to play?" "I'm easy," says Stevie. "Pick a night!"

❋ A teacher at a blind school is taking the soccer team to an away game. They stop for a roadside break and the team has an impromptu practice in a nearby pasture. The bus driver comes over to the teacher and asks how he taught blind kids to play soccer. "We made a special ball for them with a bell in it," replies teacher. Just then a farmer comes along—"Hey!" he shouts. "Are you the guy with those damn blind kids from the bus?" "Yes," says teacher. "What about it? You got something against blind kids?" "Not ordinarily," says the farmer. "But right now they're kicking the hell out of my best milk cow!"

❋ Heckle heard from a blind man in the audience: "Get off!…Has he gone yet?"

❋ How can you tell when you have a serious acne problem? Blind people start reading your face.

❋ How do you spot a blind man on a nudist beach? It's not hard.

❋ How does a blind skydiver know if he's approaching the ground? His dog's leash goes slack.

❋ The passengers on a jet watch in horror as the pilot and co pilot walk up the boarding stairs—both are wearing dark glasses and carrying white sticks. There's a buzz of conversation as the two men enter the cockpit. Surely they can't be blind; it must be a joke. The engines fire up and the aircraft starts taxiing down the runway. The passengers are extremely nervous. The plane accelerates down the runway and the passengers watch in horror as the aircraft tears toward the fence at the end of the tarmac. Surely the pilots must see how close they are. Why don't they take off? The plane gets faster and faster as they near the end of the runway. The passengers realize they're not going to make it and start screaming. The nose of the plane lifts up and the plane takes off, missing the boundary fence by inches. The passengers breathe a sigh of relief. In the cockpit, the blind pilot turns to the blind co-pilot and says, "Y'know, one day they're going to scream too late and we're all going to die."

✳ What goes "Click—is that it? Click—is that it? Click—is that it?" A blind man with a Rubik's cube.

✳ Why are Stevie Wonder's legs always wet? Because his dog is blind too.

✳ Two men try to get into a restaurant but both have their dogs with them—a Labrador and a Chihuahua—and are refused entry by the doorman. The two men put on dark glasses and try again. "Can you let me have a table?" asks the man with the Labrador. "I know I have a dog, but I'm blind and this is my guide dog." The man is let in, and the second man tries his luck. "Can you let me have a table for me and my guide dog?" he asks. "That's not a guide dog," says the doorman. "That's a Chihuahua." "A Chihuahua!?" shouts the man. "Those bastards gave me a Chihuahua?!"

✳ Why don't blind people skydive? It scares the dog.

# DISABILITY: DEAFNESS

✳ A little boy is spending Christmas Eve at his grandma's house. When he goes to bed he hangs up his stocking and shouts, "Dear Santa! Please send me a new bike!" Grandma sticks her head around the door and says, "Hush in there! Santa isn't deaf!" "I know," says the little boy. "But you are."

✳ A marriage broker has been given the job of finding a bride for an impoverished middle-aged groom. The broker warns the man's parents that he's not much of a catch, so they'll have to make do with whatever brides are available. However, when the girl is presented, the man's parents are appalled. "Look at her," whispers the father to the mother. "She has knock-knees, cross-eyes, a mustache, a huge wart, and buck teeth." "There's no need to whisper," says the broker. "She's deaf too."

✳ Beethoven was so deaf, he thought he was a painter.

✳ If blind people wear dark glasses, why don't deaf people wear earmuffs?

# DISABILITY: LOSS OF LIMBS, ETC.

✳ "Please don't stand up on my account." *Bob Hope (to an audience of amputees)*

✳ A man working at a lumber yard accidentally shears off his fingers. He runs to the emergency room, where the doctor says, "Give me the fingers, and I'll see what I can do." The man replies, "I haven't got the fingers." The doctor says, "What do you mean, you haven't got the fingers? We could have done microsurgery. I could have put them back on. Why on earth didn't you bring the fingers?" The man replies, "I couldn't pick them up."

✳ "The other day, I saw a man with wooden legs, and real feet." *Steven Wright*

✳ A doctor visits a patient lying in a hospital ward. "I'm sorry," says the doctor, "but I have good news and bad news." "Don't hold back," says the man. "Tell me the bad news." The doctor replies, "Your illness was worse than we thought. We had to amputate both your legs." The man asks, "So what's the good news?" The doctor replies, "The man in the next bed wants to buy your slippers."

✳ My doctor says he has to amputate all of me.

# DOGS

✳ "Did you ever walk in a room and forget why you walked in? I think that's how dogs spend their lives." *Sue Murphy*

✳ "I spilled spot remover on my dog. Now he's gone." *Steven Wright*

✳ "My wife kisses the dog on the lips, yet she won't drink from my glass!" *Rodney Dangerfield*

✳ A dog goes to a telegraph office and dictates a message. "Woof, woof, woof, woof, woof, woof, woof, woof, woof." The operator reads it back then says, "Y'know, we charge per ten words. You could have an extra 'woof' for free." "No thanks," says the dog. "That would sound silly."

✳ "Some dog I got. We call him Egypt because he leaves a pyramid in every room." *Rodney Dangerfield*

✳ "What a dog I got. His favorite bone is in my arm!" *Rodney Dangerfield*

✳ "With my dog I don't get no respect. He keeps barking at the front door. He don't want to go out. He wants me to leave." *Rodney Dangerfield*

✳ A barking dog never bites. Well, at least not while it's barking.

✳ What's a Shih Tzu? A dog. No, a zoo with no animals.

✳ A dog with three legs walks into a Wild West bar and says, "I'm looking for the man who shot my paw."

✳ A mailman meets a boy and a huge dog. "Does your dog bite?" asks the mailman. "No," replies the boy. And the dog bites the mailman's leg. "You said he doesn't bite!" yells the mailman. "That's not my dog," replies the boy.

✳ A dog is sitting in a theater with its owner. The dog stares at the screen intently and growls whenever the villain appears and wags its tail whenever the hero comes on. An old lady has been watching the dog's behavior. She turns to its owner and says, "That's extraordinary behavior for a dog." "You're right," says the owner. "It is surprising – he hated the book."

✳ A man bought a dachshund for his six children so they'd have a dog they could all pet at once.

✳ A man enters a little country store and sees a sign reading, "Danger! Beware of Dog." He then sees an old hound dog lying asleep on the floor. "Is that the dog folks are supposed to beware of?" says the man to the clerk. "Yep," replies the clerk. "Before I posted that sign, everyone kept tripping over him."

✳ A man sees a sign in front of a house—"Talking Dog for Sale." He rings the bell and the owner takes him to the back yard where the dog is chained to a post. "Can you talk?" asks the man. "Yep," says the dog. "I discovered this gift when I was young. I decided to help the government, so I got in touch with the CIA. In no time they had me jetting from country to country, sitting in rooms with spies and world leaders, because no one would think a dog would be eavesdropping. I was one of their most valuable spies eight years running. The jetting around really tired me out though, I wasn't getting any younger and I wanted to settle down. So I signed up for a job at the airport to do some undercover security work, mostly wandering near suspicious characters and listening in. I uncovered some incredible dealings and was awarded a lot of medals. Later I got a wife, had some puppies, and now I'm retired." The man is amazed. He asks the owner what he wants for the dog. "Ten dollars," replies the owner. "That's a low price for such an amazing dog," says the man. "Why on earth are you selling him?" The owner replies, "Because he's such a huge liar."

✳ A man takes his Rottweiler to the vet. "My dog's cross-eyed, is there anything you can do for him?" "Okay," says the vet. "Let's have a look at him." So he picks up the dog examines his eyes and checks his teeth. Finally he says, "I'm going to have to put him down." "What? Because he's cross-eyed?" asks the man. "No," replies the vet. "Because he's really, really heavy."

✳ A man walks by a table in a casino and passes three men and a dog playing cards. "That's a very smart dog," says the man. "He's not so clever," says one of the players. "Every time he gets a good hand, he wags his tail."

✳ A man walks into a bar and says, "Who's the owner of that Great Dane tied up outside?" A man replies, "It's mine. Why do you ask?" The first man says, "I'm sorry, but my dog just killed your dog." The owner of the Great Dane is shocked. "Are you kidding? That dog was huge!" "I know," says the first man, "but he just choked on my Chihuahua…"

✳ A man walks into a bar with a small dog. The guy sits the dog on the piano stool, and the dog starts playing some great tunes. Suddenly a bigger dog runs in, grabs the small dog by the scruff of the neck, and drags it out. The bartender says, "That little dog was fantastic, but what was up with the big dog?" The man replies, "Oh, that was his mother. She wanted him to be a doctor."

✳ Bert takes his dog to the vet and says, "Can you cut off my dog's tail?" "Why do you want me to do that?" asks the vet. Bert replies, "My mother-in-law's arriving tomorrow, and I don't want her to think she's welcome."

✳ I'm opposed to the testing of dog food on animals.

✳ Harry bought a puppy going cheap at the pet shop. It cost him a fortune because it did bird impressions.

✳ Harry goes into a shop and asks for some clothes detergent to wash his dog with. The shopkeeper tells him to use shampoo instead but Harry buys the detergent anyway. A week later Harry returns to the shop to buy a paper. "How's your dog?" asks the shopkeeper. "It died," replies Harry. "I told you detergent wasn't a good idea," replies the shopkeeper. "It wasn't the soap that killed him," says Harry. "It was the spin cycle."

✳ I loathe people who own dogs. They're cowards who haven't got the guts to bite people themselves.

✳ I lost my dog. I didn't know what to do so I put an ad in the newspaper saying "Here, boy!"

✳ I think my dog must have a particularly cold nose. Whenever he walks in a room, all the other dogs sit down.

✳ I've got a dog that barks all night. I'm thinking of buying him a burglar.

✳ Man, to friend: "I've really had it with my dog: he'll chase anyone on a bike." Friend: "What are you going to do? Have him put down?" Man: "No, I think I'll just take his bike away."

✳ My dog has an ingrown tail. I have to have him x-rayed to find out if he's happy.

✳ My dog is worried about the economy because dog food is up to fifty cents a can—that's around $3.50 in dog money.

✳ My dog's very obedient. The other day I said, "Heel!" And he bit me in the heel.

✳ Outside of a dog, a book is man's best friend. Inside of the dog, it's too dark to read.

✳ Three small boys are sitting on the curb when they see a fire engine zoom past. Sitting by the driver is a Dalmatian, and the boys discuss what it might be doing there. "They use him to keep crowds back," says one boy. "He's just for good luck," says the second boy. The third boy brings the argument to a close—"They use him to find the fire hydrants."

✳ We have a watchdog that reacts instantly to intruders—it hides under the bed.

✳ Two neighbors are arguing. "And keep your animal out of my greenhouse!" says one. "It's full of fleas!" The other neighbor turns to her dog and says, "Did you hear that, Rover? Keep out of next-door's greenhouse! It's full of fleas."

✳ Two women are arguing about which has the smarter dog. The first woman says, "My dog's so smart, every morning he runs to the newsstand with money in his mouth, buys a paper, runs back, lets himself into the house, and brings it to me in bed." The second woman replies, "I know." "How could you know?" asks the first woman. The second woman replies, "My dog told me."

✳ Two women are sitting in a vet's waiting room with their dogs, one a Jack Russell, the other a Great Dane. The Jack Russell's owner says she's there because her dog humps anything that moves. "Mine's exactly the same," says the Great Dane's owner. "Oh," says the first owner. "So you're here to have him neutered?" "No," replies the second. "I'm having his toenails trimmed."

✳ We're what you might call the average family. There's me, the wife, and 2.8 kids. We used to have three kids but then we got the pit bull.

✳ What do you call a dog in jeans and a sweater? A plain-clothes police dog.

✳ What do you call a dog that's been run over by a steamroller? Spot.

✳ What do you call a dog with four-inch legs and six-inch steel balls? Sparky.

✳ What do you call a dog with no legs? It doesn't matter, he still won't come.

✳ What do you get if you cross a dog and a lion? A terrified postman.

✳ What do you get if you cross a dog and a sheep? A sheep that can round itself up.

✳ What do you get if you cross a dog with a frog? A dog that can lick you from the other side of the road.

✳ What do you get when you cross Lassie with a pit bull? A dog that bites your leg off and runs for help.

✳ What does a dog become after it is six years old? Seven years old.

✳ What happened when the dog went to the flea circus? He stole the show.

✳ What has four legs and an arm? A happy pit bull.

✳ What looks like a dog, eats dog food, lives in a doghouse, and is very dangerous? A dog with a machine gun.

✳ When does a dog go "Moo"? When it's learning a second language!

✳ What's the difference between a businessman and a warm dog? The businessman wears a suit, the dog just pants.

✳ When dog food is new and improved with a better taste, who tests it?

✳ Why aren't there any dogs on the moon? Because there aren't any trees.

✳ Why did Harry name his dog "Carpenter"? Because he was always doing little jobs around the house.

✳ Why did the dachshund bite the woman's ankle? He couldn't reach any higher.

✳ Why do dogs wag their tails? No one else will do it for them.

✳ Why do you need a license for a dog and not for a cat? Cats can't drive.

✳ Why should you watch out when it rains cats and dogs? Because you might step in a poodle.

✳ A dog goes into an employment agency and asks for a job. "Wow, a talking dog," says the clerk. "With your talent, I'm sure we can find you a job at the circus." "The circus?" says the dog. "What does a circus want with a plumber?"

＊ A man is walking through a park when he steps in a pile of dog doo. He pauses to wipe his shoe on the grass and sees another man step into the same pile. "I just did that," says the man, so the other man rubs his nose in it.

＊ After many years of service, a rich lady decides to fire her housekeeper and hire someone younger. When she hears the news, the housekeeper takes a steak out of the fridge and throws it to the family dog. "Why did you do that?" asks the lady of the house. "I never forget a friend," replies the housekeeper. "That was for his help cleaning the dishes all these years!"

＊ How can you tell if you have kinky dogs? They do it in the missionary position.

＊ Man, to friend: "The dog is just like one of the family." Friend: "Which one?"

＊ One of the great mysteries of life—why do we never see white dog shit any more?

＊ Two men are out walking their dogs. One dog raises its leg for a pee against a wall. The second dog goes to have a pee, but instead of lifting a leg, it stands up on its hind legs, leans both front paws on the wall, and relieves itself. The first dog's owner says, "Wow, how did you teach him that?" The other man replies, "I didn't. He's done that ever since a wall fell on him!"

＊ What do you call a dog that makes a bolt for the door? Blacksmith!

＊ What do you get if you cross a giraffe with a dog? An animal that barks at low-flying aircraft!

＊ What's black and white and red all over? A Dalmatian with sunburn.

＊ Harry to Tom: "Do you want to pet my new dog?" Tom: "He looks a little vicious. Sure he won't bite?" Harry: "I don't know. That's why I want you to pet him."

＊ Why didn't the boy advertise in the paper when his dog was lost? His dog never read the paper.

＊ Man to friend: "My dog has no tail." Friend: "How do you know if he's happy?" Man: "He stops biting me."

＊ Little Johnny has a sick dog called Rex. After a visit to the vet, Dad tells Johnny that Rex probably won't live for more than a month. "But Rex wouldn't want you to be sad," says Dad. "He'd want you to have happy memories of him." "Can we give him a funeral?" asks Johnny. "Sure," says Dad. "Can I invite all my friends?" asks Johnny. "Sure you can," says Dad. "And can we have cake and ice cream?" asks Johnny. "You can have all the cake you want," says Dad. "Dad," says Johnny. "Can we kill Rex today?"

# DRINK, DRINKING, AND DRUNKENNESS

✴ A train conductor asks a drunk for his ticket. He goes through all his pockets but can't find it. "It's okay," says the conductor. "I'm sure you paid." "Never mind that," says the drunk. "If I can't find it, how am I supposed to know where I'm going?"

✴ "Drinking provides a beautiful excuse to pursue the one activity that truly gives me pleasure, hooking up with fat hairy girls." *Timothy Walsh*

✴ "Twenty-four hours in a day, twenty-four beers in a case. Coincidence? I think not." *Steven Wright*

✴ "Do you drink to excess?" "I'll drink to anything."

✴ "Here's to alcohol—the cause of, and solution to, all of life's problems." *Homer Simpson*

✴ "I drink to make other people interesting." *Groucho Marx*

✴ "I never drink water. The reason being fish make love in it." *W. C. Fields*

✴ A doctor says to a patient after an examination, "There are two reasons for your poor health: it's entirely due to drinking and smoking." "That's a relief," replies the patient. "I thought you were going to say it was my fault."

✴ "It only takes one drink to get me loaded. Trouble is, I can't remember if it's the thirteenth or fourteenth." *George Burns*

✴ "My wife drives me to drink." "You're lucky. I had to walk."

✴ "Why is American beer served cold?" "So you can tell it from urine." *David Moulton*

✴ A bartender offers his customers free drinks if they can name a cocktail he doesn't know how to make. Many people try to catch him out by naming the most obscure cocktails they can think of, but the bartender knows them all. That is, until one man names a drink called a "Boston." The bartender is stumped and has to admit he's never heard of it. "So how do I make one?" he asks. "It's easy," says the man. "All you need is a large port."

✴ A biker chick is sitting at a bar drinking beer. Every time she lifts her arm to knock one back, she reveals she has an incredibly hairy armpit. A drunk at the other end of the bar watches her in fascination. Eventually he turns to the bartender and says, "Say, I'd like to buy that ballerina a drink." "What makes you think she's a ballerina?" replies the bartender. "Hell," says the drunk. "Any gal who can raise her leg that high has to be a ballerina!"

✳ A drunk falls down the steps of the Hilton hotel, crawls to a waiting cab, and says to the driver, "Hey, take me to the Hilton." "We're already there," replies the cabby. "That's great," slurs the drunk. "Only next time—don't drive so fast."

✳ A drunk goes to court. The judge says, "You've been brought here for drinking." The drunk says, "Great. Let's get started."

✳ A drunk goes up to a parking meter, puts in a quarter, and watches as the dial goes to sixty. "I can't believe it," he says. "I just lost 100 pounds!"

✳ A drunk in a bar finishes his pint and slams the glass on the bar. "Piss!" he says, then asks for another. He downs this one too and, again, slams his empty glass down, saying "Piss!" This happens again and again until eventually the bartender looks the drunk in the face and says, "Piss off." The drunk replies, "Oh. In that case, I'll have a vodka."

✳ A drunk phones the police to report that thieves have been in his car. "They've stolen the dashboard, the steering wheel, the brake pedal, even the accelerator," he cries out… "Oh hang on. I'm in the back seat."

✳ A drunk phones the offices of Alcoholics Anonymous. "Is this AA?" asks the drunk. "Yes," says the switchboard operator. "Would you like to join?" "No," says the drunk. "I'd like to resign."

✳ A drunk staggers into a Catholic church late one night and collapses in the confessional. Next morning he's awoken by the sound of the priest entering the cubicle next to him. The priest addresses him through the grill. "Good morning, my son. What can I do for you?" "You got here just in time," replies the drunk. "Could you pass over some toilet paper?"

✳ A man is staggering home drunk late at night when he's stopped by a policeman. "What are you doing out here at this time of night?" asks the officer. "I'm going to a lecture," replies the man. "And who's going to give a lecture at this hour?" asks the policeman. "My wife," replies the man.

✳ A drunk stumbles on to a baptismal service by the river. The minister notices him and says, "Sir, are you ready to find Jesus?" The drunk replies, "Yesh, Your Honor, I shur am!" The minister pushes the drunk under water and pulls him up. "Have you found Jesus?" he asks. "No, I shur dint!" says the drunk. The preacher dunks him again and says, "Brother, have you found Jesus yet?" "No, I shur dint!" the drunk slurs again. The preacher holds the drunk under for half a minute and brings him up again. "Sinner, have you still not found Jesus?" The drunk wipes his eyes and says, "Nope. Are you sure this is where he fell in?"

✳ A hangover is the wrath of grapes.

✳ A man goes into a pub and says, "I'd like something tall, icy, and full of gin." The bartender turns and shouts into the kitchen, "Hey, Doris! Someone to see you!"

✳ A man orders a glass of beer, notices it tastes sour, and complains to the bartender. "What are you moaning about?" says the bartender. "You've only got a glass of that garbage, I've got three barrels full."

✳ A man spends all night drinking at a bar. When it's time to go he stands up and falls flat on his face, so he decides to crawl outside in the hope the fresh air will sober him up. Once outside he stands up and falls over, so he has to crawl the half-mile to his house. When he gets home he manages to prop himself upright so he can unlock the front door, then falls on his face again and crawls up the stairs. When he reaches his bed he tries to stand one last time but collapses and falls fast asleep. The next morning he's woken by his wife's shouting "You've been out drinking again, haven't you!" "What makes you says that?" asks the man. "Don't bother to lie about it!" shout his wife. "The bar called—you left your wheelchair behind again!"

✳ Did you hear about the drunk who thought Alcoholics Anonymous meant drinking under an assumed name?

✳ He doesn't drink anything stronger than pop. Mind you, Pop will drink anything.

✳ A man walks into a bar and finds a drunk playing with a small ball of gloop. The drunk mutters to himself, "It looks like plastic but it feels like rubber." Interested, the man looks over the drunk's shoulder and takes a peek at the strange substance. "It's weird stuff," says the drunk. "It looks like plastic but it feels like rubber." "That's unusual," says the man. "I'm a pharmacist, perhaps I can tell what it is." The drunk hands the man the gloop and he rolls it between his fingers. "You're right," he says. "It does look like plastic but feel like rubber. Do you know where it came from?" "Sure," replies the drunk. "It just fell out of my nose."

✳ A policeman is staking out a bar looking for drunk drivers. At closing time, he sees a man stumble out of the bar, trip on the curb, and fumble for his keys for five minutes. When he finally gets in his car, it takes the man another five minutes to get the key in the ignition. Meanwhile, everybody else leaves the bar and drives off. When the man finally pulls away, the policeman is waiting for him. He pulls him over and gives him a Breathalyzer test. The test shows he has a blood alcohol level of zero. "That can't be right," says the policeman. "Yes, it can," says the man. "Tonight I'm the designated decoy."

✳ A policeman spots a man driving very erratically. He pulls the man over and asks him if he's been drinking. "Yeah," replies the man. "Me and my friends stopped by this bar where I had six or seven beers. Then we went to a bar where they serve these great margaritas, so I had four of those. Then I stopped on the way home, got a bottle of whiskey, and drank that too." The policeman says, "Sir, you need to step out of the car and take a Breathalyzer test." Indignantly, the man replies, "Why? Don't you believe me?"

✳ A short-sighted priest finds a drunk trying to climb the stairs in a block of apartments. The drunk tells him he lives on the top floor, so the priest helps him up the stairs, shows him to the door of his apartment, then goes downstairs. On the ground floor the priest finds another drunk who also lives on the top floor. The priest helps the second drunk climb the stairs and shows him the door to his apartment. However, when he returns to the ground floor, he finds yet another drunk staggering around. "I suppose you live on the top floor too," says the priest. "Yes," replies the drunk. "But every time I get there some bastard pushes me down the elevator shaft."

✳ A flight attendant approaches a passenger on a flight. "Would you care for an orange juice, sir?" The passenger replies, "Sure, if it needed me."

✳ A woman is chatting with her friends when she points at a man in the street, "That's my next-door neighbor. He's an alcoholic!" One of her friends asks, "How do you know that?" The woman replies, "Yesterday he was at the bar drinking next to me all night."

✳ Beer: helping ugly people have sex since 3000 BC.

✳ He drank like a fish. Which would have been okay if he'd drunk what the fish drinks.

✳ He's donating his body to science. And he's preserving it in alcohol until they can use it.

✳ He's such an alcoholic, when pink elephants get drunk, they see him.

✳ I feel sorry for people who don't drink. When they wake up in the morning, that's as good as they're going to feel all day.

✳ I never drink unless I'm alone or with somebody.

✳ It's night, and a couple are sleeping in bed when there's a knock on the front door. The man gets out of bed and hurries downstairs. He opens the door and finds a drunk waiting outside. "Hey," says the drunk. "Be a pal and give me a push." "No!" shouts the man. "Do you know what time it is?" The man slams the door, goes back to bed, and explains what happened to his wife. "You should be ashamed of yourself," says his wife. "That man was asking for our help and you turned him down flat. I don't care if he was drunk, go out and help him push his car." The man gives in, puts on some clothes, and goes out to find the drunk. He opens the front door and calls out into the darkness. "Hey!" he shouts. "Do you still want a push!?" "Yesh!" shouts back the drunk. "I'm over here on your swing!"

✳ One cure for a cold consists of three shots of whiskey. There are better remedies, but most people don't want to hear them.

✳ It's night and a drunk is crawling along the pavement looking for something. A passerby offers to help and asks what's missing. The drunk replies that he's lost his watch. "And whereabouts did you lose it?" asks the passerby. "About half a mile up the road," replies the drunk. "So why are you doing down here?" asks the passerby. The drunk replies, "Down here the lighting is better."

✳ My wife hates the sight of me when I'm drunk, and I hate the sight of her when I'm sober.

✳ One night Harry had been drinking so much, he came home and was sick all over the cat. He looked down at it and said, "I don't remember eating that."

✳ Rehab is for quitters.

✳ Response to a heckle—"Listen to him. I thought alcoholics were meant to be anonymous."

✳ Sean gets home in the early hours of the morning after a night at the bar. He makes such a racket that he wakes up his missus. "What on earth are you doing down there?" she yells down from the bedroom. "Get yourself to bed and don't wake the neighbors!" "I'm trying to get a barrel of Budweiser up the stairs," shouts Sean. "Leave it till the morning," she yells back. "I can't," he shouts. "I've drunk it."

✳ Sometimes too much to drink isn't enough.

✳ The Australian rugby team is being driven through Dublin. The driver shouts out, "And if you look to your left you'll see we're going past the biggest pub in the city." A voice from the back shouts, "Why?"

✳ To be intoxicated is to feel sophisticated, but not be able to say it.

✳ Tom is walking home from the bar late one night when he takes a short cut across a cow field. Halfway across he drops his hat. He has to try on fifty others before he finds it again.

✳ Two drunks are walking down the street when they come across a dog, sitting on the curb, licking its privates. They watch for a while before one of them says, "I sure wish I could do that!" The other looks at him and says, "Wouldn't you like to make friends with him first?"

✳ We call my father-in-law the exorcist. Every time he visits, he rids the house of spirits.

✳ Two drunks get talking in a bar. The first man says, "Where are you from?" "I'm from Ireland," replies the second man. "You don't say," says the first man. "I'm from Ireland too! Let's have a drink." They both knock back their drinks and the first man asks, "Where in Ireland are you from?" "Dublin," comes the reply. "I can't believe it," says the first man. "I'm from Dublin too! Let's have another drink!" The first man asks, "So what school did you go to?" "Saint Mary's," replies the second man. "This is unbelievable," replies the first man. "I went to Saint Mary's as well! Let's have another drink!" One of the other customers says to the bartender, "What are those two celebrating?" "Nothing," replies the bartender. "It's just the O'Mally twins getting drunk again."

✳ What's the difference between a drunk and an alcoholic? A drunk goes to work.

✳ Why did Tom come home drunk and leave his clothes on the floor? He was in them.

✳ Why has Guinness got a white head on it? So when you're drunk you know which end to start on.

✳ Wine improves with age—the older you get the more you like it.

✳ "He's so full of alcohol, if you put a lighted wick in his mouth, he'd burn for three days." *Groucho Marx*

✳ "You can't be a real country unless you have a beer and an airline. It helps if you have some kind of a football team or some nuclear weapons, but at the very least you need a beer." *Frank Zappa*

✳ A drunk staggers to the men's room of a large restaurant. On his way back to his seat, he stops and asks a young woman if he stepped on her foot a few minutes ago. "Yes," she replies testily. "Yes, you did." "Great," he replies. "I knew my table was around here somewhere."

✳ A man is having a pint in a bar when a little gremlin comes in and orders a pint for himself. The gremlin sits on the bar slurping beer. Then it suddenly dashes over to the man and sticks its head in his beer. The man is surprised by this but says nothing, and the gremlin runs back to its drink. This happens a few more times, and the man slowly gets angrier and angrier. When the gremlin sticks its head in the man's beer for the sixth time, the man grabs it and says, "Look, you! If you do that one more time, I'm going to pull your dick off." "You can't," replies the gremlin. "I haven't got a dick." "Haven't you?" says the man. "Then how do you go to the toilet?" "Like this," says the gremlin, and sticks his head in the man's beer.

✳ A man leaves his local bar hoping he can get home early enough not to annoy his wife. However, when he gets home, he finds his boss in bed with his wife. Later, back at the bar, the man tells the story to the bartender. "Hey, that's awful," says the bartender. "What did you do?" "Well," says the man. "They hadn't seen me, so I snuck back out the door. They were only just getting started, so I reckon I've got time for a couple more beers."

✳ A rabbit manages to break free from a research laboratory and finds a group of wild rabbits living in a field. He joins them and spends the day eating grass, stealing carrots and lettuce from a farmer's field, and mating like crazy with all the female rabbits. However, as evening falls, the rabbit turns his back on his wild friends and heads back to the laboratory. "What's the matter?" says one of the wild rabbits, "Don't you like it out here?" "I love it," replies the lab rabbit. "But I'm dying for a cigarette."

✳ He doesn't like to drink. It's just something to do while he gets drunk.

✳ I gave up alcohol last year. It was the longest twenty minutes of my life.

✳ One tequila, two tequila, three tequila, FLOOR.

✳ To some it's a six-pack; to me it's a support group.

✳ Two drunks are sitting in a bar when one throws up over himself. "Damn," he says, "My wife is going to kill me when she sees this." "It's not a problem," says the second drunk. "Just put $20 in your shirt pocket. When she asks what it's for, say a man threw up on you and gave you $20 to get your shirt cleaned." "That's a great idea," says the first drunk, and to celebrate they both buy each other many drinks. Later, the first drunk returns home. "Look at the state of you!" shouts his wife. "You're covered in vomit!" "It's not my fault," replies the drunk. "A man threw up on me and gave me $20 to get it cleaned up." Saying this, the drunk hands his wife some money. "What do you mean $20?" says his wife, "There's $40 here." "Oh yes," replies the drunk. "I forgot to mention, he crapped in my pants too."

✳ Two drunks are sitting side by side in a bar. One of the drunks goes to the bathroom but neglects to button up his fly when he's finished. He staggers back to the bar, sits on a barstool, and his penis flops out on the bartop. The other drunk yells, "Snake!" and hits the penis with a bottle. The first drunk shouts, "Hit it again! It just bit me!"

✳ Two Kennedy Airport baggage handlers, Bill and Fred, hear that aircraft fuel gives cocktails an extra kick, so they steal some to liven up a night's drinking. Sure enough, the fuel cocktails taste great, and the pair get plastered. The next day Bill is awakened by the phone. He answers it and hears Fred on the other end. "How do you feel?" asks Bill. "Not bad," replies Fred. "But tell me, have you farted this morning?" "No," says Bill. "Well don't," replies Fred. "I did and I ended up in Chicago."

✳ Whiskey is a great drink—it makes you see double and feel single.

✳ I drink to steady my nerves. Last night I got so steady I couldn't move.

✳ It's late evening and Tom's wife catches him pouring six cans of beer down the toilet. "What on earth are you doing?" she says. Tom replies, "Well, it seems a waste, but I thought it'd save me getting up in the night."

✳ Dick goes into a rough bar and orders a drink. A man sidles up to him and says, "I can see you're a stranger in here." "Why, yes," says Dick. "How could you tell?" The man replies, "You've taken your hand off your glass."

✳ A policeman has just stopped a drunk driver and given him a Breathalyzer test. "I'm sorry, sir," says the policeman. "But this bag tells me you've been drinking too much." "What a coincidence!" exclaims the driver. "I've got a bag at home that does the exact same thing!"

✳ A husband goes out on the town on Friday night and has far too much to drink. When he eventually comes around, he discovers it's Sunday afternoon. He struggles to come up with a good explanation for his wife, then has a stroke of genius. He calls home and shouts into the phone, "Darling! Don't pay the ransom! I've escaped!"

✳ A fire engine speeds down the road with all bells ringing. Behind it, a drunk tries to chase the engine on foot. The engine turns a corner and zooms out of sight. The exhausted drunk collapses on the ground and shouts, "All right then! Keep your stupid ice cream!"

✳ Sign over a pub bar: "Due to the recent water shortage, beer will now be served at full strength."

✳ Why did the idiot put starch in his whiskey? He needed a stiff drink.

✳ Harry, to Tom: "I went to the dentist this morning." Tom: "So does your tooth still hurt?" Harry: "I don't know; he kept it."

✳ It's nighttime, and two drunks are walking down the road. One looks up in the sky and says, "Here, is that the moon up there?" The second drunk replies, "I don't know. I'm a stranger around here."

# DRINK, DRINKING, AND DRUNKENNESS: BARS

✳ A bear walks into a bar and says to the bartender, "I'll have a whiskey and........ soda." The bartender says, "Why the big pause?" "Dunno," says the bear. "I've always had them."

✳ A fish walks into a bar. The bartender says, "What do you want?" The fish croaks, "Water."

✳ A grasshopper walks into a bar. The bartender looks at him and says, "Did you know there's a drink named after you?" "Really?" says the grasshopper. "There's a drink called Jeremy?"

✳ A group of fonts walk into a bar. "Get out of my bar!" shouts the bartender. "We don't serve your type in here."

✳ A horse walks into a bar and orders a drink. The bartender says, "Why the long face?"

✳ A little pig walks into a bar, orders a drink, and asks direction to the restroom. The bartender tells him where it is, and the pig hurries off to relieve himself. A second little pig then comes in, orders a drink, and asks for the restroom. Again the bartender tells the pig where to go, and the pig hurries away. A third little pig then appears and orders a drink. "I suppose you'll want to know where the men's room is," says the bartender. "No," replies the pig. "I'm the one that goes wee-wee-wee all the way home."

✳ A skeleton walks into a bar and says, "I'd like a beer and a mop…"

✳ "I was tired one night and I went to the bar to have a few drinks. The bartender asked me, 'What'll you have?' I said, 'Surprise me.' He showed me a naked picture of my wife." *Rodney Dangerfield*

✳ A man is sitting in a bar, staring at his drink. After staring at it for half an hour without taking a sip, one of the bar regulars decides to have some fun with him. He picks up the man's drink and knocks it back. The man starts crying. "Don't take it like that," says the regular. "It was a joke. I'll buy you another one." "It's not just that," replies the man. "This day has been the worst one of my life. First I oversleep and get into work late. My boss fires me and, when I leave the building, I find my car had been stolen. I get a cab home but leave my briefcase on the back seat with my wallet in it. Then, when I get home, I find my wife in bed with the gardener. After all that I come to this bar and then, when I've just made up my mind to end it all, you show up and drink my poison…"

✳ A man sits at a bar. "What'll you have?" asks the bartender. "A Scotch, please," replies the man. The bartender hands him the drink, and says, "That'll be five dollars." The man replies, "What are you talking about? I don't owe you anything for this." A lawyer, sitting nearby says to the bartender, "He's right. In the original offer, which constitutes a binding contract upon acceptance, there was no stipulation of remuneration." The bartender is not impressed and tells the man to finish his drink and get out. The next day the man returns. "What the hell are you doing back?" says the bartender. "I can't believe you've got the nerve to show your face here!" The man replies, "What are you talking about?

I've never been in this place in my life!" "I'm very sorry," says the bartender. "But the resemblance is uncanny. You must have a double." So the man says, "Thanks. Make it a Scotch."

✳ A man walks into a bar and orders a drink, then discovers he has to go to the bathroom. To stop anyone stealing his drink, he puts a note on it saying, "I spat in this beer." When he returns he finds another note saying, "So did I!"

✳ A man walks into a bar and orders six whiskies. He lines them up in a row and knocks back the first, third, and fifth glasses. Then he gets up to leave. "Don't you want the others?" asks the bartender. "You've only had three of your whiskies." "Best not," replies the man. "My doctor said it was only okay to have the odd drink."

✳ A man walks into a bar and sees a cow serving behind the counter. "What are you staring at?" says the cow. "Never seen a cow serving drinks before?" "It's not that," replies the man. "I just never thought the moose would sell this place."

✳ A priest, a rabbi, and a minister walk into a bar. The bartender says, "Is this some kind of joke?"

✳ A man walks into a bar and the bartender notices he has a steering wheel stuck down the front of his pants. "Hey," says the bartender. "What's that steering wheel doing down your pants?" "Oh, don't start me on that," says the man. "It's driving me nuts!"

✳ A piece of string goes into a bar and orders a glass of whiskey. When the drink arrives, the string gulps it down in one go then runs out without paying. Outside, the string ruffles itself and ties itself up, then goes back in the bar and orders another whiskey. "Here!" says the bartender. "Aren't you that piece of string that just ran out without paying?" The string replies, "No, I'm a frayed knot."

✳ A woman walks into a bar and asks for a double entendre—so the bartender gives her one.

✳ Descartes walks into a bar. The bartender asks, "Can I get you a drink?" Descartes replies, "I think not"…and disappears.

✳ Man, to bartender: "Do you serve women in this place?" Bartender: "No. You have to bring your own."

✳ A Frenchman walks into a bar with a toad on his head. "What the hell is that?" asks the bartender. The toad replies, "I don't know—it started as a wart on my ass and grew."

✳ A man walks into a bar and orders twenty glasses of Guinness. He lines them up on the bar and announces that he'll give $100 to the man who can drink all of them. Patrick sticks up his hand and says he'd like a go if the man can wait half an hour. Patrick then leaves the pub, comes back thirty minutes later and downs the twenty glasses one after another. The man is impressed and hands over the money, "But tell me," he asks. "Where did you go to for that half an hour?" "Ah, well," says Patrick. "Before I took your bet, I popped to the bar next door to see if I could do it."

✳ A man walks into a bar and says to the bartender, "I want you to give me twelve-year Scotch, and don't try to fool me, because I can tell the difference." The bartender is skeptical and decides to try to trick the man with five-year Scotch. The man takes a sip, scowls, and says, "Bartender, this crap is five-year Scotch. I told you I want twelve-year Scotch." The bartender tries once more with eight-year Scotch. The man takes a sip, grimaces and says, "Bartender, I don't want eight-year Scotch. Give me twelve-year Scotch!" Impressed, the bartender gets the twelve-year Scotch. The man takes a sip and sighs, "Ah, now that's the real thing." A drunk has been watching this with great interest. He stumbles over, sets a glass down in front of the man, and says, "Hey, try this one." The man takes a sip and immediately spits it out again, "Yechhh! This stuff tastes like piss!" The drunk says, "Yeah. Now how old am I?"

✳ A man walks into a bar with a lump of tarmac under his arm. "What would you like?" asks the bartender. The man replies, "A glass of beer and one for the road."

✳ The Loch Ness Monster squeezes into a Soho bar and orders a shot of whiskey for $8. "You're really an unusual sight if you don't mind me saying so, sir," said the bartender. "We don't get many monsters in here." The monster replies, "Aye, and at your prices I'm noo surprised."

✳ Shakespeare walks into a bar and asks the bartender for a beer. "I can't serve you," says the bartender. "You're Bard!"

✳ A penguin walks into a bar, goes to the counter and says to the bartender, "Have you seen my brother?" The bartender says, "I don't know. What does he look like?"

# DRUGS

✳ "Why are there no recreational drugs taken in suppository form?" *George Carlin*

✳ A friend of mine confused her Valium with her birth control pills. She now has fourteen kids—but doesn't really care.

✳ Drugs may lead to nowhere, but at least it's the scenic route.

✳ I said "no" to drugs, but they just wouldn't listen.

✳ I say that if a rock star is found to have used illegal drugs, the Olympic commission should strip him of his gold discs.

✳ In the '60s, people took acid to make the world appear weird. Now the world is weird, people take Prozac to make it normal.

✳ If you really want to get stoned, drink wet cement.

✳ Some people think its clever to take drugs. Most of them are customs officers.

✳ I tried sniffing coke once, but the ice cubes got stuck in my nose.

# DUMB

✳ A woman is at a soda vending machine in a casino. She sticks a quarter in, pushes the button, and catches the can when it pops out. Then she puts another quarter in and does the same, then again, and again, and again. Eventually the casino manager comes over and says, "Hey, you must be really thirsty." "Not really," replies the woman, "but I don't want to stop while I'm winning."

✳ A woman sees a sign reading "Press bell for night watchman." She does so, and after a few seconds she hears the watchman clomping down the stairs. He then proceeds to unlock first one gate, then another, then shut down the alarm system, and finally makes his way through the revolving door. "Well," he says. "What do you want?" The woman replies, "I just wanted to know why you can't ring the bell yourself?"

✳ Four exuberant partiers come into a bar and order champagne. The corks are popped, the glasses are filled, and they begin chanting, "51 days, 51 days, 51 days!" Three more partiers arrive, take up their drinks and the chanting grows, "51 days, 51 days, 51 days!" Two more partiers show up and join in as well, "51 days, 51 days, 51 days!" Finally a tenth partier comes in holding a picture. He walks over to the table, sets the picture in the middle, and everyone starts dancing around it chanting, "51 days, 51 days, 51 days!" The bartender walks over to the table and sees that the picture is a framed children's jigsaw puzzle. The bartender says to one of the partiers, "What's all the fuss about?" The partier replies, "Everyone thinks that we're dumb. So we decided to set the record straight. Ten of us got together, bought that puzzle, and put it together!"

✳ A nerd and a slacker are watching an evening news story about a man about to jump off a bridge. The nerd turns to the slacker and says, "I bet you $50 the man is going to jump." The slacker accepts the bet and, sure enough, the man jumps. The slacker gives the nerd $50. "I can't accept your money," says the nerd, "I watched the midday news and saw the man jump then." "I watched the midday news too," replies the slacker, "I didn't think he'd do it twice in one day."

✳ A dumb person comes to a river and sees another dumb person on the opposite bank. "Yoo-hoo!" she shouts. "How can I get to the other side?" The other dumb person looks around then shouts back, "You are on the other side!"

✳ A woman in a bar is hunched over her martini spearing at the olive with a cocktail stick. A dozen times the olive eludes her until a man sitting next to her grabs the stick and skewers it for her. "That's the way to do it," he says. "Big deal," replies the woman. "You'd never have got it unless I'd tired it out first."

✳ A man keeps checking his mailbox. A neighbor notices his repeated trips to the curb and asks if he's waiting for a special delivery. "No," he replies. "But my computer keeps telling me I have mail."

✳ A man on vacation in Louisiana tries to buy some alligator shoes. He goes into a shoe shop and finds a nice pair, but is not prepared to pay their high price. Determined to get some, he decides to catch an alligator himself and takes a club into the swamp. Curious, the owner of the shoe shop follows him and eventually tracks him down by a lake. On the lakeside is a large pile of dead alligators and the shop owner watches as the man beats another one to death in the water. Eventually he kills the 'gator and drags it to shore. He looks at its feet and says, "Damn, this one isn't wearing shoes either!"

✳ One day a man takes up ice fishing. He gets to the pond and starts to cut a hole in the ice, when he hears a loud disembodied voice say "There's no fish there…!" Puzzled, the man picks up his ice saw and cuts another hole a few feet away. Again, he hears the voice say, "There's no fish there…!" The man moves another ten feet and begins to cut another ice hole. "There's no fish there…!" says the voice. The man looks up and says, "Are you God?" "No!" replies the voice. "I'm the manager of the ice rink!"

✳ A woman goes to the hospital to give blood and is asked what type she is. She tells them she's an outgoing cat-lover.

✳ A man wanders into a library and says, "Can I have a burger and fries?" The librarian says, "I'm sorry, but this is a library." The man whispers, "Can I have a burger and fries?

# DYSLEXIA

❊ A dyslexic man walks into a bra...

❊ Did you hear about the atheist dyslexic? He didn't believe there was a dog.

❊ Dyslexics have more fnu!

❊ Dyslexics of the world, untie!

❊ Man, to job applicant: "The spelling in your resume is very erratic. Are you sure you don't have dyslexia?" Applicant, "Have it? I can't even smell it."

❊ What does DNA stand for? The National Dyslexics Association.

❊ Why is dyslexia so hard to spell?

❊ Did you hear about the dyslexic devil worshiper? He sold his soul to Santa.

❊ Did you hear about the dyslexic pimp who bought a warehouse?

# EDUCATION

❊ "And who can tell me the name of the Speaker of the House?" asks the fourth-grade teacher. Billy's hand shoots up—"Mommy."

❊ "Our bombs are smarter than the average high school student. At least they can find Kuwait." *A. Whitney Brown*

❊ "She sends me to the principal's office. I get there and sit down, and he looks at me and says, 'Emo, Emo, Emo...' I said, 'I'm the one in the middle, you drunken slob.'" *Emo Phillips*

❊ A boy is doing badly in mathematics, so his parents send him to a strict Catholic boarding school. To his parents' delight, his grades skyrocket. On their next visit they ask him what his new school does that the old one didn't. "They're much tougher here," he says. "As soon as I saw that guy nailed to the giant plus-sign, I knew they meant business."

✳ A class has been photographed and teacher is trying to persuade them to buy a copy of the group picture. "Just think how nice it will be to look at it when you are all grown up and say 'There's Jennifer—she's a lawyer' or 'That's Michael—he's a doctor.'" A small voice calls out, "And there's Teacher—she's dead!"

✳ A couple send their dumb son to a special tutor to help him catch up on his schoolwork. After a month they ask for a progress report. "He's getting straight As," says the tutor. "That's fantastic," say the parents. "Yes, they're great," says the tutor. "But his Bs are still a little shaky."

✳ A private school raises its fees but sends out letters mistakenly saying that the new fees will be paid "per anum" rather than the correct "per annum." One parent writes back to say that he agrees to the new fees but would rather continue paying through the nose.

✳ Father, to son: "Let me see your report card." Son: "You can't. My friend just borrowed it. He wants to scare his parents."

✳ I never learned to spell at school, the teachers kept changing the words.

✳ A small boy is being tested on the Kings and Queens of England. "And who followed Edward the Sixth?" asks the teacher. "Mary," replies the boy. "And who followed her?" asks the teacher. The boy replies, "Her little lamb."

✳ A small boy is walking slowly to school. "Hurry up! You'll be late!" shouts out his mother. "There's no rush," he replies. "They're open till three-thirty."

✳ A teacher is trying to explain addition to a young boy. "Johnny, if I laid two eggs over there and two eggs over here, how many would I have?" "I don't know," says Johnny. "Let's see you do it first."

✳ Make little things count. Teach arithmetic to dwarves.

✳ An English teacher says to her pupils, "There are two words I don't allow in my class. One is gross, and the other is cool." From the back of the room a voice calls out, "So, what are the words?"

✳ An English teacher notices a boy staring out of the window and calls out a question, "You, boy! Give me two pronouns." The boy looks around and says, "Who? Me?"

✳ Dolly Parton tried working as a schoolteacher for a while but it was no good. Every time she turned around, she wiped everything off the blackboard.

✳ Father, to son: "How do you like going to school?" Son: "The going part and the coming home part are fine, but I'm not keen on the time in between."

✳ I woke up and realized I didn't have to go to school today. I was so happy—then I remembered I'm an unemployed forty-three-year-old.

✳ I've got degrees in biology and metalwork. So if you need someone to weld your parrot, I'm your man.

✳ Little Johnny's second-grade teacher is quizzing them on the alphabet. "Johnny," she says, "What comes after 'O'?" Johnny says, "Yeah?"

✳ Mother, to daughter: "What was the first thing you learned in class?" Daughter: "How to talk without moving my lips!"

✳ Man, to friend: "My uncle was the only truant at his correspondence school." Friend: "How can you be a correspondence school truant?" Man: "Easy, you send back empty envelopes."

✳ Mother, to son: "What did you learn in school today, dear?" Son: "How to write." Mother: "And what did you write?" Son: "I don't know, they haven't taught us to read yet."

✳ Teacher asks her class to come up with a story that has a moral. Little Billy stands up and says, "Last week we were driving back from the market with a basket of eggs. We hit a bump in the road and some of the eggs got broke. The moral is—don't put all your eggs in one basket." Little Susie then stands up and says, "My grandma had five chicken eggs. She put them in an incubator but only three hatched. The moral is—don't count your chickens before they're hatched." Little Johnny stands up and says, "My Uncle Jim was in Vietnam. One day his helicopter crashed behind enemy lines, and all he had was a machine gun, a knife, and a crate of beer. He drank all the beer then killed thirty Viet Cong with his gun. Then he ran out of bullets, so he stabbed another twenty Viet Cong with his knife. Then he lost the knife and strangled another ten with his bare hands. Then he got sent home." "I see," says teacher. "And what's the moral of that?" Little Johnny replies, "Don't mess with Uncle Jim when he's drunk."

✳ Mother, to son: "Why did you just swallow the money I gave you?" Son: "You said it was my lunch money!"

✳ Professor, to medical student: "What happens when the human body is immersed in water?" Student: "The telephone rings."

✳ Teacher is giving one of her students, Patty, a math lesson. "Patty, If I give you two rabbits and two rabbits and another two rabbits, how many rabbits have you got?" Patty replies, "Seven!" "No," says teacher. "Listen carefully. If I give you two rabbits and two rabbits and another two rabbits, how many rabbits have you got?" "Seven!" replies Patty. "Let's try this another way," says teacher. "If I give you two apples and two apples and another two apples, how many apples have you got?" "Six," says Patty. "Good," says teacher. "Now if I give you two rabbits and two rabbits and another two rabbits, how many rabbits have you got?" Patty replies, "Seven!" Teacher is getting cross—"How on earth do you work out that three groups of two rabbits is seven?" Patty replies, "Because that's six rabbits plus the one I've already got at home!"

✳ Teacher: "Can anyone tell me how many seconds there are in a year?" Student: "Twelve. The second of January, the second of February…!"

✳ Teacher: "Who can tell me where Hadrian's Wall is?" Student: "I expect it's around Hadrian's garden!"

✳ Teacher: "Class, we'll have only half a day of school this morning…" Class: "Hooray!" Teacher: "We'll have the other half this afternoon!"

✳ Teacher: "Jimmy, how do you manage to get so many things wrong in a day?" Jimmy: "I start early."

✳ Teacher: "Tommy, this letter from your father looks like it was written by you." Tommy: "That's because he borrowed my pen to write it."

✳ Teacher: "What does the 1286 BC. inscribed on the mummy's tomb indicate?" Student: "Is it the registration number of the car that ran him over?"

✳ Teacher: "When was Rome built?" Student: "At night." Teacher: "Why did you say that?" Student: "Because my dad always says that Rome wasn't built in a day!"

✳ Teacher: "Why can't you ever answer any of my questions?" Student: "Well, if I could, there wouldn't be much point in my being here!"

✳ Teacher: "How much is half of eight?" Student: "Up and down or across?" Teacher: "What do you mean?" Student: "Well, up and down makes three and across the middle leaves a zero."

✳ Teacher, to class: "Can someone tell me what happens to a car when it gets old and starts to rust?" Student: "My dad buys it."

✳ Teacher, to student: "When you yawn, you're supposed to put your hand to your mouth!" Student: "What? And get bitten!"

✳ Teacher, "Johnny, give me a sentence starting with 'I.'" Little Johnny replies, "I is…" Teacher interrupts, "No, Johnny. Always say 'I am.'" Johnny replies, "Okay. I am the ninth letter of the alphabet."

✳ Teacher: "Didn't you hear me call you?" Student: "You said not to answer you back!"

✳ Teacher, to student: "Can you name an animal that lives in Iceland?" Student: "A reindeer." Teacher: "Can you name another?" Student: "Another reindeer."

✳ Teacher, to student: "Where's the English Channel?" Student: "I don't know, my TV doesn't pick it up."

✳ The headmistress of a girls' school asks the local minister to give her pupils a talk on Christianity and sex. The minister is happy to do so, but doesn't want to upset his prudish wife, so he tells her he'll be giving the girls a talk about sailing. A week later the headmistress meets the minister's wife in the street and tells her what a good talk her husband gave. "I can't imagine it was that good," says the wife. "He's only ever done it twice. The first time, he was sick, and the second time, his hat blew off."

✳ They did a raffle at my daughter's school. First prize was a place at a better school.

✳ He was a slow starter. At kindergarten he was different from all the other five-year-olds—he was eleven.

✳ What does a math graduate say to a sociology graduate? "I'll have the burger and fries, please."

✳ What's the difference between a university and a junior college? At a university they tell you to wash your hands after visiting the toilet. At a junior college they teach you not to pee all over your fingers.

✳ Why did the cross-eyed teacher get fired? He couldn't control his pupils.

✳ "Just look at this report card!" yells the angry father. "Your friend John doesn't come home with C's and D's on his report cards!" "No," comes the reply. "But he's different. He's got smart parents!"

✳ A nursery school teacher is telling her class about the three little pigs. She gets to the part where the first pig is collecting material for his house. "And when the first little pig went to the store, what did he ask the man for?" Little Susie puts up her hand and says, "He asked if he could have some straw to build his house." "That's right," says the teacher. "And what do you think the man said back to him?" Little Johnny sticks up his hand and says, "Holy crap, a talking pig!"

✳ Boy to father: "Can you sign your name without looking?" Father: "Yes, I think so." Boy: "Then shut your eyes and sign my report card."

✳ A small boy comes back to school after a vacation in the country. His teacher asks him what he saw. "I saw a sty." says the boy. "And what was in the sty?" asks the teacher. The boy replies, "A lot of very small piggy banks robbing a big piggy bank."

✴ Mother, to son: "What did you learn in school today?" Son: "Not enough, I have to go back tomorrow!"

✴ Teacher poses a problem to his class: "Suppose there were a dozen sheep and six of them jumped over a fence. How many would be left?" "None," answers little Norman. "None?" says teacher. "Norman, you don't know your arithmetic." Norman replies, "And you don't know your sheep. When one goes, they all go!"

✴ Teacher: "Now, class, when I ask a question, I want you all to answer at once. How much is six plus four?" Class: "At once!"

✴ Teacher: "Okay, Johnny, if you added 4,308 to 3,804, divided the total by four, then multiplied it by three, what would you end up with?" Johnny: "The wrong answer."

✴ Teacher to child: "Do you know how to spell 'banana'?" Child: "Yes, but I just don't know when to stop."

✴ Teacher to student: "I asked you to draw a cow eating grass while I was out of the room. You've only drawn a cow." Student: "You were out so long the cow ate it all."

✴ Teacher to student: "You aren't paying attention to me. Are you having trouble hearing?" Student: "No, I'm having trouble listening!"

✴ A teacher goes up to a child in the woodwork class. "What are you making?" she asks. "It's a portable," replies the child. "A portable what?" says the teacher. "I don't know," says the child. "So far I've only made the handle."

✴ "Going to school is a waste of time," says Little Johnny. "I can't read, I can't write, and they won't let me talk."

✴ Teacher to student: "What's a comet?" Student: "A star with a tail." Teacher: "And can you name one?" Student: "Mickey Mouse."

✴ Chemistry teacher to student: "What's the chemical composition of water?" Student: "H-I-J-K-L-M-N-O." Teacher: "What? Whatever gave you that idea?" Student: "You said so yesterday. You said water was 'H to O.'"

# EDUCATION: ABSENTEES

✴ Father to son: "I hear you skipped school to play football." Son: "No, I didn't, and I have the fish to prove it."

✴ Teacher, to student: "Good morning, and why weren't you at school yesterday?" Student: "Sorry, Miss, but my granddad got burned." Teacher: "Oh dear, he wasn't burned too badly, was he?" Student: "Oh yes. They really know what they're doing at those crematoriums."

✳ Teacher to student: "Why were you late?" Student: "Sorry, sir, I overslept." Teacher: "You mean you need to sleep at home too?"

✳ Teacher to student: "You missed school yesterday didn't you?" Student: "Yes, but not very much!"

✳ The phone rings in the school office. "I'm sorry," says the voice on the phone. "But little Tommy won't be coming in to school today as he's not feeling well." "Who's speaking?" asks the headmaster. "It's my father," says the voice.

✳ Son to father: "I can't go to school today." Father: "Why not?" Son: "I don't feel well." Father: "Where don't you feel well?" Son: "In school!"

# EDUCATION: COLLEGE

✳ What's the difference between a university and a mental institution? To get out of a mental institution, you have to show some improvement.

✳ A chemistry professor is demonstrating the properties of various acids. "Now I've put this solid silver coin in this glass of acid. Will it dissolve?" says the professor. "No, sir," calls out a student. "If it would, you wouldn't have dropped it in there."

✳ A university lecturer addresses a class for the first time—"If there are any idiots in this room, stand up now." One of the students stands up. "That's interesting," says the lecturer. "Why do you consider yourself to be an idiot?" "I don't," replies the student. "But I hated to see you standing there all by yourself."

✳ On the first day of college, the Dean addresses the students, pointing out some of the rules, "The female dormitory will be out of bounds for all male students, and the male dormitory, to the female students. Anybody caught breaking this rule will be fined $20 the first time. Anybody caught breaking this rule the second time will be fined $60. Being caught a third time will cost you $180. Are there any questions?" A student shouts from the back, "How much for a season pass?"

✳ Student, to friend: "How's your history paper coming?" Friend: "Well, my history professor suggested that I use the internet for research and it's been very helpful." Student: "Really?" Friend: "Yes! So far I've found seventeen people who sell them!"

✳ An attractive female student approaches her lecturer. "I'd do anything to pass this exam, Professor," she says. "Anything at all…" "You'd really do anything I wanted?" asks the lecturer. "Oh yes, Professor…" pants the student. "Would you…study?" asks the lecturer.

✳ A professor stands before a philosophy class and picks up an empty mayonnaise jar. He then proceeds to fill it with golf balls and asks the students if the jar is full. They agree that it is. The professor then picks up a box of pebbles and pours them in the jar. He shakes the jar, and the pebbles roll into the open areas between the golf balls. He then asks the students if the jar is full. They agree that it is. The professor next picks up a box of sand and pours it into the jar. He asks once more if the jar is full, and the students agree that it is. The professor then picks up two cans of beer, opens them and pours them into the jar. "Now," says the professor. "I want you to recognize that this jar represents your life. The golf balls are the important things—your family, your children, your health, your friends. If everything else were lost and only they remained, your life would still be full. The pebbles are the other things that matter like your job, your house, your car. The sand is everything else—the small stuff. If you put the sand into the jar first, there's no room for the pebbles or the golf balls. And remember, no matter how full your life might seem, there's always room for a couple of beers."

# EDUCATION: DUMB EXAM ANSWERS

✳ Describe the functions of the human spine: "The spinal column is a long bunch of bones. The head sits on the top and you sit on the bottom."

✳ Explain one of the processes by which water can be made safe to drink: "Filtration makes water safe to drink because it removes large pollutants like grit, sand, dead sheep, and kayakers."

✳ Give the meaning of the term "Caesarian Section": "The Caesarian Section is a district in Rome."

✳ How can you delay milk turning sour?: "Keep it in the cow."

✳ In a democratic society, how important are elections?: "Very important. Sex can only happen when a male gets an election."

✳ Name the four seasons: "Salt, pepper, mustard, and vinegar."

✳ Use the word "diploma" in a sentence: "Our pipes were leaking so my dad called diploma."

✳ Use the word "information" in a sentence: "Geese sometimes fly information."

✳ Use the word "judicious" in a sentence: "Hands that judicious can be as soft as your face."

✳ What does the word "benign" mean?: "Benign is what you will be after you be eight."

✳ What is a Hindu?: "It lays eggs."

✳ What is a seizure?: "A Roman emperor."

✳ What is a terminal illness?: "When you are sick at the airport."

✳ What is a turbine?: "Something an Arab wears on his head."

✳ What is artificial insemination?: "When the farmer does it to the bull instead of the cow."

✳ What is the fibula?: "A small lie."

✳ Where was the Magna Carta signed?: "At the bottom."

✳ Which English King invented the fireplace?: "Alfred the Grate."

✳ Who invented fractions?: "Henry the 1/8."

✳ Who invented King Arthur's round table?: "Sir Circumference."

✳ Who succeeded the first president of the United States?: "The second one."

✳ Who was the Black Prince?: "The son of Old King Cole."

✳ Why does history keep repeating itself?: "Because we weren't listening the first time."

✳ Why was George Washington buried at Mount Vernon?: "Because he was dead."

✳ Why were the early days of history called the Dark Ages?: "Because there were so many knights."

✳ Give an example of a fungus. What is a characteristic feature?: "Mushrooms. They always grow in damp places and so they look like umbrellas."

✳ What guarantees may a mortgage company insist on?: "If you're buying a house, they will insist you are well endowed."

✳ Use the word "fascinate" in a sentence: "I have a coat with nine buttons, but I can only fascinate."

✳ What does "varicose" mean?: "Nearby."

* When did Julius Caesar die?: "A few days before his funeral."

* Why did Robin Hood only rob the rich? "Because the poor didn't have anything worth stealing."

# EDUCATION: EXAMS

* A student taking a philosophy class had a single question in his final exam: "What is courage?" The student wrote: "This," signed it, and handed it in.

* Father, to son: "Why did you get such a low score in that test?" Son: "Absence." Father: "You were absent on the day of the test?" Son: "No, but the boy who sits next to me was!"

* Son, to father: "I failed every subject except for algebra." Father: "How did you keep from failing that?" Son: "I didn't take algebra."

* Teacher: "I hope I didn't see you looking at Fred's test paper." Student: "I hope you didn't see me either!"

* Teacher: "Johnny, I believe you copied off Jimmy in the exams." Johnny: "How can you tell?" Teacher: "Whenever Jimmy's written 'I don't know' next to a question, you've put 'Neither do I.'"

* "I was thrown out of NYU in my freshman year. I cheated on my metaphysics final in college, I looked within the soul of the boy sitting next to me." *Woody Allen*

* A man reports for a university exam that consists of yes/no questions. He takes his seat in the exam room, opens the test paper, and starts tossing a coin. If he tosses heads, he marks an answer "yes," if it's tails, he marks it "no." The man finishes the test quickly and spends the time left rereading the paper, tossing the coin, and occasionally swearing under his breath. The moderator goes over to see what's the matter. "It's okay," says the man. "I finished the exam half an hour ago. Now I'm checking my answers."

# EDUCATION: HOMEWORK

* A little boy is called up by his teacher. "This essay you've written about your pet dog," says the teacher. "It's word for word exactly the same essay as your brother wrote." "Well of course it is," says the boy. "It's the same dog."

* A little boy is doing his homework. He says to himself, "Two plus five, the son of a bitch is seven. Three plus six, the son of a bitch is nine." His mother hears this and gasps,

"What are you saying?" The little boy answers, "I'm doing my homework. This is how my teacher taught me to do it." Infuriated, the mother confronts the teacher the next day. "What are you teaching my son in arithmetic? He's been saying two plus two, the son of a bitch is four?" The teacher replies, "Oh dear. What I taught them was, two plus two 'the sum of which' is four!"

✳ Student, to teacher: "Would you punish me for something I didn't do?" Teacher: "No, of course I wouldn't." Student: "That's good, because I didn't do my homework."

✳ Son, to father: "Dad, can you help me find the lowest common denominator in this problem?" Father: "Don't tell me that they haven't found it yet! I remember looking for that when I was a boy!"

✳ Teacher: "Did your parents help you with these homework problems?" Student: "No, I got them all wrong by myself!"

✳ Teacher, to student: "Did your father help you with your homework last night?" Student: "No. He did all of it."

✳ A small boy is struggling with his homework. "Dad, can you help me with my math?" asks the boy. "I could," replies his father. "But it wouldn't be right, would it?" "Probably not," says the boy. "But you could at least give it a try."

# ELECTRICIANS AND ELECTRICAL ITEMS

✳ "There was a power outage at a department store yesterday. Twenty people were trapped on the escalators." *Steven Wright*

✳ "I bought some batteries but they weren't included. So I had to buy them again." *Steven Wright*

✳ A man gets stuck on an escalator during a power outage. A security guard comes up to him and says, "Why don't you just walk down?" He replies, "I can't. I'm going up!"

✳ A bricklayer, a carpenter, and an electrician are arguing about which has the oldest profession. "We built the pyramids," says the bricklayer. "We must have been the first." "We built Noah's Ark before the pyramids," says the carpenter. "We were first." The electrician says, "You're both wrong. When God said, 'Let there be light,' it came on right away. We must have been there to put in the wiring."

✴ My wife has an electric blender, an electric toaster, and an electric bread maker. Then she says, "There are too many gadgets, and no place to sit down!" So I bought her an electric chair.

# ELEPHANTS

✴ How can you tell if an elephant is sitting behind you in a bathtub? You can smell the peanuts on his breath.

✴ How do you get down off an elephant? You don't, you get down off a duck.

✴ How do you know if an elephant is in your bed? You'll see the "E" embroidered on his pajamas.

✴ How do you know when there's an elephant under your bed? When your nose touches the ceiling!

✴ "I once shot an elephant in my pajamas. How he got into my pajamas, I'll never know." *Groucho Marx*

✴ How does an elephant get down from a tree? He sits on a leaf and waits till autumn!

✴ Jumbo the elephant has lived at the zoo for ten years, but in all that time, he's failed to mate with Mrs. Jumbo. In the end the zookeeper calls in an expert on elephant sexual behavior to see if he can help. The expert demonstrates how to get Jumbo in the mood by using a long wooden pole to stimulate him. A few weeks later the expert phones the zoo to see if there's been a change in Jumbo's behavior. "There certainly has," said the zookeeper. "Now we can't get him away from the TV when pool comes on."

✴ What do elephants have for lunch? Forty minutes, like everybody else.

✴ What do you do if an elephant comes through your window? Swim!

✴ What do you get if you cross a worm and an elephant? Big holes in your garden.

✴ What do you get if you cross an elephant and a kangaroo? Big holes all over Australia!

✴ What time is it when an elephant sits on the fence? Time to get a new fence!

✴ What's the difference between an elephant's rear end and a mailbox? If you don't know, I'm not giving you any letters to mail.

✴ How do you know if elephants have been making love in your kitchen? The trash can liners are missing.

* How does an elephant hide in a cherry tree? He climbs to the top and paints his nuts red.

* What do you get if you cross a spider and an elephant? I'm not sure, but if you see one walking across the ceiling, run before it falls on you.

* What's the difference between an elephant and a flea? An elephant can have fleas, but a flea can't have elephants.

* Two elephants walk off a cliff…boom, boom!

* How do you know when you've passed an elephant? You can't get the toilet seat down.

# ENGINEERS AND ENGINEERING

* The optimist says the glass is half full. The pessimist says the glass is half empty. The engineer says the glass is twice as big as it needs to be.

* Three engineering students are arguing over who designed the human body. One student insists that the human body was designed by an electrical engineer, because of the perfection of the nerves and synapses. The second disagrees, and exclaims that it was a mechanical engineer who designed the human body as an ingenious system of levers and pulleys. The third student says, "You're both wrong. The human body was designed by a civil engineer. Who else would have put a toxic waste pipe through a recreation area?"

* Yesterday I couldn't spell engineer—today I are one.

# ETHNIC: AUSTRALIAN

* A Texan goes into an outback pub in Australia and says, "Y'know, this country might be big, but back home I've got a horse that takes a whole week to ride around my ranch." The bartender replies, "I know what y' mean, mate. I had a horse like that once—I had to shoot the lazy bastard."

* What's the definition of Australian aristocracy? A man who can trace his ancestry back to his father.

* An Aussie sees a gorgeous woman at a party and asks if she'd like to have sex. "Certainly not," replies the woman. "Fair enough," replies the Aussie. "But would you mind lying down while I have some?"

✳ Do people in Australia call the rest of the world "up over"?

✳ Why is an Australian lover like a wombat? He eats, roots, shoots, and leaves.

✳ An Englishman is applying for emigration to Australia. "Do you have a criminal record?" asks the emigration official. "No," says the Englishman. "Do I need one?"

# ETHNIC: CANADIAN

✳ Canada could have had British democracy, French culture, and American know-how. Instead it ended up with British know-how, French democracy, and American culture.

# ETHNIC: CHINESE

✳ No matter how great your triumphs or how tragic your defeats, approximately one billion Chinese couldn't care less.

# ETHNIC: FRENCH

✳ What do you call 100,000 Frenchmen with their hands up? The Army.

✳ What do you call a French man in sandals? Philippe Philoppe.

✳ "Boy, those French, it's like they have a different word for everything!" *Steve Martin*

# ETHNIC: GERMAN

✳ "A German joke is no laughing matter." *Mark Twain*

# ETHNIC: RUSSIAN

✳ A Polish soldier is asked whom he'd shoot first if he came across a Russian soldier and a German soldier. "The Russian soldier," replies the Pole. "Business before pleasure."

# ETHNIC: SCOTTISH

✳ McTavish is on his death bed. He calls over his friend Hamish and says, "I have a bottle of twenty-five-year-old whiskey under my pillow. When I'm dead, would you do me a kindness and pour it over my grave?" "Of course I will," replies Hamish. "Though I might be passing it through my kidneys first."

✳ A Yankee and a Scot are walking in the mountains of Scotland. The Scot, wishing to impress his visitor, produces a famous echo to be heard in that place. The echo returns after nearly four minutes. The proud Scotsman turns to the Yankee and says, "There, ye canna show anything like that in your country." "Oh, I don't know," says the American. "Back in the Rockies, when I go to bed, I just lean out the window and shout, 'Time to get up!' Eight hours later the echo comes back and wakes me."

# EVIL

✳ Of the choice of two evils, I pick the one I've never tried before.

# EXCUSES

✳ "Why did I sit with her? Because she reminds me of you, that's why I'm here with you, because you remind me of you, your eyes, your throat, your lips, everything about you reminds me of you—except you. How do you account for that? (If she figures that one out she's good.)" *Groucho Marx*

✳ "Why was I with her? She reminds me of you. In fact, she reminds me more of you than you do!" *Groucho Marx*

# EXERCISE

✳ "If God had intended Jewish women to exercise, he would have put diamonds on the floor."*Joan Rivers*

✳ "I ran three miles today, finally I said, 'Lady, take your purse.'" *Emo Phillips*

✳ "I'm not into working out. My philosophy is no pain, no pain." *Carol Leifer*

✳ "You have to stay in shape. My grandmother started walking five miles a day when she was sixty. She's ninety-seven today and we don't know where the hell she is." *George Carlin*

✳ I joined a health club last year, spent about four hundred bucks. Haven't lost a pound. Turns out you have to show up.

✳ An old woman goes to a health club and asks if she can join an aerobic class. "I'm not sure if that's a good idea," says the instructor. "How flexible are you?" "Oh, very," replies the old woman. "But I can't make Tuesdays."

✳ How do men exercise on the beach? By sucking in their stomachs every time they see a bikini.

✳ I have to exercise early in the morning—before my brain figures out what I'm doing.

✳ I like long walks, especially when they're taken by people who annoy me.

✳ If a jogger runs at the speed of sound, can he still hear his iPod?

✳ If God meant us to touch our toes, he would have put them further up our body.

✳ If you jog backward, will you gain weight?

✳ My doctor told me if I took up jogging, it could add ten years to my life. And he was right. I now feel ten years older.

✳ One day as I came home early from work, I saw a guy jogging naked. I said to the guy, "Hey buddy, why are you doing that?" He said, "Because you came home early." *Rodney Dangerfield*

✳ Running feels awful, but it will let you live longer—so, life will feel awful, but at least it will last longer.

✳ The advantage of exercising every day is that you'll die healthier.

✳ The only reason I would take up jogging is so that I could hear heavy breathing again.

✳ The other night I went for a walk. My girlfriend asked me how long I was going to be gone, and I said, "The whole time." *Steven Wright*

✳ Tom was advised by his doctor to go to a health club and lose some weight. He lost 20 pounds in one day—the jogging machine tore his leg off.

✳ Two old women are sitting on a bench talking. One says to the other, "How's your husband holding up in bed these days?" The second replies, "He makes me feel like an exercise bike. Each day he climbs on and starts pumping away, but we never seem to get anywhere."

✳ Why did the aerobics instructor cross the road? Some people on the other side could still walk.

✳ How do you get a man to do sit-ups? Put the remote control between his toes.

✳ If swimming is good for your shape, why do whales look the way they do?

✳ The only exercise she gets is jumping to conclusions.

✳ Harry gets a lot of exercise. Last week he was out seven nights running.

# EXPLORERS

✳ A French explorer, an English explorer, and a New York explorer are captured by a fierce tribe. The chief says, "We're going to kill you, then use your skins to build a canoe. However, you get to choose how you die." The Frenchman says, "I take ze poison." The chief gives him some poison. The Frenchman drinks it down shouting, "Vive la France!" The Englishman says, "A pistol for me, please." The chief gives him a pistol. The Englishman shouts, "God save the Queen!" And blows his brains out. The New Yorker says, "Gimme a fork." The chief is puzzled, but he shrugs and gives him a fork. The New Yorker takes the fork and starts jabbing himself all over. "What are you doing?" shouts the chief. The New Yorker says, "So much for your canoe, asshole!"

# FAIRY TALES

✳ "I used to be Snow White, but I drifted." *Mae West*

✳ Did you hear about the giant who threw up? It's all over town.

✳ Little Red Riding Hood is walking through the woods when she sees the wolf hiding behind a bush. Playfully she slips behind him and taps him on the shoulder—"My, what big eyes you have!" she says. The wolf runs off and hides behind another bush. Little Red Riding Hood follows him and taps him on the shoulder again—"My, what a big nose you have!" she says. The wolf yelps and dashes off to hide behind another bush. Little Red Riding Hood sneaks up on him yet again, and again taps him on the shoulder. "My, what big teeth you have!" she says. The wolf turns on her and shouts, "Do you mind? I'm trying to take a crap!"

# FAMILIES

٭ "Happiness is having a large, loving, caring close-knit family—in another city." *George Burns*

٭ Families are like fudge—mostly sweet, with a few nuts.

٭ This advice has been passed down from generation to generation. Okay, it's never been used.

٭ A psychiatrist is interviewing a patient in a psychiatric institution. "How did you get here?" he says. "What is the nature of your illness?" The patient replies, "Well, it all started when I married a widow with a grown daughter. My dad came to visit us, fell in love with my lovely step-daughter, then married her. So my step-daughter was now my step-mother. Soon, my wife had a son who was, of course, my daddy's brother-in-law, since he is the half-brother of my step-daughter, who is now, of course, my daddy's wife. Now, since my new son is brother to my step-mother, he also became my uncle. As you know, my wife is my step-grandmother, since she is my step-mother's mother. So since I'm married to my step-grandmother, I am not only the wife's grandson and her hubby, but I am also my own grandfather. And if that's not enough to drive you crazy, what is?"

٭ A little boy goes up to his father and asks what an ancestor is. "Well," replies father. "I'm your ancestor and so's your granddad." "Okay," replies the boy. "So why do people boast about them?"

# FAMILIES: PARENTING

٭ A young couple bring their new baby home and the wife suggests that her husband try his hand at changing a diaper. "I'm busy," he says. "I'll do the next one." Next time the baby's diaper needs changing, she asks him again. The husband says, "I didn't mean the next diaper. I meant the next baby."

٭ "My father told me all about the birds and the bees, the liar—I went steady with a woodpecker till I was twenty-one." *Bob Hope*

✳ "When I was ten, my pa told me never to talk to strangers. We haven't spoken since."
*Steven Wright*

✳ A father and son are out fishing. The boy says, "Dad, how do boats float?" "I don't know," replies Dad. The boy then asks, "How do fish breathe?" "I don't know," replies Dad. "Why is the sky blue?" asks the boy. "I don't know," replies Dad. "Dad," says the boy. "I hope you don't mind me asking you all these questions?" "Of course not," replies Dad. "If you don't ask questions how will you ever learn anything?"

✳ A man is helping one of his cows give birth, when he notices his four-year-old son watching from the fence. The man thinks, "Great. He's four, and I'm gonna have to start explaining the birds and bees. No need to jump the gun. I'll just let him ask, and I'll answer." After everything is over, the man walks over to his son and says, "Well, son, do you have any questions?" "Just one," gasps the wide-eyed lad. "How fast was that calf going when he hit the cow?"

✳ A vest is something a boy wears when his mother feels cold.

✳ A woman goes to her psychiatrist. "I can't sleep at night," she says. "When I'm in the next room, I have this dreadful fear I won't hear the baby if he falls out of the crib. What can I do?" "Easy," replies the doctor. "Take the carpet off the floor."

✳ A small boy is sent to bed by his father. Five minutes later the boy cries out, "Da-ad!" "What?" shouts back his father. "I'm thirsty," says the boy. "Can you bring me a drink of water?" "No," says Dad. "You had your chance. Lights out!" Five minutes pass. "Da-aaaad!" shouts the boy. "What?" says Dad. "I'm thirsty," says the boy. "Can I have drink of water?" "I said no!" shouts back the father. "And if you ask again, I'll smack your bottom!" Five minutes later. "Daaaa-aaaa!" shouts the boy. "What?" yells his father. "When you come in to smack me, can you bring a drink of water?"

✳ If you have any advice to pass on to your children, do it while they're still young enough to think you know what you're talking about.

✳ Mothers of teenagers know why some animals eat their young.

✳ I never knew the identity of my real parents. I wasn't adopted, it was just that whenever I got home from school, they put on masks and pretended to be French.

✳ I remember Dad coming home, telling Mom the plant was closing, and there'd be no more work. Then he sat down in his chair and screamed at the top of his lungs—it was possibly the wrong moment to have played the "drawing pin on the seat" gag.

✳ My mother never saw the irony in calling me a son of a bitch.

✳ Never raise a hand to your children—it leaves your groin unprotected.

✳ There are three ways to get something done: do it yourself, hire someone, or forbid your kids to do it.

✳ What did the girl band member's mother say to her before she went out? "If you're not in bed by midnight, you have to come home."

✳ What never made much sense to me is why people without any children and those with children both feel sorry for each other.

✳ Two little girls are in the lunchroom of the Beverly Hills Elementary School. "Guess what?" says one. "My mommy's getting married again and I'm going to have a new daddy." "Really?" says the other. "Who's she marrying?" "Winston James," says the first girl. "He's a famous director." The second girl smiles. "Oh, you'll like him. He was my daddy last year."

✳ A father is a man with pictures in his wallet where he used to keep his money when he was single.

✳ I bought my son a pet rabbit after he promised he'd take care of it. As I expected, I ended up with the responsibility. Exasperated, I said, "How many times do you think that rabbit would have died if I hadn't looked after it?" My son replied, "Only the once."

✳ You know your children are growing up when they stop asking you where they came from and start refusing to tell you where they're going.

# FARMING

✳ A farmer buys a new rooster that turns out to be a sex maniac. It tears around mating with all the chickens, then, when they're exhausted, has a go at the ducks, the geese, and the turkeys. It even tries to jump on the farm cat. The rooster is insatiable and, after a week of frantic sex, the farmer is not surprised when he finds the bird lying flat on its back with a couple of buzzards circling over it. "I knew your heart would give out sooner or later," says the farmer. The rooster opens an eye, looks at the buzzards, and whispers, "Get lost, you'll scare them away."

✳ A farmer decides to breed his three sows with his neighbor's stud pig. The farmer drives the sows to his neighbor's farm, leaves them there for the day, then drives them back home in the evening. The next day the farmer looks at his sows to see if they're grazing on grass—a sure sign that they're pregnant. The sows aren't grazing, so the framer puts them in his truck and drives them to the stud farm a second time. Next morning he looks at his sows and sees them sitting around as usual, so he loads them on the truck and drives them to stud a third time. This goes on for two weeks, and the sows never seem to get pregnant. One morning the farmer decides to give up, stop driving his pigs around, and sleep in instead. The farmer's wife hears a noise and looks out of the window. "You should see this," says his wife. "Those sows are acting very strange." "Are they grazing on grass?" asks the hopeful farmer. "No," says his wife. "Two are sitting in the back of the truck, and the third is in the front honking the horn."

✳ A farmer has a big watermelon patch but is disturbed by some local kids who sneak on to his land at night and eat his crop. One day he hatches a plan to scare them off and sticks a sign in his field reading "Warning! One of these watermelons has been injected with cyanide." Next day the farmer looks at his field and sees the kids have stuck up their own sign—"Now there's two of them!"

✳ A handsome blonde man is looking for a bride when he comes across a farmer with three gorgeous blonde daughters. He can't decide which to have as his wife so takes out each one in turn. After taking out the first daughter, the farmer asks for the man's opinion. "Well," says the man. "She's just a weeeeee bit, not that you could hardly tell, knock-kneed." The man then takes out the second daughter and, again, the farmer asks for the man's opinion. "Well," the man replies, "She's just a weeeee bit, not that you can hardly tell, cross-eyed." The man then takes out the third daughter. The next morning the man rushes to the farmer exclaiming, "She's perfect, just perfect! She's the one I want to marry!" The man and the farmer's daughter marry, but six months later, his new bride gives birth to an ugly red-haired baby. The man goes to his father-in-law to ask how such a thing could happen. "Well," explains the farmer. "When you met her she was just a weeeee bit, not that you could hardly tell, pregnant."

✳ A man complains to his friend that he's having trouble keeping his neighbor's free range chickens out of his flower beds. A couple of weeks later his friend notices the flower beds are doing great and asks how he managed to keep the birds away. "It wasn't all that hard," says his friend. "One night I hid half a dozen eggs under a bush by my flower bed, and the next day I let my neighbor see me pick them up. I wasn't bothered after that."

✳ A man moves to the country and decides to buy some livestock. He goes to a farmer and says, "I want to buy a rooster, a chicken, and a donkey." "Sure," says the farmer. "But there's things you should know. Around here we call a rooster, a cock. A chicken, a pullet. And a donkey, an ass. Now I can sell you all three, but you mind the ass, he's a mite bad-tempered and if he tries to bite you, you have to scratch his ears to calm him down." So the man tucks the pullet and the cock under his arms and starts to ride the ass home. Unfortunately the ass starts trying to bite the man, so he stops and gets off. He remembers the advice about scratching the ears, but can't do anything as he has a bird under each arm. At this moment a little old lady passes by. "Excuse me," says the man. "Could you do me a favor? I need someone to hold my cock and pullet while I scratch my ass…"

✳ A man sees a farmer walking a pig and notices that the animal has a wooden leg. Curious, he asks the farmer how the pig lost its limb. "Well," says the farmer. "One night the wife and I were asleep when the pig saw the house was on fire. It broke down the door, ran up the stairs, and dragged me to safety. Then it went back in and carried out my wife, then it went in a third time and rescued my four children. We'd all be dead if it weren't for this pig." "So did the pig get its leg burned in the fire?" asks the man. "Oh, no," says the farmer. "But when you've got a pig like this, you don't eat it all at once."

✳ I know a farmer who's invented a scarecrow that's so hideous, none of the local crows will touch his corn—a few of them have even brought back the corn they stole last year.

✳ Farmer Giles had a very attractive young wife. He discovered he couldn't keep his hands off her—so he fired them.

✳ Farmer Giles used to take his pigs to market every Wednesday but never sold a single animal. Years later he discovered his mistake—market day was Friday.

✳ Man, to farmer: "You were going to start marketing cow dung when I last saw you. How's that going?" Farmer: "Great, it's one of the phew things that sell."

✳ Man, to friend: "Jones makes a very good living with his pen." Friend: "I didn't know he was a writer." Man: "He's not, he breeds pigs."

✳ The teacher asks Little Johnny why he wasn't at school the previous day. "Our cow was in heat," says Johnny. "So I had to take her to the bull." "I'm sure your father could have done that," says the teacher. "Oh no, ma'am," says Johnny. "It has to be the bull."

✳ Why was the farmer hopping mad? Someone stepped on his corn.

✳ Zeke has a mule and a stable to keep it in, but the mule's ears are so long, they brush the door as it walks in. This makes the mule kick dangerously, so Zeke decides to rebuild the stable with a higher entrance. After struggling with a saw, hammer, and nails all afternoon, Zeke's neighbor Leroy comes along and says, "Y'know, rather than lifting the door frame, it would be a lot easier if you dug out the doorway and made it deeper." "Don't be an idiot," replies Zeke. "It's his ears that are too long, not his legs."

✳ A farmer is drowning his sorrows in a bar. The bartender asks him what's the matter. "I was milking my cow, Daisy, this morning," says the farmer, "when she kicked her left leg and knocked the bucket over." "That's not so bad," says the bartender. "No," replies the farmer. "But I tied her left leg to a post to stop her doing it again, and she kicked over the bucket with her right leg, so I tied that to another post." "That's not so bad," says the bartender. "No," says the farmer. " But then she knocked over the bucket with her tail, so I took off my belt and tied it up out of the way." "That's still not so bad," says the bartender. " No," replies the farmer. "But that's when my pants fell down and my wife walked in."

✳ Did you hear about the farmer who won an award? He was outstanding in his field.

✳ Sandra lost her job as a herdswoman because she couldn't keep her calves together.

✳ What do you call an Arab dairy farmer? A milk sheikh.

✳ Did you know it takes forty pigs to make 4,000 sausages? Isn't it amazing what you can teach them?

# FEMINISTS

✳ A feminist gets on a bus and is disgusted when a little old man stands up to give her his seat. "Patronizing old fool," she mutters as she pushes him back down. A minute later another woman gets on, and the old man rises to his feet once more. "Male chauvinist pig," seethes the feminist as she pushes him back down again. The bus stops again, more women get on, and once more the little old man attempts to stand up. "You're living in the Stone Age," hisses the feminist as she pushes him down. "For God's sake!" wails the little old man. "Will you let me get off? I've missed three stops already!"

✳ I don't know what feminists are going on about when they say television never shows any positive, dynamic female role models. I mean, what was Lassie all about?

✳ Pick-up line guaranteed not to work: "So you're a feminist…Isn't that cute."

# FIRE AND FIREFIGHTING

✳ A woman phones the fire brigade—"Help me! My house in on fire!" "Tell me your address and we'll be there as soon as possible," replies the operator. "I can't tell you that, I'm too confused to think straight," complains the woman. "Then how do you expect us to get there," replies the operator. "What do you mean?" says the woman. "Don't you have those big red trucks?"

✳ I remember when the candle store burned down. Everyone stood around singing "Happy Birthday."

✳ If there's H2O on the inside of a fire hydrant, what's on the outside? K9P.

✳ My dad used to say "Always fight fire with fire." Which is probably why he got thrown out of the fire brigade.

✳ A forest fire is raging out of control, and the local volunteer firefighters are drafted in to help. One ancient volunteer fire engine hurtles down a track toward the flames, but the Fire Chief realizes that the wagon is too old and dilapidated to be of any help, so he flags it down to stop. To his astonishment, the wagon hurtles past and shoots into the center of the inferno. The volunteers leap out and manage to extinguish the fire in minutes. The Fire Chief is very impressed. He goes up to the head of the fire crew and gives him a check for $10,000. "That's for some new equipment," he says. "If you can fight a fire with that ancient equipment, just think what you can do with some new gear." "Thanks," says the fireman. "But before I buy any new equipment, I'll be getting some new brakes for the damn truck."

✳ Ted bought himself a new smoke alarm. He stuck it on the ceiling then read the instructions—"Now test your alarm is working properly." So he set fire to his sofa.

# FISH AND FISHING

✳ A man is ice-fishing on a frozen lake and not having much luck. A small boy comes along, bores a hole in the ice a short distance away, and starts fishing himself. After a few minutes the boy catches a huge fish. A few minutes later another large fish is caught, then another, then another. The man is mystified and, after the boy has caught his fifth fish, he goes over to investigate. "Hey, son," says the man. "What's your secret?" The boy replies, "Yu haf tu kip yr wrms wrm." "What was that?" says the man. The boy spits into a bucket—"I said, "You have to keep your worms warm."'

✳ What can you do in radiation-contaminated rivers? Nuclear fission.

✳ Give a man a fish and he will eat for a day. Teach him how to fish, and he will sit in a boat and drink beer all day.

✳ Mother, to son: "Have you put fresh water in the goldfish's bowl?" Son: "Why should I? It hasn't finished the last bowl yet."

✳ The only time a fisherman tells the truth is when he calls another fisherman a liar.

✳ There are two kinds of fishermen: those who fish for sport and the ones who actually catch something.

✳ There's a fine line between fishing and just standing on the shore like an idiot.

✳ Two fish are in a tank. One turns to the other and says, "Do you know how to drive one of these things?"

✳ There are two periods when fishing is fun: before you get there and after you leave.

✳ I know a very good salmon river. In fact, it's so good none of them will leave it.

✳ Two fish swim into a concrete wall. One turns to the other and says, "Dam!"

✳ Two men go on a week-long fishing trip and spend a fortune renting their gear and accommodation. All week they fish but don't catch a thing. On their last day they finally catch one small fish but then have to pack up and go home. On the drive back, both men are very depressed. One turns to the other and says, "Do you realize that one lousy fish we caught cost us fifteen hundred dollars?" The other man perks up and says, "Really? Then it's a good thing we didn't catch any more!"

✳ Who sleeps at the bottom of the sea? Jack the kipper!

✳ I'm trying to get my pets to exercise more, so I put my goldfish out on the lawn—he managed about ten sit-ups and gave up.

✳ Two men are out fishing in a boat and having great luck. In fact, they catch so much, they have to go back early. "This is great," says the first man. "We should mark the spot so we can come here again." "You're right," says the second man, who promptly dives over the side and paints a big "X" on the bottom of the boat. They head for land, but just as they're about to dock, the first man looks at the second and says, "I just thought of something. What if we don't get the same boat tomorrow?"

✳ A single herring can produce over a million offspring. God knows how many the married ones can churn out.

✳ Fisherman, to friend: "I've caught as many as fifteen trout in an hour. Can you say the same?" Friend: "Yes. But not with a straight face."

# FLASHERS

✳ Did you hear about the flasher who was thinking of retiring? He finally decided to stick it out for one more year!

✳ It was so cold last week, the local flasher had to go around describing himself to people.

✳ Three old women are sitting on a park bench when a man jumps out and flashes at them. Two of the women immediately have a stroke. The other one couldn't quite reach.

# FLATULENCE

✳ "How dare you break wind before my wife," says the host to his dinner guest. "I'm sorry," replies the guest. "I didn't realize it was her turn."

✳ A man walks into a doctor's. "Doctor, I'm suffering from silent gas emissions. All day at work, I have these silent gas emissions. Last night during a movie, I had ten silent gas emissions. On the way to your office, I had five silent gas emissions. And while sitting in your waiting room, I had three silent gas emissions. As a matter of fact, I've just had two more." The doctor replies, "Well, the first thing we're going to do is check your hearing."

✳ How do you tell if a girl is wearing pantyhose? Her ankles swell when she farts.

✳ How does a man take a bubble bath? He eats beans for dinner.

✳ Ted, suffering from continual flatulence, goes to the doctor's. The doctor asks him to take off his pants and lie down on the couch. Then, to Ted's horror, he produces a six-foot pole. "What are you going to do with that?" asks Ted. "I'm going to open a window," says the doctor.

✳ A male fly and a female fly are feeding on a cow pat when the male fly farts. The female fly says, "Do you mind. I'm eating!"

✳ A man goes to pick up his date for the evening. She's not ready, so he has to sit in the living room with her parents. He has a bad case of wind and needs to relieve some pressure. The family dog jumps up on the couch next to him. He decides that he can let out a little fart and if anyone notices they'll think the dog did it. He farts, and the mother yells, "Spot, get down from there." The man thinks, "Great, they think the dog did it." He releases another fart, and the mother again yells for the dog to get down. This goes on for a couple more farts. Finally the mother yells, "Dammit Spot, get down before that bastard craps on you."

✳ An old married couple have lived happily together for years. The only friction in their marriage is caused by the husband's habit of breaking wind every morning. The wife complains about this habit and often warns her husband that one day he'll "fart his guts out." However, he ignores her and keeps on farting. One day, after cleaning out a chicken, the wife decides to play a trick on her windy husband. That night she takes the chicken giblets and, when her husband has fallen asleep, slips then under the bedsheets, between his legs. Next morning she wakes up and asks her husband how he slept. "Fine till this morning," he replies. "Then I discovered you were right all along. I did fart my guts out." "Don't you think you should see a doctor?" asks his wife. "Nah," replies the husband. "It took a while, but I managed to poke them all back up again."

✳ There was a woman who loved eating baked beans. Unfortunately, after a meal of beans, she always suffered an embarrassing, violent, and rather smelly reaction. But then one day she met a man and fell in love. When it became apparent that they would marry, she thought she would make the supreme sacrifice for him—she gave up her beans. Then, one year on her birthday, she decided to treat herself on her way home from work. She stopped at a café on the way home and, before she knew it, she had scarfed down three large orders of baked beans. When she got home, she felt reasonably sure she could keep the commotion in her bowels under control, but her husband greeted her at the door, very excited to see her. "Darling," he said, "I have a surprise for dinner tonight." He blindfolded her and led her to her chair at the table. She seated herself and just as he was about to remove the blindfold, the telephone rang. He made her promise not to take the blindfold off until he got back from answering the phone. By now, though, the beans were causing almost unbearable pressure. So while her husband was out of the room, she shifted her weight to one leg and let fly. Then she shifted to the other cheek and blasted out three more sustained and pungent gusts. Keeping her ears tuned for hubby's return, she put her legs up on the table and carried on. She went on like this for another ten minutes, firing away with hardly a pause. When she heard hubby finishing on the phone, she quickly fanned the air and was the picture of innocence when he came back in. He asked her if she had peeked, and she assured him that she had not. At this point, he removed the blindfold, and she was surprised to see all her friends and family around the table in party hats, ready to wish her a happy birthday.

✳ Two old ladies are discussing the benefits of stockings over tights. "I much prefer stockings," says one. "Do you find them more elegant?" asks the other. "Oh yes," replies the first. "And if I fart wearing tights, I usually blow my slippers off."

✳ Fart in church and you'll sit in your own pew.

# FOOD AND DRINK

✳ "The remarkable thing about my mother is that for thirty years she served us nothing but leftovers. The original meal has never been found." *Calvin Trillin*

✳ "We've got a new toaster," said a little boy to his friend. "It's really clever. When the toast is done, a bell rings." "Ours is better," says his friend. "When the toast's done, it sends out smoke signals."

✳ A lady is picking through the frozen turkeys at the grocery store, but can't find one big enough for her family. She calls over the grocer and says, "Do these turkeys get any bigger?" The shopkeeper replies, "No, they're dead."

✳ A Frenchman is staying in a Scottish guesthouse. On his first day he comes down to breakfast and sees his first ever bowl of steaming hot porridge oats. Horrified by the sight of this strange concoction, he turns to his host and says, "You're not really going to eat that are you?" Then adds, "...or have you had it already?"

✳ A hungry termite walks into a bar and says, "Is the bar tender here?"

✳ A little old lady orders a burger in a café. She then watches as the cook grabs a hunk of chopped meat, stuffs it in his bare armpit, pumps his arm a few times, then tosses it on the grill. The old lady says, "That's the most disgusting thing I've ever seen!" The waitress replies, "Yeah? You should see him making the donuts!"

✳ A lord dines with an elderly duchess one evening. Next day a friend asks him if he enjoyed himself. "Well," says the lord. "If the melon had been as cold as the soup, and the soup had been as warm as the wine, and the wine had been as old as the chicken, and if the chicken had been as young as the maid, and the maid had been as willing as the duchess then, yes, I would have had a very good time indeed."

✳ A man goes into a restaurant and orders an appetizer. The waitress brings him a bowl of soup, but the man notices she has her thumb stuck in it. When the soup is finished, the waitress suggests beef stew as a main course. The man agrees, but when she brings the stew to the table, he notices she has her thumb stuck it that too. Once the stew is finished, the waitress suggests hot apple pie as a dessert. The man agrees, but again, the waitress brings him his plate with her thumb stuck in his food. "Look!" says the man. "I wasn't going to mention it, but every time you bring food to my table you've got your thumb stuck it in it." "Sorry," says the waitress. "But my thumb's got an infection. My doctor says I have to keep it in a warm, moist place." "Well, why not stick it up your ass!" says the man. The waitress replies, "Where d'you think I've been putting it when I'm in the kitchen?"

✳ A man goes into a restaurant and says, "How do you prepare the chicken?" "We don't," replies the waiter. "We just tell it straight that it's going to die."

✳ A man orders a pizza and the clerk asks if he should cut into six pieces or twelve. "Make it six," says the man. "I could never eat twelve."

✳ A man orders steak at a restaurant but notices that the waiter bringing it to his table is pressing the steak to the plate with his thumb. "That's very unhygienic," complains the man. "It'll be more unhygienic if I drop it again," replies the waiter.

✳ A man visiting his wife's "organic" vegetarian parents is sent out to buy some food. "These are for my mother-in-law," he says to the grocer. "Are you sure they haven't been sprayed with dangerous pesticides?" "Quite sure," replies the grocer. "You'll have to do that yourself."

✳ A man walks into a Bangkok bar and sees a sign reading "Cheese Sandwich: $1.50. Chicken Sandwich: $2.50. Hand Job: $10.00." The man beckons to one of the barmaids. "I was wondering," he says. "Are you the one who gives the hand jobs?" "Yes," she purrs. "That's me." "Then go wash your hands," says the man. "I want a cheese sandwich."

✳ A man walks into a café and asks for hot chili. The waitress says, "The woman next to you got the last bowl." The man looks over and sees that the woman has finished her meal, but the chili bowl is still full. "Are you going to eat that?" asks the man. "No," says the woman. "Help yourself." The man starts eating. He gets halfway through the chili when he sees a dead mouse and throws up into the bowl. The woman says, "That's about as far as I got, too."

✳ A mother is getting her small son, Willie, ready to go to his first party. "And remember, Willie," says his mother, "if you're offered a second piece of cake, be grown-up and refuse it as politely as your father would." Later Willie returns, and his mother asks him if he's behaved as she'd asked him to. "Oh yes, Mother," replies Willie. "When I was offered more cake I answered just as Daddy would have—'Christ no! Get that crap out of my sight!'"

✳ A man walks into a seafood restaurant and sees a sign saying "Lobster Tails $1 each." The man goes up to the waitress and says, "Those must be very small tails if you're selling them so cheaply." "No," replies the waitress. "They're normal size." "Then they have to be pretty old," says the man. "No," replies the waitress. "They're fresh today." "There must be something wrong them," says the man. "No," replies the waitress. "They're just regular lobster tails." "Okay," says the man. "I'll have one." So the waitress takes the man's money sits him down and says, "Once upon a time there was a big red lobster…"

✳ A restaurant customer asks to see the manager and says, "This place is filthy." "That's an outrageous statement," replies the manager. "You could eat your dinner off our floor." "That's the problem," replies the customer. "It looks as if someone has."

✳ A wife hears a noise in the kitchen one morning. She goes downstairs and finds her husband slumped at the table, stinking of booze and with lipstick stains all over his shirt. "I hope you've got a good reason for being here at seven in the morning," she glowers. "I certainly do," replies her husband. "Breakfast."

✳ A wife is nagging her husband at the company picnic. "Doesn't it embarrass you that people have seen you go up to the buffet table five times!" "Not at all," replies the husband. "I just tell them I'm filling up the plate for you!"

✳ Eating prunes gives you a good run for your money.

✳ A woman is preparing a French dinner for her parents and sends her husband out to buy some fresh snails. The husband buys the snails then pops into a bar for a quick drink. One thing leads to another, and he stays for a few rounds—so many in fact, that by the time he leaves, it's nine in the evening. Realizing he's extremely late, the husband runs home, pours the snails over the path leading to his house, then rings the bell. His furious wife opens the door. "Where the hell have you been?" she screams. The husband waves back to the snails, "Come on, guys!" he shouts. "We're nearly there!"

✳ A sandwich walks into a bar. The bartender says, "Sorry, we don't serve food in here."

✳ Did you hear about the sword swallower who went on a diet? He had pins and needles for months.

✳ Good King Wenceslas calls his local pizza parlor: "The usual please. Deep pan, crisp, and even."

✳ Harry is a very noisy eater. When he started drinking soup in the restaurant, six couples got up and started to dance.

✳ He attended the karate school of cooking. He could kill with just one chop.

✳ He had an accident boiling an egg this morning. He held the egg in his hand and boiled his watch.

✳ He never criticizes his wife's cooking. He just looks at his plate and says things like "What happened? Was the dog not hungry?"

✳ Her cooking wasn't exactly cordon bleu. It was more cordon noir.

✳ How do you keep flies out of the kitchen? Put a pile of manure in the living room.

✳ I wouldn't say it was a bad restaurant, but they've only just started a same-day service.

✳ I bought some of that Pedigree chow they keep advertising. It was terrible. In the end, I had to give it to the dog.

✳ I didn't fight my way to the top of the food chain to be a vegetarian.

✳ I drive way too fast to worry about cholesterol.

✳ I feel great because I eat nothing but organic food these days. The only thing is, when I die, my entire body will apparently decompose completely in under twenty-four hours.

✳ I love defenseless animals, especially in a good gravy.

✳ I found this marvelous stuff recently. It's sugar free, low in fat, and you can have as much as you want without putting weight on. I don't know why crack isn't more popular.

✳ I love cooking with wine. Sometimes I even put it in the food.

✳ I saw a café serving an all-day breakfast. But I didn't really have that much time.

＊ I think the chef here does a marvelous job. For a man with his skin condition.

＊ I went into McDonald's yesterday and said, "I'd like some fries." The girl at the counter said, "Would you like some fries with that?"

＊ I wouldn't say she's unhygienic, but the only time she washes her ears is when she eats a slice of watermelon.

＊ If they don't have chocolate in heaven, I'm not going.

＊ If white wine goes with fish, do white grapes go with sushi?

＊ If you ate pasta and antipasta, would you still be hungry?

＊ Thank you for the magnificent dinner—it will always have a place in my heartburn.

＊ Man, to friend: "Hot milk makes me sleepy, but cold milk keeps me awake." Friend: "How come?" Man: "Our milkman comes around at 4:30 in the morning."

＊ Red meat may be bad for you, but fuzzy green meat is even worse.

＊ Sign in a baker's window: "Cakes like your mom used to make—$2. Cakes like she thought she used to make—$5."

＊ There's not much Harry doesn't know about horses—he spent five years working in a French restaurant.

＊ The chicken we had for dinner last night was so old, they had to bring it to our table in a wheelchair.

＊ Two bachelors are talking about cooking. "I got a cookbook once," says one. "But I could never do anything with it." "Were the recipes too hard?" asks the other. "No," he replies. "But each of the recipes began the same way—take a clean dish..."

＊ When I wake up in the morning, I just can't get started until I've had that first, piping hot pot of coffee. Oh, I've tried other enemas...

＊ Two foreign tourists arrive in the United States and are astonished to see a man selling hot dogs. "I never realized Americans ate dogs," says one. "But since we're here, we might as well try some." The pair order a couple of "dogs" then sit down to see what they've got. The first tourist opens his bun and looks inside. He pulls a face then turns to his friend and says, "Well I'm not eating mine. What part of the dog did you get?"

＊ Two chips were walking down the road. One was assaulted.

＊ Two old ladies are swapping news. One old lady says, "The other day, my Harold went into the vegetable patch to pull up a cabbage, and he dropped dead of a heart attack."

"Oh dear," says her friend. "Whatever did you do?" The old lady replies, "I had to defrost some peas."

✳ "McDonald's 'Breakfast for under a dollar' actually costs much more than that. You have to factor in the cost of coronary bypass surgery." *George Carlin*

✳ What did the apple say to the orange? Nothing, apples don't talk.

✳ What do you call it when you pass out after eating too much curry? A korma!

✳ What do you get if you cross a door knocker with some zucchinis, onions, tomatoes, and garlic? Rat-a-tat-a-touille.

✳ What food will decrease a woman's sex drive by 70 percent? Wedding cake.

✳ What's the best way to open a jar with a stuck lid? Put it on the table and tell the kids to leave it alone.

✳ When I came home last night, the wife complained that the cat had upset her—but she really shouldn't have eaten it in the first place.

✳ Where there's smoke, there's dinner.

✳ Who is the most popular man in a nudist colony? The one who can carry two large coffees and a dozen doughnuts. Who is the most popular woman in a nudist colony? The one who can eat the last two doughnuts.

✳ "I'll tell you what I like about Chinese people, they're hanging in there with those chopsticks. They've seen the fork. And the spoon. I don't know how they missed it— Chinese farmer, getting up, working in the field with a shovel all day. Hello…shovel! There it is! You're not plowing forty acres with a couple of pool cues." *Jerry Seinfeld*

✳ A little old lady gets home after a game of bridge with her friends and discovers she has nothing in the pantry for her husband's dinner. All she can find is a can of cat food, an egg, and a lettuce leaf. There's no time to go shopping, so she stirs the egg into the cat food, quickly cooks it in a pan, puts it on a plate and garnishes it with the lettuce leaf. Her husband comes home, eats the meal, and declares it's the best thing he's ever tasted. The next week the old lady is playing bridge with her pals and she tells them about her culinary experiments. "He seems to love cat food," she tells them. "He's had egg and cat food every day this week. He can't get enough of it." "You can't feed your husband cat food!" declares one of her friends. "You'll kill him." Sure enough, next week the old lady informs her friends that her husband has passed away. "We told you cat food would kill him," says one. "It had nothing to do with it," replies the old lady. "He died when he fell off the fence." "What was he doing up there?" asks the friend. The old lady replies, "He was trying to lick his rear end."

✳ A man in a fish restaurant is waiting for his meal. The waiter comes over and says, "I'm sorry for the delay with your order, sir. It should be with you shortly." The man replies, "That's okay, but if you don't mind my asking, what sort of bait are you using?"

✳ A man walks up to the counter and asks for a plate of potatoes. The women serving says, "Oh, you must be from Ireland." The man is furious, "What sort of stereotypical remark is that? If I walked in here and asked for a haggis, would you assume I was Scottish?" "Well, no," says the woman. "And if I walked in here and asked for some chow mein, would you think I was Chinese?" asks the man. "No, I suppose not," replies the woman. "So why do you automatically assume I'm Irish when all I want is a plate of potatoes," asks the man. The women replies, "Because this is a hairdressers."

✳ A platoon of soldiers is stranded in the desert. After a week with no sign of rescue, the sergeant sends out two men to look for supplies. After a day they return. "We've got good news and bad news, Sarge," says one of the soldiers. "What's the bad news?" asks the sergeant. "All we found to eat is camel shit," replies the soldier. "And the good news?" asks the sergeant. "We found tons of the stuff," says the soldier.

✳ A tourist goes into a restaurant in Madrid and sees a dish called "cojones" on the menu. The man asks the waiter what a "cojone" is. The waiter replies, "They are the testicles of a fighting bull that has died in the arena." The man looks a little squeamish at this news, but decides to give them a try. He orders them and finds they taste really good. The next day he returns to the restaurant and, again, orders cojones. However, when they arrive he finds the cojones are the size of small walnuts, not the huge juicy testicles he had yesterday. He calls the waiter over, "What's the meaning of this?" he says. "These cojones are tiny. What sort of bull had these?" "The bull didn't have those," replies the waiter. "The bull doesn't always lose."

✳ Harry keeps a record of everything he eats. It's called a tie.

✳ I always take my wife to the finest restaurants; one day I might let her inside one.

✳ I went to a seafood disco yesterday. I managed to pull a mussel.

✳ The three bears go into their dining room. "What's this?" says the daddy bear. "I've no porridge. Who's been eating my porridge?" The baby bear peers into its bowl and says, "Look, I've no porridge either. Who's been eating my porridge?" Mommy bear shouts, "Shut up! I haven't made the damn porridge yet! Do we have to go through this every single morning?!"

✳ Two muffins are in the toaster. The first muffin says, "Boy, it's hot in here. " The second muffin says, "I don't believe it! A talking muffin!"

✳ What's the difference between snot and beets? Kids will eat snot.

✳ I bought a box of those animal crackers. They're great. They're chocolate crackers all in the shape of different animals. But it said on the box "Do not eat if the seal is broken." And when I opened them up, would you believe it…

✳ Two fat guys are in a bar. One says to the other, "Your round." The other replies, "So are you, you fat bastard!"

✳ Practice safe eating—always use condiments.

✳ I ordered a thin and crispy Supreme from my local pizza shop—they sent me Diana Ross.

✳ My wife is a terrible cook. Absolutely terrible. Last night I came home and she was in tears. "It's a disaster," she said. "The cat's eaten your dinner!" "Cheer up," I said. "I'll buy you a new one."

✳ Wife, to husband: "I've made the chicken soup." Husband: "Oh thank God! I thought that muck was for us."

✳ What do you say to a hamburger? "How now, ground cow?"

✳ Father O'Leary invites Rabbi Levy over for tea and offers him a ham sandwich. "It looks very tempting," says the rabbi. "But you know I can't eat ham." "Ah go on," says the Father. "Just a little bit. To be sure it won't do you any harm." "No, I'd better not," says the rabbi. "Oh go on," insists the Father. "Don't be so old-fashioned now." "All right," says the rabbi. "I will have one—at your wedding."

# FOOD AND DRINK: CONVENIENCE FOOD

✳ "I bought some powdered water. But I don't know what to add." *Steven Wright*

✳ "I once put instant coffee in a microwave and almost went back in time." *Steven Wright*

✳ "I have a microwave fireplace. I can lie down in front of the fire for the evening in eight minutes." *Steven Wright*

# FOOD AND DRINK: DIETING

✳ "I'm not feeling well," says a patient to his doctor. "Do you think it might be my diet?" "What have you been eating?" asks the doctor. "Pool balls," replies the patient. "I have two reds for breakfast, three blues for lunch. And five browns, and a pink for dinner." "I think I see what the problem is," replies the doctor. "You're not eating enough greens."

✳ A balanced diet is chocolate in each hand.

✳ My doctor's put me on a stable diet—hay and oats three times a day.

✳ She's a light eater. When it gets light, she starts eating.

✳ My wife is on a new diet. Coconuts and bananas. She hasn't lost weight, but can she climb a tree!

✳ A dietitian is lecturing an audience. "The food we eat is enough to have killed most of us years ago," he says. "Red meat is dangerous. Vegetables are often sprayed with pesticides, and our drinking water is frequently polluted. However, there is one foodstuff far more dangerous than all of them combined. Who can tell me what it is?" There's a long pause, then a man in the front row sticks his hand up and says, "Wedding cake?"

✳ A man rushes to his dietitian. "You've got to help me. This diet you've put me on is making me irritable. Yesterday I bit someone's ear off." "Oh dear," says the dietitian. "That's a lot of calories."

✳ An old couple die in an accident and are transported to Heaven. The wife is amazed at the beauty of the place, and the peace and the contentment she feels. Her husband, on the other hand, is furious. "What's the matter?" she asks. "Don't you like it here?" "Of course I like it here," snaps the husband. "And if it weren't for your damn health foods, I'd have been here twenty years ago."

✳ Have you heard about the new Chinese diet? You're allowed to eat whatever you want, but you're only allowed one chopstick.

✳ She's on a seafood diet. If she sees food she eats it.

✳ Why do people order double cheeseburgers, large fries, and a Diet Coke?

✳ First man: "I've got a terrible fat belly." Second man: "Have you tried to diet?" First man: "Yes, but whatever color I use, it still looks fat!"

✳ The cardiologist's diet: If it tastes good, spit it out.

✳ Seconds count—especially when you're dieting.

* Lots of people are lousy at counting calories—and they have the figures to prove it.

* I wouldn't say she is thin, but when she goes to the park, the ducks throw her bread.

# FOOD AND DRINK: EATING DISORDERS

* Did you hear about the guy who's a dyslexic-bulimic? He eats, and then he sticks his finger up his backside.

* Just think, if Momma Cass had shared her ham sandwich with Karen Carpenter, they might both be alive today.

# FOOD AND DRINK: PACKED LUNCHES

* A man goes shopping and sees a Thermos flask. He asks a sales clerk what it does. "It keeps hot things hot and cold things cold," replies the clerk. He buys one and takes it to work the next day. "Look at this," he says to his coworker. "It's a Thermos. It keeps hot things hot and cold things cold," "What have you got in it?" asks his friend. "Two cups of coffee and a chocolate ice cream."

* Why does Harry have a see-through lunch box lid? So when he's on the train, he can tell if he's going to work or coming home.

# FRIENDSHIP

* A good friend is always there to bail you out of jail. Your best friend is in the cell next to you saying "Damn, that was fun!"

* We have been friends for a very long time—what say we call it quits?

* You are such a good friend that if we were on a sinking ship and there was only one life jacket, I'd miss you tons and think of you often.

# FROGS

* A frog's perspective on life: time's fun when you're having flies.

# GAMBLING

* A man goes into a butcher shop. The butcher points to some beef hanging from the rack and says, "I bet you $10 that you can't touch that meat." "No thanks," replies the man. "The steaks are too high."

* After examining a 3,000-year-old mummy, an archaeologist announces that it's the body of a man who died of a heart attack. "How can you tell?" asks one of his students. "I examined a piece of parchment found in the mummy's hand," replies the archaeologist. "It was a betting slip that said '5,000 on Goliath.'"

* For months, a little boy has been pestering his father to take him to the zoo. Eventually Dad gives in, and off they go. When they get back, the boy's mother asks him if he had a good time. "It was great," replies the boy. "And Daddy had fun too, especially when one of the animals came home at thirty to one."

* Harry is walking down the street with a bag of donuts when he meets Tom. "Tell you what," says Tom. "If I can guess how many donuts are in that bag you're carrying, you give me one of them." "That'd be a good trick," says Harry. "In fact, if you can guess how many's in this bag, I'll give you both of them." "Okay," says Tom. "Four."

* I made so much money betting on the Democrats to win the election that I was able to become a Republican.

* Two casino workers are waiting for someone to try their luck at the craps table. An attractive woman comes in and puts down a twenty-thousand-dollar bet on a single roll of the dice. "I hope you don't mind," says the woman. "But I feel much luckier when I'm bottomless." With this, she strips naked from the waist down and rolls the dice, yelling, "Momma needs a new pair of pants!" The dice fall and the lady jumps up and down shouting, "Yes! I win! I win!" She then picks up her winnings and leaves. The casino workers look at each other. One says, "So what did she roll anyway?" The other replies, "I don't know. I thought you were watching the dice!"

* Two men are in a bar on the twentieth floor of a building. The first man says to the second man, "I bet you $100 I can jump out of that window and jump straight back in." The second man takes the bet and watches as the first man jumps out of the window, disappears for a second, then jumps back inside. The second man is astonished and

decides to go double or nothing. Again the first man jumps out of the window, disappears for a second, then jumps back in. The second man is thinking there must be a simple trick involved and decides to try it himself. "I'll bet you $500 I can do that too," he says. The first man takes the bet and watches as the second man leaps out of the window and plummets to his death. A waitress turns to the first man and says, "Gee, you can be a real bastard when you're wasted, Superman."

✳ A man goes to a pet shop, where he sees a talking dog. After chatting with it for ten minutes, he buys it. Later he goes to the bar and says, "I bet everyone $5 this dog can talk." A number of people take the bet, but the dog remains silent, and the man is forced to pay out. Puzzled, the man takes the dog home, where it starts chatting away again. The next day the man returns to the bar and bets everyone $10 the dog can talk. To the man's astonishment, the dog clams up and won't say a word. After paying out on his bets, the man takes the dog outside and says, "I'm taking you back to the shop. You're absolutely useless!" "Wise up," says the dog. "Think of the odds we'll get tomorrow."

✳ Why do the people who run the Football Pools always have check books four feet wide?

✳ How do you leave Las Vegas with a small fortune? Go in with a big one.

# GAMES AND PUZZLES

✳ "My wife made me join a bridge club. I jump off next Tuesday." *Rodney Dangerfield*

✳ A group of chess enthusiasts are standing in a hotel lobby discussing tournament victories. After an hour, the manager comes by and asks them to go to their rooms. "But why?" they ask, as they move off. "Because," he says. "I can't stand chess nuts boasting in an open foyer."

✳ A man swallowed all the tiles from a Scrabble set. Doctors said the problem will eventually work itself out, but not in so many words.

✳ Harry got very excited after finishing a jigsaw in only six months. On the box it said, "From two to four years."

✳ Harry to Tom: "I was playing cards with Dick and some of the guys last night, but Dick kept cheating." Tom: "How could you tell?" Harry: "He didn't play the cards I dealt him."

# GANGS

✳ "Our neighborhood was tough. We had the typical gang. You know, Shorty, Fats, Skinny, Stinky. Then there were the boys." *Bob Hope*

# GARBAGE COLLECTION

✳ A garbage man is collecting the cans when an old woman comes out of her house in her nightgown and curlers. "Am I too late for the trash?" she asks. "Course not, dear," says the garbage man. "Hop in."

✳ Junk is something you've kept for years—then throw away a week before you need it.

✳ Tom to Harry: "What does your son want to be when he grows up?" Harry: "He wants to be a garbage man." Tom: "Why does he want to do that?" Harry: "He thinks they only work on Tuesdays!"

# GARDENING

✳ A husband and wife are standing at the window admiring their garden. "Sooner or later you're going to have to make a proper scarecrow to keep the birds off the flower beds," says the wife. "What's wrong with the one we've got?" asks the husband. "Nothing," replies the wife. "But Mother's arms are getting tired."

✳ A little boy goes up to Old Ned the gardener and says, "What do you put on your celery?" "Well, usually rotted horse manure," replies Old Ned. "We have ranch dressing," says the little boy.

✳ A parson is congratulating a parishioner on his success at transforming an abandoned plot of land into a beautiful garden. "It's wonderful what man can achieve with the help of the Almighty," says the parson. "Yes," replies the parishioner. "Mind you, you should have seen the state it was in when He had it all to Himself."

✳ Did you hear about the successful bonsai tree grower? He got so good, he ended up looking for a house with a smaller garden.

✳ The seeds I planted didn't look nearly as good as the ones on the packet. It turned out those pictures had been posed by professional vegetables.

✳ Gardens need a lot of water—most of it sweat.

✳ The good thing about snow is that it makes my garden look as good as my neighbor's.

✳ The manager of a garden center overhears one of his employees talking to a customer. "No, we haven't had any of that in ages," says the employee. "And I don't know when we'll be getting any more." The customer leaves and the manager walks over to give him a telling off. "Never tell a customer we can't get them something," he says. "Whatever they want, we can always get it on order and deliver it. D'you understand?" The employee nods. "So what did he want?" asks the manager. "Rain," replies the nurseryman.

✳ Two gardeners have entered their potatoes in a vegetable show. One is declared the winner and swaggers over to boast of his success to the other gardener. "Not surprised I won, to be honest," he says. "I thought yours were looking a little on the small side." "That's true," says the other gardener. "Mind you, I grew them to fit my mouth, not yours."

✳ Man, to neighbor: "Can I borrow your lawnmower?" Neighbor: "No, she's not home yet."

✳ A small boy is helping his grandfather dig up potatoes. "What I want to know," he says, "is why you buried the damn things in the first place."

✳ A garden is a thing of beauty and a job forever.

✳ A wise man will never plant more vegetables than his wife can take care of.

✳ How do you stop moles digging in your garden? Hide their shovels.

✳ Harry's invented a new spray to kill the aphids on his rose bushes. His formula kills the roses and the aphids starve to death.

# GASTROPODS

✳ What sort of animal is a slug? A snail with a housing problem.

✳ A man hears a knock on his back door and goes to answer it. There's no one there, but the man notices a snail on his doorstep, so he kicks it to the bottom of his garden. Five years later there's another knock on the door. The man answers it to find the snail on his doorstep again. "Hey!" says the snail. "What the hell was that about?"

✳ A snail is crossing the road. As he's about to get to the other side, a turtle runs him over. The paramedics transport the unconscious snail to the hospital. The doctors work to revive the snail and, when he awakens, the doctor asks him what happened. The snail replies, "I don't know, it all happened so fast!"

✳ Two slugs are slithering along the pavement. They go around a corner and get stuck behind two snails. "Oh no!" says one. "Caravans."

# GENIES AND WISHES

✳ A man finds an odd-looking bottle and rubs it. Much to his surprise, a genie appears. "For releasing me from the bottle, I will grant you three wishes," says the genie. "But there's a catch. For each of your wishes, every lawyer in the world will receive double what you ask for." First the man wishes for a Ferrari. Poof! A Ferrari appears in front of him. "Now, every lawyer in the world has been given two Ferraris," says the genie. "What is your next wish?" "I could really use a million dollars," replies the man. Poof! One million dollars appears at his feet. "Now every lawyer in the world is two million dollars richer," the genie reminds him. "What is your third wish?" The man thinks and says, "Well, I've always wanted to donate a kidney…"

✳ A man finds an old bottle. He rubs it and is astonished to see a pixie emerge from the bottle's mouth. "You look tense," says the pixie. "Would you like a back rub?" "Well, I'd prefer a million dollars," says the man. "I can't give you any money," says the pixie. "But how about I rub your back?" "Well, how about you fix me a date with a *Playboy* centerfold?" asks the man. "Sorry," says the pixie. "But why don't I work on those shoulders of yours?" "Can't you make me taller?" asks the man, "I'd prefer to be six foot six." The pixie replies, "Lie down and I'll get started on your scapulas." "Hang on a minute," says the man. "What's with the back rubs? I thought genies were meant to grant three wishes?" "Who said I was a genie?" replies the pixie. "I'm a massage in a bottle."

✳ A man goes into a bar with a lamp. After he's had a few drinks, the man says to the bartender, "This lamp is magic, y'know. If you rub it, a genie comes out and grants you a wish." "Oh yes?" replies the bartender. "Let's try it then." He rubs the lamp with a bar rag, and out pops a genie. "Fantastic," says the bartender. "It works. Uh, let's see. Can I have a million bucks, please." "As you wish," replies the genie and the bar is suddenly full of ducks. "I forgot to mention," says the man. "He's a little deaf."

✳ A man is sitting at home when a genie pops up out of a bottle. "And what will your third wish be?" asks the genie. The man replies, "What? How can I be getting a third wish when I haven't had a first or second wish?" "You've had two wishes already," replies the genie. "But your second wish was for me to put everything back the way it was before you made your first wish. "Okay," says the man. "I don't believe any of this, but what the hell. I wish I were irresistible to women." "That's funny," says the genie as it fades from sight. "That was your first wish too."

✳ A man is walking along a beach when he comes across a lamp. He picks it up, rubs it, and a genie pops out. As is customary, the genie grants him three wishes. The guy says, "I'd like a million dollars." Poof! A million dollars appear at his feet. "I'd like a new Mercedes," says the guy. Poof! A Mercedes appears in front of him. Finally the guy says, "I want to be irresistible to women." Poof! He turns into a box of chocolates.

✳ A Scotsman and an Englishman are strolling along the beach when they find a lamp. They clean it up, and out pops a genie. "I'll give you each one wish for freeing me," says the genie. The Englishman says, "I'm sick and tired of Scots coming into England. I wish there was a huge wall around England to keep them out." Poof! And it's done. The Scotsman says, "So tell me about this wall, genie." "Well," says the genie. "It's 500 feet high and a third of a mile thick. Nothing can get in, and nothing can get out." "Right," says the Scotsman. "Fill it with water."

✳ Harry and Tom are adrift in a lifeboat. Harry finds a lamp and, giving it the customary rub, is not surprised when a genie appears. The genie apologizes to Harry and Tom and says that, due to cut-backs, it can only grant them one wish. Harry doesn't think, he just knows he's thirsty so he blurts out, "Turn the entire ocean into beer!" The genie claps its hands, the salt water changes to beer, and the genie vanishes. There's a pregnant pause as Harry and Tom consider their new circumstances. Tom looks at Harry with disgust, "Well isn't that great," he says. "Now we're going to have to pee in the boat."

✳ Harry is walking down the street when he sees a man who has an orange for a head. "What happened to you?" asks Harry. The man replies, "I released a genie from a magic lamp, and it gave me three wishes. My first wish was that I wanted to be incredibly rich, and my second wish was that I would be irresistible to women." "Okay," say Harry. "But what was your third wish?" "Isn't it obvious?" says the man. "I wished I had an orange for a head."

✳ Paddy finds an old lamp and starts to polish it. Poof! A genie appears and grants Paddy three wishes. "Well now," says Paddy. "I've always liked my Guinness in bottles, so I'd like a bottle of Guinness that will never be empty." Poof! There it is. Paddy opens the bottle and takes a drink. "Oh that's grand," says Paddy. "Did you say I get three of these wishes?" "Yes indeed," says the genie. "Great," says Paddy. "I'll take two more of these then."

✳ A project manager, a software engineer, and a hardware engineer take a break from work and go to the beach for a walk. They find an old lamp, rub it, and a genie pops out. "In return for rescuing me I'll grant you each one wish," says the genie. The software engineer says, "I'd like to be a millionaire who owns a luxury beach resort in the Caribbean." Poof! he disappears. The hardware engineer says, "I'd like to be a millionaire too, but I want to own the world's greatest ski resort." Poof! he disappears. The genie turns to the project manager and says, "So, what do you want?" The manager replies, "I want those two straight back after lunch."

# GENIES AND WISHES: OF A SEXUAL NATURE

＊ A man finds a magic lamp and rubs it. A genie appears and grants him one wish. The man is embarrassed about his wish, so he leans down and whispers it in the genie's ear. The genie looks surprised but shrugs his shoulders and says, "Okay. If that's what you want. Your wish will be granted at midnight." That night the clock strikes twelve, and the man hears someone knocking on his front door. He answers it and finds two slaughterhouse men standing outside holding a rope. "Hello," says one. "Are you the man who wants to be hung like a donkey?"

＊ A man finds an old lamp and rubs it. Sure enough, a genie appears and says, "Thank you, Master, for freeing me. In return, I can offer you three wishes!" The man thinks then says, "Thanks. But I really don't know what I'd like." The genie says, "Wish for money, that's what most people want." The man replies, "I lead a simple life. I don't need more money." The genie says, "How about travel? I can take you anywhere you want in an instant." The man replies, "No, I've traveled enough, and I like it here." The genie says, "How about sex? How often do you make love in a week?" "Oh, once or twice," says the man. "Ah-ha!" exclaims the genie. "I can make it much, much better than that." "Well, gee," says the man. "I thought once or twice a week was pretty good for a priest in a town this small."

＊ An old lady is polishing a lamp when a genie suddenly appears and offers her three wishes. "I'd like to be young and beautiful again," says the old lady. "I'd like this cottage to be a fine mansion, and I'd like my cat, Tiddles, to be a handsome prince." The genie grants these wishes and the old lady, the cottage, and Tiddles are all transformed. The beautiful young woman swoons into the handsome prince's arms, and he gently whispers in her ear, "Now I bet you wish you hadn't taken me to the vet for that little operation."

＊ Mr. Bear and Mr. Rabbit live in the same forest, but don't like each other. One day they come across a magic golden frog who tells them it will give them each three wishes. Mr. Bear wishes that all the other bears in the forest are females. Mr. Rabbit wishes for a crash helmet. Mr. Bear then wishes that he has unrelenting sexual stamina. Mr. Rabbit wishes for a motorcycle. Mr. Bear makes his final wish—that he is irresistible to all female bears. The magic frog replies that it has been done. "Okay," says Mr. Bear to Mr. Rabbit. "You wasted your other two wishes, what are you going to waste your last wish on?" Mr. Rabbit puts on the helmet, climbs on the bike, revs the engine, then tears off down the road. Over his shoulder he shouts, "I wish Mr. Bear was gay!"

＊ Tom walks into a bar and sees a man 12 inches tall playing the piano. "Where did he come from?" says Tom to the bartender. "I wished for him," says the bartender. "I've got a magic beer bottle that grants requests. Rub it and see what happens." So Tom rubs the bottle and a genie pops out. "I can grant you one wish," says the genie. "What would you like?" Tom thinks then says, "I'd like a million bucks please." "Okay," says the genie and—poof!—the genie vanishes and the bar is filled with a million ducks. Tom looks at the bartender and says, "Hey, I didn't want a million ducks." The bartender says, "And you think I wanted a 12-inch pianist?"

✳ A man finds a magic lamp, rubs it, and releases a genie. "What is your wish?" asks the genie. "Well I'm a real sex maniac," says the man. "So I wish that I'm always hard and I get more ass than any man who ever lived." So the genie turns him into a toilet bowl.

# GIRAFFES

✳ Why do giraffes have such long necks? Their feet smell.

✳ What's the loudest noise in the jungle? A giraffe eating cherries.

# GOLF

✳ A female physical therapist tees off on the golf course but she slices her shot and hits a man standing on the next green. The man collapses with his hand between his legs. The physical therapist runs over and says, "Don't worry, I have medical training. I can help reduce the pain." So saying she opens his pants and massages his privates. After a minute she says, "Does that feel better?" The man replies, "Yes, thank you. But I think you broke my thumb."

✳ A golfer drives his new Honda into a gas station. An attendant comes over and the golfer asks him to fill up the tank. As he fills up, the attendant sees a couple of tees on the passenger seat. "What are those things for?" asks the attendant. "They're called tees," replies the golfer. "What are they for?" asks the attendant. The golfer replies, "They're for resting my balls on when I drive." "Jesus," says the attendant. "Those Japanese have thought of everything."

✳ "I asked my good friend Arnold Palmer how I could improve my game, he advised me to cheat!" *Bob Hope*

✳ A golfer is being given a lesson by a pro, but on his first swing, he hits the ball in the path of a bus. The ball smashes the windshield of the bus and knocks out the driver. The bus hurtles off the road into a reservoir and disappears in a seething mass of bubbles.

"Oh my God," says the golfer. "What am I going to do?" The pro replies, "Well, I'd loosen your grip and keep your back straighter."

✳ A golfer is bemoaning his lack of skill to his caddie. "I'm awful. There can't be any golfers worse than me," he says. "Oh there are," replies the caddie. "It's just they don't play any more."

✳ A golfer is playing a disastrous round when he slices his shot, hits two trees, and sends the ball into the middle of a swamp. The golfer tuts and turns to his caddie, "Golf. Funny old game isn't it?" "Yes," replies the caddie. "But it's not meant to be."

✳ A golfing coach puts his finger on his pupil's main failing. "The problem is that you're standing too close to the ball—after you've hit it."

✳ A group of businessmen are playing a round of golf when a funeral procession drives slowly alongside the green. One of the men takes off his cap and bows his head. "It's nice to see someone showing some respect for the dead," comments one of the players. "It's only proper," replies the man. "After all, we were married for twenty-five years."

✳ A husband and wife are playing a round of golf when one of the husband's shots lands the ball into the doorway of a greenhouse. The wife holds the greenhouse door open for her husband but he misjudges the swing, hits her on the head, and kills her. A couple of years later the husband, returns to the same golf course with his new wife. He slices the same shot and, again, puts the ball in the doorway of the greenhouse. "Shall I hold the door open for you, dear?" asks his wife. "No way," replies the man. "I tried that shot two years ago and I ended up taking a triple bogie."

✳ A man and a priest are playing golf. The man takes his first shot, misses, and says, "Jesus dammit, I missed." The priest is shocked, "Don't use that kind of language, or God will punish you." The man takes his second shot but misses again. Under his breath he says, "Jesus effing Christ..." The priest overhears him and says, "My son, please refrain from blasphemy or God will surely punish you." The man takes a third shot and misses again. He can't help himself and mutters, "Jesus H. Christ I missed again..." Suddenly a bolt of lightning strikes down and kills the priest. From the clouds a booming voice mutters, "Ahh, Jesus, missed again..."

✳ A man has been drinking at the golf club. On his way home his car is pulled over by the police, who tell him he's too drunk to drive. "Too drunk to drive?" responds the drunk. "I can barely putt."

✳ A man comes across four golfers in a bunker. One of the golfers is lying on the sand and the other three are arguing. "What's the matter?" asks the man. One of the golfers turns to him and says, "These swine will do anything to win a game. My partner's just had a stroke, and they want to add it to our score."

✳ A man finishes a terrible round of golf. He turns to his caddie and says, "I've never played that badly before." "Really, sir," replies the caddie. "So you've played before?"

✳ A man is marooned on a desert island for ten years. One day a beautiful woman is washed ashore and the man tells her his story. "You mean you've been on this island all that time?" says the woman. "Tell me, did you smoke cigarettes before you were marooned?" "Why, yes, I did," says the man. "Here, have one of mine," says the woman pulling a packet out of her pocket. "Say, were you a drinking man before you got shipwrecked?" asks the woman. "Why, yes, I was," says the man. The women reaches into her pocket and produces a small flask. "Help yourself," says the woman. "Say. Since you've been alone all that time, I guess you haven't played around in ten years, have you?" says the woman. "Good God!" says the man. "You don't mean you've got a set of golf clubs in there as well?"

✳ How did the bad golfer hit two good balls? He stood on a rake.

✳ A man takes his friend, a trader on the stock exchange, for his first game of golf. The man tees off and shouts, "Fore!" The trader shouts back, "Three ninety-five!"

✳ A terrible golfer hits his ball into a large bunker. "Which club should I use for this one?" he asks his caddie as he prepares to step into the sand. "I wouldn't worry about the club," replies the caddie. "Just make sure you take in plenty of food and water."

✳ A woman is accompanying her husband on a round of golf. At the first stroke he hits the ball in the rough. She shakes her head in sympathy. On the second stroke he hits the ball into a bunker. She shakes her head and sighs. On the third stroke the man knocks the ball on the green, and it rolls into the hole. "Oh boy," says his wife. "Now you're in real trouble."

✳ An avid golfer is so obsessed with the game, he can't stand the idea of not playing when he's dead. To put his mind at rest he goes to a psychic to try and find out if there's golf in Heaven. The psychic communes with the spirits, then says, "I have good news and bad news." "What's the good news?" asks the man. "Heaven does indeed have a golf course," says the psychic. "It's a beautiful course with thirty-six holes, twenty-four-hour access, and the most magnificent clubhouse you can imagine." "Wow," says the man. "So what's the bad news?" The psychic replies, "You're booked in for a game next Tuesday."

✳ Every year, Billy's father asked him what he wanted for his birthday, and every year, Billy said he wanted a pink golf ball. For years and years, this was the only gift he ever requested. If it was his birthday, he wanted a pink golf ball, if it was Christmas, he only ever wanted a pink golf ball. Nothing else would tempt him. Eventually Billy's father got tired of buying his son pink golf balls, so for his eighteenth birthday he got him a surprise present—a car. Billy liked the car and took it into town for a spin. Passing a sporting goods store, he saw they had some pink golf balls in the window, so he parked on the curb and crossed the road to take a closer look. Halfway across the road, he was hit by a truck. Billy's father came to see him in the hospital. He knew Billy wasn't going to make it and he wanted to ask his son one question before he died. "Billy," he said. "You've never played golf, so why for all these years did you only ever want pink golf balls as gifts?" Billy looked up at his father, opened his mouth to speak, then died. And the moral of this story is, you should always look both ways before crossing the street.

✳ Golfer, to caddy: "Say, do you think my game is improving?" Caddy: "Certainly. You miss the ball much closer than you used to."

✳ Why do golfers carry a spare sock? Because they might get a hole in one.

✳ On their honeymoon, a husband confesses a secret to his new wife. "Darling, I'm a golf addict," he says. "You'll never see me on the weekends and all our vacations will be at golfing resorts." "I've got a confession too," replies his new wife. "I'm a hooker." "That's not a problem," replies the husband. "Just keep your head down and your arm straight."

✳ Harry and Tom are on the golf course when Harry slices a shot deep into a wooded ravine. He takes his eight iron and clambers down the embankment in search of his lost ball. After fifteen minutes hacking at the underbrush, Harry spots something glistening among the leaves. He gets closer and discovers that it's an eight iron in the hands of a skeleton. Harry calls out to Tom, "Hey! I've got trouble down here!" "What's up?" shouts back Tom. "Bring me my wedge!" replies Harry. "You can't get out of here with an eight iron!"

✳ Harry and Tom are on the golf course. "I wish my wife had never taken up golf," says Harry. "She spends so much time practicing, she's cut down our sex life to once a week." "Count yourself lucky," replies Tom. "She's cut some of us out altogether."

✳ Harry is on the golf course lining up a perfect drive when a voice from the clubhouse calls out, "Will the gentleman on the ladies' tee please move back to the men's tee!" Harry ignores the voice and continues his practice swings. The voice calls out again, "Sir, will you please obey club rules and use the men's tee!" Harry prepares to take a swing when the voice calls out again, "The player on the ladies' tee must move back to the men's tee immediately!" Harry's had enough, he turns and shouts back, "Do you mind shutting up while I take my second shot!"

✳ Jill takes up golf and has many lessons with her golf pro before embarking on her first game. Unfortunately she soon hits her ball into the rough and, while trying to find it, gets stung by a bee. She runs back to the clubhouse for help and sees her pro at the bar. "Have you got any first aid? I got stung by a bee," says Jill. "Whereabouts?" asks the pro. "Between the first and second hole," she replies. "Dammit, Jill," says the pro. "We really need to work on your stance."

✳ One Sunday morning a priest decides to sneak off to play golf. He leaves a note on the church door saying he's too ill to read the Sunday sermon, then sneaks off to the golf course. God and Saint Peter are watching this from above. "I hope you're going to punish that man," says Saint Peter. "Watch this," says God. The priest tees off, and his first ball ricochets off three trees, skips across a pond, bounces off a boulder, loops the loop, and drops neatly into the hole. "I thought you were going to punish him?" says Saint Peter. "I have," says God. "Who's he going to tell?"

✳ Why did the idiot golfer invent green golf balls? So he could find them easier in the sand traps.

✳ Tom and Dick are on the golf course. "That's a funny-looking golf ball you've got there." says Tom. "It's the latest thing," replies Dick. "It's fantastic, a completely unlosable golf ball. If it goes in the bushes, it lights up. If it lands in the water, a flag pops up. If you lose it at night, it emits a bleeping sound till you track it down." "That's amazing," says Tom. "Where did you get it?" "I found it," replies Dick.

✳ "How was your golf game, dear?" asks Jack's wife. "Well," says Jack. "I was hitting pretty well, but my eyesight's got so bad I couldn't see where the ball went." "Why don't you take my brother, Scott, along?" suggests his wife. "He's eighty-five but he's got perfect eyesight." So the next day Jack tees off with Scott looking on. Jack swings, and the ball disappears down the middle of the fairway. "Do you see it?" asks Jack. "Yup," Scott answers. "Well, where is it?" says Jack, peering off into the distance. "Where's what?" says Scott.

✳ A golfer is taking a long time teeing off, and his friend asks him what's the matter, "My wife is watching from the clubhouse," he says. "So I want to make sure this is a good one." "You're crazy," replies the friend. "The clubhouse has to be 500 yards away. You'll never hit her from this distance."

✳ A man goes to confession and tells the priest that he used the "f" word, "But I had a good reason," says the man. "There's never a good reason for bad language," replies the priest. "But if you wish, you may tell me what happened." "Well," says the man. "I was playing golf when I hooked my first shot…" "Is that when you swore?" asks the priest. "No, Father," says the man. "When I got to my ball, I saw I had a clear shot to the green, but before I could take a swing, a squirrel came along, grabbed my ball, and ran up a tree…" "And is that when you swore?" asks the priest. "No, Father," says the man. "An eagle snatched the squirrel out of the tree together with my ball…" "And is that when you swore?" asks the priest. "No, Father," says the man. "A low-flying jet frightened the eagle, and it dropped the squirrel…" "And is that when you swore?" asks the priest. "No, Father," says the man. "The squirrel dropped the ball as it fell, and it landed three inches from the hole…" "Sweet Jesus," says the priest. "Don't tell me you missed the fucking putt!"

✻ After a long day on the course, the exasperated golfer turns to his caddie and says, "You must be the worst caddie in the world." "No, I don't think so," replies the caddie. "That would be too much of a coincidence."

✻ Harry's car breaks down, so he has to take the bus to his local golf course. His golf bag is full, so he stuffs a couple of extra balls in his pants pockets. On the bus an old lady starts staring at the strange bulge in his trousers. "Don't worry," says Harry. "They're only my golf balls." "Oh dear," says the old lady. "Is that like tennis elbow?"

✻ Golfer to caddy: "That can't be my ball. It looks far too old." Caddy: "Well, it's a long time since we started."

✻ Angry golfer to wife: "One day you'll drive me out of my mind." Wife: "That would be a putt, dear."

✻ A golfer is thrashing through the bushes, looking for a lost ball. An old lady watches him as she sits on a bench knitting. After half an hour the golfer is just about to give up when the old lady says, "Excuse me. But is it against the rules if I tell you where it is?"

✻ Golfer to caddy: "I'd move heaven and earth to be able to break one hundred on this course." Caddy: "Try heaven. You've already moved most of the earth."

# GOODWILL TO ALL MEN

✻ Before you criticize someone, you should walk a mile in their shoes. That way, when you criticize them, you're a mile away and you have their shoes.

✻ I love mankind. It's people I can't stand.

✻ If you can't laugh at yourself, make fun of other people.

✻ If you can't say anything nice, you probably don't have many friends.

✻ If you have nothing good to say about someone, go on an afternoon talk show and say it anyway.

✻ If you think there's good in everybody, you haven't met everybody.

✻ I'm not prejudiced. I hate everyone equally.

✻ Some people are alive only because it's illegal to kill them.

✻ If you can't say anything good about someone, sit right here by me.

# GOSSIP

✳ A woman says to her friend, "Peggy told me that you told her the secret I told you not to tell her." "Well," replies her friend in a hurt tone, "I told her not to tell you I told her." "Oh dear!" says the woman. "Well, don't tell her I told you that she told me."

✳ As you well know, I never repeat gossip. So listen very carefully; I'm only going to tell you this once…

# GRAFFITI

✳ Graffiti in a toilet: "I like grils." Somebody had written underneath "You mean girls, stupid." And underneath that someone else had written "What's the matter with us grils?"

✳ On a wall in a ladies' room: "My husband follows me everywhere." Written just below it: "No. I don't."

✳ Written in a women's toilet: "Friends don't let their friends take home an ugly man."

✳ Written over a mirror in a men's toilet: "No wonder you always go home alone."

✳ Written over a mirror in a women's toilet: "You're too good for him."

✳ Written over a urinal: "Express lane—five beers or less."

✳ Written in a men's toilet: "Don't forget, no matter how good she looks, there's some other guy somewhere who's sick and tired of her shit."

✳ Written in a women's toilet: "If it has tires or testicles, you're going to have trouble with it."

✳ Written over a urinal: "What are you looking up here for? The joke's in your hand."

# HAIR AND/OR THE LACK OF IT

✳ A bald man sees a sign outside a barber's shop saying "Baldies! Instant treatment! A head of hair just like mine for $5,000!" Underneath the sign is a picture of the barber with a fine mane of luxuriant hair. The bald man goes in and says, "Can you guarantee my head will look like yours, instantly, for $5,000?" "I sure can," says the barber. "It'll only take a few seconds for us to look exactly alike." So the bald man hands over the $5,000, and the barber shaves his own hair off.

✳ A girl is at the hairdresser's chatting with her stylist. "My boyfriend has terrible dandruff," she says. "Is there anything you can suggest?" The stylist replies, "Why don't you give him Head & Shoulders?" The girl thinks for a moment then says, "So how do you give shoulders?"

✳ How did they know the shark attack victim had dandruff? They found his head and shoulders on the beach.

✳ I do sometimes bleach my hair. It's the only way I can get it clean.

✳ It's such a shame to ruin such beautiful blonde hair by dying the roots black.

✳ She waxed the hair off her legs, she waxed the hair off her armpits, she waxed the hair off her bikini line. But when she tried to wax the hair out of her nostrils, she asphyxiated herself.

✳ Tom sees Harry on the street and shouts, "What did you do to your hair? It looks like a wig!" Harry looks embarrassed and says, "Well, it is a wig." Tom replies, "You know what, you'd never be able to tell."

✳ What is the only true cure for dandruff? Baldness.

✳ What should you buy if your hair falls out? A good vacuum cleaner.

✳ Women will never be equal to men until they can walk down the street bald and still think they're gorgeous.

✳ "He looks like an explosion in a pubic hair factory." *Jonathan Miller*

✳ Men, don't worry if your hair is getting thin on top; fat hair is unhealthy.

✳ I'm not bald; I've just got flesh-colored hair.

✳ Little boy to grandfather: "Are you still growing, Granddad?" Grandfather: "I don't think so. Why do you ask?" Boy: "It's just that the top of your head's coming out through your hair."

# HAIRDRESSERS

✳ A man and a boy go into a barber's. The man has a trim then says to the boy, "You get your hair cut while I go to the supermarket and do some shopping." The boy has his hair, cut but the man does not return. "Looks like your dad's forgotten you're here," says the barber. "That wasn't my dad," replies the boy. "That guy grabbed me on the street, said 'How would you like a free haircut' and dragged me in here."

✳ A man enters a barber's for a shave. While the barber is foaming him up, the man mentions the problem he has getting a close shave around his cheeks. "I have just what you need," says the barber, giving him a small wooden ball. "Just place this between your cheek and gum." The man does so, and the barber gives him the closest shave the man has ever experienced. After a few moments the client says, "Hey, what if I swallow this thing?" "No problem," replies the barber. "Just bring it back tomorrow like everyone else."

✳ A man goes into a barber's and asks for a haircut that leaves his fringe at different lengths round his head, creates two bald spots near the back, a spiky bit at the side, and leaves a large nick on his ear. "I'm not sure we could manage that," says the barber. "It sounds pretty tricky." "I don't see why," says the man. "It's the same haircut you gave me the last time I was here."

✳ A man goes into a barber shop and notices that a little dog is watching the barber intently. "That dog seems very interested in what you're up to," says the man. "He's hoping for a treat," replies the barber sharpening his razor. "If I sneeze, he sometimes gets a bit of ear."

✳ A man goes into a hairdresser's for a cut and shave and starts flirting with the girl doing his hair. "What time do you finish tonight?" he asks. "Half past five," says the girl. "How about coming for a drink with me?" he says. "I'm married," says the girl. "What would I tell my husband?" "Tell him anything," says the man. "Tell him you're going out with a friend." "I've got an idea," says the girl. "Why don't you tell him yourself. He's the one over there sharpening the razor."

✳ I went into the barber's and noticed he had dirty hands. "I can't help it," said the barber. "No one's been in for a shampoo today."

✳ When one barber cuts another's hair, which one does the talking?

✳ While getting his hair trimmed, Patrick tells his barber about a planned vacation to Rome. "Who knows," says Patrick. "I might even get to meet the Pope." "You'll never meet the Pope," says the barber. "He's much too important to mix with the likes of you." "But I might meet him," replies Patrick. "It's not impossible." "Bullshit," says the barber. "I'll bet you a hundred dollars you don't meet him." "Okay," says Patrick. "You're on." A month later Patrick comes back and says, "You owe me a hundred dollars. I was walking around St. Peter's Square when the Pope saw me from his balcony, invited me into the Vatican, and asked me a question." "My God," says the barber. "What did he say?" Patrick replies, "He said, 'Where in Christ's name did you get that awful haircut?'"

✳ "How do you get your barber to cut your hair that way?" "I insult him."

✳ A man walks into a barber shop and asks how many people are waiting to be served. "I've got three cuts and a shave booked this morning," replies the barber. The man leaves but comes back the next day. "How many are waiting today?" he asks. "I've got two cuts, a dye-job, and a shave," replies the barber. Next day the man is back with the same question, and the barber tells him, "Four cuts and a wash." This goes on for weeks until the barber gets suspicious—perhaps the man is a rival planning on opening his own barber shop in the area. Perhaps he wants to find out how much business he can expect. To solve the mystery, he gets his assistant to follow the man the next time he drops by. The next day the man comes in, asks his usual question and leaves, this time trailed by the assistant. When the assistant gets back, the barber says, "Well? Who is he? Where did he go?" The assistant replies, "I don't know who he is, but he seems to be a friend of your wife. He just went around to your house."

✳ Harry went to a new barber and was horrified to find that a trim would be $20. "But I'm practically bald," says Harry. "How can it cost $20?" The barber replies, "To be honest, the cut is only $5. The other $15 is a search fee."

# HAPPINESS

✳ "Some cause happiness wherever they go; some whenever they go." *Oscar Wilde*

✳ "What's the use of happiness? It can't buy you money." *Henny Youngman*

✳ Happiness: good health and a bad memory.

✳ "When you wake up in the morning, smile—and get it over with." *W.C. Fields*

✳ Remember, the person who's always happy might just be too dumb to complain.

✳ But I'll tell you what I love doing more than anything: trying to pack myself in a small suitcase. I can hardly contain myself.

# HARDWARE AND DIY

✳ "If you nail a tool shed closed, how do you put the hammer away?" *George Carlin*

✳ I got a self-assembly dresser. It didn't work. I got it out of the box, it didn't do a thing.

✳ I used some of that quick drying wood stain the other day and, like they say, it did exactly what it said on the can. It caused nausea and vomiting when ingested.

✳ I was doing some decorating, so I got out my stepladder. I don't get on with my real ladder.

✳ My boyfriend's really into DIY. He's just built a set of shelves for our house, and now he's writing some books to put on them.

✳ A man goes into a hardware store and asks to buy a chainsaw. The sales clerk sells him one that is guaranteed to fell even the largest tree in under a minute. The man takes it home but comes back the next day to complain. "A minute, my ass," he says. "I started cutting down a tree yesterday lunchtime, and by six in the evening, I'd only managed to get half-way through the trunk." The sales clerk apologizes. "I'm sorry," he says. "Perhaps the engine's air-to-fuel ratio is out of adjustment. I'll just check." So saying, he pulls the starter cord and the chainsaw roars into life. "Jesus!" exclaims the startled man. "What's that noise!?"

✳ Last week I replaced every window in my house. Then I discovered I had a crack in my glasses.

✳ I have six locks on my door. When I go out, I lock every other one. I figure no matter how long somebody stands there picking the locks, they're always locking three of them.

✳ I need a trash compactor because my trash is too heavy to carry up the driveway.

# HEALTH AND DOCTORS

✳ A half-drowned man washes up on a beach outside a hospital. A medical team rushes out, gives him the kiss of life, then pumps out his stomach to get rid of any seawater. The pump brings up gallons of water, some seaweed, a number of small fish, and some crabs. The medical team keeps pumping, but after five minutes, the brine, the fish, the seaweed, and the shellfish still keep coming in an endless stream. Finally a bystander taps one of the doctors on the shoulder and says, "Excuse me, but should you be doing that while he's still sitting in the water?"

✳ A health expert is giving a talk on well-being in a town hall. "The best way to start the day is to do five minutes light exercise, and five minutes of deep breathing," says the expert. "Then I take a short hot shower, and feel rosy all over." A voice from the back of the hall shouts, "Tell us more about Rosie!"

✳ A man answers a knock at his front door. Outside is a six-foot ladybug which proceeds to head-butt him, kick him in the crotch, and stamp on his head. The man wakes up in the hospital where he describes his ordeal to the doctor, "You're the sixth case like this we've had in today," says the doctor. "There's a nasty bug going around."

✳ A man goes to a psychiatrist. "You've got to help me," says the man. "I can't stop deep-frying things in batter. I get up in the morning and deep-fry my boiled egg. I've deep-fried all my clothes and shoes. I've even deep-fried my bike and battered the cat! What's wrong with me?" "It's obvious," replies the psychiatrist. "You're frittering your life away."

✳ A man goes to the doctor and says, "Doctor, I can't pronounce my Fs, Ts or Hs." "Well," says the doctor. "You can't say fairer than that."

✳ How do you stop a head cold going to your chest? Tie a knot in your neck!

✳ I'm taking prenatal breathing classes. I'm not having a baby, I'm just having trouble breathing.

✳ A man is sitting in a doctor's waiting room. Every so often he says, "Lord, I hope I'm sick!" After his saying this about six or seven times, the receptionist says, "Excuse me, but why in the world would you want to be sick?" The man replies, "I'd hate to be well and feel this crappy."

✳ A man walks into a doctor's office. The doctor says, "I haven't seen you in a long time." The man replies, "I know, I've been ill."

✳ A rat catcher walks into a doctor's office, "I was putting down some poison when one of the little buggers bit off my finger." "Which one?" asks the doctor. "How should I know?" says the rat catcher. "They all look the same to me."

✳ An old man goes to a school reunion where he finds that his surviving classmates are only interested in talking about their ailments: kidney stones, heart murmurs, liver pains, etc. When he gets home, his daughter asks him how it went. "It wasn't much of a reunion," he replies. "It was more like an organ recital."

✳ Doctors can be frustrating. You wait a month and a half for an appointment and he says, "I wish you'd come to me sooner."

✳ It was recently discovered that research causes cancer in rats.

✳ I've got no faith in my doctor. All his patients are ill.

✳ Jack Benny, receiving a showbusiness award: "I don't deserve this. But I have arthritis and I don't deserve that either."

✳ My doctor said he would have me on my feet in two weeks. He did, I had to sell my car to pay his bill.

✳ Tom, to Dick: "Who gave you that black eye?" Dick: "Nobody. I had to fight for it."

✳ Tom spent many years trying to find a cure for his halitosis and acne, only to find people didn't like him anyway.

✳ Never go to a doctor whose office plants have died.

✳ What good is mouthwash that kills germs? Who wants a mouth full of dead germs?

✳ Sam and John are at work in the lumberyard when John accidentally chops his arm off with a saw. Sam wraps the arm in a plastic bag and takes John to a surgeon. Four hours later Sam is amazed to see John in the pub throwing darts. "Wow!" thinks Sam. "That surgeon is great." A few weeks later John cuts his leg off. Sam puts the leg in a plastic bag and takes John back to the surgeon. That evening he's amazed to see John playing soccer. "Wow!" thinks Sam. "That surgeon is amazing." A few weeks later John cuts his head off. Sam puts the head in a plastic bag and carries John to the surgeon. The next day the surgeon calls Sam and says, "I'm sorry, but John is dead." "Don't blame yourself," says Sam. "I'm sure you did all you could." "I'm not blaming myself," says the surgeon. "I'm blaming you. If you'd put some holes in that plastic bag, the poor bastard wouldn't have suffocated!"

✳ A foreman hires a man to do a job, but he calls up and complains he's feeling too unwell to work. "Tell you what," says the foreman, "When I'm feeling ill I have sex with my wife. It soon perks me up. Try it and let's see how you feel." A few hours later the hiree calls back and says, "I had sex just like you said. Now I feel great. You have a very nice house."

✳ A guy walks into a crowded doctor's office and says to the receptionist, "There's something wrong with my dick." The receptionist looks up and says, "You shouldn't say things like that in a public area. Please leave, and when you come back, say there's something wrong with your ear, or something like that." The guy walks out, then walks back in and says, "There's something wrong with my ear." "And what's wrong with your ear?" says the receptionist. The man says, "It hurts when I piss out of it."

✳ A man walks into a doctor's office. "What seems to be the problem?" asks the doctor. "I have five penises," replies the man. "Jesus!" says the doctor. "How do your pants fit?" The man replies, "Like a glove."

✳ A man walks into a doctor's office. He has a cucumber up his nose, a carrot in his left ear, and a banana in his right ear. "Ah! I can see what's the matter with you," says the doctor. "You're not eating properly."

✳ A medical student holding a syringe approaches a patient. "Don't worry," he says. "It's just a little prick with a needle." "I can see that," replies the patient. "I'm just wandering what you're going to do with the needle."

✳ At a medical convention, a male doctor, Tom, and a female doctor, Janet, start eyeing each other. Tom asks Janet to dinner and she accepts. After dinner, one thing leads to another, and they end up in her room. However, just as things get hot, Janet stops to go and wash her hands. She comes back and they go for it. After sex, Janet gets up and washes her hands again. Tom says, "I bet you're a surgeon. You're always washing your hands. "That's very clever," says Janet. "And I bet you're an anesthesiologist." "Wow," says Tom. "You're right. How did you guess?" Janet replies, "Because I didn't feel a thing."

✳ I'm not an organ donor, but I once gave an old piano to the Salvation Army.

✳ Joe suffers from very bad headaches and eventually finds a doctor who offers a solution. "The good news is that I can cure your headaches," says the doctor. "The bad news is that it will require castration. You have a rare condition which causes your testicles to press against the base of your spine. It's that pressure that causes the headaches." Joe is shocked but decides he has no choice but to go under the knife. After the operation, Joe feels much better and decides to treat himself to a new suit. He goes into a tailor's to see what's on offer. The tailor looks at him and says, "Let's see. I'd guess you take a size 44 long?" Joe laughs, "That's right. How did you know my exact size?" "It's my job to know," says the tailor. "How about a new shirt to go with it? I'd say you take a 34 sleeve and a 16 neck." "Right again," says Joe. "How did you know?" "It's my job," says the tailor. "How about some new underwear as well? Let's see, I'd say you're a size 36." Joe laughs, "Got you that time. I'm actually a 34. I've worn size 34 since I was eighteen." The tailor tuts, "You shouldn't do that, sir. You see, a size 34 would press your testicles against your spine and give you terrible headaches."

✳ Nurse: "Doctor, the man you just gave a clean bill of health to dropped dead as he was leaving the surgery." Doctor: "Turn him around. Make it look like he was walking in."

✳ What do a near-sighted gynecologist and a puppy have in common? A wet nose.

✳ What's the difference between an oral thermometer and a rectal thermometer? The taste.

✳ Dick to wife: "Darling, I'm not feeling well. Can you call me a vet." Wife: "A vet? Don't you mean a doctor?" Dick: "I think a vet's more appropriate. After all, I work like a horse, I live like a dog, and I sleep with a cow."

✳ Harry to doctor: "I don't understand it. My wife's pregnant, but we haven't had sex in a year!" Doctor: "It's what we call a 'grudge pregnancy'—someone's obviously had it in for you."

✳ Doctor to hospital patient: "Your coughing seems to be easier this morning." Patient: "It should be. I've been practicing all night."

✳ Medicine has now advanced to the point where it is impossible for a doctor to examine someone without finding something wrong with them.

# HEALTH AND DOCTORS: ALTERNATIVE THERAPY

✳ "A friend of mine is into voodoo acupuncture. You don't have to go. You'll just be walking down the street, and…'Oh, that's much better.'" *Steven Wright*

✳ "I went to a massage parlor. It was self-service." *Rodney Dangerfield*

✳ I went to one of those people who sort out your problems with alternative remedies. He played some new age music, applied essential oils, did some acupuncture, and massaged my butt with licorice. It didn't work—the washing machine still won't drain.

✳ Why did the pregnant woman eat rubber? So she'd have a bouncing baby.

# HEALTH AND DOCTORS: DISEASES

✳ A man bumps into a friend who's been recovering from the flu. The man asks how he's feeling. "I'm better, thanks," replies his friend. "It was actually a wonderful experience." "Wonderful?" says the man. "How can the flu be wonderful?" "I learned my wife really loves me," explains the friend. "She was so excited I was home, every time the postman, milkman, or garbageman came by, she'd run out shouting, "My husband's home! My husband's home!"'

✳ A worried father telephones his doctor and tells him that his teenage son has come down with a sexually transmitted disease. "He thinks he caught it from the housekeeper," says the father. "Don't worry too much," says the doctor. "These things happen." "I know," says the father. "But I've been sleeping with the housekeeper too. And now I seem to have the same symptoms." "That's unfortunate," says the doctor. "But try not to get distressed." "That's not all," says the man. "I think I've passed it to my wife." "Christ Almighty!" shouts the doctor. "That means we all have it!"

✳ What do you give a man who has everything? Antibiotics.

# HEALTH AND DOCTORS: DOCTOR, DOCTOR...

✳ "Doctor, doctor, I have a ringing in my ears." "Don't answer!"

✳ "Doctor, doctor, I've hurt my arm in several places." "Well, don't go there any more."

✳ "Doctor, doctor, I think I'm shrinking!" "Now, settle down. You'll just have to be a little patient."

✳ "Doctor, doctor, can I have second opinion?" "Certainly. Come back tomorrow!"

✳ "Doctor, doctor, I feel like a pack of cards." "I'll deal with you later!"

✳ "Doctor, doctor, can you cure my sleepwalking?" "Try these." "Are they sleeping pills?" "No. They're thumbtacks. Sprinkle them on the floor."

✳ "Doctor, doctor, everyone I meet thinks I'm a liar!" "I'm sorry, but I can't believe that!"

✳ "Doctor, doctor, everyone keeps ignoring me." "Next please!"

✳ "Doctor, doctor, have you got something for a headache?" "Yes. Take this hammer and hit yourself on the head."

✳ "Doctor, doctor, I can't get to sleep." "Sit on the edge of the bed and you'll soon drop off."

✳ "Doctor, doctor, I keep thinking I'm invisible." "Who the hell said that?"

✳ "Doctor, doctor, I keep thinking there are two of me." "One at a time please."

✳ "Doctor, doctor, I can't stop my hands shaking!" "Do you drink a lot?" "Of course not. I spill most of it!"

✳ "Doctor, doctor, I feel like a pair of curtains." "For goodness sake, pull yourself together."

✳ "Doctor, doctor, I feel like a pig!" "How long have you been feeling like this?" "Oh, about a weeeeeeeeeeek!"

✳ "Doctor, doctor, I feel like a spoon!" "Sit there and don't stir!"

✳ "Doctor, doctor, I get a terrible pain in my eye when I drink a cup of coffee." "Try taking the spoon out."

✳ "Doctor, doctor, I keep feeling like I'm a box of Wheat Thins!" "Oh no. You're crackers!"

✳ "Doctor, doctor, I keep thinking I'm a dog." "Sit on the couch and we'll talk about it." "I can't, I'm not allowed on the couch!"

✳ "Doctor, doctor, I think I need glasses." "You certainly do. This is a garage."

✳ "Doctor, doctor, I snore so loudly, I keep myself awake." "Have you tried sleeping in another room?"

✳ "Doctor, doctor, I think I'm a bridge." "What's come over you?" "Two cars, a truck, and a bus."

✳ "Doctor, doctor, I think I'm a dog." "How long have you felt like this?" "Ever since I was a puppy!"

✳ "Doctor, doctor, I've just swallowed a pen." "Well, sit down and write your name!"

✳ "Doctor, doctor, I think I'm a python." "You can't get around me just like that you know!"

✳ "Doctor, doctor, I think I'm suffering from déjà vu!" "Hang on! Didn't I see you yesterday?"

✳ "Doctor, doctor, I think I'm turning into an apple." "We'll have to get to the core of this!"

✳ "Doctor, doctor, I'm a kleptomaniac!" "Take these pills, and if that doesn't work, pick me up a computer."

✳ "Doctor, doctor, I've got amnesia!" "Go home and forget about it."

✳ "Doctor, doctor, I'm having trouble with my breathing." "Don't worry. I'll give you something that will put a stop to that!"

✳ "Doctor, doctor, I've got something wrong with my eyes. I keep seeing an insect spinning around my head." "Don't worry, that's just a bug going around."

✳ "Doctor, doctor, I've got terrible wind. What can you give me for it?" "Have you tried a kite?"

✳ "Doctor, doctor, I think I'm a moth." "Get out of the way, you're in my light!"

✳ "Doctor, doctor, I've had a tummy ache since I ate three crabs yesterday." "Did they smell bad when you took them out of their shells?" "What do you mean 'took them out of their shells'?"

✳ "Doctor, doctor, I've lost my memory!" "When did this happen?" "When did what happen?"

✳ "Doctor, doctor, I've swallowed a bone!" "Are you choking?" "No, I really did!"

✳ "Doctor, doctor, my baby's swallowed a bullet." "Well, don't point him at anyone until I get there!"

✳ "Doctor, doctor, my sister thinks she's an elevator!" "Tell her to come in." "I can't, she doesn't stop at this floor!"

✳ "Doctor, doctor, my son has swallowed my pen. What should I do?" "Use a pencil till I get there!"

✳ "Doctor, doctor, some days I feel like a tepee and other days I feel like a wigwam." "I think you're two tents."

✳ "Doctor, doctor, there's a strawberry growing out the top of my head." "I'll give you some cream to put on that."

✳ "Doctor, doctor, these pills you gave me for B.O. are crap!" "What's wrong with them?" "They keep slipping out of my armpits!"

✳ "Doctor, doctor, you've taken out my tonsils, my adenoids, my gall bladder, my varicose veins, and my appendix, but I still don't feel well." "That's quite enough out of you!"

✳ "Doctor, doctor, you have to help me out!" "Certainly, which way did you come in?"

✳ "Doctor, doctor, I keep seeing images of Mickey Mouse and Donald Duck!" "I see, and how long have you been having these Disney spells?"

✳ "Doctor, doctor, I feel terrible!" "What are the symptoms?" "It's a cartoon show with yellow people."

✳ "Doctor, doctor, I keep dreaming about necrophilia, sadism, and bestiality!" "Forget it, you're flogging a dead horse."

✳ "Doctor, doctor, it hurts when I do this." "Then don't do that!"

✳ "Doctor, doctor," says a patient. "I can't stop singing, 'The Green, Green Grass of Home.'" "That sounds like Tom Jones Syndrome," says the doctor. "Is it common?" asks the patient. The doctor replies, "It's not unusual."

✳ "Doctor, doctor, how do I stop my nose from running?" "Stick your foot out and trip it up!"

✳ "Doctor, doctor, I feel like a sheep." "Oh dear, that sounds baaaaaaaaaad!"

✳ "Doctor, doctor, I need something to keep my hair in." "Here's a shoe box."

✳ "Doctor, doctor, I think I'm an enormous moth. Have you got anything to help me out?" "Wait there, I'll get a big glass and sheet of paper."

✳ "Doctor, doctor, my baby is the image of his father." "Never mind, just so long as he's healthy."

✳ "Doctor, doctor, will this ointment you've given me clear up my spots?" "You know me, I never make rash promises!"

✳ Patient: "Doctor, my leg hurts. What can I do?" Doctor: "Limp!"

✳ "Doctor, doctor, I keep thinking I'm a vampire." "Necks please!"

✳ "Doctor, doctor, I've got a problem with my waterworks!" "Have you seen a plumber?"

✳ "Doctor, doctor, I have bananas growing out of both ears!" "Good God! How did that happen?" "What did you say?"

# HEALTH AND DOCTORS: EXAMINATIONS

✳ A doctor is examining a young female patient. He applies his stethoscope and says, "Big breaths." "Yeth," replies the girl. "And I'm thtill only thixteen."

✳ A doctor is holding a stethoscope to a man's chest. The man says, "Doctor, how do I stand?" The doctor says, "That's what puzzles me!"

✳ A man walks into a doctor's and asks to be examined. The doctor gives him a once-over and is astonished to find money stuffed into his ears. The money is taken out and the doctor counts it. "There's exactly one thousand, nine hundred and fifty dollars in there," says the doctor. "That sounds about right," says the patient. "I knew I wasn't feeling two grand."

✳ A private doctor says to a patient, "I'll examine you for twenty bucks." "Okay," replies the patient. "If you can find it, you can have it."

✳ Doctor to patient: "You seem to be in excellent health. Your pulse is as regular as clockwork." Patient: "That's because you've got your hand on my watch!"

✳ Doctor to patient: "Your breathing doesn't sound very good." Patient: "No. It's coming in short pants." Doctor: "Well, it should be coming from your lungs."

✳ A man goes for a check-up. The doctor says, "I'm going to need a urine sample, a semen sample, a blood sample, and a stool sample." The man replies, "I'm in a hurry. Can I just leave my underwear?"

✳ A few days before his proctological exam, a one-eyed man accidentally swallows his glass eye. In the doctor's office, the man gets undressed and bends over. The proctologist looks up the man's ass and sees the glass eye staring back at him. "You know," he says. "You really have to learn to trust me."

✳ A man goes to his doctor with a sprig of green sticking out of his bottom. "Doctor, I think I have a lettuce growing out of my rear end," he says. The doctor examines the greenery and says, "I'm afraid I have bad news—it's only the tip of the iceberg."

✳ Doctor to patient: "Don't forget to stick your tongue out when the nurse comes." Patient: "Why?" Doctor: "I don't like her."

# HEALTH AND DOCTORS: HEALTHY HABITS

✳ A reporter is interviewing a woman celebrating her hundredth birthday. "And to what do you attribute your amazing old age?" asks the reporter. "I believe in moderation in all things," says the old lady. "I eat moderately, sleep moderately, and drink moderately, and so remain in perfect health." "But I understand you've often been bedridden," says the reporter. "Well, of course I have," says the old lady. "But don't put that in your newspaper."

✳ A woman walks up to a wrinkled old man sitting on a park bench. "You look very content," she says. "What's your secret for a long, happy life?" "I smoke sixty cigarettes a day," replies the man. "I drink a crate of beer a week. Eat nothing but fatty meat, and never exercise." "That's amazing," says the woman. "And just how old are you?" The man replies, "Twenty-six."

✳ An apple a day keeps the doctor away, but an onion does the job for a week.

✳ Good health is merely the slowest possible rate at which one can die.

✳ Harry maintains that drinking a pint of beer every day is actually good for your liver. If only he had twenty-seven livers, he'd be a picture of health.

# HEALTH AND DOCTORS: HOSPITALS

✳ A hospital patient is talking with his wife. "I've got the doctors baffled," he says. "Why do you think that?" asks the wife. The husband replies, "They've put a suggestions box at the bottom of my bed."

✳ A man calls his local hospital. "How is Mr. Jackson in Ward B?" he asks. "Mr. Jackson is out of danger," replies the nurse on duty. "His test results were normal. Can I ask who's calling?" "Yes, it's Mr. Jackson in Ward B," says the man. "No one tells me anything."

✳ A seriously ill man is lying in his hospital bed on a ventilator. The man's family and the hospital chaplain gather around to comfort him. The man gestures for a pen and paper, writes a brief note, hands it to the chaplain, and passes away. The chaplain reads out the man's dying words, "Help. You're standing on my oxygen tube."

✳ Due to a mixup in Urology, orange juice will not be on the hospital menu this morning.

✳ Why did Harry get thrown out of the hospital? After two days he took a turn for the nurse.

✳ A hospital is a place where they wake you at five in the morning to give you a sleeping pill.

✳ Always guard your rear while you're in the hospital. Remember, you're in enema country.

✳ Visitor to hospital patient: "I heard they're bringing in a case of diarrhea." Patient: "Well, anything's better than the coffee they keep giving us."

# HEALTH AND DOCTORS: HYPOCHONDRIA

✳ "There's no need for me to come out to the house," says the doctor to a worried caller. "I've checked my files, and your uncle isn't ill at all, he just thinks he's sick." A week later, the same caller phones back. "And how's your uncle today?" asks the doctor. "Worse," replies the caller. "Now he thinks he's dead."

✳ Hypochondria is the only disease I haven't got.

✳ A man goes to his doctor and tells him he's suffering from a long list of illnesses. "The trouble with you," says the doctor. "Is that you're a hypochondriac." "Oh no," says the man. "Don't tell me I've got that as well."

✳ Doctor to patient: "I have good news and bad news. The good news is that you're not a hypochondriac."

✳ Harry tells the doctor he thinks he has a rare fatal disease. "You wouldn't know though," says the doctor. "If you were suffering from that disease, you'd feel no pain or discomfort at all." "I know," says Harry. "And those are exactly my symptoms."

✳ Inscription on a hypochondriac's grave: "I told you I was ill."

✳ Mrs. Smith is a hypochondriac and her doctor—fed up with her constant complaints about nonexistent illnesses—starts palming her off with a mild sedative to keep her happy. One day Mrs. Smith complains of chest pains and is prescribed her usual treatment. However, this time the pain is real, and Mrs. Smith dies of a heart attack. The doctor hears this and is so upset, he dies of shock. Mrs. Smith and the doctor are buried in adjoining plots. The next morning the doctor hears a tapping on his coffin. A muffled voice calls out, "Doctor, this is Mrs. Smith! Do you have anything for worms?"

✳ He was such a hypochondriac, he insisted on being buried next to a doctor.

# HEALTH AND DOCTORS: INAPPROPRIATE INVOLVEMENT WITH PATIENTS

✳ A woman says to her doctor, "Kiss me! Kiss me, you gorgeous stud!" The doctor replies, "I can't. It would be unethical. To be honest I shouldn't be screwing you at all…"

# HEALTH AND DOCTORS: OPERATIONS

✳ A beautiful young girl is about to undergo an operation. She's laid on a gurney and wheeled into the corridor. The nurse leaves her outside the operating room and goes to tell the surgeon she's ready. A young man in a white coat comes over, lifts up the girl's sheet, and examines her naked body. He walks away and talks to another man in a white coat. The second man comes over and performs the same examination. Then a third man comes over and lifts the sheet. The girl loses her temper—"Are these examinations absolutely necessary?" she complains. "I've no idea," replies the man. "We're just here to paint the ceiling."

✳ The colder the X-ray table, the more of your body that is required on it.

✳ A man is given a pig's ear during a transplant operation. A month later he goes back to the hospital for a check-up. "Any problems?" asks the doctor. "No, it's fine," replies the man. "Though I do get a bit of crackling."

✳ A man is going into the hospital for an operation. He asks his doctor, "Doctor, will I be able to play the piano after my operation?" The doctor says, "Certainly you will." "That's good," says the man. "I couldn't before."

✳ A surgical patient wakes up after an operation and is told he's got to be opened up again—it seems the surgical team has left a pair of rubber gloves inside him. The patient says, "Couldn't I just pay for them?"

✳ Surgeon to patient: "This is Nurse Jones, she has a severe case of halitosis and will be French-kissing you before your operation." Patient: "Why?" Surgeon: "We've run out of anesthetic."

✳ A mother takes her young son to see the doctor. "Doctor, is it possible for a twelve-year-old boy to operate on himself and take out his own appendix?" "Of course not," says the doctor. "See!" she says to the boy. "Now put it back!"

✳ Surgeon to patient: "I have good news and bad news about your operation. The bad news is that it's a risky procedure and your chances of survival are one in ninety-nine." "Oh my God," says the patient. "So what's the good news?" The surgeon replies, "The good news is that my last ninety-nine patients died."

# HEALTH AND DOCTORS: PILLS AND TREATMENT

✳ A doctor is walking down a hospital ward when he hears a shriek and sees a nun running out of another doctor's office. Curious, he steps in to find out what's going on. "Oh, I just told that nun she's pregnant," says the second doctor. "My God, is she?" asks the first doctor. "Of course not," says the second doctor. "But it cured her hiccups."

✳ "Those pills you gave me are fantastic," says a patient to his doctor. "But they make me walk like a crab." "Those will be the side effects," replies the doctor.

✳ A man is examined by his doctor. The doctor says, "Take this green pill with a glass of water when you get up. Take this blue pill with a glass of water after lunch. Then just before going to bed, take this red pill with another glass of water." "Exactly what's the matter with me?" asks the man. "You're not drinking enough water," says the doctor.

✳ A man with a persistent cough goes to a pharmacist and gets a remedy from the assistant. The next day he's back saying the cure didn't work and asks for something else. The assistant gives him another cough cure, but the next day the man is back complaining that the new medicine didn't work either. The assistant gives him another remedy, but again the man comes back the next day to complain. This continues for a week, until the head pharmacist takes over and gives the man another bottle of medicine. The next day the assistant sees the man walking very slowly down the road, his cough completely cured. "That's fantastic," says the assistant. "What cough remedy did you give him?" "I didn't give him a cough remedy," says the pharmacist. "I gave him a laxative. Now he's afraid to cough."

✳ A man with terrible back problems is forced to go to a chiropractor even though he doesn't believe in the treatments they offer. Reluctantly he gets on the examination table and lets the chiropractor get to work. Half an hour later he gets up with his problem completely cured. "So," says the chiropractor. "How do you feel about chiropractors now?" The man replies, "I stand corrected."

✳ A mother calls her doctor. "Doctor, doctor! My little Jimmy has swallowed a dozen aspirin. What should I do?" The doctor says, "Calm down. Is little Jimmy crying?" "No," replies the mother. "Is he sleeping?" asks the doctor. "No," replies the mother. "Is his face pale?" asks the doctor. "No," replies the mother. "Has Jimmy thrown up?" asks the doctor. "No," replies the mother. "Is his temperature high?" asks the doctor. "No," replies the mother. "But I'm so scared. He's had all that aspirin. Shouldn't I do something?" The doctor replies, "Well, he sounds fine but you could try giving him a headache."

✳ An old man was having some stomach problems, so his doctor told him to drink warm water with Epsom salts one hour before breakfast. At the end of a week the old man returned and said he was feeling much worse. "Really?" said the doctor. "And did you drink the warm salt water an hour before breakfast each day?" "No," replied the old man. "I could only do about fifteen minutes."

✳ A woman goes to the doctor to get some medication for her elderly husband. She's given some pills and is told that he should take two every Sunday, Tuesday, and Wednesday, and skip the remaining days in the week. A month later the woman returns to tell the doctor that her husband has died of a heart attack. "I don't understand it," says the doctor. "His heart hasn't bothered him before. I hope it wasn't a side effect of the medication." "Oh no," replies the wife. "The pills did him good, it was the skipping that killed him."

✳ A man goes into a drugstore and asks the pharmacist if he can give him something for hiccups. The pharmacist reaches out and slaps the man's face. "What did you do that for?" asks the man. "Well, you don't have the hiccups anymore, do you?" says the pharmacist. The man replies, "No, but my wife still does!"

✳ A man walks into a doctor's office. "Doctor, can you help me?" he says, "My penis has holes all up and down it. When I go to the toilet it sprays out in all directions." The doctor examines the organ and hands him a card with a name and address on it. "Is this the name of a specialist?" asks the man. "No," says the doctor. "He's a clarinet tutor. He'll teach you how to hold it."

✳ A woman is put on a course of testosterone to cure a mild hormonal imbalance. Two weeks later she comes back to her doctor for a check-up. "Since you've put me on those pills, I've noticed some extra hair growth," says the woman. "Well, that's to be expected," says the doctor. "It's nothing to worry about. Where have you noticed this hair?" The woman replies, "On my balls."

✳ Patient to doctor: "Do you mean to say that these pink pills you've given me will work a miracle cure?" Doctor: "I assume so, no one's ever come back for more."

✳ Doctor to patient: "And have you been taking your medicine after your bath as I advised?" Patient: "I try, but after so much water, there's usually no room for it."

# HEALTH AND DOCTORS: SUPPOSITORIES

✳ A man with severe bowel trouble is prescribed a series of suppositories. However, after two weeks there's been no change. "Have you been taking them regularly?" asks the doctor. "Of course I have," snaps back the man. "What d'you think I've been doing—sticking them up my ass?"

✳ Two elderly men are eating breakfast one morning. One notices something funny about the other's ear. "Hey," he says. "Did you know you have a suppository in your left ear?" His friend pulls the suppository out and stares at it. "I'm really glad you saw this thing," he says. "Now I know where my hearing aid is."

# HEALTH AND DOCTORS: TEST RESULTS

✳ A doctor is speaking to a patient. "I have good news and bad news," says the doctor. "Which would you like to hear first?" The patient asks for the bad news. "I have the results from your lab tests, and you only have twenty-four hours to live," says the doctor. "So what's the good news?" asks the patient. "You see that gorgeous busty blonde nurse at the front desk?" says the doctor. "That's my girlfriend."

✳ A man goes to his doctor for a check-up. Afterwards the doctor comes out with the results. "I'm afraid I have some very bad news," the doctor says. "You're dying, and you don't have much time left." "That's terrible!" says the man. "How long have I got?" "Ten," says the doctor. "Ten?" says the man. "Ten what? Months? Weeks? Days…?" The doctor continues, "Nine…eight…"

✳ A man goes to the doctor for his test results. The doctor says, "I've got good news and bad news." "What's the bad news?" asks the man. The doctor replies, "You've got a week to live." "What!" says the man. "So what the hell is the good news?" The doctor replies, "They're going to name the disease after you."

✳ Doctor to male patient: "You're pregnant." Patient: "How does a man get pregnant?" Doctor: "The usual way. A little wine, a little dinner…"

✳ Doctor to patient: "I have bad news. You only have three minutes to live," Patient: "Oh my God! What am I going to do?" Doctor: "How about boiling an egg?"

✳ Doctor to patient: "I have to tell you, you have acute angina." Patient: "Why thank you, doctor."

✳ Doctor to patient: "I have good news and bad news." Patient: "What's the bad news?" Doctor: "We cut off the wrong leg. But the good news is that your bad leg is getting better."

✳ Harry comes back from the hospital looking worried. "What's the matter?" asks his wife. "The doctor says I have to take a pill every day for the rest of my life," groans Harry. "Well, that's not too bad," says his wife. "Yes, it is," says Harry. "He only gave me seven."

✳ "Mr. Clark, I'm afraid I have bad news," says the doctor. "You only have six months to live." "But I have no medical insurance," replies Mr. Smith. "I can't possibly pay you in that time." "Okay," says the doctor. "Let's make it nine months."

✳ Patient to doctor: "Tell me straight. Is it bad?" Doctor: "Well, I wouldn't start watching any new soap operas!"

✳ A man goes to his doctor for a check-up. The doctor says, "I'm afraid I have bad news. First you've got cancer. Second, you have Alzheimer's Disease." "Oh, no!" says the man. "Oh no. That's awful. That's terrible. But hey! At least I don't have cancer."

✳ Doctor to patient: "You'll live to be sixty." Patient: "I am sixty!" Doctor, "See, what did I tell you?"

✳ The doctor tells his patient that he has "HAGS." "What on earth is HAGS?" asks the patient. The doctor replies, "It's a combination of herpes, aids, gonorrhea, and syphilis. The only cure is complete isolation and a diet of pancakes and bacon." "Pancakes and bacon?" asks the patient. "Yes," says the doctor. "It's the only food we can slide under the door."

# HELPFUL ADVICE

✳ Commuters: Keep the seat next to you on the train vacant by smiling and nodding at people as they walk up the aisle.

✳ A neighbor's car antenna, carefully folded, makes an ideal coat hanger in an emergency.

✳ Clean the toilet bowl at the same time as you urinate. Drink no other liquids apart from toilet cleaner.

✳ Clumsy? Avoid cutting yourself while slicing vegetables by getting someone else to hold them.

✳ Cooks: Thicken up runny low-fat yogurt by stirring in a spoonful of lard.

✳ Don't waste money buying expensive binoculars; simply stand closer to what you want to look at.

✳ Employees: Only empty your bowels at work. Not only will you save money on toilet paper, you'll also be getting paid for it.

✳ Hijackers: Avoid a long stressful wait and the risk of arrest, simply make sure you book a flight to your intended destination in the first place.

✳ Husbands: Avoid arguments with your wife about lifting the toilet seat. Just piss in the sink.

✳ Men: Create instant designer stubble by sucking a magnet and dipping your chin in a bowl of iron fillings.

✳ Drivers: Enjoy the freedom of motorcycling by removing your windshield, sticking half a melon rind on your head, then jumping red lights and driving the wrong way up one-way streets.

✳ Oversleeping? A mousetrap placed on top of your alarm clock will prevent you from going back to sleep.

✳ Pedestrians: Save time when crossing a one-way street by only looking in the direction of oncoming traffic.

✳ Swimmers: Re-create the fun of a public swimming pool by filling the bath with cold water, adding two bottles of bleach, then urinating into it.

✳ Tell me what you need, and I'll tell you how to get along without it.

✳ Before attempting to remove stubborn stains from a garment, always circle the stain in permanent pen. That way, when you remove the garment from the washing machine, you can easily check that it's gone.

✳ High blood pressure sufferers: Simply cut yourself and bleed for a while, thus reducing the pressure in your veins.

✳ Olympic athletes: Disguise the fact that you've taken anabolic steroids by running a little slower.

✳ Parents: Make the kiddies' bathtime as fun as a trip to the seaside—put a bucket of sand, a bag of salt, and a dog turd in the water.

✳ A good way to save water is to dilute it.

# HIKING

✳ A hiker is about to cross a field when he spots a bull in the far corner. He sees the farmer and says, "Excuse me, but is that bull safe?" The farmer replies, "He's as safe as houses, but I can't say the same for you if you step in that field."

✳ A man comes home from a long business trip and finds his son playing with an expensive toy. "Who bought you that?" asks Dad. " I did," replies the boy. "I bought it with the money I earned hiking." "Hiking?" asks his father. "Who pays anyone to go hiking?" "Mr. Jones next door," replies the boy. "Every time he came around to see Mommy, he gave me $5 and told me to take a hike."

✳ Two men are out hiking. One says to the other, "Wow! Did you see that eagle over there?" "No," replies the second man. A little while later the first man says, "Hey, did you see that brown bear in the ravine?" "No," replies the second man. A while later the first man says, "Look, did you see that deer by the trees?" "No," says the second man. "You should keep your eyes open," says the first man. "You're missing an awful lot." A while later the first man says, "Hey, did you see that?" "Why, yes I did," snaps the second man. "I saw it very clearly. In fact, I dare say I even saw it before you did." "I see," says the first man. "So why did you step in it?"

✳ When he goes hitchhiking, he leaves early to avoid the traffic.

✳ A hitchhiker is standing by the roadside, making rude signs at the passing cars. Another hiker approaches him. "You'll never get a lift like that," he says. "Who cares," replies the hitchhiker. "It's my lunch hour."

# HIPPOPOTAMI AND RHINOCERI

✳ How do you stop a rhino from charging? Cut up its credit card.

✳ Why did the hippopotamus fall out of the banana tree? The rhino pushed him.

# HISTORY

✳ A knight in a besieged castle offers to break out and ride for help. Unfortunately, all the horses are dead, so the knight suggests riding out on the back of a giant wolfhound. "You can't," says the lord of the manor. "My wolfhound has a sore leg. The only other dog is this Chihuahua, and I wouldn't send a knight out on a dog like this."

✳ History is something that never happened, written by someone who wasn't there.

✳ I remember exactly where I was when I heard Kennedy had been shot. I was sitting at home listening to the news.

✳ A man applying for a job is given an intelligence test by the company doctor. The doctor says, "Captain Cook went on three expeditions and died on one of them. Was it the first, the second, or the third?" The man replies, "Can I have another. I was never very good at history."

✳ It's the French Revolution and Tom, Dick, and Harry are due to be guillotined. First up on the scaffold is Tom. The revolutionaries ask him if he wants to die facing down, or facing up. "I'll lie facing up at the blade," says Tom. So they put him in the guillotine and release the blade. Luckily for Tom, the blade gets stuck halfway down and, according to custom, he's free to go. The revolutionaries tinker with the guillotine and finally fix it. Dick goes up next and he, like Tom, asks to die facing the blade. Again the guillotine drops, only to stop halfway down, and Dick too is released. The revolutionaries attempt to fix the guillotine once more, then drag Harry up the scaffold. Harry says, "Like my friends, I'll die looking up at the blade." The revolutionaries put him in the guillotine and are about to release the blade when Harry shouts, "Hang on! I think I can see what's wrong with this thing…!"

✳ I wish I'd been born 1,000 years ago—just think of all the history I wouldn't have to learn!

✳ Sir Francis Drake circumcised the world using a 40-foot clipper.

# HORSE RACING

✳ "Betting on horses is a funny old game," says a man to his friend. "You win one day and lose the next." The friend replies, "So why not bet every other day?"

✳ I bet on a great horse yesterday! It took seven horses to beat him.

✳ Man, to friend: "I don't like the chances of that horse you bet on." Friend: "Why's that?" Man: "I just saw the jockey buy a book to read on the journey."

✳ Riding the favorite at Saratoga, a jockey is well ahead of the field. Suddenly he's hit on the head by a chicken salad sandwich and coleslaw. He manages to keep control of his mount and pulls back into the lead, only to be struck by a fruit salad and a loaf of bread. With great skill he manages to steer the horse to the front of the field once more when, on the final stretch, he's struck on the head by a bottle of wine and an apple pie. Thus distracted, he only manages second place. Furious, he immediately goes to the judges to complain that he's been seriously hampered.

✳ The horse I bet on was so slow, the jockey kept a diary of the trip.

✳ What's the best way to stop a runaway horse? Bet on it.

# HORSES

✳ What has four legs and flies? A dead horse.

✳ Harry is buying a horse from Patrick. "And is he well bred?" asks Harry. "I'll say he's well bred," says Patrick. "In fact he's so well bred, if he could talk, I doubt he'd speak to either of us."

# HOTELS

✳ "I like staying in hotels, I enjoy hotels, I like tiny soap. I pretend that it's normal soap and my muscles are huge." *Jerry Seinfeld*

✳ "One time I went to a hotel. I asked the bellhop to handle my bag. He felt up my wife!" *Rodney Dangerfield*

✳ "Room service? Send up a larger room." *Groucho Marx*

✳ A bell boy is whistling in the foyer of an exclusive hotel when the manager stops him. "Don't you know that it is forbidden to whistle in the corridors of this establishment?" he says. "I wasn't whistling," replies the bell boy. "I was paging a dog."

✳ A guest at a country inn is appalled by the state of his bedroom. "This bed is a disgrace," he complains to the owner. "But it's very historic," says the owner. "Paul Revere slept in that bed!" "Yes," replies the guest. "And judging by the state of the mattress, his horse slept with him."

✳ A man books into a sleazy hotel, the desk clerk tells him that it's $20 a night, or $15 if he makes his own bed. "I suppose I can do that," says the man. "Give me a $15 room." "Here's the key," replies the desk clerk. "Pick up your timber and nails at the top of the stairs."

✳ A man is checking into a hotel. The reception clerk asks him if he'd like a room with a bath or a shower. "What's the difference?" asks the man. "You can sit down in a bath," explains the clerk.

✳ A man makes a complaint at a cheap hotel. "My room is swimming in water," he says. "Does the roof always leak like that?" "No, sir," says the receptionist. "Only when it's raining."

✳ Hotel porter, to guest: "I hope you have a good memory for faces." Guest: "Yes. Why?" Porter: "There's no mirror in the bathroom."

✳ I called the front desk of my hotel and told them I had a leak in my sink. "Okay," they said. "Go ahead."

✳ A man takes his bride to an exclusive Moscow hotel for their honeymoon. The man is paranoid about being spied on, so he checks the room to make sure there aren't any KGB bugs still lurking around. Sure enough, he finds a suspicious round metal plate in the floor under a rug. He removes the restraining screws and throws the object out of the window. A few minutes later he hears a fleet of ambulances pulling up outside. He calls down to reception to find out what's going on. "It's terrible!" says the receptionist. "One of the chandeliers in the suite below yours has fallen on a dinner party!"

✳ A married couple are traveling across country and stop off at a high-class hotel. After spending the night they check out and discover the bill is $600. "This is ludicrous!" complains the husband. "Three hundred dollars each for one night?" "The price also includes the use of the hotel sauna, complementary drinks at the bar, and our car valet service," replies the desk clerk. "But we didn't use the sauna," says the husband. "You could have used it if you'd wanted to," replies the clerk. "And we didn't have drinks at the bar," says the husband. "You could have if you'd wanted to," replies the clerk. "And we didn't have our car valeted," says the husband. "You could have if you'd wanted to," replies the clerk. "I give up," says the husband and writes a check. "Excuse me," says the clerk, "but this check is only for $100." "I know," replies the husband, "but I'm charging you $500 for sleeping with my wife." "I didn't sleep with your wife," says the clerk. "No," replies the husband, "but you could have if you'd wanted to."

✳ A woman goes to the reception desk of a hotel. The porter appears and the woman says, "Can you check me out please?" The porter looks her up and down and says, "Sure baby. You're not bad. Not bad at all …"

✳ The phone at the reception desk of a hotel starts ringing at three in the morning. The desk clerk answers it. It's a call from a drunk asking what time the bar opens. "The bar opens at noon," answers the clerk. An hour later the same man calls again. He sounds even drunker but still wants to know when the bar opens. "Same time as before," replies the clerk. Another hour passes and the drunk calls again, "Whatjoo shay the bar opens at?" he slurs. The clerk replies, "It opens at noon, but if you really can't wait, I'll have room service send you up a drink." "I don't wanna git in!" shouts the man. "Ah wanna git out!"

✳ I wouldn't say the hotel was exclusive but even room service had an unlisted number.

✳ I stayed in a really old-fashioned hotel last night. They sent me a wake-up letter.

✳ My room was so small, when I put the key in the door, I broke the window!

✳ The hotel was filthy. They change the sheets every day, but only from one room to another.

✳ The room service in this hotel is terrible—when I ordered a hot chocolate, they brought me a Hershey's bar and a match.

✳ A guest goes to the reception desk at a hotel. "Excuse me, but a card in my room said that I should alert the management of any complaints." "That's right, sir," says the receptionist. "What's the matter?" The guest replies, "Not much. Just a touch of rheumatism and some dandruff."

✳ Business at Harry's hotel was terrible. It got so bad he had to start stealing towels from the guests.

✳ The hotel bathroom was so small you couldn't brush your teeth sideways.

✳ I wouldn't say my hotel room was damp, but I found a goldfish in the mousetrap.

✳ It was a very fancy hotel. They even made you wear a tie in the shower.

✳ The walls in our hotel were very thin. If I ever called out a question to my wife, I'd get three different answers.

✳ I was staying in a really sleazy hotel. At two in the morning the manager pounded on my door asking if I'd got a girl in there. I said I hadn't, so he asked me if I'd like one.

# HOUSEWORK

✳ "I'm an excellent housekeeper. Every time I get a divorce, I keep the house." *Zsa Zsa Gabor*

✳ A woman is complaining to her friend about the amount of housework she has to do, "I spend all day at the office, then come home and wash the clothes and dishes. And every weekend, I have to wash the kitchen floor and all windows." "But what about your husband?" asks her friend. "I make him wash himself," says the woman.

✳ My idea of housework is to sweep the room with a glance.

✳ You know the greatest labor-saving device around the house—tomorrow.

✳ "My second favorite household chore is ironing, my first being hitting my head on the top bunk bed until I faint." *Erma Bombeck*

✳ I always thought that the braille writing on bottles of bleach was a safety warning for blind people, but it's a really nasty trick. Apparently it says "Drink me."

✳ I'm not saying our house is a mess, but vandals broke in last week and redecorated it.

* Help keep the kitchen clean—eat out.

* "You make the beds, you do the dishes, and six months later you have to start all over again." *Joan Rivers*

# HUMILITY AND EGOTISM

* Humility is no substitute for a good personality.

* I am a nobody, and nobody is perfect; therefore, I am perfect.

* I know for a fact he's a genius. He told me so himself.

* One nice thing about egotists: they don't talk about other people.

* People who think they know everything are particularly annoying to those of us who actually do.

* What is the height of conceit? Calling out your own name during orgasm.

# HUNTING

* A couple of rednecks are hunting in the woods when one suddenly collapses. His friend dials 9-1-1 on his cell phone and shouts to the operator, "Help me. My friend is dead! What can I do?" The operator tries to calm him down. "Take it easy," she says. "The first thing to do is make sure he really is dead." Next thing, the operator hears the man putting the phone down, then a rifle shot. The man picks up the phone again, "Okay. So what next…?"

* The Alaskan hunters usually dined on deer in the evenings—it was far too cold to hunt bear.

* A hunter goes into a butcher's shop and asks for a duck. "I'm sorry," says the butcher. "We're out of duck. How about a chicken?" "Oh, yes." replies the hunter. "And how do I tell my wife I shot a chicken?"

* A man takes his wife hunting for the first time. He impresses upon her the need to claim a kill quickly before anyone has the chance to step in and bag your deer. The wife is suitably impressed by this, and they both stalk off into the woods. A little while later the wife shoots and makes a kill. The brush is too thick for the husband to see what's going on, but he can hear his wife arguing with another man. "This is my kill," shouts his wife.

"There is no other hunter in the vicinity and I can categorically prove that my bullet killed this deer." "I'm not arguing with you," says the man. "But can I take my saddle off your deer, before you take it home?"

✻ A rich lawyer is grouse shooting when one of his birds falls in an adjacent field. The lawyer sees an old yokel standing in the field and asks him to pick up the grouse. "Not doing that," says the old man. "This here's my field, so that there's my bird." This infuriates the lawyer. "Listen," he says. "I know the law, and that bird belongs to me. If you don't hand it over, I'll sue you." The old man replies, "Around here we settle things with the Three Wack Rule. I gives you three whacks with my stick, then you give me three whacks. Whoever gives the biggest whacks wins." The lawyer is sure he can whack harder than the old yokel, so he agrees. The old man takes his walking stick and gives the lawyer a terrific whack across the legs, then another across his nose, and another across the back of his head. The lawyer has been knocked to his knees but manages to stagger to his feet, "Right. My turn," he says. "Naahh," says the old yokel. "You win. Keep the damn bird."

✻ A young man from the city goes to visit his farmer uncle. For the first few days, the uncle shows him the usual things; chickens, cows, crops, etc. However, it's obvious the nephew is getting bored, so the uncle suggests he go on a hunt. "Why don't you grab a gun, take the dogs, and go shooting?" This cheers up the nephew, and off he goes with the dogs in tow. After a few hours, the nephew returns. "Did you enjoy it?" asks his uncle. "It was great!" exclaims the nephew. "Got any more dogs?"

✻ Tom and Dick go hunting in the woods and get lost. Tom remembers that the international SOS signal in this situation is to fire three shots in the air. Dick fires three shots, and they wait, but no one comes. Tom fires three shots—again they wait, but still no one comes. It starts to snow heavily, and the sun is fast dropping below the horizon. "Well, this is it," says Dick. "If this doesn't work we're done for. We only have three arrows left."

✻ Two hunters are dragging a dead deer back to their truck, when a man approaches them and says, "Y'know it's much easier if you drag it the other way—then the antlers won't dig into the ground and slow you up." The hunters try this method and make good progress. The first hunter says to the other, "That guy really knew what he was talking about, didn't he?" "Yes," replies the second hunter. "But on the other hand we are getting further away from the truck."

✻ What has one hundred balls and screws rabbits? A shotgun cartridge.

✻ Obituary: Mr. Thomas Gunner died in a hunting accident last Thursday. He is survived by a wife, two sons, and a rabbit.

✳ "I ask people why they have deer heads on their walls. They always say because it's such a beautiful animal. I think my mother is attractive, but I have photographs of her." *Ellen DeGeneres*

✳ Two hunters rent a moose costume in the hope they can get close enough to a bull moose to kill it. They creep up on a huge bull moose but find that the costume's zipper is stuck. Suddenly there's a loud bellow, and the hunter in the front of the costume sees that the bull moose is approaching them with a huge erection. "What are we going to do now?" asks the hunter in the back of the costume. "I'm going to nibble some grass," replies the other. "You'd better brace yourself."

✳ I'm against fox hunting. In fact I'm a hunt saboteur. I go out the night before and shoot the fox.

✳ Two Irishmen are out hunting duck. One shoots at a flying bird, and it falls dead at his feet. "You could've saved yourself a shot there," says the other. "From that height, the fall alone would've killed it."

# IDEAS AND INVENTIONS

✳ "I had a great idea this morning but I didn't like it." *Samuel Goldwyn*

✳ Man to friend: "Did you hear about the man who invented a rubber suit to protect construction workers if they fell off tall buildings?" Friend: "Did it work?" Man: "Yes, but when he tried it out, he bounced around for so long he starved to death."

✳ Tom made a fortune in the dog food business. He invented a canned meat that tastes just like a mailman's leg.

✳ When he was younger, Harry invented a two-rung ladder—it was for women who wanted to elope from bungalows.

✳ Harry has invented a device for looking through walls. He calls it a window.

# IMPONDERABLES

✳ "No one can ever know for sure what a deserted area looks like." *George Carlin*

✳ After eating, do amphibians have to wait one hour before getting out of the water?

✳ Can a half-wit work part-time for NASA?

✳ Do illiterates get the full effect of Alphabet Soup?

✳ Does killing time damage eternity?

✳ How can you identify a person using their dental records? If you don't know who they are, you certainly won't know who their dentist is.

✳ Doesn't expecting the unexpected make the unexpected become the expected?

✳ Have you ever imagined a world without hypothetical situations?

✳ How can you have a self-help group?

✳ How can you tell when you're out of invisible ink?

✳ How come Superman could stop bullets with his chest, but always ducked when someone threw a gun at him?

✳ How come wrong numbers are never busy?

✳ How do "Keep off the grass" signs get where they are?

✳ How do you know when it's time to tune your bagpipes?

✳ How does the man who drives the snowplow get to work?

✳ How is it that an "all-butter" croissant isn't just a big pile of butter?

✳ If a man stands in the middle of a forest and there is no woman to hear him, is he still wrong?

✳ If a person owns a piece of land, do they own it all the way down to the core of the earth?

✳ If a pig loses its voice, is it disgruntled?

✳ If Barbie is so popular, why do you have to buy her friends?

✳ If corn oil is made from corn, and vegetable oil is made from vegetables, what's baby oil made from?

✳ If gravity exists, why is it harder to drop a girl than to pick one up?

✳ If I save time, when do I get it back?

✳ If love is blind, why is lingerie so popular?

✳ If nothing sticks to Teflon, how does it stay on the pan?

✳ If one synchronized swimmer drowns, do all the rest have to drown too?

✳ If Polish people are called Poles, why aren't people from Holland called Holes?

✳ If someone with a multiple personality disorder threatens to kill himself, is it considered a hostage situation?

✳ If the number 2 pencil is the most popular, why is it still number 2?

✳ If you choke a Smurf, what color does it turn?

✳ If you try to fail but succeed, which have you done?

✳ If you're born again, do you end up with two bellybuttons?

✳ Is French-kissing in France just called kissing?

✳ Is it bad luck to be superstitious?

✳ Is it possible to be totally partial?

✳ Just before someone gets nervous, do they have cocoons in their stomach?

✳ We know the speed of light, but what's the speed of dark?

✳ What did people go back to when development of the world's first-ever drawing board failed?

✳ What do chickens think we taste like?

✳ What do little birdies see when they get knocked unconscious?

✳ What do people in China call their good plates?

✳ Who was the first person to look at a cow and say, "I think I'll squeeze these dangly things here and drink whatever comes out"?

✳ What do you do when you see an endangered animal eating an endangered plant?

✳ What do sheep count when they can't get to sleep?

✳ What happens if you get scared half to death twice?

✳ What if the hokey pokey really is what it's all about?

✳ What was the best thing before sliced bread?

✳ What would a chair look like if your knees bent the other way?

✳ What would Geronimo say if he jumped out of an airplane?

✳ What's happened to all the gruntled employees?

✳ When you open a bag of cotton balls, is the top one meant to be thrown away?

✳ Where do forest rangers go to "get away from it all"?

✳ Why are there disabled parking places in front of a skating rink?

✳ Why are there interstate highways in Hawaii?

✳ Why are they called stairs inside but steps outside?

✳ Why can't a woman put on mascara with her mouth closed?

✳ Why did kamikaze pilots wear helmets?

✳ Why didn't Noah swat those two mosquitoes?

✳ Why do bankruptcy lawyers expect to be paid?

✳ Why do banks leave both doors open and chain the pens to the counters?

✳ Why do they put braille dots on the keypad of the drive-up ATM?

✳ Why do people point to their wrist when they're asking you the time? Do I point to my crotch when I ask people where the bathroom is?

✳ Why do supermarkets make sick people walk to the back of the store to get their prescriptions, while the healthy ones can buy cigarettes at the front?

✳ Why do they lock gas station toilets? Are they afraid someone will clean them?

✳ Why do they sterilize needles for lethal injections?

✳ Why do we buy hot dogs in packs of ten and buns in packs of eight?

✳ Why do we leave cars worth thousands of dollars in the driveway and put our junk in the garage?

✳ Why do we use answering machines to screen calls and then have call waiting so we won't miss a call from someone we didn't want to talk to in the first place?

✳ Why do we wait until a pig is dead to "cure" it?

✳ Why do we wash bath towels? Aren't we clean when we use them?

✳ Why does mineral water that "has trickled through mountains for centuries" have a sell-by date?

✳ Why don't they make the rest of the airplane out of whatever they make the black box out of?

✳ "If toast always lands butter-side down, and cats always land on their feet, what happens if you strap toast on the back of a cat and drop it?" *Steven Wright*

✳ Why does the TV news bother reporting power failures?

✳ Why does your gynecologist leave the room when you get undressed?

✳ Why is it called Alcoholics Anonymous when the first thing you do is stand up and say "My name is Bob, and I'm an alcoholic"?

✳ Why doesn't glue stick to the inside of the bottle?

✳ Why does no one ever say "It's only a game" when their team is winning?

✳ Why don't you ever see the headline "Psychic Wins Lottery"?

✳ Why is a boxing ring square?

✳ Why is bra singular and panties plural?

✳ Why is a carrot more orange than an orange?

✳ Why is it called tourist season if we can't shoot at them?

✳ Why is it that night falls but day breaks?

✳ Why is lemon juice mostly artificial ingredients, but dishwashing liquid contains real lemons?

✳ Why is the third hand on the watch called a second hand?

✳ Would a fly without wings be called a walk?

✳ "After they make Styrofoam, what do they ship it in?" *Steven Wright*

✳ Do pediatricians play miniature golf on Wednesdays?

✳ Does fuzzy logic tickle?

✳ How come a pizza can get to your house faster than an ambulance?

✳ How much deeper would the ocean be if there weren't any sponges in it?

✳ If crime fighters fight crime, and fire fighters fight fire, what do freedom fighters fight?

✳ If quizzes are quizzical, what are tests?

✳ Why is it that when someone tells you that there are over a billion stars in the universe, you believe them, but if they tell you there is wet paint somewhere, you have to touch it to make sure?

✳ If we're here to help others, then what are the others here for?

✳ Is Disney World a people-trap operated by a mouse?

✳ Should crematoriums give discounts for burn victims?

✳ What are occasional tables the rest of the time?

✳ What hair color do they put on the driver's licenses of bald men?

✳ When sign makers go on strike, is anything written on their signs?

✳ Why are they called apartments when they're all stuck together?

✳ Why do croutons come in airtight packages? Aren't they just stale bread to begin with?

✳ Why do toasters have a setting that burns toast to a horrible crisp?

✳ Why do you need a driver's license to buy alcohol when you can't drink and drive?

✳ Why does the twenty-four-hour store have a lock on the door?

✳ Why doesn't Tarzan have a beard?

✳ Why is it called lipstick if you can still move your lips?

✳ Why is there a light in the fridge and not in the freezer?

# INQUIRIES

✳ "People come up to me and say, 'Emo, do people really come up to you?'" *Emo Phillips*

# INSECTS

✳ What do you get if you cross a firefly and a moth? An insect that can find its way around a dark closet!

✳ A woman walks into the kitchen to find her husband stalking around with a fly swatter. "Have you killed any?" she asks. "Yep," replies her husband. "Three males and two females." "How can you tell?" she says. He replies, "Three were on a beer can, two were on the phone."

✳ "Time flies like an arrow. Fruit flies like a banana." *Groucho Marx*

✳ A boy fly sees a cute girl fly land on a pile of crap. He buzzes down and says, "Excuse me, miss. Is this stool taken?"

✳ A couple of fleas are planning a trip to the far side of a house. One turns to the other and says, "Shall we hop or take the cat?"

✳ What goes zzub, zzub? A bee flying backward!

✳ What's a myth? A female moth!

✳ What's green and can jump a mile in a minute? A grasshopper with hiccups!

✳ What's the last thing to go through an insect's brain when it hits your car windshield? Its rear end.

✳ Why do bees hum? Because they don't know the words.

✳ How do you know if you have a tough mosquito? You slap him and he slaps you back.

✳ What's worse than finding a maggot in your apple? Finding half a maggot.

✳ How did the firefly burn himself to death? Trying to screw a lit cigarette.

✳ I bought some mothballs the other day. Talk about useless. Have you ever tried to hit a moth with one of those things?

✳ A woodworm bumps into another woodworm: "How's life?" he asks. "Boring," replies the other.

# INSULTS

✳ "I have had a perfectly wonderful evening—but this wasn't it." *Groucho Marx*

✳ "There's no beginning to your talents." *Clive Anderson to Jeffrey Archer*

✳ "You know, I could rent you out as a decoy for duck hunters." *Groucho Marx*

✳ Any friend of yours—is a friend of yours.

✳ Any similarity between you and a human being is purely coincidental.

✳ Are you the first in your family to be born without a tail?

✳ At least you're not obnoxious like so many other people—you're obnoxious in different and worse ways!

✳ Before you came along we were hungry. Now we are fed up.

✳ Did the aliens forget to remove your anal probe?

✳ Do you want me to accept you as you are, or do you want me to like you?

✳ God could still use you for miracle practice.

✳ "He is a modest man who has a good deal to be modest about." *Winston Churchill*

✳ "Do you think I can buy back my introduction to you?" *Groucho Marx*

✳ Don't you realize that there are enough people to hate in the world already without your working so hard to give us another?

✳ He could be described as charming, intelligent, and witty. And who knows, perhaps one day he will be.

✳ Don't get me wrong. I'm not trying to make a monkey out of you. I can't take the credit.

✳ Here's twenty cents. Call all your friends and bring back the change!

✳ He's a difficult man to forget. But well worth the effort.

✳ He's a lesson to us all. He's a man who started out with nothing and to this day he still has most of it.

✳ He's a man of hidden talents. As soon as we find one, we'll let you know.

✳ His own father looks on him as the son he never had.

✳ I believe in respect for the dead—in fact I could only respect you if you were dead!

✳ I bet I know what you use for contraception. Your personality.

✳ I can tell you always manage to keep your head above water—just by the color of it.

✳ I can't seem to remember your name—please don't help me!

✳ I hear the only place you're ever invited is outside.

✳ I knew the day would come when you would leave me for my best friend. So here's his leash, water bowl, and chew toys.

✳ I know you're a self-made man—it's nice of you to take the blame!

✳ I like your approach—now let's see your departure.

✳ I must admit, you brought religion into my life. I never believed in Hell till I met you.

✳ I see you in my dreams—if I eat too much.

✳ I thought of you all day today. I was at the zoo.

✳ I used to think you were a pain in the neck. Now I have a much lower opinion of you.

✳ I thought I saw your name on a loaf of bread this morning. But when I looked again, what it actually read was "Thick cut."

✳ I want nothing out of you but breathing, and very little of that!

✳ I won't mind your talking as long as you won't mind my not listening.

✳ I'd like to give you a going-away present—but you have to do your part.

✳ I'd like to leave you with one thought—but I'm not sure you have a place to put it!

✳ I'd like to see things from your point of view, but I can't seem to get my head that far up my ass.

✳ If God tried to help you, we'd have an eight-day week.

✳ If I said anything to you that I should be sorry for, I'm glad.

✳ If I throw a stick, will you leave?

✳ If truth is stranger than fiction, you must be truth!

✳ If we killed everybody who hates you, it wouldn't be murder; it would be genocide!

✳ If you ever had a bright idea, it would be beginner's luck!

✳ If you think people are the same as you, you have a very low opinion of them.

✳ I'm busy now—can I ignore you some other time?

✳ I'm not rude. You're just insignificant.

✳ I'm so miserable without you, it's almost like you're here.

✳ The ultimate proof of the overwhelming nature of the sex drive is the fact that someone was willing to father you.

✳ I'm trying to imagine you with a personality.

✳ Instead of being born again, why don't you just grow up?

✳ It's mind over matter—I don't mind, because you don't matter.

✳ I've only got one nerve left—and you're getting on it.

✳ I've seen people like you before—but I had to pay admission!

✳ Just because you have one doesn't mean you have to act like one!

✳ Keep talking—I always yawn when I'm interested.

✳ Learn from your parents' mistakes—use birth control!

✳ Nice suit. Were you there for the fitting?

✳ Of all the people I've met, you're certainly one of them.

✳ One day you stopped to think, then forgot to start again.

✳ Ordinarily people live and learn—you just live.

✳ Pardon me, but you've obviously mistaken me for someone who gives a damn.

✳ People can't say that you have absolutely nothing—you have inferiority!

✳ Please breathe the other way—you're bleaching my hair.

✳ She's a treasure. I wonder who dug her up?

✳ Some people are one in a million. He was won in a raffle.

✳ Some people say you're superficial—but that's just on the surface.

✳ Someone said you're not fit to sleep with pigs. I stuck up for the pigs.

* Sorry if I looked interested. I'm not.

* The more I think of you, the less I think of you.

* The only thing you brought to your job was your car.

* The smaller the pip, the louder the squeak.

* There's nothing wrong with you that reincarnation won't cure.

* There's one too many in this room, and I think it's you.

* We all sprang from the apes—but you didn't spring far enough.

* We have been friends for a very long time, what say we call it quits?

* We know you'd go to the end of the world for us—but would you stay there?

* We think of you when we are lonely. Then we are content to be alone.

* You used to be arrogant and obnoxious, now you're the opposite—obnoxious and arrogant.

* When they made him, they kept the mold and threw him away.

* When you ran away from home, your folks sent you a note saying "Don't come home and all will be forgiven."

* When you were a child, your mother tried to hire someone to take care of you—but the Mafia wanted too much.

* Whoever told you to just be yourself couldn't have given you worse advice.

* Why don't you bore a hole in yourself and let the sap run out?

* You are a prime candidate for natural deselection.

* You couldn't hit sand if you fell off a camel.

* They say opposites attract. I hope you find someone good-looking and intelligent who doesn't stink.

* You did some soul searching, but didn't find one.

* You don't know the meaning of the word fear, but then again, you don't know the meaning of most words.

* You fear success, but really have nothing to worry about.

* You got into the gene pool while the lifeguard wasn't watching.

* You have a great deal of pride, but very little to be proud of.

* You have a lot of well-wishers—they'd all like to throw you down one.

* You have a mechanical mind. Too bad you forgot to wind it up this morning.

* You have a nice personality, but not for a human being.

* You have a room-temperature IQ.

* You have an inferiority complex—and it's fully justified.

* You have an inferiority complex, but not a very good one.

* You have delusions of adequacy.

* You have depth, but only on the surface. Down deep inside, you're shallow.

* You have nothing to say, but delight in saying it.

* You let your mind wander, and it hasn't come back yet.

* You remind me of the ocean—you make me sick.

* You took an IQ test and the results were negative.

* You were the life and soul of the party. Which tells us a lot about the party.

* You'll never be the man your mother was!

* Your future is behind schedule.

* Your only purpose in life is to serve as a warning to others.

* Your personality's split so many ways, you can go to group therapy by yourself.

* You're a peripheral visionary.

* You're about as useful as a chocolate teapot.

* You're about as useful as an ashtray on a motorcycle.

* You're living proof that manure can grow legs and walk.

* You're living proof that nature does not abhor a vacuum.

* You're not as bad as people say—you're worse!

✳ You're the answer to my prayers. Unfortunately I was praying to see if things could get any worse.

✳ You're not yourself today—I noticed the improvement immediately.

✳ You're the best at all you do—and all you do is make people hate you.

✳ You've been called rude, cold, egotistical, self-centered, and arrogant. But that's just your family's opinion.

✳ You've been compared to many great men. Unfavorably. But you have been compared to them.

✳ You've got your head so far up your ass, you could chew your food twice.

✳ "I never forget a face, but in your case I'll make an exception." *Groucho Marx*

✳ As an outsider, what do you think of the human race?

✳ For him, it's a night out. For his family, it's a night off.

✳ He's a man of hidden shallows.

✳ I don't have an attitude problem. You have a perception problem.

✳ I hear you had an asshole transplant—and the asshole rejected you.

✳ I only know you superficially. But to be honest, I think that's enough.

✳ I wouldn't piss in your ear if your brain was on fire!

✳ If I want any crap out of you, I'll squeeze your head.

✳ If I wanted to hear from an ass, I'd fart.

✳ I'll never forget the first time we met—although I'll keep trying.

✳ It's hard to believe you beat 1,000,000 other sperm.

✳ I've hated your looks from the start they gave me.

✳ Nobody thinks more highly of him than I do. And I think he's a dumbass.

✳ People tend to take an instant dislike to you—which isn't very nice, but it does save time.

✳ The good news is that Jesus loves you. I, on the other hand, think you're a jerk.

✳ They say one day he'll be president. And one day will be quite enough.

* You are a hemorrhoid on the ass of the world.

* When people first meet you, they don't like you. When they get to know you better, they hate you.

* You are overdue for reincarnation.

* You have a good weapon against muggers—your face.

* You have an ego like a black hole.

* You look like a talent scout for a cemetery.

* Your men would follow you anywhere, but only out of morbid curiosity.

* You're down to earth—but not quite far enough.

* You're the goalie for the dart team.

* Jane and Mary meet in the street. "My God," says Jane. "It must be ten years since I last saw you. You're looking much older." "You too," replies Mary. "In fact if it weren't for your dress and shoes I wouldn't have recognized you at all."

* As the days go by, I think of how lucky I am that you're not here to ruin it for me.

* I've always wanted to have someone to hold, someone to love. Having met you, I've changed my mind.

* You do a very good impression of a river—small at the head and big at the mouth.

# INSULTS: EUPHEMISMS

* Your dock doesn't quite reach the water.

* Your elevator doesn't go all the way to the top floor.

* Your lights are on but no one's at home.

* Your wheel is spinning but the hamster is dead.

* You've got both oars in the water but they're on the same side of the boat.

* You're a few green beans short of a casserole.

* You're a few sandwiches short of a picnic.

* You've got lots of bricks, but no cement.

✳ Your driveway doesn't quite reach the garage.

✳ You're all crown and no filling.

# INSULTS: STUPIDITY

✳ "To call you stupid would be an insult to stupid people." *John Cleese*

✳ A guy with your IQ should have a low voice too!

✳ Are you always so stupid, or is today a special occasion?

✳ Don't go to a mind reader—go to a palm reader. I know you've got a palm.

✳ Don't let your mind wander too far. It's too little to be out alone.

✳ Go ahead, tell them everything you know. It'll only take ten seconds.

✳ Have you considered suing your brains for non-support?

✳ He has to be careful. He's not allowed anything sharp—like a mind.

✳ I bet your brain feels as good as new, seeing that you've never used it.

✳ Clearly your behavior is the result of a childhood trauma from the time your parents spanked you for landing on your head and breaking the concrete.

✳ I don't think you're a fool. But then, what's my opinion against thousands of others?

✳ I must say you're very open-minded. So much so, your brains have fallen out.

✳ I refuse to enter a battle of wits with you—I can't attack an unarmed person.

✳ I would like to insult you, but with your intelligence, you wouldn't get offended.

✳ If brains were dynamite, you'd have nothing to worry about.

✳ If I gave you a penny for your thoughts, I'd get change back.

✳ If idiots could fly, this would be an airport.

✳ If intelligence were rain, you'd be holding an umbrella.

✳ If what you don't know can't hurt you, you're practically invulnerable.

✳ If you stand close enough to your head, you can hear the ocean.

✳ If you were any more stupid, you'd have to be watered twice a week.

✳ I'm glad to see you're not letting your education get in the way of your ignorance.

✳ Looking on the bright side, you're immune from serious head injury.

✳ Please sit down and give your mind a rest.

✳ Stupidity does not qualify as a handicap—park elsewhere!

✳ There sits a man with an open mind—you can feel the draft from here.

✳ What you lack in intelligence, you more than make up for in stupidity.

✳ "You've got the brain of a four-year-old boy, and I'll bet he was glad to get rid of it." *Groucho Marx*

✳ What's on your mind, if you'll forgive the overstatement?

✳ What's the latest dope—besides yourself?

✳ When I look into your eyes—I see the back of your head.

✳ Why don't you go to the library and brush up on your ignorance?

✳ Would you cover one of your ears, please? You're causing a draft.

✳ You have an IQ one lower than it takes to grunt.

✳ Your brain waves fall a little short of the beach.

✳ Your mouth's in gear, but your brain's in neutral.

✳ Your reaction time is longer than your attention span.

✳ Your verbosity is exceeded only by your stupidity.

✳ You're always lost in thought—it's unfamiliar territory.

✳ You're nobody's fool—let's see if we can get someone to adopt you.

✳ You're not a complete idiot—some parts are missing.

✳ You're not as dumb as you look, but then again, that would be impossible.

✳ You're so dense, light bends around you.

✳ I don't know what makes you so stupid, but it really works.

✳ If brains were taxed, you'd get a rebate.

* If ignorance is bliss, you must be experiencing a near constant orgasm.

* I'll try being nicer if you'll try being smarter.

* Too bad stupidity isn't painful.

* Y'know, I'd love to screw your brains out, but it seems someone beat me to it.

* You're as bright as Alaska in December.

# INTERNATIONAL RELATIONS

* Doris goes to the doctor with morning sickness and discovers she's pregnant. "When did you last have a check-up?" asks the doctor. "Never," replies Doris. "But I think the last one might have been a Frenchman."

# I.T.

* I've got one those special filters on my internet access. It's really handy, it blocks out everything except porn sites.

* A computer programmer has been missing from work for over a week. Finally someone notices and calls the police. They break down the door of his apartment where they find him dead in the shower, an empty bottle of shampoo next to his body. The programmer seems to have died from a combination of exposure and exhaustion. The puzzle is explained when the police read the instructions on the shampoo bottle—"Wet hair. Apply shampoo. Rinse. Repeat."

* A Microsoft support technician goes to a shooting range. He shoots ten bullets at the target 50 yards away. The supervisors check the target and see that there's not even a single hit. They shout to him that he missed completely. The technician tells them to recheck, and gets the same answer. The technician then aims the gun at his finger and shoots, blasting it off. He shouts back, "It's working fine here! The problem must be at your end!"

* A new army computer is put through its paces. An officer types in a question—"How far is it from the barrack gate to the armory?" The computer replies, "Seven hundred." The officer types, "Seven hundred what?" The computer replies, "Seven hundred, sir!"

* Computers make very fast, very accurate mistakes.

✳ An artist, a lawyer, and a programmer are discussing the merits of a mistress. The artist tells of the passion, the thrill that comes with the risk of being discovered. The lawyer warns of the difficulties. It can lead to guilt, divorce, and bankruptcy. The programmer says, "It's the best thing that's ever happened to me. My wife thinks I'm with my mistress. My mistress thinks I'm home with my wife, and I can spend all night on the computer!"

✳ An engineer, a manager, and a programmer are driving down a steep mountain road. The brakes fail, and the car careens down the road until it hits a tree. They all get out and discuss how to fix the car. The manager says, "To fix this problem, we need to organize a committee and develop a mission statement." The engineer says, "That would take too long. I have my penknife here. I'll take apart the brake system, isolate the problem, and correct it." The programmer says, "No, I think we should push the car back up the road and see if it happens again."

✳ What do you get when you cross an apple with a nun? A computer that won't go down.

✳ At a recent software engineering management course, the participants were given an awkward question to answer. "If you had just boarded an airplane and discovered that your team of programmers had been responsible for the flight control software, how many of you would get off immediately?" Among the forest of raised hands, only one man sat motionless. When asked what he would do, he replied that he would be quite content to stay onboard. With his team's software, he said, the plane was unlikely to even taxi as far as the runway, let alone take off.

✳ Fed up with your computer winning at chess? Try it at kick-boxing instead!

✳ Jesus and Satan are arguing as to who is the better programmer. They decide to have a contest with God as the judge. They start and type furiously, lines of code streaming up the screen but, seconds before the end of the contest, a bolt of lightning strikes the power cable. When the power is restored, God announces the contest is over. He asks Satan to show what he's come up with. Satan says, "I've got nothing. I lost it all when the power went out." God then goes to Jesus's computer. Jesus enters a command, and the screen comes to life in a vivid display, an angelic chorus pouring from the speakers. Satan is astonished—"How did he manage that?" God replies, "You might have lost everything, but Jesus saves."

✳ Someday, the people who know how to use computers will rule over those who don't. And there will be a special name for them—executive assistants.

✳ What's the difference between a car salesman and a computer salesman? The car salesman can probably drive!

✳ Tech Support to customer: "I need you to right-click on the open desktop." "Okay," says the customer. Tech Support: "Did you get a pop-up menu?" "No," replies the customer. Tech Support, "Okay. Right-click again. Do you see a pop-up menu?" "Not at all," replies the customer. Tech Support, "Okay, sir. Can you tell me what you have done up until this point?" "Sure," replies the customer. "You told me to write 'click' so I wrote down 'click.'"

✳ Three female friends are comparing their sex lives. The first says, "My husband is an architect. Our lovemaking has power, form, and function." The second says, "My husband is an artist. Our lovemaking has passion, emotion, and vision." The third woman says, "My husband works for Microsoft. When we make love, he sits at the end of the bed in the dark telling me how great it will be when we finally get started."

✳ Tom is trying to get his new computer working. He's having trouble, so he calls over Harry to give him a hand. Harry switches on the computer, then asks Tom if he wants it password protected. "Oh yes, I read about that in the manual. I think the password I'll have is 'DaffyDuckBugsBunnyTomandJerry.'" "That's a very long password," says Harry. "Yes," replies Tom. "But the manual says it has to be at least four characters."

✳ Why computers are male: 1) In order to get their attention, you have to turn them on. 2) They have a lot of data but are still clueless. 3) They are supposed to help you solve your problems, but half the time they are the problem. 4) As soon as you commit to one, you realize that, if you had waited a little longer, you might have had a better model. Why computers are female: 1) No one but their creator understands their internal logic. 2) The native language they use to communicate with other computers is incomprehensible to everyone else. 3) Even your smallest mistakes are stored in long-term memory for later retrieval. 4) As soon as you make a commitment to one, you find yourself spending half your monthly salary on accessories for it.

✳ A businessman is invited for an audience with the Pope but finds it clashes with a meeting he has with Bill Gates. The businessman asks his assistant which appointment he should go to. "Definitely the Pope," replies the assistant. "He'll only expect you to kiss his hand."

✳ Computer users are divided into three types: novice, intermediate, and expert. Novice users: people who are afraid that simply pressing a key might break their computer. Intermediate users: people who don't know how to fix their computer after they've just pressed a key that broke it. Expert users: people who break other people's computers.

✳ Harry is having trouble with his computer so he calls Suzie, the computer expert, over to his desk. Suzie clicks a couple buttons and solves the problem. "So, what was wrong?" asks Harry. Suzie replies, "It was an ID ten T error." "So what's that?" asks Harry. "Write it down," says Suzie. "You'll figure it out."

✳ Where do you go if you become "at one" with your computer? Nerdvana.

✳ A TV can insult your intelligence, but nothing rubs it in like a computer.

# KANGAROOS

✳ A kangaroo keeps getting out of his enclosure at the zoo. Knowing how high he can jump, the zookeepers put up a 10-foot fence. However, next morning the kangaroo is out again. The next time they try putting up a 20-foot fence but, again, the kangaroo is out the next morning. Frustrated, the zookeepers build a 40-foot-high fence. A camel in the next enclosure says to the kangaroo, "How much higher do you think they'll go?" The kangaroo replies, "About a 1,000 feet, unless somebody remembers to lock the gate!"

✳ What do you call a kangaroo at the North Pole? Lost.

✳ A mother kangaroo leaps in the air with a yelp. She looks into her pouch and says, "How many times do I have to tell you? No smoking in bed!"

# KIDNAPPING

✳ "I remember the time I was kidnapped and they sent a piece of my finger to my father. He said he wanted more proof." *Rodney Dangerfield*

✳ "When I was a kid I got no respect. The time I was kidnapped and the kidnappers sent my parents a note, they said, 'We want five thousand dollars or you'll see your kid again.'" *Rodney Dangerfield*

✳ I was a lovely baby. My parents used to fake my kidnapping just to see my picture in the papers.

# LANGUAGE AND LINGUISTICS

✳ What's the difference between a Northern fairytale and a Southern fairytale? A Northern fairytale starts, "Once upon a time…" A Southern fairytale begins, "Y'all ain't gonna believe this shit…"

✳ There ain't no reason to use no double negatives, not never.

✳ An English professor writes the sentence "A woman without her man is nothing" on the chalkboard and tells his students to punctuate it. A male student writes "A woman, without her man, is nothing." A female student writes "A woman: without her, man is nothing."

✳ "I had a linguistics professor who said that it's man's ability to use language that makes him the dominant species on the planet. That may be, but I think there's one other thing that separates us from animals—we aren't afraid of vacuum cleaners." *Jeff Stilson*

✳ Three language professors are walking through town when they see a group of streetwalkers plying their trade. This leads to a discussion about the collective noun for prostitutes. One suggests a jam of tarts. The second suggests a flourish of strumpets. While the third says, "There's already a collective noun for this profession. It's an anthology." "Anthology?" says one of his colleagues, "Where on earth did you get that from?" "Never heard of an anthology of prose?" replies the professor.

✳ I call English my mother tongue, as Father rarely got a chance to use it.

✳ Tom decided to improve his vocabulary by learning three new words every day. After a week, none of his friends could understand anything he said.

# LANGUAGE AND LINGUISTICS: ETYMOLOGICAL CONUNDRA

✳ Is there another word for synonym?

✳ When a building's completed, shouldn't it be called a built?

✳ Whose idea was it to have a letter "s" in the word "lisp"?

✳ Why has the word "monosyllabic" got five syllables?

✳ Why is "abbreviation" such a long word?

✳ Why is it so hard to remember the spelling of "mnemonic"?

✳ Why is it that the word "big" is smaller than the word "little," while the words "small" and "large" are the same size?

✳ Why is the word "synonymous" spelled differently than the word "same"?

✳ Why isn't phonetic spelled the way it sounds?

✳ Why do "overlook" and "oversee" mean opposite things?

✳ Why is there no other word for "thesaurus"?

# LANGUAGES: FOREIGN

✳ A foreign visitor to America was having trouble with the pronunciation of words like "enough," "bough," and "though." He thought he was getting the hang of it until he saw the newspaper headline "Fete pronounced success."

✳ "English? Who needs that? I'm never going to England!" *Homer Simpson*

✳ "I bought a self-learning record to learn Spanish. I turned it on and went to sleep. During the night, the record skipped. The next day I could only stutter in Spanish." *Steven Wright*

✳ An English cat, called One-two-three, and a French cat, called Un-deux-trois, decide to having a swimming race across a lake. Which cat won? The English cat—Un-deux-trois catre cinq.

✳ An Irish professor of linguistics is chatting with a Spanish counterpart when the latter asks him if there's an Irish equivalent of "mañana." The Irishman thinks for a moment and says, "Yes, but it doesn't convey the same sense of urgency."

✳ Well…that was easier said than sung in Russian.

✳ At an international medical conference, two African surgeons are having an argument. "I tell you it sounds like 'wooooom.'" says one. "You're wrong," says the other. "It sounds like 'woombba.'" "You're both wrong," says a passing French surgeon. "In English it is pronounced 'womb.'" "Ridiculous," replies one of the Africans. "I wager that you have never even seen a wild hippopotamus, let alone heard one fart underwater."

✳ I speak Spanish like a native—a native Hungarian.

# LATIN MOTTOS

✳ Volvo, Video, Velcro (I came, I saw, I stuck around.

# LAW AND ORDER

✳ A bank had been robbed three times by the same bandit. An FBI agent interviews one of the bank tellers looking for clues. "Have you noticed anything distinctive about the man?" he asks. "Not really," replies the teller. "But each time he turns up, he's better dressed."

✳ A government inspector visits a prison. After being shown around, he meets with the Governor. "You seem to have a lot of social events here," says the inspector. "Do we?" asks the Governor. "Well, yes," says the inspector. "One of the prisoners sold me a ticket for the Warden's Ball. Didn't you know about it?" "Well, yes I did," says the Governor. "But that's not a dance, that's a raffle."

✳ A man walks into a police station and drops a dead cat in front of the desk sergeant. "Someone threw this in my front garden," says the man. "I'll take your name, sir," says the sergeant. "And if no one claims it in three months, you can keep it."

✳ A bank was held up by a criminal with a sawed-off shotgun. Luckily no one was injured—he'd sawed off the wrong end.

✳ A man is about to be put into the electric chair and the prison chaplain asks him if there's anything he can do for him in his dying moments. "Yes," says the man. "Will you hold my hand?"

✳ A masked man runs into a bank and points a banana at the cashier. "This is a fuck-up!" he shouts. "Don't you mean a hold-up?" asks the cashier. "No," says the man. "It's a fuck-up. I left the gun on the bus."

✳ A school class goes on a field trip to the local police station where they see pictures of the country's ten most wanted criminals. A little boy points to a picture and asks if it really is the photo of a wanted person. "Yes," said the policeman. "The detectives want to capture him very badly." The boy replies, "So why didn't you keep him when you took his picture?"

✳ A sleuth is a detective who discovers who slue who.

✳ My grandfather was the unluckiest criminal in the country. He made a deathbed confession of all his crimes—then got better.

✳ My grandmother gave me $1 and said, "Not a word about this to your parents." I said, "It's going to cost you a lot more than that."

✳ The police have reported the theft of a shipment of filing cabinets, document folders, and labeling machines—it's believed to have been the work of organized crime.

✳ To find out which is the best law enforcement agency, the president sets a test for the CIA, the FBI, and the LAPD. He releases a rabbit in a forest and challenges them to find it. The CIA goes in first and, after months of interviewing forest dwellers and conducting forensic tests, they deduce that the rabbit never existed. The FBI go in next and burn down half the forest, claiming the rabbit provoked them. The LAPD go in last, and after half an hour, drag out a badly beaten bear yelling, "Okay, okay. I'm a rabbit, I'm a rabbit…"

✳ We have 35 million laws to enforce the Ten Commandments.

✳ What did the idiot burglar do when he saw his "Wanted" poster outside the police station? He went in and applied for the job.

✳ Why did the doctor fail when he turned kidnapper? No one could read his ransom notes.

✳ Why did the escaped convict saw the legs off his bed? He wanted to lie low.

✳ Why in movies are detectives only able to solve cases once they've been suspended from duty?

✳ A man is standing at a urinal when he notices he's being watched by a little person. After a few seconds the little person drags a small stepladder next to the man, climbs it, and proceeds to look at his privates at close range. "Don't be embarrassed," says the little person. "I'm a doctor and I couldn't help noticing that you have a slight swelling of the testicles. It might be nothing to worry about but would you mind if I examined them?" The man is rather startled by this request but tells the little person to go ahead. The little person reaches out, gets a tight grip on the man's balls, and says, "Okay, now hand over your wallet or I jump!"

✳ A woman goes into a police station and says, "I've just been molested by a laundry worker." "How do you know he works in a laundry?" asks the desk sergeant. The woman replies, "Because he did the whole thing by hand."

✳ A young couple buy a new car and take it for a spin in the countryside. Feeling romantic, they try to have sex inside the car but find it's too small. Instead they squeeze underneath the car and start going at it there. After a few minutes a policeman walks by and tells them he's going to arrest the couple for indecent exposure. "But I'm not doing anything illegal under here," complains the man. "I'm just fixing my car." "You're having sex," replies the policeman. "And I can tell that for three reasons. Firstly you have no tools out. Secondly, I can see a second pair of legs outside of yours. And thirdly, your car's been stolen."

✳ Tom is walking down the road with a computer under one arm, a swivel chair under the other, and a desk strapped to his back. A policeman stops him and says, "'I'm arresting you for impersonating an office, sir."

✳ What's the difference between unlawful and illegal? Unlawful means against the law, illegal is a sick bird.

# LAW AND ORDER: COURT

✳ Judge to defendant: "Is it true that you owe your neighbor a thousand dollars?" Defendant: "Yes, it's true." Judge: "Then, why don't you just pay him back?" Defendant: "Because it wouldn't be true any more."

✳ A judge is speaking to three men brought before him for a misdemeanor. He asks the first man why he's there. The man replies, "For throwing peanuts in the lake." The judge asks the second man why he's there. The man replies, "For throwing peanuts in the lake." The judge asks the third man why he's there. He says, "I'm Peanuts."

✳ Judge to man: "Are you the defense lawyer?" Man: "No, I'm the guy who stole the chickens."

✳ After his motion to suppress evidence was denied by the court, the attorney addressed the judge—"Your Honor. What would you do if I called you a stupid, degenerate old fool?" The judge replies, "I would hold you in contempt and seek to have you suspended from practicing before this court again!" "What if I only thought it?" asks the attorney. "In that case," says the judge, "there is nothing I could do. You have the right to think whatever you like." "I see," says the attorney. "Then, if it pleases the court, I 'think' you're a stupid, degenerate old fool."

✳ "Being a miner, as soon as you're too old and tired and ill and sick and stupid to do the job properly, you have to go. Well, the very opposite applies with judges." *Peter Cook*

✳ A man has to appear in court for a minor traffic summons. He grows increasingly restless as he waits hour after hour for his case to be heard. When his name is called, it's late in the day, and he stands before the judge only to hear that the court is going be adjourned until the next day. "What for?" he snaps at the judge. The judge shouts back, "Twenty dollars—contempt of court. That's why!" Then, noticing the man checking his wallet, the judge relents, "That's all right. You don't have to pay now." The man replies, "I'm not paying. I'm just seeing if I have enough for two more words."

✳ A man is on trial for murder. There's strong evidence of guilt, but no corpse. In the defense's closing statement, the man's lawyer says, "Ladies and gentlemen of the jury, I have a surprise for you. Within one minute, the person presumed dead in this case will walk into this courtroom." The jury watch the door, but after a minute has passed, the lawyer says, "Ladies and gentlemen, I made up the previous statement. But you all watched the door in anticipation. I therefore put it to you that there is reasonable doubt as to whether anyone was killed and insist that you return a verdict of not guilty." The jury retires to deliberate. A few minutes later, they return and the foreman declares a verdict of guilty. "What?" says the lawyer. "You must have had some doubt; You were all staring at the door." The foreman replies, "Yes, we were all looking, but your client wasn't."

✳ Accused to judge: "As the Lord is my judge, I am not guilty." Judge: "He's not, I am, you are, six months."

✳ A prosecutor is cross-examining a witness. "You strike me as an intelligent, honest man, Mr. Smith. One who wouldn't cheat or lie." "Thank you," replies Mr. Smith. "I'd say the same about you if I wasn't under oath."

✳ Lawyer to witness: "And did you actually see the accused bite off Mr. Smith's nose?" Witness: "No, but I saw him spit it out."

✳ Clerk: "Prisoner at the bar, how do you plead, guilty or not guilty?" Prisoner: "How can I tell till I've heard the evidence?"

✳ Judge to accused: "You admit murdering that old lady for a paltry fifty cents?" Accused: "Fifty here, fifty there. It soon adds up."

✳ Judge to disruptive witness: "Are you showing contempt for this court?" Witness: "No, I'm doing my best to hide it."

✳ Two judges are arrested for being drunk and disorderly, but agree to try each other's cases the next morning. The first judge fines the second $2, but when it is the first judge's turn, he gets a $50 fine "Why did you do that?" says the first judge. "I only fined you $2." "I know," says his friend. "But there's far too much of this behavior going on these days. Yours is the second case this morning."

✳ When you go into court, you are putting yourself in the hands of twelve people who weren't smart enough to get out of jury duty."

✳ Jury foreman to judge: "We find the accused not guilty by reason of insanity." Judge: "What, all twelve of you?"

✳ Judge to defendant: "You have been found not guilty of robbery and can leave this court without a stain on your character." Defendant: "Great! Does that mean I can keep the money?"

# LAW AND ORDER: JAIL

✳ A group of prisoners passes the time telling jokes to each other. Unfortunately their repertoire is limited, and they soon know all of them by heart; indeed, they even start referring to the jokes by number. One prisoner says, "D'you remember number thirteen?" And everyone chuckles. Another says, "That reminds me of joke number six!" Again everyone laughs. "Or how about number twelve?" says another. Everyone chuckles except for one prisoner who starts having hysterics. He laughs until tears fall down his cheeks and his sides hurt. He falls on the floor, rolls about, and slaps his thighs, cackling uncontrollably. Finally he calms down and notices his friends looking at him stony-faced. "Sorry," he says. "First time I'd heard that one."

✳ Three men are sentenced to twenty years of solitary confinement. However, they're each allowed one luxury to take to their cells. The first man asks for a stack of law books. The second man asks for a pile of medical books. And the third man asks for two hundred cartons of cigarettes. At the end of the twenty years, they open up the first man's cell. He comes out and says, "I studied so hard, I can now qualify as a lawyer." They open up the second man's door. He says, "After all the learning, I can now become a doctor." They open up the third man's door. He comes out and says, "Anybody got a match?"

✳ A guy escapes from prison and goes home. His wife says, "Where have you been? You escaped eight hours ago!"

# LAW AND ORDER: MURDER

✳ Tom, Dick, and Harry are about to tee off on the golf course when a stranger asks if he can join them. Being friendly, types they let him, and the conversation soon turns to professions. The stranger reveals that he's a hitman and is actually carrying his gun in his golf bag. Tom doesn't believe him and asks to see it. Sure enough, inside the golf bag is a rifle with a huge telescopic sight. Harry asks if he can look through it. "Wow!" says Harry, "I can see my house with this. Look there's my bedroom window! I can even see my wife sitting on the bed." Suddenly he turns pale. "Oh my God, she's in there with our neighbor and they're both stark naked." Furious, Harry turns to the hitman and says, "Okay, how much to shoot my lying wife in the mouth and my cheating neighbor in the dick?" The hitman replies, "I get $1,000 every time I pull the trigger." "It's a deal," says Harry. "Do it now." The hitman picks up his rifle, takes aim, and waits. A few seconds pass. "What are you waiting for?" asks Harry, "Shhh," says the hitman. "I'm trying to save you a thousand dollars."

✳ A defense lawyer meets with his client. "The blood tests have come back, and we have good news and bad news." "So what's the bad news?" asks the client. "Your DNA matches the blood found on the victim, the murder weapon, and the getaway car." "Okay," says the defendant. "So what the good news?" The lawyer replies, "Your cholesterol is down to 120."

✳ I'd like to smother my mother-in-law in diamonds. Then again, there has to be a cheaper way to do it.

✳ Mr. Smith to judge: "Your Honor, my wife is being ridiculous. Most women would love to have a chivalrous husband. Who could object to having a car door opened for them?" "Mr. Smith," replies the judge. "It might be chivalrous to open a car door for your wife, but not when you're driving at 65 miles per hour."

✳ An old man is given twenty-five years for murder. "Twenty-five years?" he complains. "I'll never live that long!" The judge replies, "Well, never mind, old man. Just do what you can."

# LAW AND ORDER: POLICE

✳ A hole has appeared in the ladies' changing rooms at the fitness club. The police are looking into it.

✳ A salesman, tired of his job, gives it up to become a policeman. Several months later a friend asks him how he likes it. "Well," he replies. "The pay is good and the hours aren't bad, but what I like best is that the customer is always wrong."

✳ A woman finds her house has been robbed, so she calls the police and demands they send a patrol car immediately. The dispatcher tells her that the only patrol car near her home is a canine car. She yells, "I don't care, just send him over!" The car stops by, but when the woman sees the officer get out of the car with his German shepherd, she wails, "Just my luck! My house gets robbed and they send me a blind policeman!"

✳ A police officer stops a woman and asks for her license. He reads it and says, "Lady, it says here that you should be wearing glasses." The woman answers, "I have contacts." "I don't care who you know!" says the officer. "You're getting a ticket!"

✳ A policeman is at the scene of a terrible accident. Body parts are everywhere and the officer is making notes of what is where. He comes across a head and writes in his notebook "Head on boolevard." This doesn't look right, so he crosses it out and writes "Head on bullevard." That doesn't look right either, so he writes "Head on boullavard," which still doesn't seem right. The officer looks around to make sure no one is watching and kicks the head. Then he writes, "Head in garden."

✳ One evening a man looks out of his window and sees that burglars are in his garage. He calls the police, but they tell him they don't have a car in his area. The man hangs up, counts to thirty, and calls the police again. "Hello," he says. "I called a few seconds ago about the burglars in my garage. Well, you don't have to worry now—I've just shot them all." Within five minutes there are half a dozen police cars outside his house, and they catch the burglars red-handed. One of the policemen approaches the man and says, "I thought you said you'd shot them!" The man replies, "And I thought you said there was no one available!"

* Police arrested two kids yesterday; one was drinking battery acid, the other was eating fireworks. They charged one and let the other off.

* A police officer pulls over a driver for speeding. As he writes out the ticket he keeps swatting at a fly circling around his head. "What kind of damn fly is that anyhow?" he says. The driver replies, "That's a circle fly." "I've never heard of a 'circle fly,'" says the cop. The driver says, "Circle flies are usually found circling around a horse's ass." The police officer is furious, "Hey! Are you calling me a horse's ass!?" The driver replies, "Oh, no, sir. But it sure is hard to fool those flies."

* The police station toilet has been stolen. The cops have nothing to go on.

* A man taking a bus ride in a totalitarian country taps a fellow passenger on the shoulder. "Excuse me," he says. "But are you a member of the Secret Police?" "No," replies the passenger. "Are any of your family in the Secret Police?" asks the man. "No," replies the passenger. "So do you know anyone in the Secret Police?" asks the man. "No, I don't," replies the passenger. "Oh good," says the man. "In that case, would you mind getting off my damn foot?"

# LAW AND ORDER: PUNISHMENT

* "My uncle's dying wish was to have me sitting on his lap. He was in the electric chair."
*Rodney Dangerfield*

* What is the maximum sentence for bigamy? Two mothers-in-law.

* A prisoner on death row is about to be put to death by firing squad. As the blindfold is being put on, the guard asks him if he has a last request. The prisoner thinks for a moment, then says, "One thing I'd really like to do is to sing my favorite song, from beginning to end, without any interruptions." "Okay," says the guard. So the prisoner sings, "One billion bottles of beer on the wall. One billion bottles of beer..."

* Two prisoners are shown into a new cell. "How long are you in for?" says the first to the second. "Twenty years," replies the second. "How about you?" "I'm in for twenty-five," replies the first. "But since you're getting out first, you'd better have the bed by the door."

# LAW AND ORDER: THEFT

✳ I'm a kleptomaniac, but I'm taking something for it.

✳ The darkest hour is just before dawn. So if you're going to steal your neighbor's milk, that's the time to do it.

✳ The people around here are so warm and friendly and trusting. It makes robbing them a piece of cake.

✳ A little girl is chatting with her teacher—"My daddy just got a new car." "That's nice," says the teacher. "Is he excited?" "Oh yes," says the little girl. "He spent all last night painting it and changing the license plates."

✳ A couple are walking down the street when the girl stops in front of a jewelry store and says, "Honey, look at that necklace! It's so beautiful." "No problem," replies her man, throwing a brick through the window and grabbing the necklace. A little later the girl points to a bracelet in the window of another shop. "Ooh, honey," she says. "I'd love that too." "No problem," says her boyfriend and, again, throws a brick through the window. A little later they pass another shop when she sees a diamond ring. "Oh honey. Isn't that lovely!" she says. "Hang on!" he says. "What do you think I am? Made of bricks?"

✳ A burglar is robbing a house when he hears someone say "Jesus is watching you." To his relief, he realizes it's just a parrot. The burglar says to the parrot, "What's your name?" The parrot says, "Moses." The burglar says, "Moses? What sort of person calls their parrot Moses?" The parrot replies, "The same sort of person who calls his Rottweiler Jesus."

✳ A man is walking down a dark alley when he's approached by a stranger, "Please, sir. Could you spare something for a man down on his luck? All I have in the world is this small gun."

✳ Husband to police officer: "I want to talk to the guy you arrested for breaking in my house last night." Officer: "What for?" Husband: "I want to know how he got in without waking my wife."

✳ There is justice in the world. Yesterday the man stealing my tires was run over by the man stealing my car.

✳ Did you know that your car is most likely to be stolen when it's parked outside your house—that's why I park outside my neighbor's house.

✳ He was a crook from the moment he was born. The midwife said, "Oh look. He's got his father's nose, his mother's hair, and the doctor's watch."

✳ A robber points a gun at a bank cashier. "Give me all the money or you're geography!" he shouts. "Don't you mean history?" asks the cashier. "Don't change the subject!" shouts the robber.

✳ "The other day, everything in my apartment was stolen and replaced with an exact replica. I couldn't believe it. I said to my roommate, 'Can you believe this? Everything stolen and replaced with exact replicas.' He said, 'Do I know you?'" *Steven Wright*

✳ Tom and Dick are robbing an apartment in a block of high rises when they hear police sirens. "Quick, let's jump out of the window!" says Tom. "Are you crazy?" replies Dick. "This is the thirteenth floor." "Don't be ridiculous," says Tom. "This is no time to be superstitious."

✳ A man walks into a tackle shop to buy some worms. He also takes the opportunity to slip an expensive fishing reel into his pocket. The shopkeeper spots the theft but decides not to make a big deal of it. He simply rings it up on the register, saying, "That's $3 for the worms and $60 for the reel." The man is so embarrassed at being caught, he tenses up and lets off a fart. The shop keeper rings up a new total—And another $10 for the duck call."

✳ Sherlock Holmes and Doctor Watson go camping. Sometime in the middle of the night, Holmes wakes Watson up. "Watson, look up at the stars, and tell me what you deduce." Watson says, "I see millions of stars, and if even a few of those have planets, it's quite likely there are some planets like earth, and if there are a few planets like earth, there might also be life." Holmes replies, "No, Watson, the correct deduction is that somebody has stolen our tent!"

✳ A man runs up to Harry in the street and says, "Quick! Have you seen a policeman?" "Sorry, no," says Harry, "There's never one around when you need one, is there?" "Very true," replies the man, taking a gun out of his pocket. "Now hand over your wallet."

# LAWYERS

✳ A doctor and a lawyer are involved in a car crash. The lawyer, seeing that the doctor is a little shaken up, offers him a drink from his hip flask. The doctor accepts, has a drink, and hands back the flask. The lawyer puts it in his pocket. "Aren't you having one yourself?" asks the doctor. "Sure," says the lawyer. "But I'll wait till after the police leave."

✳ A widow goes to her doctor and asks him to explain the human reproductive process. "But you've been married three times," says the doctor. "Surely you've had sex?" "Never," replies the woman. "My first husband was a gynecologist, and all he did was look at it. My second husband was a psychiatrist, and all he did was talk about it. And my third husband was a explorer who was never around to do it." "So why do you want to know

now?" asks the doctor. "I'm getting married to a lawyer," replies the woman. "So I'm bound to get screwed somehow."

✳ A lawyer with insomnia consults his doctor. "Which side is it best to lie on?" he asks. "The side that pays your fee," replies the doctor.

✳ A doctor and a lawyer are talking at a party, but their conversation is constantly interrupted by people asking the doctor for free medical advice. After an hour of this the doctor says to the lawyer, "What do you do to stop people from asking you for legal advice when you're out of the office?" "I give it to them," replies the lawyer. "Then I charge them for it." The doctor is shocked. "Does that really work?" "Certainly does," replies the lawyer. "And that'll be $400, thank you."

✳ A lawyer buys a farm as a weekend retreat. While walking around his new property he looks down and sees that his feet are in the middle of a huge cow pat. The lawyer starts yelling, "Oh my God! Help me, help me!" His wife runs up and asks what's the matter. The lawyer points to his feet and screams, "I'm melting! I'm melting…!"

✳ A lawyer dies in a car accident on his fortieth birthday and finds himself greeted at the Pearly Gates by a brass band. Saint Peter runs over, shakes his hand, and says, "Congratulations!" "Congratulations for what?" asks the lawyer. "We're celebrating the fact that you lived to be 160 years old." "But that's not true," says the lawyer. "I only lived to be forty." "That's impossible," replies Saint Peter. "We've added up your time sheets."

✳ A lawyer is paid $950 in new bills but, on counting the money, he discovers that two notes have stuck together, and he's been overpaid by $50. This leaves him with an ethical dilemma—should he tell his partner?

✳ A lawyer opens the door of his BMW. Another car speeds by and hits the door, ripping it off completely. When the police arrive, the lawyer is complaining bitterly. "Officer, look what they've done to my car!" he whines. "You lawyers are so materialistic, you make me sick," replies the officer. "You're so worried about your stupid car, you haven't even noticed your left arm was ripped off!" "Oh my God!" replies the lawyer. "Where's my Rolex?"

✳ A woman drives home with the front of her car covered in branches, sticks, leaves, mud, and lots of blood. "I'm really sorry about the car," says the woman to her husband. "But I hit a lawyer on the way home." "Well, that explains the blood," says the husband. "But what about the other stuff?" "I had to chase him through the park," says the woman.

✳ A man is stuck in a traffic jam. Looking out of his car window he sees a kid on a skateboard weaving his way toward him. "Hey, what's the hold up?" he asks. "It's some crazy lawyer," replies the boy. "He's lying in the middle of the road. He's doused himself with gas and is threatening to set fire to himself. We're taking up a collection for him."

"How much have you got so far?" asks the man. The boy replies, "About thirty boxes of matches and twenty-three lighters."

✳ A man walks into a bar with an alligator. He says to the bartender, "Do you serve lawyers here?" "Sure do," replies the bartender. "Good," says the man. "Give me a beer, and a lawyer for my 'gator."

✳ A man wanders into an antique shop in San Francisco's Chinatown. He picks through the curios on display and comes across a bronze sculpture of a rat. The craftsmanship is very good, and the price is low, so he buys it. Taking the rat statue outside, the man walks toward the waterfront but is alarmed when he realizes he's being followed by a pair of real rats. Soon the two rats are joined by others, then more arrive, until a horde of rats is following the man. Terrified, the man starts to run, and the rats run after him, more joining all the time. Finally the man reaches a pier where he's cornered by a host of rats. Figuring this behavior has something to do with the bronze rat sculpture, the man throws it into the sea. Immediately all the rats fling themselves into the water and drown. The man rushes back to the antique shop and accosts the old Chinese man who owns it. "About that statue..." gasps the man. "Yes, I probably should have warned you," says the owner. "The statue is cursed..." "Never mind that," says the man. "Have you got any statues of lawyers?"

✳ A woman is told she needs two pounds of brain for a transplant. She's informed that two pounds of doctor brain will cost $500, and the two pounds of architect brain will cost $600. She replies that, since her father was a famous lawyer, she'd prefer a lawyer's brain. "Okay," says the doctor. "That'll cost you $10,000." "What?" she says. "How can two pounds of lawyer's brain cost $10,000?" The doctor replies, "Do you have any idea how many lawyers we have to pop open to get that much?"

✳ An incompetent attorney can delay a trial for months or years. A competent attorney can delay one even longer.

✳ A young lawyer is defending a wealthy businessman in a complicated lawsuit. Unfortunately, the evidence is against his client, and he fears the worst. He asks a senior partner of his law firm if it would be appropriate to send the judge a box of Havana cigars. The partner is horrified. "The judge is an honorable man," he exclaims. "If you do that, I can guarantee you'll lose the case!" Weeks later the judge rules in favor of the lawyer's client. The partner takes him to lunch to congratulate him. "Aren't you glad you didn't send those cigars to the judge?" he says. "I did send them," replies the lawyer. "I just enclosed the plaintiff's lawyer's business card!"

✳ He was a very clever lawyer—he even named his daughter "Sue."

✳ After having a big operation, a lawyer slowly comes out of anesthesia. He looks around his room and says, "Doctor, why are all the blinds drawn in my room?" "There's a big fire across the street," replies the doctor. "We didn't want you to think the operation had been a failure."

✷ An airliner is having engine trouble. The pilot instructs the cabin crew to prepare for an emergency landing. A few minutes later the pilot asks the flight attendants if everyone is buckled in and ready. "All set back here, Captain," comes the reply. "Except one lawyer. He's still going around passing out business cards."

✷ An elderly patient needs a heart transplant and discusses his options with his doctor. The doctor says, "We have three possible donors. One is a young, healthy athlete. The second is a middle-aged businessman who never drank or smoked, and the third is an attorney who just died after practicing law for thirty years." "I'll take the lawyer's heart," says the patient. "Why?" asks the doctor. The patient replies, "It's never been used."

✷ Did you hear about the lawyer who was hurt in an accident? The ambulance he was chasing stopped too suddenly.

✷ How can you tell when a lawyer is lying? His lips are moving.

✷ If a lawyer and a tax official were both drowning, and you could only save one of them, what would you do—go to lunch or read the paper?

✷ How do you stop a lawyer from drowning? Shoot him before he hits the water.

✷ How do you stop a lawyer from drowning? Take your foot off his head.

✷ How many lawyers does it take to stop a moving bus? Never enough.

✷ If an apple a day keeps the doctor away, how many orchards does it take for a lawyer?

✷ If it weren't for lawyers, we wouldn't need them.

✷ Lawyer's creed—a man is innocent until proven broke.

✷ Man to lawyer: "If I give you $500, will you answer two questions?" Lawyer: "Absolutely. What's the other question?"

✷ Lawyer: "Let me give you my honest opinion." Client: "No, no. I'm paying for professional advice."

✷ Jerry is charged with stealing a Mercedes Benz, and after a long trial, the jury acquits him. Later that day Jerry comes back to speak to the judge that tried his case. "Your Honor," he says. "I want to get out a warrant for that dirty lawyer of mine." "Why?" asks the judge. "He won your acquittal. Why do you want to have him arrested?" Jerry replies, "I didn't have the money to pay his fee, so the bastard went and took the car I stole."

✳ Mr. Smith is on his deathbed and comes up with a plan to take some of his wealth with him. He calls for the three men he trusts most—his lawyer, his doctor, and his clergyman. "I'm going to give you each $30,000 in cash before I die," says Mr. Smith. "At my funeral, I want you to place the money in my coffin so that I can try to take it with me." At the funeral, each approaches the coffin and places an envelope inside. Later, while riding in the limousine to the cemetery, the clergyman says, "I have to confess I only put $20,000 in the coffin. The church needs a new baptistery very badly, so I took $10,000 out of the envelope." The doctor says, "Well, I didn't put the full $30,000 in the coffin either. I used $20,000 of the money to buy a dialysis machine for the hospital." The lawyer then says, "I'm ashamed of both of you. When I put my envelope in that coffin, it held my personal check for the full $30,000."

✳ Santa Claus, the tooth fairy, an honest lawyer, and a drunk are in a bar when they spot a hundred dollars on the floor. Who gets it? The drunk—the other three are mythological creatures.

✳ Ninety-nine percent of lawyers give the rest a bad name.

✳ Old lawyers never die, they just lose their appeal.

✳ Terrorists have hijacked a planeload of lawyers bound for a legal convention. They've threatened to start releasing the lawyers one by one until their demands are met.

✳ Three men are traveling in the countryside when their car breaks down. They go to a farmhouse to seek shelter. The farmer only has two spare beds, but says that one of the men can sleep in the barn. The first man, a rabbi, volunteers to sleep outside, but a few minutes after he leaves, there's a knock at the door. It's the rabbi. It turns out there's a pig in the barn, and the rabbi doesn't feel comfortable sleeping there. To get around the problem, the second man, a Hindu, volunteers to take the rabbi's place. He leaves for the barn, but a few minutes later, there's a knock at the door. It's the Hindu. It turns out there's also a cow in the barn, and the Hindu doesn't feel comfortable sleeping near it. The third man, a lawyer, says he doesn't have any religious hang-ups and walks out to sleep in the barn. A few minutes later the rabbi and the Hindu hear a knock. The rabbi opens the door. Standing outside are a pig and a cow.

✳ Two crooks try to hold up a lawyers' club, but the lawyers put up such a fight, the crooks have to flee before they manage to take much money. In the getaway car, they count their loot. "I've got good news and bad news," says one of the crooks. "What d'you mean?" asks the second crook. "We got away with $50," replies the first crook. "But we went in there with $75."

✳ Two doctors are having a fight in a hospital corridor. A nurse pulls them apart and asks what the trouble is. "There's a lawyer in the next ward who only has two days to live," says one of the doctors. "Well, one of you has to tell him," says the nurse. "That's the trouble," says the second doctor. "We both do."

✳ What do you call ten lawyers buried up to their necks in the sand? Soccer practice.

✳ Two lawyers are walking down the road when they see a beautiful woman walking toward them. "What a babe," one says. "I'd sure like to screw her!" "Really?" replies the other. "Out of what?"

✳ Two tigers are prowling through the jungle in single file and the one behind keeps licking the ass of the tiger in front. "Will you stop that," says the first tiger. "It's getting really annoying." "I'm sorry," says the second tiger. "But I just ate a lawyer, and I'm trying to get the taste out of my mouth."

✳ What can a goose do, a duck can't, and a lawyer should? Stick his bill up his rear.

✳ What do you call 5,000 dead lawyers at the bottom of the ocean? A good start.

✳ What do you call a lawyer with an IQ of 50? Your Honor.

✳ What happens when a lawyer takes Viagra? He gets taller.

✳ What's the difference between two lawyers in a Porsche and a porcupine? The porcupine has pricks on the outside.

✳ What's a foot long, transparent, and lies in the gutter? A lawyer once the crap's been kicked out of him.

✳ What's black and tan and looks great on a lawyer? A Doberman Pinscher.

✳ What's the difference between a dead lawyer in the road and a dead skunk in the road? There are skid marks in front of the skunk.

✳ What's the difference between a female lawyer and a pit bull? Lipstick.

✳ When a person assists a criminal in breaking the law before a crime, we call him an accomplice. When a person assists a criminal in breaking the law after a crime, we call him a defense lawyer.

✳ What's the difference between a hooker and a lawyer? The hooker will stop screwing you when you're dead.

✳ What's the difference between a lawyer and a catfish? One's a scum-sucking bottom dweller, the other's a fish!

✳ What's the difference between a lawyer and a terrorist? Terrorists have sympathizers.

＊ What's the difference between a shame and a pity? If a busload of lawyers goes over a cliff and there are no survivors—that's a pity. If there were any empty seats—that's a shame.

＊ Why do they bury lawyers in 20-foot holes? Because deep down, they're all really nice guys.

＊ Why does the Bar Association prohibit lawyers and clients from having sex? To prevent clients from being billed twice for the same service.

＊ Why don't lawyers enjoy fishing? Because it's too much like work, what with all the lying involved.

＊ Why don't you see lawyers on the beach? Cats keep covering them with sand.

＊ Lawyer: "Now that you have been acquitted, will you tell me truly? Did you steal the car?" Client: "After hearing you in court, I'm beginning to think I didn't."

＊ A man calls a lawyer's office. A voice answers, "Schwartz, Schwartz, Schwartz, and Schwartz." The man says, "Let me talk to Mr. Schwartz." "I'm sorry, he's on vacation." "Then let me talk to Mr. Schwartz." "He's on a big case, not available for a week." "Then let me talk to Mr. Schwartz." "He's playing golf today." "Okay, then, let me talk to Mr. Schwartz." "Speaking."

＊ A junior partner in a law firm is sent to represent a client accused of murder. After a long trial, the case is won and the client acquitted. The young lawyer texts his firm with the message "Justice prevailed." The senior partner texts back "Appeal immediately."

＊ A teacher asks her students what their parents do for a living. "What does you mother do all day, Billy?" Billy replies, "My mommy is a doctor." "That's wonderful," says teacher. "How about you, Amie?" Amie stands up and says, "My father is a mailman." "Thank you, Amie," says teacher. "And what about your father, Tim?" Tim stands up and says, "My daddy plays piano in a whorehouse." The teacher is aghast and promptly changes the subject. Later she phones Tim's mother to find out if it's true. "No, it's not true," says Tim's mother. "His father's a lawyer, but how can I explain a thing like that to a seven-year-old?"

＊ A woman walks into a post office and sees a man standing at the counter placing "Love" stamps on bright pink envelopes. When an envelope has been stamped, he sprays scent on it and posts it. The woman goes up to him and asks him what he's doing. The man replies, "I'm sending out 1,000 Valentine cards signed 'Guess who?'" "But why would you want to do that?" asks the woman. The man replies, "I'm a divorce lawyer."

＊ Having lawyers make laws is like having doctors make diseases.

✳ How many lawyers does it take to grease a combine? Only one if you run him through slowly!

✳ Taking his seat in his chambers, the judge faces the opposing lawyers. "Both of you have given me a bribe," he says. "You, Tom, gave me $15,000. And you, Harry, gave me $10,000." The judge reaches into his pocket, pulls out a check, and hands it to Tom. "I'm returning $5,000, and we'll now decide this case solely on its merits."

✳ Two lawyers arrange to have lunch, but one is over an hour late. Finally he turns up. "Sorry it took me so long," he says. "But I ran over a milk bottle and got a flat tire." "I'm surprised you didn't see the bottle in the road," comments the other lawyer. "I couldn't," says the first lawyer. "The kid had it under his coat."

✳ What do you have when a lawyer is buried up to his neck in sand? Insufficient sand.

✳ What's the difference between a lawyer and a bucket of shit? The bucket.

✳ I dated a lawyer until she said, "Stop, and/or I'll slap your face!"

✳ Why did New Jersey get all the toxic waste and California, all the lawyers? New Jersey got to pick first.

✳ What's the difference between a good lawyer and a great lawyer? A good lawyer knows the law; a great lawyer knows the judge.

# LAZINESS

✳ A father is lecturing his lazy son. "All you do is sit around the house all day!" "Well, what would I get if I had a job?" says the son. "You'd get a salary and pension," replies the father. "You'd be able to settle down and retire and not work any more." "Yeah," replies the son. "But I do that now."

✳ A man drives his car into a ditch and begs help from a farmer passing by with his horse. "I can give it a try," says the farmer. "Blackie here is pretty strong. She might be able to pull the car out." So saying, the farmer ties Blackie to the car and tells her to pull. "Come on Blackie! Pull harder, Rufus! Go to it, Billie! Come on, Joseph!" Eventually the car is pulled back on to the road. "Thanks," says the driver. "But tell me, why did you keep changing the horse's name while she was pulling?" "Blackie is short-sighted and a bit lazy," says the farmer. "She wouldn't even have tried to pull up that car if she thought she'd have to do it all herself."

✳ A young man goes to stay on his uncle's farm. At four in the morning the uncle wakes him up to help him with the barley harvest. "Excuse me," says the young man. "But is barley dangerous?" "No," says the farmer. "It's harmless." "Well, in that case," says his nephew, "why do we have to sneak up on it in the dark?"

\* He's not lazy. He's a relaxaholic.

\* He's very religious. He won't work if there's a Sunday that week.

\* Harry was so lazy, if he dropped something, he wouldn't pick it up again till his shoelaces needed tying.

\* He was so lazy, he had his window box concreted over.

\* Frowning uses more muscles than smiling. That's why you're smiling. You're not happy. Just lazy.

\* Hard work will pay off in the future, but laziness pays off now.

\* Harry is so lazy, if you shot him, he'd probably ask someone to help him to the floor.

\* My dog is so lazy, he won't even bark he just waits for another dog to bark, then nods.

\* Our neighbor is so lazy, he'll do anything to get out of a job. He even married a widow with four children.

\* Procrastination is the art of keeping up with yesterday.

\* Talk about lazy. He's the only person I know who's got a smoke alarm with a snooze function.

\* Ted knows that hard work never killed anyone, but he still thinks it's best not to take any chances.

\* The trouble with doing nothing is you never know when you've finished.

\* There's no excuse for laziness, but I'm working on it.

\* A man tells his doctor he's not nearly as active as he used to be. The doctor examines him, and the man says, "Doctor, tell me in plain English what's wrong with me." "Well, in plain English," the doctor replies, "you're just lazy." "Okay," says the man. "Now give me a fancy medical term I can tell my wife."

\* He works almost every day. He almost works on Monday, he almost works on Tuesday, he almost works on Wednesday…

\* He's not much of a housekeeper. His broom has moss growing on the north side of it.

\* Boy to father: "What does 'procrastinate' mean?" Father: "I'll tell you later."

# LEPERS

✳ How can you tell if a letter is from a leper? The tongue is still in the envelope.

✳ What goes "Ha-ha-ha-ha-thump"? A leper laughing his head off.

✳ Why did they call time-out in the lepers' hockey match? There was a face-off in the corner.

# LIBRARIES AND LIBRARIANS

✳ A man is crossing the road when he's run over by the mobile library. He lies in the road, groaning in agony, till the librarian jumps out and says, "Shhhhh!"

✳ What happens when you cross a librarian and a lawyer? You get all the information you want, but you can't understand it.

✳ A man storms up to the library front desk and shouts, "I have a complaint! I borrowed a book last week, and it was horrible! It had too many characters and there was no plot!" The librarian says, "Are you the person who stole our phone directory?"

✳ "New York's such a wonderful city. Although I was at the library today. The guys are very rude. I said, 'I'd like a card.' He said, 'You have to prove you're a citizen of New York.' So I stabbed him." *Emo Phillips*

# LIFE

✳ Life may not be worth living, but what else can you do with it?

✳ The first half of life if ruined by your parents, the second by your kids.

✳ There's one good thing about life. It's only temporary.

✳ "Two babies were born on the same day at the same hospital. They lay there and looked at each other. Their families came and took them away. Eighty years later, by a bizarre coincidence, they lay in the same hospital, on their deathbeds, next to each other. One of them looked at the other and said, 'So, what did you think?'" *Steven Wright*

✳ "I'm going to live forever, or die trying." *Joseph Heller*

✳ "I've found the secret of eternal youth. I lie about my age." *Bob Hope*

# LIGHT BULB

✳ How many boring people does it take to change a light bulb? One.

✳ Do you know how many musicians it takes to change a light bulb? No, but you hum it, and I'll play it.

✳ How many actors does it take to change a light bulb? Only one. They don't like to share the spotlight.

✳ How many chiropractors does it take to change a light bulb? Only one, but it takes fifteen visits.

✳ How many Christian Scientists does it take to change a light bulb? Just one, to heal the old light bulb.

✳ How many civil servants does it take to change a light bulb? Forty-five. One to change the bulb, and forty-four to do the paperwork.

✳ How many existentialists does it take to change a light bulb? Two. One to screw it in, the other to observe how the light bulb symbolizes a single, incandescent beacon of subjective reality in a netherworld of endless absurdity.

✳ How many consultants does it take to change a light bulb? I'll have an estimate for you a week from Monday.

✳ How many cops does it take to screw in a light bulb? None. It turned itself in.

✳ How many divorced men does it take to screw in a light bulb? Who knows, they never get the house.

✳ How many divorced women does it take to screw in a light bulb? Four. One to screw in the bulb, and three to form a support group.

✳ How many economists does it take to screw in a light bulb? None. If the light bulb really needed changing, market forces would have already caused it to happen.

✳ How many folk singers does it take to screw in a light bulb? Two: one to change the bulb, and one to write a song about how good the old one was.

✳ How many football coaches does it take to change a light bulb? Who knows, they're never around long enough for anyone to find out.

✳ How many Hollywood directors does it take to change a light bulb? One, but he'll want to do it nineteen times.

✳ How many Jewish mothers does it take to change a light bulb? "Never mind me, I'll just sit here in the dark…"

✳ How many jugglers does it take to change a light bulb? One, but it takes at least three light bulbs.

✳ How many managers does it take to change a light bulb? Three. One to get the bulb, and two to get the phone number to dial one of their subordinates to actually change it.

✳ How many L.A. cops does it take to change a light bulb? Five. One to screw in a new bulb, and four to beat the crap out of the old one.

✳ How many Marxists does it take to screw in a light bulb? None, the seeds of revolution and change are within the light bulb itself.

✳ How many medical students does it take to change a light bulb? Five. One to change the bulb, and four to pull the ladder out from under him.

✳ How many men does it take to screw in a light bulb? One. He holds it and waits for the world to revolve around him.

✳ How many men does it take to screw in a light bulb? One. Men will screw anything.

✳ How many necrophiliacs does it take to screw in a light bulb? None. Necrophiliacs prefer dead bulbs.

✳ How many New Yorkers does it take to screw in a light bulb? None of your damn business!

✳ How many Oregonians does it take to screw in a light bulb? Five. One to change the bulb, and four to chase away the Californians who come to relate to the experience.

✳ How many witches does it take to change a light bulb? Into what?

✳ How many pessimists does it take to change a light bulb? None, the old one is probably screwed in too tight.

✳ How many people from New Jersey does it take to change a light bulb? Three. One to change the light bulb, one to be a witness, and the third to shoot the witness.

✳ How many philosophers does it take to replace a light bulb? Three. One to change it, and two to argue over whether or not the light bulb really exists.

✳ How many poets does it take to change a light bulb? Three. One to curse the darkness, one to light a candle, and one to change the bulb.

✳ How many politicians does it take to change a light bulb? It depends on how many it took under the previous government.

✳ How many nihilists does it take to change a light bulb? There is nothing to change.

✳ How many preservation society members does it take to screw in a light bulb? One, but it takes a year to find an antique Edison light bulb so it'll be aesthetically accurate.

✳ How many professors does it take to change a light bulb? Only one, but they get three tech reports out of it.

✳ How many programmers does it take to change a light bulb? None. That's a hardware problem.

✳ How many psychiatrists does it take to change a light bulb? Only one. But the light bulb has really got to want to change.

✳ How many punk rockers does it take to change a light bulb? Two. One to change the bulb, and one to eat the old one.

✳ How many stockbrokers does it take to change a light bulb? Two. One to take out the bulb and drop it, and the other to try and sell it before it crashes (knowing that it's already burned out).

✳ How many Roman Catholics does it take to change a light bulb? Two. One to do the screwing, and one to hear the confession.

✳ How many stand-up comedians does it take to change a light bulb? Two, one to screw it in, and another to say, "Sock it to me."

✳ How many straight San Franciscans does it take to change a light bulb? Both of them.

✳ How many surrealists does it take to change a light bulb? Two. One to hold the giraffe, and the other to fill the bathtub with brightly colored machine tools.

✳ How many telemarketers does it take to change a light bulb? One. But he has to do it while you're having dinner.

✳ How many televangelists does it take to screw in a light bulb? None. Televangelists screw in motels.

✳ How many gorillas does it take to screw in a light bulb? One, but it takes a lot of bulbs!

✳ How many lawyers does it take to change a light bulb? How many can you afford?

✳ How many Marines does it take to change a light bulb? Fifty. One to screw in the bulb, and forty-nine to guard him.

✳ How many mathematicians does it take to screw in a light bulb? One. He gives it to six Californians, thereby reducing the problem to an earlier joke.

✳ How many Californians does it take to change a light bulb? Twenty-five. One to change it, and twenty-four to sing about the experience.

✳ How many Dadaists does it take to screw in a light bulb? To get to the other side.

✳ How many Freudian analysts does it take to change a light bulb? Two. One to change, the bulb, and one to hold the penis…ladder, I mean ladder.

✳ How many gay men does it take to screw in a light bulb? One, but it takes a whole emergency room to get it out again.

✳ How many gay men does it take to screw in a light bulb? Two. One to screw it in, and the other to say "Fabulous."

✳ How many men does it take to change a light bulb? Three. One to put in the bulb, and two to listen to him brag about the screwing.

✳ How many mice does it take to screw in a light bulb? Two. Just drop them in, and they go right at it.

✳ How many nuclear engineers does it take to change a light bulb? Seven. One to install the new bulb, and six to figure out what to do with the old one for the next 10,000 years.

✳ How many politicians does it take to change a light bulb? Two. One to change it, and another one to change it back again.

✳ How many systems programmers does it take to change a light bulb? None. You'll never find one who'll admit it went down in the first place.

✳ What is the difference between a pregnant woman and a light bulb? You can unscrew a light bulb.

# LIONS

＊ A hiker comes across an old man sprinkling powder on the ground around his cottage. "What are you doing?" asks the hiker. "Just spreading this anti-lion powder on my garden," says the old man. "But there aren't any lions around for thousands of miles!" exclaims the hiker. "I know," replies the old man. "Works real good, don't it."

＊ A lion is roaming the jungle looking for something to eat. He comes across two men, one sitting under a tree reading a book and the other typing away at his typewriter. The lion quickly pounces on the man reading the book and eats him—because even the King of the Jungle knows that readers digest and writers cramp.

＊ Zoo owner, to new keeper: "You idiot. You left the door to the lions' cage open all night." Keeper: "So what? Who's going to steal a lion?"

＊ A lion is walking through the jungle when it comes across a monkey. "Who's the King of the Jungle?" says the lion. "You are, Sire," says the monkey, hurrying up a tree. Next the lion comes across a hippo in a river. "Who's the King of the Jungle?" says the lion. "You are, Sire," says the hippo, ducking under the water. Next, the lion comes across an elephant. "Who's the King of the Jungle?" says the lion. The elephant lets out a bellow, grabs the lion by the tail and starts beating it against a tree. "Now…look…here," says the lion. "There's…no need…to get…testy…just… because you…don't know… the answer…"

# LOGIC

＊ I think sex is better than logic, but I can't prove it.

＊ Someone who thinks logically provides a nice contrast to the real world.

# LOST AND FOUND

＊ "I was walking down the street and saw a sign on a post. It said 'Reward. Lost $50. If found, just keep it.'" *Steven Wright*

＊ A man walks up to a house and says, "Hello. I'm looking for the people who live here." "Well," says the man at the door. "You've come to the right place."

✳ Of course the thing you've lost is going to turn up in the last place you look. You're not going to keep looking for it once you've found it, are you?

✳ "Once when I was lost I saw a policeman, and asked him to help me find my parents. I said to him, 'Do you think we'll ever find them?' He said, 'I don't know, kid. There are so many places they can hide.'" *Rodney Dangerfield*

✳ A man loses his donkey and gets down on his knees to thank God. A passerby asks, "Why are you thanking God when you've lost your donkey?" The man replies, "Well, thank goodness I wasn't on it at the time or I'd be lost too."

✳ Two little boys come home with a football. "Where did you get that from?" asks their mother. "We found it," they say. "Are you absolutely sure it was lost?" asks Mom. "Yes," say the kids. "We saw the people looking for it."

✳ "I was walking down Fifth Avenue today and I found a wallet. I was gonna keep it rather than return it, but I thought: well, if I lost $150, how would I feel? And I realized I would want to be taught a lesson." *Emo Phillips*

# LUCK

✳ I don't believe in luck, but then how else do you explain other people doing so well?

✳ I'm so unlucky—when my ship finally came in, I was waiting at the airport.

✳ My luck is so bad—if I bought a cemetery, people would stop dying.

✳ "I busted a mirror and got seven years bad luck, but my lawyer thinks he can get me five." *Steven Wright*

# LYING

✳ "Who are you going to believe, me or your own eyes?" *Groucho Marx*

✳ All the years he lived, a lie never once passed his lips. He talked through his nose.

✳ The only thing that stops him from being a bare-faced liar is his mustache.

✳ Woman, to friend: "Does your husband lie awake at night?" Friend: "Yes, and he lies in his sleep as well."

✳ Don't talk to me about lie detectors; I married one.

# MAGIC

✳ A couple go to see a magic show in Vegas. After one especially amazing feat, the man yells, "How'd you do that?" "I could tell you, sir," replies the magician, "but then I'd have to kill you." After a pause the man yells back, "Okay, then. Just tell my wife!"

✳ A magician walks into a booking agent's office and enthuses about his marvelous new act. "I can saw a woman in half," he announces proudly. "You'll have to do better than that," replied the agent. "It's the oldest trick in the book." "Oh yes?" says the magician. "Lengthways?"

✳ A magician works on a cruise ship. The audience is different each week, so he does the same tricks over and over again. However, the captain's parrot sees the same show every week and starts to get bored. It even starts heckling and giving away the magician's secrets. "Look, it's not the same hat! He's hiding the flowers under the table. Hey, why are all the cards the ace of spades?" etc. The magician is furious but can't do anything, and the situation continues until the ship hits a reef and sinks. The magician finds himself floating on a piece of wreckage with, as fate would have it, the parrot. They both stare at each other in hatred but don't utter a word. This goes on for a whole day, then another, then another. On the fourth day the parrot can't contain itself any longer. "Okay," it says, "I give up. What did you do with the damn ship?"

# MAIL AND MAIL CARRIERS

✳ "I can't understand why you don't get any mail from me—perhaps it's because I haven't been writing." *Groucho Marx*

✳ People usually get what's coming to them—unless it was mailed.

✳ Mailman, to farmer: "I've had to walk five miles to deliver this letter to your farm." Farmer: "That's stupid. You should have mailed it."

✳ Two mailmen are standing on the sidewalk, chatting after finishing their routes, when one notices a slug crawling by. In a rage he stomps on the poor creature. "That was cruel," says the other mailman. "Why'd you do that?" The first mailman replies, "That son of a bitch has been following me all day!"

✳ What will Postman Pat be called when he retires? Pat.

✳ Wouldn't a self-addressed envelope be addressed "Envelope"?

✳ What does it mean when the flag outside the Post Office is flying at half mast? They're hiring.

# MARINE LIFE

✳ How do you circumcise a whale? You send down four skin divers.

# MARRIAGE

✳ "Before we were married, you told me you were well off." "Yes. Unfortunately I didn't realize just how well off."

✳ "Husbands are like fires. They go out when unattended." *Zsa Zsa Gabor*

✳ "I was married by a judge. I should have asked for a jury." *Groucho Marx*

✳ A couple come across a wishing well. The husband leans over, makes a wish, and throws in a penny. The wife makes a wish too, but she leans over too far, falls into the well, and drowns. The husband says, "Wow! It really works!"

✳ "My marriage is on the rocks again. Yeah, my wife just broke up with her boyfriend." *Rodney Dangerfield*

✳ "Why do you and your wife fight all the time?" "I don't know. She never tells me."

✳ A husband and wife are driving along when they see an injured skunk lying by the roadside. They decide to take it to a vet but don't have anything to carry it in. "Why not wrap it in your skirt?" suggests the husband. "What about the stink?" protests his wife. Her husband replies, "It'll just have to get used to it."

✳ A man is on his deathbed. "Grant me one last wish, my dear," he gasps pitifully to his wife. "Six months after I die, I want you to marry Joe." "But I thought you hated Joe," says his wife. "I do," says the man.

✳ A husband and wife visit a marriage guidance counselor. The wife complains that her husband doesn't pay her enough attention, so the counselor decides on some shock treatment. He leans over the desk and gives the woman a long passionate kiss. He then turns to the husband and says, "Your wife needs that kind of attention at least twice a week." "Okay," replies the husband. "But I can only get her here Tuesdays and Thursdays."

* A husband is living proof that a wife can take a joke.

* A husband says to his wife, "I was a fool when I married you." "I know," she replies. "But I was in love and didn't notice."

* A little boy says, "Dad, I've heard that in some parts of Africa, a man doesn't know his wife until he marries her." "Son," says the dad. "That happens everywhere."

* A little girl runs into her parents' room and demands that her mother tells her a story. "It's three in the morning, dear," says her mother. "Can't you just go back to bed?" The girl replies, "I tried, Mommy, but I can't sleep. Please tell me a story." Mother sighs and says, "Tell you what, you jump in bed with me, and when your daddy finally gets home, we'll both get to hear a story!"

* A man approaches a beautiful woman in a supermarket. "I've lost my wife somewhere," he says. "Do you mind if I talk to you for a moment?" "Okay," replies the woman. "But how's that going to help you find your wife?" "Easy," replies the man. "She always turns up when I start chatting with strange women."

* A man boards a plane. Sitting next to him is an elegant woman wearing the largest, most stunning diamond ring he's ever seen. He asks her about it. "This is the Klopman diamond," she says. "It's beautiful, but there is a terrible curse that goes with it." "What's the curse?" asks the man. The woman replies, "Mr. Klopman."

* A man has a check-up and the doctor finds something seriously wrong. He decides the news is too bad to tell the man directly so he breaks it to his wife. "Your husband is seriously ill," says the doctor. "The only way you can save his life is to offer him a completely stress-free existence. You must not contradict him in any way. He must give up his job so he can concentrate on restful hobbies. He must have three home-cooked meals every day, and live in an environment that is as tranquil, tidy, and germ-free as possible." In the car ride home, the husband says, "So what's going to happen to me?" The wife answers, "You're going to die."

* A woman marries a man expecting he will change, but he doesn't. A man marries a woman expecting that she won't change, and she does.

* A woman puts an ad in the paper saying, "Husband wanted." The next day she gets a hundred letters all saying the same thing: "You can have mine."

* A man is walking down the street when he hears a voice shouting, "Stop! Take one more step and you'll be killed!" The man stops and a brick crashes on to the path in front

of him. The man looks around but can't see who shouted the warning. A few moments later the man is crossing a road when the same voice yells, "Stop! Don't step off the curb!" A car jumps a red light and zooms past, just missing the man. Again he looks around but can't see who shouted. An hour later the man is getting on a ferry when the voice yells, "Don't do it! You'll drown!" The man steps off the ferry then watches it sink midstream a few minutes later. The man looks around but still can't see who shouted. He calls out, "Who's there?" "It's me. Your guardian angel," replies the voice, "I watch over everything you do." "You rotten bastard!" shouts the man. "What d'you mean?" replies the voice. "I just saved your life three times." "Yes," replies the man, "but where were you on my wedding day?"

✳ A man rushes into his house and yells to his wife, "Martha, pack up your things! I just won the lottery!" Martha shouts back, "Shall I pack for warm weather or cold?" The man replies, "I don't care, just as long as you're out of the house by noon!"

✳ A policeman on a motorcycle pulls over a car. "What's up?" says the driver. "Your wife fell out the passenger door three miles back," says the policeman. "Thank goodness for that," says the driver. "I thought I'd gone deaf."

✳ Priest to woman: "I don't think you'll ever find another man like your late husband." Woman: "Who's going to look?"

✳ A prospector in the Wild West is crossing the mountains in a horse and wagon. With him is his daughter and $10,000 in cash. Suddenly the pair are stopped by a bandit who searches the wagon then rides off with it. "Dang it!" says the prospector. "There goes my $10,000!" "No, Pa," says his daughter. "Look. I managed to hide the money in my mouth." "Jeepers!" says the prospector. "If only your ma were here, we could have saved the horse and wagon too!"

✳ A third-grade teacher is getting to know her pupils on the first day of school. She turns to one little girl and says, "And what does your daddy do?" The girl replies, "Whatever Mommy tells him to."

✳ A woman worries about the future until she gets a husband. A man never worries about the future until he gets a wife.

✳ A tramp approaches a man in the street and asks for money. "Will you spend the money on drink?" asks the man. The tramp shakes his head. "Will you waste it on card games?" asks the man. The tramp shakes his head. "Then come home with me," says the man. "Why?" asks the tramp. The man replies, "I want my wife to meet the kind of man who doesn't drink or gamble."

✳ A widower goes to a psychic to see if he can contact his late wife. The séance starts and he finds himself talking to her. "Honey," he says. "Are you happy?" "Yes, my husband," replies his wife. "Happier than you were with me?" asks the husband. "Much,

much happier," replies his wife. "Heaven must be an amazing place," says the husband. "I'm not in Heaven," replies his wife.

✳ A woman finds her husband sobbing in the kitchen. "What's the matter?" she asks. "You remember when your father found out you were pregnant and threatened me with twenty years in jail if I didn't marry you," says the husband. "Yes," says the woman. "Well, today was my release date."

✳ A woman is sick of her husband's drinking and decides to teach him a lesson. She dresses up like Satan, and when her husband returns after another bender, she jumps out on him from behind the door. "You don't scare me," slurs the man. "I married your sister."

✳ Attending a wedding for the first time, a little girl whispers to her mother, "Why is the bride dressed in white?" Mother decides to keep things simple and replies, "Because white is a happy color and today is the happiest day of her life." The girl thinks for a second, then says, "So why is the groom wearing black?"

✳ A woman turns to her husband on their silver wedding anniversary and says, "Darling, will you still love me when my hair turns grey?" Her husband replies, "Why not? I stuck with you through the other six shades."

✳ A woman's house has been ransacked but she doesn't report the crime till the next day. When a police officer comes around, he asks her why she delayed reporting the robbery. "I didn't know I had been robbed," replies the woman. "When I came in I thought my husband had been looking for a clean shirt."

✳ According to the latest survey, married men's favorite fantasy when making love is that their wives aren't fantasizing.

✳ Any married man should forget his mistakes—it's no use having two people remember the same thing.

✳ Going to a party with your wife is like going fishing with a game warden.

✳ Courtship is like looking at the pictures in a seed catalog. Marriage is what comes up in your garden.

✳ For sale: Twenty-volume encyclopedia. Good condition. No longer needed. Wife knows everything.

✳ For twenty years my wife and I were very happy. Then we met.

✳ Getting married is very much like going to a restaurant with friends. You order what you want, then when you see what the other person's got, you wish you'd ordered that.

✳ Harry invites his friend Dick for dinner. At the dinner table Harry talks to his wife using endearing terms such as Honey, My Love, Darling, Sweetheart, Pumpkin, etc. When Harry's wife is out of the room Dick says, "That's really nice. After all these years of marriage, you still call your wife pet names." Harry whispers back, "It sounds good, but to tell the truth, I forgot her real name three years ago."

✳ Harry went into town and got a bottle of wine for his wife—it was one of the best deals he'd ever made.

✳ He asked for her hand in marriage after an evening in the bar. It was very romantic. He actually climbed up on one knee to propose.

✳ He joined the Foreign Legion to forget his wife; unfortunately, the sergeant major looked just like her.

✳ He never got married. He said he didn't want to make the same mistake once.

✳ He was in a position to marry anyone he pleased. Unfortunately, he didn't please anyone.

✳ I got married to Miss Right. I just didn't realize her first name was "Always."

✳ Husband to wife: "I hear you've been telling everyone that I'm an idiot." Wife: "Sorry, I didn't know it was a secret."

✳ Husband to wife: "Put your coat on, I'm going to the bar." Wife: "Oh that's nice, are you taking me for a drink?" Husband: "No, I'm turning the heat off."

✳ Husband to wife: "You have a flat chest and hairy legs. Tell me, have you ever been mistaken for a man?" "No," replies his wife. "Have you?"

✳ I joined Bachelors Anonymous. Every time I feel like getting married, they send around a woman in curlers to nag me for a while.

✳ I live like a medieval knight. Every night I go to sleep with a battleaxe at my side.

✳ I never married because there was no need—I have three pets that serve the same purpose as a husband. I have a dog that growls every morning, a parrot that swears all afternoon, and a cat that comes home late every night.

✳ I take my wife everywhere, but she keeps finding her way back.

✳ I took two marriage vows. Silence and poverty.

✳ I wouldn't say she's been married a lot, but the church is trying to get her to pay for a new aisle carpet.

✳ If it weren't for marriage, men would go through life thinking they had no faults at all.

✳ If you want to drive your wife crazy, don't talk in your sleep, just smile.

✳ It's not true that married men live longer than single men. It only seems longer.

✳ If you want your wife to pay attention to every word you say, try talking in your sleep.

✳ I've been happily married for ten whole years. And ten out of thirty isn't bad.

✳ I've been very depressed lately. My wife's threatened to leave me. But even that hasn't cheered me up.

✳ I've often wanted to drown my troubles but I can't get my wife to go swimming.

✳ Ladies, don't forget the garage sale. It is a good chance to get rid of those things not worth keeping around the house. Bring your husbands.

✳ Lady Astor to Winston Churchill: "If you were my husband, I'd poison your brandy." Churchill: "If you were my wife, I'd drink it."

✳ Losing a wife can be hard. In most cases, it's damned near impossible.

✳ Love may be blind, but marriage is a real eye-opener.

✳ Make love, not war. Or if you want to do both—get married!

✳ Man is incomplete until he's married. Then he's finished.

✳ Man to friend: "When did you first realize your wife had stopped loving you?" Friend: "When she pushed me through the window and wrote for an ambulance."

✳ Marriage is a bed of roses—without the flowers.

✳ Marrying a man for his good looks is like buying a house for its paint.

✳ Marriages are made in Heaven—but then again, so are thunder and lightning.

✳ Marriage is love. Love is blind. Marriage is an institution. Therefore: Marriage is an institution for the blind.

✳ Marriage is not a lottery—you get a chance in a lottery.

✳ My wife and I have agreed never to go to bed angry with one another. So far we've been up for three weeks.

✳ "One night I came home. I figured, let my wife come on. I'll play it cool. Let her make the first move. She went to Florida." *Rodney Dangerfield*

✳ My wife and I have the secret to making a marriage last. Two times a week, we go to a nice restaurant and have a little wine and good food. She goes Tuesdays, I go Fridays.

✳ My wife and I lead a quiet life. The last time we went out together was when the gas boiler exploded.

✳ My wife constantly complains that I never listen to her…or something like that.

✳ My wife has a contract to give lectures—it's called a marriage license.

✳ On the way home from a party, a wife says to her husband, "Have I ever told you how handsome, sexy, and irresistible to women you are?" The husband is very flattered, "Why no, I don't think you have." His wife replies, "Then what in hell's name gave you that idea at the party?"

✳ Remember your wife is a romantic who still loves flowers and chocolates. Show her you remember as well by referring to them occasionally.

✳ She has her husband eating out of the palm of her hand—it saves on the washing-up.

✳ The best way to get your husband to do something is to suggest he's too old to do it.

✳ The husband who wants a happy marriage should learn to keep his mouth shut and his checkbook open.

✳ Since I got married I haven't looked at another woman. My wife put me off them.

✳ The trouble with some women is that they get all excited about nothing—and then they marry him.

✳ A woman applies for a job in a lemon grove. "Have you got any experience picking lemons?" asks the foreman. "I certainly have," says the woman. "I've been married four times."

✳ There's a lot to be said about marriage, but we try not to say it in front of the children.

✳ They are a fastidious couple. She's fast and he's hideous.

✳ Two married men are talking over the telephone. One says, "Ever since we got married, my wife has tried to change me. She got me to stop drinking, smoking, and running around until all hours of the night. She taught me how to dress well, enjoy the fine arts, gourmet cooking, classical music, even how to invest in the stock market." "Sounds like you may be bitter because she changed you so drastically," remarks his friend. "I'm not bitter," replies the first. "It's just—now that I'm so improved, I've realized she isn't good enough for me."

* Two strangers, a man and a woman, find themselves in the same sleeping car of a train. They both go to sleep, the man on the top bunk, the woman on the bottom. In the middle of the night, the man leans over and says, "I'm sorry to bother you, but I'm really cold and I was wondering if you could possibly get me another blanket?" "I have a better idea," replies the woman with a glint in her eye. "Just for tonight, let's pretend that we're married." "Sounds good to me," says the man. "Great," replies the woman. "Now go and get your own damn blanket!"

* Two women meet on the street. One asks the other about her husband. "Well, liquor doesn't agree with him, and he doesn't know how to play poker," says the first. "That's wonderful," says her friend. "It would be," says the first woman. "If he didn't drink and play poker."

* What do you call a woman who knows where her husband is every night? A widow.

* When a woman steals your husband, there is no better revenge than to let her keep him.

* Why is marriage a three-ring circus? First the engagement ring, then the wedding ring, then the suffering.

* Wife to husband: "I need a new dress." Husband: "What's wrong with the dress you've got?" Wife: "It's too long, and the veil keeps getting in my eyes."

* Wife to husband: "Let's go out and have some fun tonight!" Husband: "Okay, but if you get home before I do, leave the hall light on."

* Wife to husband: "When I married you, you said you had an ocean-going yacht!" Husband: "Shut up and row."

* Wife to husband: "You certainly made a fool of yourself last night. I just hope nobody realized you were sober."

* "Basically my wife was immature. I'd be at home in the bath, and she'd come in whenever she felt like it and sink my boats." *Woody Allen*

* "I think men who have pierced ears are better prepared for marriage. They have experienced pain and bought jewelry." *Rita Rudner*

* A little boy comes home from school and tells his mother he's been given a part in the school play. "That's wonderful," says his mother. "Who are you playing?" The boy says, "I'm playing the husband!" The mother scowls and says, "Go back and tell your teacher you want a speaking part."

* "Why don't you go home to your wife. Better yet, I'll go home to your wife and, outside of the improvement, she won't notice any difference." *Groucho Marx*

✳ A man enters a bar and orders a double martini. After he has finished the drink, he looks inside his shirt pocket, then orders another double martini. After he has finished it, he looks inside his shirt pocket again and orders yet another double martini. The bartender says, "Why do you look inside your shirt pocket every time you order a refill?" The man replies, "I'm looking at a photo of my wife. When she starts looking good, I know it's time to go home."

✳ A woman goes to the doctor for a check-up. When she gets home, her husband asks, "So how did the appointment go?" She replies, "He said, I have the body of a twenty-year-old." Her husband says, "Oh yeah? And what did he have to say about your forty-year-old ass?" The woman replies, "Your name didn't come up."

✳ A woman is talking with her new neighbor—"I hope you don't mind my saying, but you and your husband don't seem to have an awful lot in common. Why on earth did you get married?" "It was the old business of 'opposites attract,'" replies the neighbor. "He wasn't pregnant and I was."

✳ After a whirlwind romance, a woman and an older millionaire decide to get married. The woman is worried that they don't know enough about each other, but the millionaire believes it will be more fun to discover each other in wedlock. On their honeymoon, the millionaire leaps from the diving board of their hotel pool and executes a perfect dive. "I used to be a diving champion when I was younger," he tells his wife. "Y'see, I told you it would be fun getting to know each other this way." The woman agrees, then gets in the pool and does fifty lengths in a row. "Wow," says her husband. "I'll bet you used to be some sort of Olympic endurance swimmer." "No," replies his wife. "I was a whore in Venice who used to work both sides of the canal."

✳ An old man and his wife are having their first argument after many years of marriage. He says, "When we got married, you promised to love, honor, and obey!" "I know," replies his wife. "But I didn't want to start an argument in front of all those people."

✳ Girl to fiancé: "When we're married, I want to share all your troubles and worries." Fiancé: "But I don't have any troubles and worries." Girl: "I know, but we're not married yet."

✳ Little Mary is at her first wedding. When it's over, she asks her mother, "Why did the lady change her mind?" "What do you mean?" asks mother. "Well," replies Mary. "She went down the aisle with one man and came back with another."

✳ He named the street he built after his wife. It was very apt, as she was cold, hard, cracked, and only got plowed around Christmas.

✳ I can remember where I got married. I can remember when I got married. I just can't remember why.

✳ If your dog was barking at the back door and your wife was knocking on the front door, who would you let in first? The dog—at least he would shut up once he was in.

✳ Marriage certificate—another name for a work permit.

✳ My husband has a split personality—and I hate both of them.

✳ My wife keeps telling me I shouldn't pee in the bath—or if I really have to I should at least wait till she gets out.

✳ Personally, I think one of the greatest things about marriage is that, as both husband and father, I can say anything I want to around the house. Of course, no one pays the least bit of attention.

✳ The old couple next door are having a "Football Romance"—each is waiting for the other to kick off so they can get some action.

✳ Things have reached crisis point in Beryl's marriage. "If things are so bad," her friend advises her. "Then you should leave your husband." "I would," says Beryl. "If only I could think of a way of doing it that wouldn't make him happy."

✳ Three women are talking about their love lives. The first says, "My husband is like a Rolls Royce, smooth and sophisticated." The second says, "Mine is like a Porsche, fast and incredibly powerful." "Mine's like an old Chevy," says the third. "It needs a hand start. Then you have to jump on quick once you've got it going."

✳ Tom and Harry are each having a shave at the barber's. Tom's barber starts slapping after-shave on his face. "Don't do that," protests Tom. "My wife will think I smell like a brothel." Harry looks up at his barber and says, "You can put as much on me as you want—my wife doesn't know what a brothel smells like."

✳ What's it called when a woman is paralyzed from the waist down? Marriage.

✳ Wife to husband: "One more word and I'm going straight back to Mother!" Husband: "Taxi!!"

✳ If it weren't for marriage, women would have to spend most of their adult lives arguing with complete strangers.

✳ A wife tries to explain the purchase of a set of expensive underwear to her husband. "After all, dear," she says. "You wouldn't expect to find fine perfume in a cheap bottle, would you?" "No," replies her husband. "And I wouldn't expect to find gift-wrapping on a dead beaver."

✳ My husband and I married for better or worse. He couldn't do better, and I couldn't do worse.

✳ I know of no one who is happily married, except my husband.

✳ Marriage is a little like having a meal at a self-service buffet: you get exactly what you want, but when you see what another man's got on his plate, you want a bit of that as well.

✳ "I love being married. I was single for a long time, and I just got so sick of finishing my own sentences." *Brian Kiley*

✳ Harry is strolling through a cemetery when he comes across a man weeping over a grave. "Why did you have to go?" sobs the man. "Why? Why?" Harry stops to offer some words of comfort. "I'm so sorry for your loss," he says. "Is that your wife's grave?" "No," sniffles the man. "It belongs to her first husband."

✳ Tom was a model husband. Mind you, he wasn't a working model.

✳ My wife is temperamental. Fifty percent temper and 50 percent mental.

✳ My wife has given me a reason to live—revenge.

✳ My wife treats me like a god—every evening at dinner I get a burnt offering.

✳ I fell in love with my wife at second sight. The first time, I didn't know she had money.

✳ "A man in love is incomplete until he's married. Then he's finished." *Zsa Zsa Gabor*

✳ After my honeymoon I felt like a new man. Unfortunately, so did my wife.

✳ Man to friend: "My wife's a peach." Friend: "Because she's so soft and juicy?" Man: "No, because she has a heart of stone."

✳ A wife and her husband are arguing. "When we got married, you said you'd die for me!" shouts the woman. "Well, now's the time!"

✳ Looking back over the years that we've been together, I can't help but wonder: what the hell was I thinking?

# MARRIAGE: ADULTERY

✳ "Eighty percent of married men cheat in America. The rest cheat in Europe." *Jackie Mason*

✳ "Men would like monogamy better if it sounded less like monotony." *Rita Rudner*

✳ A couple are celebrating their golden wedding anniversary when the husband asks his wife if she's ever been unfaithful. "Three times," answers the wife. "Remember when you needed money to start up your business and no one would give you any? Well I slept with the bank manager to secure you a loan." "You made that sacrifice for me?" asks the astonished husband. "That was wonderful of you. What was the second time?" "Remember that operation you needed that no one would perform because it was too dangerous? Well, I slept with the surgeon so he'd do it." "Oh my God," says the husband. "You saved my life. And what was the third time?" "Well," says his wife. "Remember when you wanted to be president of the golf club and you were fifty-two votes short…?"

✳ A couple are sitting in a restaurant when the man suddenly slips under the table. His female companion doesn't seem to notice, so the waiter says, "Madam. Is your husband all right? He's slipped on the floor." The woman replies, "He's not my husband. My husband just walked through the door."

✳ A husband and wife are trying to save for their vacation. The husband suggests that he put a $20 note in a jar every time they have sex. Three months later the man counts the money and finds over $700. "How did that happen?" asks the husband. "We only had sex six times." His wife replies, "Yes, but not everyone's as stingy as you are."

✳ A farmer comes home from the fields early and sees a light on in his bedroom. Suspecting foul play, he grabs his shotgun and creeps up the stairs. He bursts into the bedroom and finds one of his farmhands naked, in bed with his wife. The farmhand stands up and shouts, "Don't shoot! For God's sakes give me a chance!" The farmer aims his gun and says, "Okay, I'll give you a chance—now swing 'em!"

✳ A husband suspects his wife is having an affair. He needs to go on a business trip for several days, so he sets a trap for her. He puts a bowl of milk under the bed. From the bed springs, he suspends a spoon. He has it calibrated so that her weight on the bed will not drop the spoon into the milk. But, if there is any more weight than that, the spoon will drop into the milk, and he will detect it upon his return. He comes home several days later. The first thing he does is reach under the bed and retrieve the bowl—which is now full of butter.

✳ A farmer's son accompanies his father on a trip to buy a cow. The farmer prods the cow all over, strokes its sides, looks in every nook and cranny, and even lifts its tail so he can peer up its rear end. "Y'see," explains the farmer. "You have to give it a real going over before you know if it's worth paying money for." The next day the boy runs up to his father and says, "Dad! I just saw Mommy and the mailman behind the barn. I think he's planning on buying her!"

✳ A husband comes home early and finds his wife, Mary, lying naked on the bed, dying of a heart attack. He picks up the phone to call the doctor when his young son shouts out, "Dad! There's a nude man in the closet!" The husband opens the closet door and finds his best friend naked inside. "I don't believe it!" shouts the man. "Mary's dying on the bed and you're playing games with the kids?"

✳ A knight goes off on the Crusades, but defends his wife's honor by equipping her with a chastity belt embedded with razor blades. A year later he returns and orders all his retainers to drop their pants. They do so and the knight sees that all but one man have shredded privates. He stands before the unshredded man and says, "For your loyalty I shall give you my best horse and one hundred acres of land." The man replies, "Oh, hank u ery uch."

✳ A little boy goes to his mother and says, "Mommy, every night I hear you and Daddy making noises and when I look in your room you're bouncing up and down on him." His mother thinks quickly and says, "Oh, well, I'm bouncing on Daddy's tummy because he's fat and that makes him thin again." The boy says, "Well, that won't work." "Why not?" asks his mother. The boy replies, "Because the lady next door comes by every afternoon and blows him back up again!"

✳ A little girl goes up to her father and says, "Daddy, when my cat died, why did it lie on its back with its legs in the air?" Daddy replies, "Well, its legs were up like that to make it easier for Jesus to grab hold of him and pull him up to Heaven." "Oh my gosh," says the girl. "That means Mommy almost died this morning!" "What d'you mean?" asks Dad. "Well," replies the girl. "When I looked into Mommy's room, she was lying on the bed with her legs in the air shouting 'Jesus! Jesus! I'm coming!' and if it hadn't have been for the mailman holding her down, He would have gotten her!"

✳ A Mafia don is on his death bed and calls his eldest son to him. "My boy," he says. "I want you to have this family heirloom." So saying, he pulls out a gun and hands it to his boy. "Gee, Pop," replies the son. "Y'know I don't like guns. If you want to leave me something, why not give me your watch?" "I see," says the indignant don. "You don't want my gun, huh. So tell me, when you get home and find your wife in bed with the mailman, wadya going to do? Shoot him? Or point at your watch and say, 'Hey, buddy, time's up'?"

✳ A man comes home and finds his best friend in bed with his wife. "You bastard," he says. "I've known you since school. You were my best man and my son's godfather. I lent you money…Stop doing that when I'm talking to you!"

✳ A man comes home and finds his wife in bed with the milkman. "What are you doing?" shouts the man. The woman turns to the milkman and says, "There. I told you he doesn't know the first thing about sex."

✳ A man wants to find out if both his wife and his mistress are faithful to him, so he sends them on the same cruise. When they're back he casually asks his wife about the behavior of the passenger he knew to be his mistress. "She was terrible," replies his wife. "She slept with every man on the ship." The disappointed man then asks his mistress about the passenger he knew was really his wife. "She was a real lady," says the mistress. "She came on board with her husband and never once left his side."

✳ A man goes into a magic shop and sees a pair of "nudie" glasses for sale. "What do they do?" asks the man. "They let you see everyone in the nude," says the storekeeper. "Why not try them on?" So the man tries on the glasses, and immediately everyone he looks at is in the nude. The storekeeper is nude, his assistant is nude, even a passerby looking in the window is nude. The man buys the glasses and goes out into the street to look at everyone in the nude. After an hour of fun he decides to sneak home and surprise his wife with his new toy. He gets back, creeps in the living room, and finds his wife and his neighbor nude on the couch. "Surprise!" he shouts, coming into the room. "What do you think of my new glasses?" He takes them off and is surprised to see that his wife and neighbor are still naked. "Damn!" he says. "I've only had them an hour and they're broken already!"

✳ "Last night my wife met me at the front door. She was wearing a sexy negligee. The only trouble was, she was coming home." *Rodney Dangerfield*

✳ A man is in the back of his car having sex with a woman he picked up in a bar. The woman is insatiable and keeps demanding more. Finally the man has to have a break and steps out to smoke a cigarette. Once out of the car he notices a man nearby struggling to change the tire on his pick-up truck. The first man goes over and says, "Look, I've got a really hot date in that car and I can't keep up with her. If I change your tire, will you go in there and have sex with her? I really need a rest. It's pitch black in there, so she won't know the difference." The second man agrees and jumps in the back of the car, which soon starts to rock rhythmically. A passing policeman spots this and shines a flashlight in the back of the car. "What's going on in there?" he says. The man replies, "I'm having sex with my wife." "Why can't you do that at home?" asks the policeman. The man replies, "Because I didn't realize it was my wife till you shone that flashlight in her face."

✳ A marine is stationed on a remote Pacific island. He writes to his wife, asking for something to while away the hours and keep his mind off all the beautiful native women. His wife sends him a harmonica and suggests he learn to play it. A year later the marine comes home to his wife and says, "Baby, I'm so love-starved! Let's go to bed right now!" "Sure," she says. "But first, play me something on the harmonica."

✳ A man walks into a bar and orders a beer. "Certainly, sir," replies the bartender. "That'll be one penny." "One penny for a beer!" exclaims the man. "That's incredible! How much is the food in this place?" "I'd recommend the steak dinner," says the bartender. "You get a 16-ounce steak, potatoes, salad, and a dessert for three pennies." "That's amazing," says the man. "How do manage to make a profit with such low prices?" "You'd have to ask the owner," replies the bartender. "But he's not here right now, he's upstairs with my wife." "What's he doing up there?" asks the man. "The same as I'm doing to his business," replies the bartender.

✴ A pair of newlyweds are arguing on their honeymoon. The couple promised to be open and honest with each other, but the husband still won't tell his wife how many sex partners he's had. "Look," he says. "If I tell you, you'll just get angry." "No, I won't," she replies. "Cross my heart and hope to die." "Okay, then," says the man. "Let me think. There was one, two, three, four, five, you, seven, eight…"

✴ A police officer gets off work four hours early and gets home at two in the morning. Not wanting to wake his wife, he undresses in the dark, creeps into the bedroom, and starts to climb into bed. As he does so his wife says, "Dear, would you go down to the all-night drugstore and get me some aspirin? I've got a splitting headache." "Certainly, honey," says the policeman and, feeling his way across the dark room, he gets dressed and walks over to the drugstore. When he arrives, the pharmacist looks at him in surprise, "Don't I know you?" he says. "I thought you were a policeman?" "I am a policeman. What about it?" says the officer. "Just curious," replies the pharmacist. "I just wondered what the heck you're doing dressed like a fire chief?"

✴ A private detective is reporting to his female client. "Yesterday I followed your husband to two bars on Elm Street, three on Maple, and finally to the Humpmore Motel," he says. "I see," says the woman. "And d'you think that's enough grounds for divorce?" "I'm not sure," says the detective. "After all he was following you at the time."

✴ A woman is in bed with her husband's best friend. The phone rings, and the friend hears her say, "Uh-huh, sure, wonderful. Okay. Uh-huh. Yep. That's fine. Okay, bye." She turns to her lover and says, "That was John. Don't worry, he won't be home for hours — he's out playing cards with you."

✴ A wife is in bed with her lover when they hear hubby coming up the stairs. There's no time to get dressed. The man runs to hide in the en suite bathroom while the wife pushes his clothes under the bed. The husband bursts through the bedroom door. "What are you doing lying naked on the bed?" he asks. "Darling, I heard you coming and got ready to receive you," she replies. "Great," says her husband. "I'll just go into the bathroom to clean up." The husband goes into the bathroom and finds a man clapping his hands together in midair. "Who the hell are you?" he asks. "I'm from the exterminator company," replies the man. "Your wife called me in to get rid of these pesky moths." The husband yells, "But you've got no clothes on!" The man looks down at his body, jumps backward in surprise and shouts, "The little bastards!"

✴ A woman is in bed with her lover when she hears her husband come in the front door. There's no time for the lover to escape, so the wife makes him stand in the corner and covers him with talcum powder. "Just stay still and pretend you're a statue," she tells him. The husband comes in and his wife says, "Hello, dear. I was just admiring our new statue.

You remember the Smiths bought one for their bedroom? Well, I thought we could have one for ours." The husband admires the statue, then the couple go downstairs for dinner. An hour later, the husband returns with a glass of milk and a sandwich. He puts them on a table and says, "There you go. When I was playing statues at the Smiths, I stood there for three days without so much as a drink of water."

✳ After twenty years of marriage, they are still in love. She loves the gardener, and he loves the lady next door.

✳ Harry goes to confession and tells the priest he's been having affairs with four different women from the neighboring villages. "How could you do such a thing?" asks the priest. "It's easy," says Harry. "I've got a moped."

✳ An artist and his model are kissing on the sofa when they hear the front door open. "Oh my God! It's the wife," shouts the artist. "Quick! Get your clothes off!"

✳ Bob calls home one afternoon to see what his wife is making for dinner. "Hello?" says a little girl's voice. "Hi, honey, it's Daddy," says Bob. "Is Mommy near the phone?" "No, Daddy," says the girl. "She's upstairs in the bedroom with Uncle Frank." Bob says, "But you don't have an Uncle Frank." "Yes, I do," says the girl. "He's upstairs in the bedroom with Mommy!" "Okay, then," says Bob. "Here's what I want you to do. Put down the phone, knock on the bedroom door, and shout to Mommy and Uncle Frank that Daddy's car has just pulled up outside the house." A few minutes later the little girl comes back to the phone. "I did what you said, Daddy. When they heard me, Mommy jumped out of bed and ran around screaming. Then she tripped over the rug and fell out of the window and now she's dead." "Oh my God!" says Bob. "And what about Uncle Frank?" "He jumped out the back window into the swimming pool," says the girl. "But he must have forgotten that you took out all the water last week, so now he's dead as well." There's a long pause, then Bob says, "Swimming pool? Is this 555-7039?"

✳ I have the most wonderful wife in the whole world. I just hope her husband never finds out.

✳ Contrary to popular belief, Harry's mother and father were married. Not to each other. But they were married.

✳ Dick and Harry die and go to Heaven. Saint Peter meets them at the Pearly Gates and tells them that they will each get a car depending on how faithful they were in life. Harry's record is very good, he was married for twenty-four years and was completely faithful, so he gets a Rolls-Royce. Dick, on the other hand, had five affairs during his marriage and only gets a third-hand Ford Fiesta. A week later Dick is driving through Heaven when he passes Harry crying by the roadside. "What's the matter?" asks Dick. "I thought you'd be really enjoying that Rolls-Royce." "I was," sobs Harry. "But then I saw my wife on a skateboard."

✳ I got home and found a man in bed with my wife. I said, "Who said you could sleep with my wife?" He said, "Everybody."

✳ In all my years of marriage, I've never stopped being romantic, but if my wife finds out, she'll kill me.

✳ Harry's wife decides to take him to a lap-dancing club as a surprise birthday present. Harry protests, but his wife drags him along anyway. At the entrance, the manager greets him saying, "Hello, Harry. How you doing?" "How does he know your name?" asks Harry's wife. "Uh, I knew him from school," explains Harry. Inside the club, the coat check girl says, "Good evening, Harry. How are you tonight?" Harry hurriedly explains that she's a friend of a coworker. When they sit down, the waitress comes up and says, "Great to see you, Harry. Would you like your usual?" Harry tells his wife that she's a member of his tennis club. Finally a pole dancer walks past and says, "Hi, Harry! Stay there and I'll come by and do you a special." This is too much for Harry's wife, who drags him outside and starts screaming at him. The doorman hails them a taxi. "Oh boy, Harry," he says. "You sure picked an ugly one tonight."

✳ Lawyer to woman: "Your husband says you deceived him." Woman: "On the contrary, he deceived me. He said he'd be out all night but came home suddenly at eight-thirty."

✳ Man to friend: "Last month I met the most beautiful girl in the world. I wanted to marry her, but her family objected." Friend: "Didn't her parents like you?" Man: "They liked me, but her husband and children didn't."

✳ Little Johnny runs into class late. "I'm sorry, Miss," he says, "I'm late because I had to make my own breakfast this morning." Teacher accepts this excuse, but as a punishment, makes him stand at the front of the class and answer some geography questions. "Now, Johnny," says the teacher, "Tell me where the Canadian border is." "In bed with Mom," replies Johnny. "That's why I had to make my own breakfast."

✳ Married men have two ages. When they want to remain faithful but don't, and when they want to be unfaithful but can't.

✳ On the day of their wedding, a groom makes his bride promise never to look in the top drawer of his desk. She agrees, and twenty-five years pass before curiosity overcomes her and she has a peek inside. In the desk, she's surprised to find three golf balls and a huge pile of cash. Later that day she confronts her husband and demands to know what is going on. "I'll confess," says the husband. "Every time I've had an affair, I've put a golf ball in the desk." "You've had three affairs?" says the wife. "Well, I'm not happy, but after twenty-five years, I suppose I can live with it. Now tell me, where did all that money came from?" "Well," says the husband. "Every time I collected a dozen balls, I sold them."

✳ One day Tom notices that his coworker, Bob, has started wearing an earring. "Hey, Bob," says Tom. "I didn't know you were into earrings." "Yeah, sure," says Bob. "So how long have you been wearing one?" asks Tom. Bob replies, "Ever since my wife found it in our bed."

✳ One night, Little Johnny's father overhears his son saying his prayers. "God bless Mommy, Daddy, and Granny. Good-bye Grampa." The next day Grandfather dies. A month or so later his father again overhears Little Johnny at prayer. "God bless Mommy and Daddy. Good-bye Granny." The next day Grandmother dies. Father begins to worry. Two weeks later he again hears Little Johnny praying—"God bless Mommy. Good-bye Daddy." Father nearly has a heart attack and spends all the next day in fear of his life. However, he manages to survive and returns home after work. "I had a really bad day today," he says to his wife. "Don't tell me about bad days," replies his wife. "This morning the mailman dropped dead on the porch!"

✳ Three men are talking in a bar. "I think my wife is having an affair with an electrician," says one. "I found a pair of pliers under our bed, and they certainly aren't mine." "I think my wife is having an affair with a plumber," says the second. "I found a blow-torch under our bed, and it sure isn't mine." "I think my wife is having an affair with a horse," says the third. "When I got home yesterday, there were two jockeys in the closet."

✳ Tom and Dick are playing a round of golf when they get stuck behind a pair of female players. Eventually Tom gets tired of waiting and walks over to ask if they can play through. However, he soon scuttles back. "When I got closer, I realized it was my wife and mistress," says Tom. "You go and ask them instead." Dick walks over to the women, but he too soon hurries back. "Small world," he says.

✳ Looking very concerned, Tom comes home to his wife. "I've just been told our milkman has made love to every woman in this street apart from one." "Really," says his wife. "I bet it's that snooty cow at number 27."

✳ Wife to husband: "Y'know I can still get into the same skirts I wore before we got married." Husband: "I wish I could."

✳ Two men are sitting at a bar. One says to the other, "I heard about this great place. You get all your drinks paid for, and at the end of the evening, you get laid for free." "That sounds fantastic," says his friend. "Have you ever been?" "No," says the first. "But my wife goes there all the time."

✳ "People have different opinions on things. For example, to me, my girlfriend is the most wonderful beautiful person in the world. But to my wife…" *Jackie Mason*

✳ A psychiatrist is talking to a female patient about her sex life. "When you make love, do you ever look your husband in the face?" "I only did it once," replies the woman. "But he looked very angry." "And why do you think that was?" asks the psychiatrist. The woman replies, "Because he was looking in through the window at the time."

✳ After twenty years of marriage, a woman discovers that her husband is impotent. In fact, all their married life, he'd been pleasuring her with a strap-on dildo. "That's awful," says the wife. "How could you deceive me like that?" "I'm sorry about the dildo," replies her husband. "But I'm kind of interested in hearing you explain our three children."

✳ Always talk to your wife when you're making love—assuming there's a phone handy.

✳ An infamous stud with a long list of conquests walks into his local bar and orders a drink. The man looks worried, and the bartender asks him if anything is wrong. "Some pissed-off husband wrote to me and said he'd kill me if I didn't stop screwing his wife." "So why don't you just stop?" says the bartender. "I can't," says the man. "He didn't sign his name!"

✳ Arriving home unexpectedly, a tired executive is shocked to discover his wife in bed with his neighbor. "Since you're in bed making love to my wife!," shouts the furious man. "I'm going next door to sleep with yours!" "Go ahead," replies the neighbor. "The rest will do you good."

✳ I don't mind this role reversal business at all. I'm happy to stay at home while my wife goes out to work. I'm happy to do the dishes and the rest of the housework—and besides, our milkman is fantastic in bed.

✳ I had two women in my bed the other day. I got home from work and discovered my wife is having a lesbian affair.

✳ Harry goes up to Dick and says, "Hey, d'you like women with big sagging boobs and hairy nipples?" "No," replies Dick. "And do you like women with spotty backsides and stretch-marked stomachs?" continues Harry. "No," replies Dick. "And do you like women with bad breath and yeast infections?" "Certainly not," replies Dick. "Good," says Harry. "Then you won't mind staying the hell away from my wife."

✳ Harry walks into the bar. "Hi, Harry," say his buddies. "You put on a great show with your old lady last night. You left the light on in your bedroom and we could see everything going on projected on the curtains." "Sorry, guys," says Harry. "The joke's on you—I wasn't home last night."

✳ Man to friend: "I had it all—money, a huge house, a big car, the love of a beautiful woman, then pow! It was all gone!" Friend: "What happened?" Man: "My wife found out."

✳ Some husbands come in handy around the house. Others come in unexpectedly.

✳ Two women go for a girls' night on the town and get plastered. Staggering home, they become desperate for a pee and duck into a cemetery to relieve themselves. When they've finished, the first woman uses her panties to wipe herself then throws them away. The other woman is wearing expensive panties, so wipes herself with a card from a nearby wreath. The following morning the two husbands are comparing notes over the phone. One says, "I think we need to start keeping a closer eye on our wives. My wife came home without any panties on." The other replies, "Tell me about it. My wife came home with a card stuck to her fanny that read 'We will never forget you.'"

✳ "There is one thing I would break up over, and that is if she caught me with another woman. I won't stand for that." *Steve Martin*

# MARRIAGE: ANNIVERSARIES

✳ A sixty-year-old couple are celebrating their fortieth wedding anniversary. During the celebration, a fairy appears and says that, since they have been such a loving couple, she'll give them each one wish. The wife wishes to travel around the world. The fairy waves her wand and poof! She has a handful of plane tickets. Next, it's the husband's turn. He pauses for a moment, then says, "I'd like to have a woman thirty years younger than I." So the fairy picks up her wand and poof! He's ninety.

✳ A couple married for forty years are revisiting the places they went to on their honeymoon. As they drive through the countryside, they pass a ranch surrounded by a deer fence. The wife says, "Sweetheart, let's do the same thing we did right here forty years ago." So the couple get out of the car and make frantic love against the fence. Back in the car, the husband says, "Darling, you went crazy out there! You sure never moved like that forty years ago—or any time since!" The wife replies, "Yeah? Well, forty years ago that fence wasn't electrified!"

✳ A farmer and his wife are preparing their wedding anniversary dinner. The wife says, "Should I go out and kill a chicken?" The husband replies, "Why blame a bird for something that happened twenty years ago?"

✳ He asked how they should celebrate their twenty-five years of marriage. She suggested a two-minute silence.

✳ On their fortieth wedding anniversary, a man says to his wife, "Whatever you want, just name it, and I'll buy it for you. It doesn't matter how much it costs. Just say what you'd like for our anniversary." She replies, "A divorce." "To be honest," he says. "I wasn't thinking of spending quite that much."

✳ Tom says to Harry, "You're having an anniversary soon, aren't you?" "Yes," says Harry. "A big one, twenty years." "Wow," says Tom. "What gift are you going to get your wife?" Harry replies, "A trip to Australia." "That's impressive," says Tom. "But how will you top that on your twenty-fifth anniversary?" "Don't know," says Harry. "I'll probably pay her fare back."

✳ A couple decide to celebrate their sixtieth wedding anniversary by booking the suite where they had their honeymoon. They have breakfast in bed, and the wife says, "My dear, this is so romantic. My breasts feel all warm and tingly." "I'm not surprised," replies her husband. "One's hanging in your coffee and the other's lying on my bacon."

# MARRIAGE: BIGAMY

✳ A bigamist is a man who leads a double wife.

✳ "Bigamy is having one wife too many. Monogamy is the same." *Oscar Wilde*

# MARRIAGE: DIVORCE

✳ "As soon as I get through with you, you'll have a clear case for divorce—and so will my wife." *Groucho Marx*

✳ "Instead of getting married again, I'm going to find a woman I don't like and give her a house." *Lewis Grizzard*

✳ A doctor tells a woman she can no longer touch anything alcoholic—so she gets a divorce.

✳ A man goes to court to get a divorce. "Why do you want a divorce?" asks the judge. The man replies, "Because I live in a two-story house." "That's not much of a reason to leave your wife," responds the judge. "Sure it is," replies the man. "Whenever I want some action in bed, she just has two stories; either she has a headache, or it's her time of the month."

✳ A quarter of all married men kiss their wife goodbye when they leave the house. Of these same men, 90 percent will kiss their house goodbye when their wife leaves.

✳ After forty years of marriage, Harry asks his wife, June, for a divorce. "A divorce? After all these years?" says June. "After we've been through so much together? What about the time you had your heart attack, who nursed you back to health? When your business went bust, who convinced the bank manager to give you a loan? After the house burned down, who helped you rebuild? After your sister died, who helped you get over it? What would you have done without me?" "Probably a lot better," says Harry. "After all these years I've finally figured out you're bad luck."

✳ An elderly man and his wife tell a friend they're getting divorced. "But you're ninety-five, and your wife is ninety-three. You've been married for seventy-two years!" says the friend. "Why do you want to separate now?" The wife replies, "To be honest, we haven't been able to stand the sight of each other for a long time. But we thought we should wait till all the children died before we split up."

✳ Dick had been trying to lose annoying weight for some time; unfortunately he couldn't afford to get divorced.

✳ Did you hear about the new "divorced" Barbie doll? It comes with all of Ken's stuff.

✳ Hell hath no fury like the lawyer of a woman scorned.

✳ Judge, to woman: "On what grounds do you wish to divorce your husband?" "Adultery," says the woman. "On what evidence?" queries the judge. The woman replies, "I'm certain he's not the father of my fourth child."

✳ Keep your marriage license in a very safe place. It's one of the most important documents you'll ever have. You can't get a divorce without it.

✳ My friend is engaged in a major custody battle. His wife doesn't want him, and his mother won't take him back.

✳ What do a hurricane, a tornado, a fire, and a divorce have in common? They are four ways you can lose your house!

✳ Why would you ever want to remarry an ex-husband? It's like finding some sour milk, putting it in the trash for a couple of days, and then saying to yourself, "Gee, I wonder if it'll taste any better now?"

✳ Woman, to lawyer: "I want to divorce my husband. He has a lousy memory!" Lawyer: "Why would you want to divorce him for that?" Woman: "Every time he sees a young woman, he keeps forgetting he's married!"

✳ "Divorce, from the Latin word meaning to rip out a man's genitals through his wallet." *Robin Williams*

✳ A newly divorced husband is attending a hearing to discuss his alimony payments. "After considering the matter, I've decided to award your wife $1,000 a month," says the

Judge. "That's very generous of you," says the man. "I might even slip her a few bucks myself."

✳ I knew a couple who broke up before their wedding photographs were developed. And they were taken with a Polaroid.

✳ Good: Your husband is not talking to you. Bad: He wants a divorce. Ugly: He's a lawyer.

# MARRIAGE: NEWLYWEDS

✳ A man returns from his honeymoon and his friend asks him how it went. "Terrible," replies the man. "On the first night I got up to go to the bathroom and, without thinking, I put a $50 note on her pillow." "Well, that's not so bad," replies the friend. "If she's upset, tell her it was a joke." "She wasn't upset," replies the man. "I got upset when she gave me $30 change."

✳ For a brief period, we were lovers. It was for the two weeks after we got married.

✳ Two newlyweds are on their honeymoon. As they undress for bed, the husband tosses his pants to his bride, saying, "Here, put these on." She puts them on but the waist is twice the size of her body. "I can't wear your pants," she says. "That's right," says her husband. "And don't you ever forget it. I wear the pants in this family." With that the bride throws him her panties. "Try these on," she says. The husband tries them on but finds he can only get them as far as his knees. "Hell," he says, "I can't get into your panties!" His bride replies, "That's right, and that's the way it's going to stay until you change your attitude."

✳ You know the honeymoon is pretty much over when you start to go out with the boys on Wednesday nights—and so does she.

✳ Michael gets married, but he's led a sheltered life and is unsure what to do on his wedding night. "For goodness sake!" shouts his wife. "Take your things off and put that thing you play with in the place where I pee!" So Michael does just what she says. He gets undressed and puts his accordion in the sink.

✳ Two brides meet in a honeymoon hotel. One says, "Does your husband snore in his sleep?" The other replies, "I don't know. We've only been married three days."

✳ Two bridegrooms in a honeymoon hotel compare notes on their first night. "How did you leave your wife this morning?" asks one. "On the bed, smoking," replies the other. "Wow," says the first. "Mine was just a little sore!"

# MARRIAGE: PROPOSALS

✳ "Marry me and I'll never look at another horse!" *Groucho Marx*

✳ A young lady comes back from a date looking sad. She says to her mother, "Jeff proposed to me." "Then why are you so sad?" asks her mother. "Because he also told me he was an atheist," says the girl. "He doesn't even believe there's a hell." Her mother replies, "Marry him anyway. Between the two of us, we'll show him how wrong he is."

# MARRIAGE: SERIAL MARRIAGE

✳ "How many husbands have you had?" "Do you mean apart from my own?" *Zsa Zsa Gabor*

✳ A twice-married wife runs up to her twice-married husband and says, "Come home quick! Your kids and my kids are beating up our kids."

✳ He's been married so often, his wedding certificate says "To whom it may concern..."

✳ He's been married so often, they don't issue him with a new marriage license now. They just punch the old one.

✳ Marriage is the triumph of imagination over intelligence. A second marriage is the triumph of hope over experience.

✳ She's been married so many times she has rice marks on her face.

✳ He's been married so often, he signs the wedding certificate in pencil.

# MARRIAGE: SEX

✳ "Before I got married to you, you said you were oversexed." "No. I said I was over sex."

✳ A man complains to his friend that sex with his wife has become boring. "Use your imagination," says the friend. "Why not try playing doctor for an hour? That's what I do." The man replies, "Wow, a whole hour. How do you make it last that long?" "It's easy," replies the friend. "I just keep her in the waiting room for fifty-six minutes."

✳ Did you hear about the new magazine for married men published by *Playboy*? It has the same pictures month after month after month after month after month…

✳ Dick asks Tom how he can put the spark back in his marriage. "Try being more daring and romantic," suggests Tom. "When you go home tonight, give her a big box of chocolates and a bottle of champagne then strip her down and make love to her on the living-room rug." Dick agrees to give it a try and goes home. The next day Tom asks how it went. "Did you surprise your wife like I suggested?" he asks. "Yes," replies Dick. "But I'm not sure who was the more surprised, my wife or her bridge group."

✳ Husband to wife: "After I shave in the morning, I feel ten years younger." Wife: "So why not try shaving before you go to bed?"

✳ Husband to wife: "Y'know darling, I can't remember the last time we made love." Wife: "I can. That's why we're not doing it again."

✳ Mandy to Sandra: "What do you think our husbands talk about when they're down at the bar?" "Probably the same things we talk about," replies Sandra. Mandy thinks for a moment then says, "Oh, the dirty bastards."

✳ A doctor is doing the rounds of a maternity ward. "And when is Mrs. Smith's baby due?" he asks the nurse. "The fifth of September," replies the nurse. "I see," says the doctor. "And how about Mrs. Jones?" "She's due on the fifth too," replies the nurse. "And Mrs. Evans?" says the doctor. "She's also due on the fifth," says the nurse. "And—don't tell me—Mrs. Brown is due on the fifth as well," says the doctor. "I don't think so," replies the nurse. "She didn't go on the church picnic."

✳ A doctor tells his patient that, after a long and active sex life, his penis is burned out, and he can only use it another thirty times. The man goes home and tells his wife the bad news. "That's terrible," she says. "With so few left we can't waste any. Let's make a list of special occasions." "Sorry," replies the man. "I already made a list. You're not on it."

✳ A husband has been having sex with his wife for thirty minutes when she looks up at him and says, "What's the matter, Fred. Why are you taking so long?" "Sorry," he says. "I just can't think of anyone…"

✳ A man comes home and finds his wife having sex with a bum. "How could you?" exclaims the husband. "It just sort of happened," replies his wife. "He came around asking for food, so I gave him last night's dinner that you didn't want. Then I thought he might as well have that shirt you don't like. Then I offered him those new brown shoes you never wear. Then he asked me if there was anything else you didn't use…"

✳ A man in a hotel bar sees a beautiful woman sitting alone at a table and goes over to chat her up. After talking to her for a while, he invites her back to his room. "I can't," says the woman. "I'm saving my virginity until I meet a man I can truly love." "That must be hard," says the man." "Oh I don't mind so much," says the woman. "It's my husband who's really pissed off."

✳ A man walks into a whorehouse and lays down $200. He says, "I want a girl that'll go to bed and just lie still!" The madam says, "But, sir, for $200, you could have the best girl in the house!" "No, thank you," replies the man. "I'm not horny, I'm just a little homesick!"

✳ A woman goes to see her doctor. "I've got a problem," she says. "Every time we're in bed and my husband climaxes, he lets out this ear-splitting yell." "That's quite natural," replies the doctor. "I don't see what the problem is." The woman replies, "The problem is, it wakes me up."

✳ How can you tell if your husband is dead? The sex is the same, but you get the remote.

✳ Husband to wife: "Dear, tonight why don't we try changing positions?" Wife: "Okay, you stand by the sink, and I'll lie on the sofa."

✳ Tom, Harry, and their wives decide to spice up their sex lives by swapping partners. Later that night Tom rolls over in bed and says, "Hey, Harry. What d'you suppose our wives are up to?"

✳ Two married friends are out drinking. One says to the other, "I can never sneak into the house after I've been out all night. I've tried everything. I turn the headlights off before I get to the driveway. I shut off the engine and coast into the garage. I take my shoes off and creep up the stairs. I get undressed in the bathroom. I do everything, but my wife still wakes up and yells at me for staying out so late." His friend replies, "Do what I do. I screech into the driveway, slam the front door, storm up the steps, throw my shoes into the closet, jump into bed, slap my wife's ass, and say, 'How about a blow job?' and she always pretends she's asleep."

✳ Two men are discussing their sex lives. "Does your wife ever let you do it doggie style?" asks the first. "Not exactly," replies the second, "She's more into the trick dog aspect of it." "I see," says the first. "Kinky stuff, is it?" "No," replies the second. "Whenever I make a move, she rolls over and plays dead."

✳ Why does a bride smile when she walks up the aisle? She knows she's given her last blow job.

✳ Woman to husband: "Why don't you ever call out my name when we're making love?" Husband: "I don't want to wake you."

# MARRIAGE: WEDDINGS

✳ "Now what is a wedding? Well, *Webster's* dictionary describes a wedding as the process of removing weeds from one's garden." *Homer Simpson*

✳ A couple apply for a wedding license. "Can I have your name?" asks the clerk. "David Smith," replies the man. "Jenny Smith," replies the woman. "Any connection?" asks the clerk. "Only the once," replies the woman. "That's when he knocked me up."

✳ A man goes up to a priest and says, "Excuse me, Reverend, but do you think a man should profit by the mistakes of others?" "No, I don't think he should," replies the priest. "In that case can I have my $40 back?" says the man. "$40? What d'you mean?" replies the priest. The man says, "That's what you charged for my wedding ceremony."

✳ I like to watch my wedding video running backward so I can watch myself walk out of the church a free man.

✳ The marriage got off to a bad start during the wedding service. The priest said, "You may now kiss the bride." And she said, "Not now. I've got a headache."

✳ A police officer stops a driver speeding down Main Street. "But Officer," the man says, "I can explain—" "Be quiet," snaps the officer. "I'm going to let you cool your heels in jail until the chief gets back." "But, Officer, I just wanted to say—" says the driver. "And I say keep quiet! You're going to jail!" replies the officer. A few hours later the officer looks in on his prisoner and says, "Lucky for you, the chief is at his daughter's wedding. He'll be in a good mood when he gets back." "Don't count on it," answers the driver. "I'm the groom."

✳ If "I am" is the shortest sentence in the world, what's the longest sentence? "I do!"

✳ I got a note from the bride thanking me for the wedding present I sent. She said it was just what she wanted and she'd use them every time she entertained guests. I'm a little worried. I gave her bedsheets.

# MARTIAL ARTS

✳ "Karate is a form of martial arts in which people who have had years and years of training can, using only their hands and feet, make some of the worst movies in the history of the world." *Dave Barry*

✳ My brother-in-law died. He was a karate expert who joined the army. The first time he saluted, he killed himself.

# MATH

✳ A mathematician and a farmer are traveling by train. They pass a flock of sheep in a meadow and the mathematician says, "There are 1,248 sheep out there." The farmer replies, "Amazing. By chance, I know the owner, and that figure is absolutely correct. How did you count them so quickly?" The mathematician replies, "Easy, I just counted the number of legs and divided by four."

✳ A zero and an eight are walking down the street. The zero turns to the eight and says, "Hey. Why have you got your belt pulled so tight?"

✳ There are ten kinds of people who understand binary—those who do and those who don't!

# MEDIA: NEWSPAPER HEADLINES

✳ Astronaut Takes Blame for Gas in Spacecraft.

✳ Chef Throws His Heart into Helping Feed Needy.

✳ Cold Wave Linked to Temperatures.

✳ Deer Kill 17,000.

✳ Drunk Gets Nine Months in Violin Case.

✳ Eye Drops off Shelf.

✳ Grandmother of Eight Makes Hole in One.

✳ Hospitals Sued by Seven Foot Doctors.

✳ If Strike Isn't Settled Quickly, It May Last a While.

✳ Include Your Children When Baking Cookies.

✳ Iraqi Head Seeks Arms.

✳ Is There a Ring of Debris Around Uranus?

✳ Kids Make Nutritious Snacks.

✳ Lansing Residents Can Drop Off Trees.

* Local High School Dropouts Cut in Half.

* Lung Cancer in Women Mushrooms.

* Man Struck by Lightning Faces Battery Charge.

* Milk Drinkers Are Turning to Powder.

* Miners Refuse to Work after Death.

* New Study of Obesity Looks for Larger Test Group.

* Panda Mating Fails; Veterinarian Takes Over.

* Plane Too Close to Ground, Crash Probe Told.

* Prostitutes Appeal to Pope.

* Queen Mary Having Bottom Scraped.

* Red Tape Holds Up New Bridge.

* Safety Experts Say School Bus Passengers Should Be Belted.

* Scientists Prove Sterility Is Inherited.

* Something Went Wrong in Jet Crash, Expert Says.

* Squad Helps Dog Bite Victim.

* Supreme Court Rules That Murderers Shall Not Be Electrocuted Twice for the Same Crime.

* Teacher Strikes Idle Kids.

* Hurricane Rips Through Cemetery: Hundreds Dead.

* War Dims Hope for Peace.

* William Kelly Was Fed Secretary.

# MEDIA: NEWSPAPERS

* A champion football team loses its best player, Roger Dicks, to a sports injury. The next day the newspaper headline reads "Team Will Play Without Dicks." The manager complains about this wording and the editor agrees to change it. The next day the headline reads "Team To Play With Dicks Out."

✳ A tourist is walking through a town in Alabama when he sees a dog mauling a child. The dog is extremely vicious, and the man has to kill it with a spade before it will let the child go. A newspaper editor runs up to the man and says, "That was the bravest thing I ever saw; tomorrow morning, the headline of my paper will read 'Local Man Slays Rabid Beast.'" "Thanks," says the man. "But I'm not local. I'm not from this town." The editor replies, "Then the headline will read 'Gallant Southern Gentleman Saves Child.'" "Actually, I'm not Southern," replies the man. "I'm from New York." Next morning, the headline reads "Yankee Murderer Executes Family Pet."

✳ To raise money for a new church roof, a priest buys a racehorse. However, when it arrives, it turns out he's bought a donkey by mistake. He decides to race the donkey anyway and is astonished when it comes in third. The next day the local paper carried the headline "Priest's Ass Shows." The next day the priest enters it in another race, and this time the donkey wins. The paper carries the headline "Priest's Ass Out In Front." The local bishop is upset by this publicity and orders the priest not to race the donkey. The paper's headline reads "Bishop Scratches Priest's Ass." Reading this, the bishop orders the priest to get rid of the donkey, so he gives it to a nun. Next day the paper reads "Nun Has Fine Ass." The outraged bishop then orders the nun to get rid of the donkey, and she sells it to a farmer. The next day the headlines read: "Nun Sells Ass For $25."

✳ I called the paper to put in an ad, but I couldn't tell the lady about it because it was classified.

✳ "Woke up, had a shave, did the *Times* crossword, had another shave." *Roger McGough*

# MENTAL HEALTH: MEMORY

✳ "I have a memory like an elephant. In fact elephants often consult me." *Noel Coward*

✳ "Men forget everything; women remember everything. That's why men need instant replays in sports. They've already forgotten what happened." *Rita Rudner*

✳ A woman is jogging through a park when he sees an old man sitting on a bench sobbing. "Can I help you?" she asks. "I don't think so," says the old man. "My life is perfect. I'm rich, I just married a twenty-year-old model, I have a beautiful house with a pool, and a private jet." "So why are you crying?" asks the woman. The old man sobs, "Because I can't remember where I live!"

✳ An old woman and her sister have been to a class designed to improve their memory. A friend asks the women what the name of their instructor was. "Oh dear," says the old woman. "What's the name of that flower with the thorns on the stem?" "D'you mean a rose?" says the friend. "That's the one," says the old woman. She turns to her sister and says, "Here, Rose! What's the name of that instructor?"

✳ I have an excellent memory except for three things; names, faces, and…something else.

✳ One good thing about extreme memory loss is that you do get to meet new people every day.

✳ In men, the first sign of a bad memory is forgetting to do up your zipper after having a pee. The second sign is forgetting to pull it down before you have a pee.

✳ Right now I'm having amnesia and déjà vu at the same time. I think I've forgotten this before.

✳ Three absent-minded professors were talking together in a bus terminal. They got so engrossed in what they were saying that they didn't notice the bus had pulled in. As the driver sang out, "All aboard," they looked up, startled, and dashed from the platform. Two of them managed to hop on the bus, but the third didn't make it. As he stood sadly watching the bus disappear into the distance, a stranger tried to cheer him up, saying, "You shouldn't feel too bad. Two out of three made it, and that's a pretty good average." The professor shook his head. "You don't understand, they came to see me off."

✳ For as long as I can remember I've had amnesia.

✳ "I'm a psychic amnesiac. I know in advance what I'll forget." *Michael McShane*

# MICE

✳ Three mice are sitting in a bar trying to impress each other. The first mouse says, "Whenever I see a mousetrap, I lie on my back and set it off with my foot. When the bar comes down, I catch it in my teeth, bench press it twenty times to work up an appetite, then take the cheese." The second mouse replies, "Yeah, well, when I see rat poison, I collect as much as I can, take it home, grind it up into a powder, and add it to my coffee each morning. It gives me a good buzz for the rest of the day." The third mouse yawns, looks at his watch, and says, "Sorry guys, I don't have time for this bullshit. I gotta go home and screw the cat."

✳ Two mice are sitting in a hole listening to the "Meow, meow…" of a prowling cat outside. Suddenly they hear, "Woof, woof, woof…!" and then silence. Thinking the cat has been chased off, they creep outside and are immediately jumped on by the cat. After its meal, the cat says to itself, "I always knew it would be useful knowing a second language."

# MISTAKES

✳ If I could live my life over again, I'd make exactly the same mistakes. But I'd start making them earlier.

✳ I've learned a lot from my mistakes, and if I could live my life again, I'm sure I could repeat them exactly.

✳ You have the capacity to learn from your mistakes. You will learn a lot today.

✳ I never made a mistake in my life. I thought I did once, but I was wrong.

✳ If each mistake you make is a new one—cheer up, you're making progress.

# MODELS

✳ Harry gets stranded on a desert island with Cindy Crawford. One day he goes up to her and asks her to put on some of his old clothes. She does so. Then he asks if he can call her Pete. Cindy is surprised but says it's okay by her. Harry then takes a piece of charcoal from the campfire and draws a mustache on Cindy's upper lip. "What on earth are you doing?" says Cindy. "Never mind that, Pete," says Harry. "Listen, you'll never believe who I've been sleeping with for the last six months…"

# MONEY

✳ "If all the nations in the world are in debt, where did all the money go?" *Steven Wright*

✳ "Money frees you from doing things you dislike. Since I dislike doing nearly everything, money is handy." *Groucho Marx*

✳ "Strange things happen when you're in debt. Two weeks ago my car broke down and my phone got disconnected. I was one electric bill away from being Amish." *Tom Ryan*

✳ "Why don't oysters give to charity? Because they're shellfish." *Jay Leno*

✳ "The United States has developed a new weapon that destroys people but it leaves buildings standing. It's called the stock market." *Jay Leno*

✻ A study of economics usually reveals that the best time to buy anything is last year.

✻ A couple are arguing over money. "Do you know," says the man. "If it weren't for my money, this house wouldn't be here at all." "Yes," says his wife. "And if it weren't for your money, neither would I."

✻ A man hails a taxi to take him to court for his bankruptcy trial. When they arrive, he says to the driver, "Well, I suppose you might as well come in too."

✻ A man is sitting in a bar drowning his sorrows. "What's the matter?" asks the bartender. "Last month my father died leaving me $15,000," says the man. "Then a week later my mother died and left me $25,000. A week after that, my auntie died and left me $40,000. This week?—nothing."

✻ A man says to his wife, "Just what have you been doing with all the grocery money I give you?" His wife says, "Try turning sideways and look in the mirror!"

✻ A redneck and a lawyer are seated next to each other on a plane. The lawyer thinks the redneck looks like an easy touch. "To pass the time, why don't we ask each other questions," he suggests. "If you don't know the answer to my question, you pay me $5 and if I don't know the answer to yours, I pay you $50. "Okay," says the redneck. "So what's your question?" "What's the distance from the earth to the moon?" asks the lawyer. The redneck shakes his head, reaches into his pocket and gives the lawyer $5. "Okay," says the lawyer. "Now what's your question?" "What goes up a hill with three legs and comes down with four?" asks the redneck. The lawyer is baffled, he thinks long and hard, but eventually has to give the redneck $50. "So what's the answer?" asks the lawyer. The redneck shrugs, reaches to his pocket, and hands the lawyer another $5.

✻ A worker approaches his employer and holds up his last paycheck. "This is two hundred dollars short," he says. "I know," says the employer. "But last week I overpaid you two hundred dollars, and you didn't say anything." "Well," says the worker. "I don't mind an occasional mistake. But when it gets to be a habit, I feel I have to call it to your attention."

✻ An economist is an expert who will know tomorrow why the things he predicted yesterday didn't happen today.

✻ Bills travel through the mail at twice the speed of checks.

✻ Harry applies for a job at a finance company, the manager tells him the job is his if he can crack their toughest account. Harry goes off and comes back two hours later having recovered the entire amount. "Amazing!" says the manager. "How did you do it?" "Easy," replies Harry. "I said that if he didn't pay us, I'd tell all his other creditors he had."

✳ Harry staggers exhausted into his house. "What's wrong with you?" asks his wife. "I thought I'd save my seventy-five-cents bus fare by running behind the bus," gasps Harry. Says his wife, "If you'd run home behind a taxi, you could've saved a ten spot."

✳ I got this antique watch from my grandfather on his deathbed—he put up one hell of a fight for it.

✳ I make money the old-fashioned way. My salary is the same as it was ten years ago

✳ I married my wife for her money. And believe me, I've earned it.

✳ I started out with nothing, and I still have most of it.

✳ Jesus saves. But wouldn't it have been better if he had invested?

✳ I'm proud to say I made my money the old-fashioned way. My dad left it to me in his will.

✳ Man, to friend: "A thief has stolen my wife's credit card. Last month he ran up a bill of over a thousand dollars." "That's terrible," says the friend. "You should report this thief to the police." "I would," says the man. "But at the moment he's spending less than my wife does."

✳ Many people get valuable furniture on payment plans; it's not that expensive when they buy it, but by the time it's paid for, it's usually antique.

✳ Money can't buy happiness, but it can rent it for a couple of hours.

✳ Money isn't everything, but at least it encourages relatives to stay in touch.

✳ Never borrow money from optimists—they always expect to get it back.

✳ Should you trust a stockbroker who's married to a travel agent?

✳ The wages of sin are death—but after taxes and SSI contributions, you'll just end up feeling a little tired.

✳ This antique pocket watch has been in my family for generations. It's true. My grandfather sold me it on his deathbed.

✳ We have our water metered and it's very expensive. The other day the house was on fire and we didn't know whether it would be cheaper to let it burn.

✳ What's the quickest way to double your money? Fold it in half!

✳ What leads most people into debt? Trying to catch up with people who are already there.

* What I want to know is how did a fool and his money get together in the first place?

* Why does E.T. have such big eyes? He saw the phone bill.

* Why is the man who invests all your money called a broker?

* "Money can't buy you happiness, but it does bring you a more pleasant form of misery." *Spike Milligan*

* "If you pick up a starving dog and make him prosperous, he will not bite you. This is the principal difference between a dog and a man." *Mark Twain*

* A journey of a thousand miles begins with a cash advance.

* A worker goes to his boss and says, "You have to give me a raise. There are three other companies after me." "Is that so?" says the manager. "And what companies are those?" The worker replies, "The electric company, the telephone company, and the gas company."

* An old miser comes into the bank with a huge bag of coins. "Gracious," says the bank teller. "Did you hoard all that yourself?" "No," replies the miser. "My sister whored most of it."

* Harry and Dick work at the same factory. Harry is a little short of money, so he decides to work overtime and asks Dick if he can stop by his house and tell his wife he'll be late home. Dick goes to Harry's house, and the door is opened by Harry's wife. Dick has always had his eye on Harry's wife, and he knows they're short on money, so he asks her if she'll go to bed with him for $100. Harry's wife is very uncomfortable about the proposition, so Dick raises his offer to $150. Harry's wife is tempted but still reluctant, so Dick makes a final offer of $200. Finally she succumbs, and they go to the bedroom for an hour of sex. Later Harry gets home and asks his wife if Dick has been around. "Yes," she replies, "He popped in a couple of hours ago." "Oh good," says Harry. "And did he drop off that $200 he owes me?"

* I love her so much, I worship the ground her father found oil on.

* Remember when we spent money like there was no tomorrow? Well, it's tomorrow.

* What's the best way to stop water coming into your house? Don't pay the water bill.

* After any salary raise, you will have less money at the end of the month than you did before.

* No matter how hard we try, we never seem to save any money. Our neighbors are always buying something we can't afford.

✳ Money is not everything. There's also MasterCard and Visa.

✳ Uncle gives little Johnny a $5 bill for his birthday. "Spend it carefully," says Uncle. "Remember—a fool and his money are soon parted." Little Johnny replies, "Well you certainly handed it over fast enough."

✳ A mink in the closet often leads to a wolf at the door.

✳ "How to make a million dollars: First get a million dollars…" *Steve Martin*

✳ Living on earth may be expensive, but it includes an annual free trip around the sun.

✳ A young man wants to be left something in his aunt's will, so every day, he goes around and takes her poodles for a walk. When she finally dies, she does indeed remember the kindness of her nephew—and leaves him the poodles.

✳ A small boy goes up to a man in the street and asks him if he's lost $5. The man checks his pockets and says, "Well, yes. I think I have lost a $5 bill. Have you found one?" The boy replies, "No. I just wanted to see how many people had lost a $5 bill today. You make seventy-two."

# MONEY: BANKS

✳ "A bank is a place that will lend you money if you can prove that you don't need it." *Bob Hope*

✳ "My father was stupid. He worked in a bank and they caught him stealing pens." *Rodney Dangerfield*

✳ A man goes into a bank and asks the cashier to check his balance, so the cashier pushes him over.

✳ A woman goes to her bank with a check from her husband. The cashier tells her it has to be endorsed, so she writes on the back "My husband is a wonderful man."

✳ A young woman comes running in tears to her father. "Dad, you gave me some terrible financial advice!" she cries. "I did? What did I tell you?" asks Dad. "You told me to put my money in that big bank, and now that big bank is in trouble." "What are you talking about?" says Dad. "That's one of the largest banks in the world. Surely there must be some mistake." "I don't think so," she sniffs. "They just returned one of my checks with a note saying 'Insufficient Funds.'"

✳ A young woman walks into a bank to withdraw some money. "Can you identify yourself?" asked the bank clerk. The young woman opens her handbag, takes out a mirror, looks into it and says, "Yes, it's me all right."

✳ "If you owe the bank $100, that's your problem. If you owe the bank $100 million, that's the bank's problem." *John Paul Getty*

# MONEY: INSURANCE

✳ A woman calls her insurance company. "Our house burned down, and I want $100,000," she says. "It doesn't work like that," replies the insurance agent. "We will only give you enough money to get another house of equal value." The woman thinks for a second, then says, "In that case, I'd like to cancel the policy on my husband."

✳ An actuary priced an automobile "fire and theft" policy with an extremely low premium. When asked why it was so cheap, he said, "Who'd steal a burned car?"

✳ Three guys are fishing in the Caribbean. One guy says, "My house burned down. I lost everything, but the insurance company paid up, and that's why I'm here." The second guy says, "My gas station blew up. I lost everything, but the insurance company paid up, and that's why I'm here." The third guy says, "My farm suffered a terrible flood. I lost everything, but the insurance company paid up, and that's why I'm here." The first guy turns to him and says, "Flood? How the hell do you start a flood?"

✳ What's the difference between an insurance company actuary and a Mafia actuary? An insurance company actuary can tell you how many people will die this year, a Mafia actuary can name them.

✳ "They moved to the suburbs and they have all kinds of status symbols. They have their own home and station wagon and fire insurance and life insurance and mutual funds and his wife has orgasmic insurance or something. If her husband fails to satisfy her sexually, Mutual of Omaha has to pay her every month." *Woody Allen*

✳ A man with a wooden leg wanted to buy fire insurance for it. The first actuary quoted an annual premium of $500, estimating that the leg would burn once in twenty years, and the value of the leg is $10,000. The second actuary quoted an annual premium of $50. When the second actuary was asked how he'd arrived at such a small figure, he replied, "This situation is in the fire schedule rating table. The object is a wooden structure with an upper sprinkler."

# MONEY: LOTTERY

✳ Did you hear about the gypsy who won the lottery? He got paid in travelers' checks.

✳ Every year Tom enters the lottery at the state fair, but since he never wins, he decides to give up. "What kind of attitude is that?" says his friend Harry. "What you need is faith. Look around and see if the Lord sends you a message." Tom walks about looking for a sign but receives no divine inspiration. Finally he passes an old lady's pie stand and sees her bending over. Suddenly a finger of fire appears in the air and etches a seven on each of the old lady's buttocks. Tom rushes to the raffle booth and plays the number "77." A few minutes later the winner is announced over the speaker: "707…"

✳ If I won the lottery, I wouldn't be one of those people who immediately quit their jobs. I'd make my boss's life a living hell for a week or two first.

✳ What's the best way to get in touch with your long-lost relatives? Win the lottery.

✳ Harry is desperate for cash and prays to God to let him win the lottery. Harry doesn't win and is forced to sell his car to pay his bills. The next week Harry prays to God to win the lottery, but again he fails to win and has to sell all his possessions to pay the bills. The next week Harry again prays to God to win the lottery. He doesn't win and has to sell his house to pay the bills. Harry is now desperate. He has no possessions or money and is starving. He looks up in the sky and says, "God, if I don't win the lottery this week I'm going to kill myself." God's voice booms back, "Harry, at least meet me halfway—buy a ticket!"

# MONEY: POVERTY

✳ A beggar walks up to a well-dressed woman out shopping. "I haven't eaten anything in four days," he says. She looks at him and says, "God, I wish I had your willpower."

✳ I have enough money to last me the rest of my life. Unless I buy something." *Jackie Mason*

✳ "I used to sell furniture for a living—unfortunately it was my own." *Les Dawson*

✳ "I was so poor growing up. If I hadn't been born a boy I'd have had nothing to play with." *Rodney Dangerfield*

✳ A man walks into a bar and orders a triple brandy with a double whiskey chaser. "You know I shouldn't really be drinking like this with what I've got," says the man to the bartender. "Why? What have you got?" asks the bartender. "Fifty cents," replies the man.

✳ Being poor has its advantages. For example, your keys are never in your other pants.

✳ Dick's family was very poor—when the wolf came to the door, they ate it.

✳ He's in debt up to his eyes. The only thing he's paid for is his hat.

✳ Money talks—all mine says is "Goodbye!"

✳ Think nobody knows you're alive? Try missing a payment.

✳ My grandfather came from a very poor family. The only time he tasted meat was when he bit his tongue.

✳ Our family was so poor, our Christmas dinner was the leftovers from our last Christmas dinner.

✳ We were so poor, our mother would send us out with a shopping list to chase the garbage truck.

✳ We were so poor, the only way I could afford to get my suit pressed was to ride the subway during rush hour.

✳ We were so poor, we couldn't get rid of the roaches in our house because they paid half the rent.

✳ We were so poor, we had to go to KFC to lick other people's fingers.

✳ "We were kind of poor and my mother hated to spend a nickel on herself, so she bought most of her things in an army surplus store. She was the only woman in Cleveland wearing khaki lipstick." *Bob Hope*

✳ He was so poor, he didn't even get a yo-yo for Christmas. His parents could only afford a yo.

✳ Our house was so small, if we got a large pizza, we had to go outside to eat it.

✳ I am currently experiencing an out-of-money experience.

✳ I wouldn't say that inflation is making my life difficult, but I'm now starving on an income I used to dream about.

# MONEY: RICH

✳ "Be careful of men who are bald and rich; the arrogance of 'rich' usually cancels out the nice of 'bald.'" *Rita Rudner*

✳ "I wasn't always rich. There was a time I didn't know where my next husband was coming from." *Mae West*

✳ A reporter asks a rich old man how he made his money. The old man replies, "Well, son, it was 1932. The depth of the Great Depression. I was down to my last nickel and I invested that nickel in an apple. I spent the entire day polishing the apple and, at the end of the day, I sold the apple for ten cents. The next morning, I invested those ten cents in two apples. I spent the entire day polishing them and sold them for twenty cents. I continued this system for a month, by the end of which I'd accumulated a fortune of $1.37. Then my wife's father died and left us two million dollars…"

✳ A sixty-year-old millionaire has just married a twenty-year-old model. "You crafty old devil," says his friend. "How did you manage to get a beautiful young wife like that?" "Easy," replies the millionaire. "I told her I was ninety-five."

✳ If you want to know God's opinion of money, just look at the people He gave it to.

✳ She was so rich, she even had monograms on the bags under her eyes.

✳ We're all self-made, but only the rich and successful like to admit it.

✳ A man wakes up after spending twenty years in a coma. One of the first things he does is call his stockbroker. "Your assets have increased considerably," says the stockbroker. "The $20,000 you had invested with us is now worth $20 million." "That's fantastic," says the man. Just then the phone starts bleeping and a recorded voice interrupts, "To continue this conversation please insert another $500,000."

✳ "If you can count your money, you don't have a billion dollars." *John Paul Getty*

✳ Uncle Harry is very rich. His dog was lonely, so he bought it a boy to play with.

# MONEY: TAXES

✳ "He's spending a year dead for tax purposes." *Douglas Adams*

✳ "I love to go to Washington, if only to be nearer my money." *Bob Hope*

✳ A boy is playing with a coin when he gets it stuck in his throat and starts to choke. His mother runs into the street, calling for help and a passing man offers his assistance. The man grabs hold of the boy, puts his mouth over the boy's mouth, and skillfully sucks the coin out of his throat. "Thank you, Doctor," says the woman. "Did you learn to do that at medical school?" "I'm not a doctor," replies the man. "I work for the IRS."

✳ A man is being audited by the tax inspector. "How have you managed to buy such a luxurious villa when your declared income is so low?" asks the inspector. "Well, it's like this," replies the man. "While I was fishing last summer, I caught a large golden fish. When I took it off the hook, the fish opened its mouth and said, 'I am a magical fish. Throw me back to the sea and I'll give you the most luxurious villa you have ever seen.' So I threw the fish back into the sea, and got the villa." The inspector is not impressed—"How do you expect to prove such a ludicrous story?" The man replies, "Well, you can see the house, can't you?"

✳ A man is called for an interview with the IRS and asks his accountant for advice. "Wear your shabbiest clothing. Let him think you're a pauper," says the accountant. The man then asks his lawyer the same question. "Don't let them intimidate you. Wear your most elegant suit and tie," says the lawyer. Confused, the man goes to his priest and asks him what should he do. "Let me tell you a story," says the priest. "A woman, about to be married, asks her mother what to wear on her wedding night. 'Wear a heavy, long, flannel nightgown that goes right up to your neck,' she tells her. But when she asked her best friend, she says, 'Wear your most sexy negligee, with a V-neck right down to your navel.'" "I don't get it," says the man. "What does all this have to do with the IRS?" "The moral of the story is this," replies the priest. "Whatever you wear, you're still going to get screwed."

✳ A man is talking to the tax inspector who's come to review his records. The inspector says, "As a citizen, you have an obligation to pay taxes, and we expect you to pay them with a smile." "Thank God for that," replies the man. "I thought you were going to ask for cash."

✳ Smile and the world audits your taxes.

✳ The best things in life are free, plus tax.

✳ The tax auditor has just read the story of Cinderella to his four-year-old daughter for the first time. The little girl is fascinated by the story, especially the part where the pumpkin turns into a golden coach. "Daddy," she says. "When the pumpkin turned into a golden coach, would that be classed as income or a long-term capital gain?"

✳ There was a fire at the local tax office, but the fire brigade managed to put it out before any serious good was done.

✳ There will always be death and taxes. However, death doesn't get worse every year.

✳ If God had meant us to pay taxes, he'd have made us smart enough to fill in the return form.

✳ Born free. Taxed to death.

# MONEY: THRIFT

✳ A man goes into a shop to get his wife a present. He points out a bottle of perfume and asks how much. "That's $50, sir," says the assistant. "Oh no. That's too much," says the man. "What about that smaller bottle?" "That's $30, sir," says the assistant. "No," says the man. "That's still too much. What about that really tiny bottle?" "That's $15," says the assistant. "No," says the man. "Still too much. I'd like to see something cheap." So the assistant hands him a mirror.

✳ A millionaire is out driving in his Rolls-Royce when he spots two men on the roadside eating handfuls of grass. The millionaire stops and asks them why. "We don't have any money for food. Grass is all we can get," says one of the men. "Then come with me," says the millionaire. "I'll help you out." "But I have a wife and two children," says the man. "Bring them too. And bring your friend here," says the millionaire. The second man replies, "Thank you, sir, but I too have a wife, and six children." "Then bring them as well," says the millionaire. "You're all coming to my mansion. The more the merrier." "God bless you for your kind heart," says the first man." "It's no trouble," says the millionaire. "My mower has broken. The grass in my garden must be three feet high."

✳ Don't spend money having your shirts laundered. Donate them to a thrift shop, then when they've cleaned them, buy them back.

✳ Harry's so cheap, he didn't buy his wife a pearl necklace, he got her a length of string and told her to start a collection.

✳ He was so cheap, he had the house sound-proofed so the children wouldn't be able to hear the ice cream truck.

✳ He was so cheap, he used to give his children $1 each instead of an evening meal, then charged them $2 for breakfast.

✳ Last year I told the kids there was no Santa Claus, this year I'm telling the wife.

✳ Man, to friend: "My wife makes terrible demands for money. Two weeks ago she asked for $50. Last week she wanted $100, and yesterday it was $150." Friend: "What does she do with it all?" Man: "I don't know. I never give her any."

✳ Misers are lousy to live with, but they make great ancestors.

✳ Three cheapskates try to figure out a way of killing themselves with one bullet—so they put their heads together.

✳ A husband gives his wife a complete mink outfit for her birthday—a twelve-bore shotgun and some traps.

✳ My uncle is very cheap. I went around the other day and found him stripping the wallpaper. He wasn't redecorating, he was moving.

✳ Getting money out of my father was like taking candy from a baby. He used to scream and cry like hell.

# MOTHERS-IN-LAW

✳ A big-game hunter goes on safari with his wife and his mother-in-law. One evening the wife wakes up to find her mother gone. She rushes to find her husband, he picks up his rifle, and they go out to look for her. In a clearing not far from the camp, they come upon a chilling sight—the mother-in-law is backed up against a rock with a fierce lion facing her. "Oh no," cries the wife. "What are we going to do?" "Nothing," says her husband. "That lion got himself into this mess. He can get himself out of it."

✳ A man is playing golf with his mother-in-law when she slices the ball into a field with a cow in it. They climb the fence and start looking for the ball. They search everywhere but can't find it. Eventually the man realizes that the one place they haven't looked is by the cow. He goes over, pokes around, then sees something sticking in the cow's backside. He lifts up the cow's tail, sees a ball lodged in the hole, and shouts over to his mother-in-law, "Hey! Does this look like yours?"

✳ A man receives a telegram informing him about the death of his mother-in-law. It also asks him whether she should be buried or cremated. The man telegraphs back, "Take no chances. Burn the body and bury the ashes."

✳ Did you know you can calculate the age of your mother-in-law by counting the rings in her bath tub?

✳ Fred, to Steve: "You're looking down in the mouth today, what's the matter?" Steve: "I had a fight with my mother-in-law. She swore she wouldn't talk to me for a month." Fred: "That's not so bad." Steve: "Yes it is, that was four weeks ago!"

✳ Of course Adam was the only married man not to have a mother-in-law. And he lived in paradise.

✳ What's the best way to talk to your mother-in-law? Through a medium.

✳ After years of marriage, Tom eventually developed an attachment for his mother-in-law. It fit over her mouth.

＊ What's the definition of mixed emotions? When you see your mother-in-law backing off a cliff in your new car.

＊ My mother-in-law paid me a compliment the other day. She called me a perfect idiot.

# MOVIES

＊ "I thought Deep Throat was a movie about a giraffe." *Bob Hope*

＊ "I would have won the Academy Award if not for one thing—my pictures." *Bob Hope*

＊ How in movies does anyone getting out of a taxi manage to pull their exact fare out of their pocket without even checking it?

＊ In movies, when you're having a fight with a large group of martial arts experts, why does each of them wait patiently until you've finished with their predecessor before attacking you themself?

＊ "One time I went to the drive-in in a cab. The movie cost me $95." *Steven Wright*

＊ Harry got a job at the film studios to get a little extra—her name was Wendy.

＊ Hollywood movies would be improved if they shot less film and more producers.

＊ It's true that in my new film, I do appear completely naked in one scene, but I felt it was artistically necessary for the story—it's about a group of Hell's Angels at a gang bang.

＊ Two goats are scavenging on some rough ground behind a Hollywood film lot when they find an old reel of celluloid film. They're munching away on the film when one goat says to the other, "Not bad is it?" "Mmmm," says the other. "It's okay, but the book was better."

＊ Why in movies are all bombs fitted with timing devices and large read-outs so you know exactly when they're due to go off?

＊ Why in movies do they always have L-shaped duvet covers that reach up to the waist on a man and up to the shoulders of the woman lying next to him?

＊ Why in movies does every window in Paris have a view of the Eiffel Tower?

＊ Harry went to Hollywood and directed two films at once, his first and his last.

＊ Never judge a book by its movie.

✳ Why in movies is it never necessary to begin or end a phone conversation with "Hello" or "Goodbye"?

✳ Why in movies, when people have just finished a dramatic phone conversation, do they spend a few moments just staring solemnly at the receiver?

# MOVING

✳ If you move, you'll end up like us: surrounded by hundreds of cardboard boxes packed by strangers. You won't be able to find anything. For example, I'm pretty sure that we used to have a seven-month-old daughter.

✳ A man goes into a pet shop and asks for fifteen cockroaches, thirty-five termites, twelve wasps and three mice. "What d'you want all them for?" asks the shopkeeper. The man replies, "I'm moving out of my apartment tomorrow, and my landlord said I had to leave it exactly as I found it."

# MOMMY, MOMMY...

✳ "Mommy, Mommy! Are you sure this is how to learn to swim?" "Shut up and get back in the sack!"

✳ "Mommy, Mommy! Can I lick the bowl?" "No, flush it like everyone else!"

✳ "Mommy, Mommy! Can I play in the sandbox?" "Not until I find a better place to bury Daddy."

✳ "Mommy, Mommy! Daddy's had a heart attack!" "Don't make me laugh; you know my lips are chapped."

✳ "Mommy, Mommy! Daddy's on fire!" "Quick, grab a burger and a frying pan!"

✳ "Mommy, Mommy! Grandma's got a big hairy wart!" "Shut up and eat around it."

✳ "Mommy, Mommy! I don't like bows in my hair!" "Shut up and lift the other arm!"

✳ "Mommy, Mommy! I don't wanna visit Grandma!" "Shut up and keep digging!"

✳ "Mommy, Mommy! I want to play with Grandpa." "Keep quiet, the coffin's staying closed!"

✳ "Mommy, Mommy! My egg tastes bad." "Stop complaining! Just eat it!" "But Mommy, do I have to eat the beak as well?"

✳ "Mommy, Mommy! What's a nymphomaniac?" "Shut up and help me get Grandma off the doorknob."

✳ "Mommy, Mommy! What happened to all your scabs?" "Shut up and eat your cornflakes!"

✳ "Mommy, Mommy! What's a lesbian?" "Ask your father. She knows."

✳ "Mommy, Mommy! What's a werewolf?" "Be quiet and go and comb your face."

✳ "Mommy, Mommy! When will the wading pool be full?" "Shut up and keep spitting."

✳ "Mommy, Mommy! When will we have that nice yellow pudding again?" "Shut up, you know Grandma's boils got better."

✳ "Mommy, Mommy! Daddy just fell off the roof!" "I know, I saw him go past the window."

# MUSIC AND MUSICIANS

✳ "Go ahead and play the blues if it'll make you happy." *Homer Simpson*

✳ "I wrote a song, but I can't read music so I don't know what it is." *Steven Wright*

✳ A drummer decides to learn how to play a "real" musical instrument. He goes into a music store and says, "I'll take that red trumpet and that accordion." The store clerk replies, "Okay, you can have the fire extinguisher, but the radiator's got to stay."

✳ A gentleman is a man who knows how to play the accordion but doesn't.

✳ A man goes on vacation on a tropical island. As soon as he gets off the plane, he hears drums. He goes to his hotel and he hears the drums. He eats lunch and he hears drums. He goes to a beach party and hears drums. He goes to the bar and he hears drums. That night he tries to go to sleep—but all can hear is the drums. This goes on for days until he finally goes to the hotel reception desk to complain. "Hey! What's with the drums?" says the man. "They're driving me mad! I can't get any sleep! Stop the damn drums!" The manager replies, "No! Drums must never stop. Very, very bad if drums stop." "Why?" asks the man. The manager replies, "Because when drums stop… bass solo begins."

✳ A little boy thanks his grandfather for the harmonica he gave him for Christmas. "It's the bestest present I ever got!" says the little boy. "It's already earned me $100." "You must have learned to play it really well," says his grandfather. "I haven't learned to play it all," replies the boy. "Mommy gives me five dollars not to play it during the day and Daddy gives me ten not to play it at night…"

✳ A man is in a restaurant where a pianist is playing in a corner. "Do you play things on request?" calls the man to the pianist. "Oh yes, sir," says the pianist. "Great," says the man. "Play dominoes."

✳ A viola player comes home and finds his house has burned down. A policeman tells him that the orchestra conductor came to the viola player's house, slaughtered his family, then burned everything he possessed. The viola players says, "Wow. Y'mean the conductor actually came to my house…"

✳ An accordion player is driving home from a late night gig. Feeling tired, he pulls over for some coffee. While waiting to pay, he remembers that he locked his car doors but left the accordion in plain view on the back seat of his car! He rushes out only to discover that he's too late—the side window of his car has been smashed and somebody has thrown in two more accordions.

✳ Are part-time bandleaders semi-conductors?

✳ Arguably he is one of the greatest singers in the country. It's not an argument that anyone's ever won, of course.

✳ Conductor, to music student: "You should have taken up singing earlier." Student: "Why? Do you think the practice would have made me really good?" Conductor: "No. But you might have given up by now."

✳ Definition of an opera: where a man gets stabbed and starts singing instead of bleeding.

✳ Definition of modern music: things that aren't worth saying put into a song.

✳ How can you tell if a bagpipe is out of tune? Someone is blowing into it.

✳ How can you tell when a drummer's at the door? He doesn't know when to come in.

✳ He really was a very talented young man. Whatever musical instrument you gave him, he'd always be able to get some kind of noise out of it. Usually a sort of snapping sound, admittedly.

✳ How can you tell when a drummer is sitting up straight? He dribbles out of both sides of his mouth!

✳ How can you tell when a drummer's at the door? The knocking speeds up.

✳ How is a drum solo like a sneeze? You can tell it's coming, but you can't do anything about it.

✳ How is playing a bagpipe like throwing a javelin blindfolded? You don't have to be very good to get people's attention.

✳ I bought my daughter a new piano the other day. The neighbors love to hear her practice; in fact, they broke all the windows so they wouldn't miss a note.

✳ I traded in my wife's piano for a clarinet. You can't sing while playing a clarinet.

✳ I went to see Pavarotti once, and I'll tell you this much, he doesn't like it when you join in.

✳ In the beginning, there were only wind instruments in the orchestra. Then they noticed that many of the people were too stupid to play wind instruments, so they gave them boxes with wires strapped across them. These people were known as "strings." Then they noticed that some people were too dumb to play strings, so they were given two sticks and were told to hit whatever they wanted. These people were known as "percussionists." Finally they noticed that one percussionist was so dumb, he couldn't even do that, so they took away one of his sticks and told him to go and stand in front of everybody. And that was the birth of the first conductor.

✳ Johnny says to his mother, "Mommy, I want to be a drummer when I grow up!" "Now, Johnny," replies Mom. "You know you can't do both."

✳ Man to bartender: "Hey buddy, how late does the band play?" Bartender: "Oh, about a half-beat behind the drummer."

✳ The trouble with life is there's no background music.

✳ Man to friend: "Your wife sings like a pirate." Friend: "What do you mean?" Man: "She's murder on the high Cs."

✳ My son is what you might call a spiritualist musician—every time he plays we hear rapping on the walls.

✳ The thing about music journalism is that writing about music is a little like dancing about architecture.

✳ Three trumpet players are in an airplane with their orchestra. One of them says, "I'll throw a hundred-dollar bill out the window and make someone very happy." The second says, "I'll throw out two fifty-dollar bills, and make two people very happy." The third says, "I'll throw out five twenty-dollar bills and make five people happy." The conductor says, "If I threw out you three, I'd make the whole orchestra very happy."

✳ Two men are sentenced to die in the electric chair on the same day. The warden says to the first man, "Do you have a last request?" The man replies, "Yes. Could you play me the Macarena one last time?" "Certainly," replies the warden. He turns to the other man and says, "And what's your final request?" The second man says, "I'd like to go first."

✳ What do violists and Mike Tyson have in common? They're both hard on the ears.

✳ What do a lawsuit and a viola have in common? Everyone is much happier when the case is closed.

✳ "I don't like country music, but I don't mean to denigrate those who do. And for the people who like country music, denigrate means 'put down.'" *Bob Newhart*

✳ What do you call someone who hangs around with musicians? A drummer.

✳ What do you get when you cross a French horn player with an ant? An ant that can't march.

✳ What's the range of a piccolo? Twenty yards on a good day.

✳ What happens when you play country music backward? You sober up, your wife comes back, and your dog un-dies.

✳ What's the definition of perfect pitch in a piccolo? When you throw it in the toilet and it doesn't hit the rim.

✳ What's the best way to confuse a drummer? Put a sheet of music in front of him.

✳ What's the definition of an optimist? An accordion player with a pager.

✳ What's the difference between a drum machine and a drummer? You only have to punch the information into the drum machine once!

✳ What's the difference between a drummer and a vacuum cleaner? You have to plug one of them in before it sucks.

✳ What's the difference between a pizza and a drummer? A pizza can feed a family of four.

✳ What's the difference between a viola and a cello? A cello burns longer.

✳ What's the last thing a drummer says in a band? "Hey, guys. Why don't we try one of my songs…?"

✳ When she sings I make my wife stand in the front garden. I don't want the neighbors to think I'm beating her.

✳ Why are an accordionist's fingers like lightning? They rarely strike the same spot twice.

✳ Why are bad drummers better than drum machines? You don't have to plug them in to get something stiff, mechanical, and uninspired.

✳ Why are harps like elderly parents? They're both unforgiving and hard to get in and out of cars.

✳ Why do viola players spend a lot of time standing outside houses? They can't find the key and don't know when to come in.

✳ Why shouldn't you drive a mini off a cliff with three violas on board? Because if you tried, you could probably squeeze another two in the back.

✳ You know that song "Broken Alarm Clock Blues"? It's the one that begins "Woke up this afternoon..."

✳ "I'm not playing all the wrong notes. I'm playing all the right notes. But not necessarily in the right order." *Eric Morecambe*

✳ A father is attending his young son's piano recital at a music competition. He turns to whisper to one of the judges, "What do you think of his execution?" The judge replies, "I'm all in favor of it."

✳ A morgue assistant examining a newly delivered corpse finds a cork up its bottom. Curious, the assistant pulls out the cork and he hears a song being sung—"My Lauri-Lou done left me. Lauri-Lou's done gone..." The astonished assistant plugs up the bottom again and calls over the coroner to listen. The assistant pulls out the cork, and once again the corpse's bottom starts singing, "My Lauri-Lou done left me. Lauri-Lou's done gone..." "Don't you think that's incredible?" says the assistant. "Nah," says the coroner. "Any asshole can sing country music."

✳ Did you hear about the woman who couldn't find a singing partner? She had to buy a duet-yourself kit.

✳ How does a woman know when she's dating a French horn player? Whenever he kisses her, he has his hand up her rear.

✳ The show I saw last week was so bad, the manager was giving people their money back while they were walking in.

✳ What do you call a drummer without a girlfriend? Homeless.

✳ What's a bassoon good for? Kindling an accordion fire.

✳ What's the difference between an accordion and a trampoline? You're supposed to take off your shoes before jumping on the trampoline.

✳ What's the difference between an orchestra and a bull? The bull has the horns in front and its ass at the back.

✳ Why do they call it rap music? The letter C fell off at the printers.

✳ I traded in my wife's piano for a clarinet. You can't sing while playing a clarinet.

✳ The kid next door can't play the piano—and I wish he'd stop trying.

✳ "I'd always thought music was more important than sex. Then I thought if I don't hear a concert for a year and a half it doesn't bother me." *Jackie Mason*

✳ I'd like to perform for you a little number I wrote myself: three and a half.

✳ Definition of a music lover: Granddad puts his ear to the bathroom keyhole when the au pair starts singing in the shower.

✳ I took a course that said "Learn the piano in ten easy lessons." It's true, I did learn in ten easy lessons, but the first 120 were really, really hard.

✳ A man is listening to a violin recital being given by his neighbor's son. "What do you think?" asks the neighbor. "Your boy reminds me of Barry Manilow," replies the man. "I didn't know Barry Manilow could play the violin," replies the neighbor. "He can't," says the man, "and neither can your son."

# NAMES

✳ What do you call a female magician? Trixie.

✳ What do you call a man buried in a garden? Pete.

✳ What do you call a man hanging on a wall? Art.

✳ What do you call a man who wears a coat? Mac. What do you call a man who wears two coats? Max.

✳ What do you call a man in a catapult? Chuck.

✳ What do you call a man in a stock pot? Stu.

✳ What do you call a man in a mailbox? Bill.

✳ What do you call a man sitting in a hole? Phil.

* What do you call a man under a car? Jack.

* What do you call a man who runs up large debts? Owen.

* What do you call a man with a collection of dolphin pictures? The Prints of Whales.

* What do you call a man with a government subsidy? Grant.

* What do you call a man with a sackful of stolen goods over his shoulder? Robin.

* What do you call a man with a seagull on his head? Cliff.

* What do you call a man with flowers and vegetables growing on his head? Gordon.

* What do you call a man with no arms and no legs in a swimming pool? Bob.

* What do you call a man with no legs? Neil.

* What do you call a man with sports equipment on his head? Jim.

* What do you call a nun with a washing machine on her head? Sister-Matic.

* What do you call a water skier with no arms and no legs? Skip.

* What do you call a woman with a beach on her head? Shelly.

* What do you call a woman with a boat on her head? Maude.

* "Going to call him William? What kind of a name is that? Every Tom, Dick and Harry's called William. Why don't you call him Bill?" *Samuel Goldwyn*

* What do you call a woman with a food mixer on her head? Belinda.

* What do you call a woman with a screwdriver in one hand, a knife in the other, a pair of scissors between the toes on her left foot, and a corkscrew between the toes on her right foot? A Swiss Army wife.

* What do you call a woman with a sheep on her head? Baa-Baa-Ra.

* What do you call an Italian with a rubber toe? Roberto.

* What do you call a girl on the horizon? Dot.

* What do you call a man in a pile of leaves? Russell.

* What do you call a man with a rabbit on his head? Warren.

* What do you call a man with no arms or legs who can swim across a pool? Clever Dick.

✳ What do you call a woman with a computerized piano on her head? Cynthia.

# NEIGHBORS

✳ A neighbor is someone who listens to you attentively—through a wall.

✳ A young man is showing off his new apartment to his friends. "What are the big brass gong and the hammer for?" asks one. "It's a talking clock," replies the man. Saying this, he proceeds to give the gong an ear-shattering pound with the hammer. Someone screams from the other side of the wall, "Knock it off, you idiot! It's two o'clock in the morning!"

✳ If you're feeling lonely, try putting a "For Sale" sign in your front lawn. It's amazing how much friendlier your neighbors get when they think you're moving.

✳ An old lady calls the police to her house. She tells them that the man next door keeps wandering around naked with his curtains open. A policeman has a look through the window. "Hang on," he says. "I can't see into his house at all from here." The old lady replies, "No. You have to climb on the dresser and look out of the skylight."

✳ Don't try keeping up with the Joneses. Drag them down to your level. It's much cheaper.

✳ Every night a couple are kept awake by the barking of their next-door neighbors' dog. Finally the man has had enough and jumps out of bed. "Right!" he says. "I'm going to teach them a lesson." So saying, he runs downstairs and comes back five minutes later. "What did you do?" asks his wife. "I've put their dog in our garden," replies the man. "Let's see how they like it."

✳ I held a Festival of Peace and Meditation, but my neighbors complained about the quiet.

✳ Last night I played a blank tape at full blast. The mime next door went nuts.

✳ Last night the sex was so good, even my neighbors had to have a cigarette afterward.

✳ My wife knows exactly what she wants, just as soon as the neighbors get one.

✳ Man, to neighbor: "Did you hear me pounding on the wall last night?!" Neighbor: "Don't worry about it. We were making quite a lot of noise ourselves."

✳ The best way to meet your neighbors—play your stereo full blast at two in the morning.

✳ A woman approaches a policeman—"I want to report my neighbor. He's always spying on me." "Why do you say that, Ma'am?" asks the policeman. The woman replies, "Every time I peer through the window at his house, he's peering back at me."

✳ I just got skylights put in at my place. The people who live above me are furious.

# NON-ATTENDANCE

✳ He would have been here tonight but for a conflict of interest—he didn't want to come.

# NOSTALGIA

✳ "Whenever I think about the past, it just brings back so many memories." *Steven Wright*

✳ Do you know, one day we'll look back on all this… and plow straight into a parked car.

✳ It's hard to be nostalgic when you can't remember anything.

✳ Nostalgia isn't what it used to be.

✳ Things have gotten so bad, the good old days were only last week.

# NUDISM, NUDITY, AND NUDENESS

✳ A streaker runs through a golf club with a towel over his face and passes three female members. "Well, that's not my husband," says the first woman. "No, it isn't," says the second woman. "He's not even a member of the club," says the third woman.

✳ At a nudist colony for intellectuals, two old men are sitting on the porch. One turns to the other and says, "Have you read Marx?" The other says, "Yes, it's these wicker chairs."

✳ If God had meant for us to be naked, we would have been born that way.

✳ Why do men and women go to nudist camps? To air their differences.

✳ Two small children are spying on the inhabitants of a nudist colony through a hole in the fence. "Are they men or ladies?" asks one. "I can't tell," replies the other. "They haven't got any clothes on."

✳ A couple take their young son to a nude beach. The boy notices that some of the ladies have boobs much bigger than his mother's and asks her why. She says, "The bigger they are, the dumber their owner." The boy goes to play in the water but returns to tell his mother that many of the men have larger penises than his dad. His mother replies, "The bigger they are, the dumber their owner." Satisfied with this answer, the boy goes for a walk. Shortly after, the boy returns. "Mommy," he says. "I saw Daddy talking to the dumbest girl on the beach. And the longer they talked, the dumber he got."

✳ According to a new survey, women say they feel more comfortable undressing in front of men than they do undressing in front of other women. They say that women are too judgmental, whereas men are just grateful.

✳ What do you call a Spanish streaker? Señor Willy.

✳ In the school playground, little Johnny goes up to little Timmy and says, "Here, have you got any nude pictures of your mom?" "No!" replies little Timmy. Little Johnny says, "So do you want to buy some?"

# OPTICAL ILLUSIONS

✳ It is not an optical illusion, it just looks like one.

# OPTICIANS AND EYESIGHT

✳ "I got contact lenses recently, but I only need them when I read, so I got flip-ups." *Steven Wright*

✳ "I have bad eyesight. When I go to the optician's he points to the chart, reads them out himself and says, 'True or false?'" *Woody Allen*

✳ A man goes to an optician. "I keep seeing spots in front of my eyes," says the man. "Have you ever seen a doctor?" asks the optician. The man replies, "No, just spots."

✳ A man goes to the doctor's. The doctor says, "I'm afraid you need new glasses." "But I haven't told you what's wrong with me yet," says the man. "You didn't have to," says the doctor. "I could tell as soon as you walked in through the window!"

✳ A Polish woman with poor eyesight decides to have her vision tested. The optician shows her a wall chart with the letters C K O P V W X S C Z Y, and asks her if she can read it. "Sure I can read it," the woman replies. "But how did you know my maiden name?"

✳ An optician is speaking to a patient—"When did you last have your eyes checked?" The patient replies, "Never, they've always been brown."

✳ He has contact lenses, but he only needs them for reading. So he wears them on a chain around his neck.

✳ I've bought myself some glow-in-the-dark contact lenses. When I close my eyes, I can still see.

✳ My eyes are very bad. I have to wear contact lenses just so I can find my glasses.

✳ Sign at an optometrist's office "If you don't see what you're looking for—you've come to the right place."

✳ Yo momma's glasses are so thick, when she looks at a map she sees people waving.

✳ "Grandma, why do you have three pairs of glasses?" "One pair is for reading the paper, the second is for watching the television, and the third is to help me keep track of the other two."

✳ Carrots are very good for the eyes. Did you ever see a rabbit wearing glasses?

# OPTIMISM AND PESSIMISM

✳ "There is no sadder sight than a young pessimist, except an old optimist." *Mark Twain*

✳ Remember, whenever one door closes, another slams in your face.

✳ You should always borrow money from pessimists. They don't expect it back.

✳ I believe that for every drop of rain that falls…someone gets wet.

✳ What's a pessimist? A well-informed optimist.

✳ Today may be the first day of the rest of your life, but on the other hand, it's also the last day of your life so far.

✳ Pessimist: a person who looks both ways when crossing a one-way street.

# ORPHANS

✳ "When they asked Jack Benny to do something for the actors' orphanage, he shot both his parents and moved in." *Bob Hope*

# PARTYING

✳ She'd turn up to the opening of an envelope.

✳ Nothing is more irritating than not being invited to a party that you wouldn't be caught dead at.

# PERFUME

✳ "Is that a new perfume I smell?" "It is, and you do!"

✳ If you have everything, gloat. When that gets boring, start your own line of perfumes.

# PERSONAL HYGIENE

✳ A couple have just got married but they each have a terrible secret. He has smelly feet and she has bad breath. As they get ready for bed on their wedding night, he throws his socks in the bath and she sprays in some breath freshener. Once in bed he decides to make a confession. "Darling! I think there's something you should know. I have very smelly feet." "I have a confession for you as well," says his wife. "I think I know what it's going to be," said her husband. "You've eaten my socks, haven't you?"

✳ How do you get a hippie out of the bath? Turn on the water.

✳ How do you starve a hippie? Hide his sandwich under the soap.

✳ I tried some of that revitalizing shampoo. My hair was awake all night.

✳ If your slippers smell, fill them with cat litter then leave them overnight. By morning, all the odor will have been absorbed—as long as you don't have a cat.

✳ They show you how detergents take out bloodstains, but if you've got a T-shirt with bloodstains all over it, maybe your laundry isn't your biggest problem.

✳ "My grandmother took a bath every year, whether she was dirty or not." *Brendan Behan*

✳ Her armpits were so stinky, she put on Right Guard and it went left.

✳ Why did the baker have smelly hands? Because he kneaded a poo.

# PERSONALITY QUIRKS

✳ "Some people are afraid of heights. Not me, I'm afraid of widths." *Steven Wright*

✳ My auntie was a very cautious character; she even looked both ways before crossing her legs.

✳ She's so tidy, she puts a sheet of newspaper under the cuckoo clock.

# PHARMACISTS

✳ A Swedish man walks into a pharmacy and says, "I would like to buy some deodorant, please." "Certainly, sir," says the pharmacist. "Ball or aerosol?" "Neither," says the man. "It's for my armpits."

✳ A man walks into a pharmacy and asks for an anal deodorant. The pharmacist explains that they don't stock them. The man insists that he bought his last one from this store. The pharmacist asks the man to bring in his last purchase and he will try to match the product. The next day the man returns and shows the deodorant to the pharmacist. The words on the label read "To use, push up bottom."

# PHONES

* "If I called a wrong number, why did you answer it?"

* "My phone number is seventeen. I got one of the early ones." *George Carlin*

* I called up the phone company to report a crank caller. They said, "Not you again."

# PICK-UP LINES

* "Tell me about yourself—your struggles, your dreams, your phone number." *Peter Arno*

* "Why don't we break away from all this and lodge with my fleas in the hills—I mean, flee to my lodge in the hills." *Groucho Marx*

* Baby, I'm like milk—I'll do your body good.

* Excuse me, I just noticed you noticing me and I just wanted to give you notice that I noticed you too.

* Hi, I'm new in town. Can I have directions to your house?

* Hi. I suffer from amnesia. Do I come here often?

* I want to melt in your mouth, not in your hand.

* I'd look so good on you.

* Inheriting eighty million dollars doesn't mean much when you have a weak heart.

* Baby, you're so fine, I want to pour milk all over you and make you part of my complete breakfast.

* I seem to have lost my number. Can I have yours?

* Three guys go out on the town. The first picks up a cute brunette, and they go off to her place. The second soon finds a willing redhead, and they check into a motel. The third eyes an attractive blonde and asks if she wants to come back to his apartment. "I'd love to," she says. "But I'm on my menstrual cycle." "That's all right," says the man, "I came on a moped."

# PICK-UP LINES: EXTRA BOLD

* Do you have any Irish in you? Would you like some?

* Do you sleep on your stomach? Can I?

* Do you want to see something swell?

* Do you work for the post office? I could have sworn I saw you checking out my package.

* Hey baby, why don't you sit on my lap, and we'll talk about the first thing that pops up.

* Hey, baby, can I tickle your belly button from the inside?

* Hey, baby, let's play army. I'll lie down, and you can blow me up.

* Hey, that dress looks nice. Can I talk you out of it?

* Hi, I've been undressing you with my eyes all night long—it's time to see if I'm right.

* How about you sit on my lap, and we'll straighten something out?

* I love every bone in your body—especially mine.

* I lost my puppy, can you help me find him? I think he went into a cheap motel room.

* If I said you had a beautiful body, would you hold it against me?

* If your left leg is Thanksgiving, and your right leg is Christmas, can I visit you in-between the holidays?

* I may not be Fred Flintstone, but I sure can make your bed rock.

* I want to kiss you passionately on the lips and then move up to your belly button.

* If it's true that we are what we eat, then I could be you by morning.

* If you were a car door, I'd slam you all night long.

* Is that a keg in your pants? 'Cuz I'd just love to tap that ass!

* Is that a mirror in your pants? Because I can see myself in them.

* I've got the hot dog and you've got the buns.

* I've just received government funding for a four-hour expedition to find your G-spot.

✳ Man: "My magic watch tells me you aren't wearing underwear." Woman: "Well, your 'magic watch' is wrong." Man: "Oh, I'm sorry. It must be an hour fast…"

✳ What's a nice girl like you doing in a dirty mind like mine?

✳ Why don't we go back to my place and do the things I'm going to tell people we did anyway?

✳ You know, if I were you, I'd have sex with me.

✳ My face is leaving in fifteen minutes, be on it!

✳ Nice legs—what time do they open?

✳ Screw me if I'm wrong, but is your name Helga?

✳ That outfit would look great in a crumpled heap on my bedroom floor tomorrow morning.

✳ The word of the day is "legs." Let's go back to my place and spread the word.

✳ What do you say we go back to my room and do some math: Add a bed, subtract our clothes, divide your legs, and multiply.

✳ Will you be my love buffet, so I can lay you out on a table and take anything I want?

✳ You with those curves, and me with no brakes…

✳ You're like a championship bass. I don't know if I should mount you or eat you.

✳ You've got 206 bones in your body. Would you like one more?

✳ You. Me. Whipped cream. Handcuffs. Any questions?

✳ I'd really like to see how you look when I'm naked.

# PICK-UP LINES: EXTRA CHEESY

✳ Are those pants from outer space? 'Cuz that ass is out of this world.

✳ Are we near the airport, or is that just my heart taking off?

✳ Are you a parking ticket? Because you have fine written all over you.

✳ Are you from Tennessee? Because you're the only ten-I-see!

✳ Do you believe in love at first sight, or should I walk by again?

✳ Do you know CPR? Because you take my breath away.

✳ If I could rearrange the alphabet, I'd put U and I together.

✳ If I had eleven roses and you, I'd have a dozen.

✳ Is it hot in here or is it just you?

✳ Is your dad a terrorist? Because you're a bomb!

✳ Is your name Gillette? You're the best a man can get.

✳ You're so sweet, you're giving me a toothache.

# PICK-UP LINES: PUT DOWNS

✳ Man: "Haven't I seen you somewhere before?" Woman: "Yeah, that's why I don't go there any more."

✳ Man: "Hey, baby, what's your sign?" Woman: "Do not enter."

✳ Man: "Hey, come on, we're both at this bar for the same reason." Woman: "Yeah! Let's pick up some chicks!"

✳ Man: "I want to give myself to you." Woman: "Sorry, I don't accept cheap gifts."

✳ Man: "I'd go through anything for you." Woman: "Good! Let's start with your bank account."

✳ Man: "I'd go to the end of the world for you." Woman: "Yes, but would you stay there?"

✳ Man: "I'd like to call you. What's your number?" Woman: "It's in the phone book." Man: "But I don't know your name." Woman: "That's in the phone book too."

✳ Man: "If I could see you naked, I'd die happy." Woman: "Yeah, but if I saw you naked, I'd probably die laughing."

✳ Man: "So what do you do for a living?" Woman: "I'm a female impersonator."

✳ Man: "So, wanna go back to my place?" Woman: "I don't know. Will two people fit under a rock?"

✳ Man: "Your body is like a temple." Woman: "Sorry, there are no services today."

✳ Man: "Your place or mine?" Woman: "Both. You go to yours and I'll go to mine."

* Man: "You're one in a million." Woman: "So are your chances."

* Man: "You're trying to imagine me naked aren't you?" Woman: "No. I'm trying to imagine you with a personality."

* Man: "How do you like your eggs in the morning?" Woman: "Unfertilized!"

* Man: "I know how to please a woman." Woman: "Good, I guess that means you'll leave me alone."

* Man: "I'd really like to get into your pants." Woman: "No thanks. There's already one asshole in there."

* Man: "Is this seat empty?" Woman: "Yes, and mine will be too if you sit down."

# PIRATES

* A pirate is talking with the new cabin boy. "How did you lose your leg?" asks the boy. "We was sailing the high seas," says the pirate, "when a squall blows up and knocks me into the water. It was there that a shark got me leg." "And how did you lose your hand?" asks the cabin boy. "We was out collecting fresh water from a stream when a crocodile bit it off," replies the pirate. "And how did you lose your eye?" asks the cabin boy. "I was on deck one evening when a seagull pooped in my face," replies the pirate. "Are you telling me you were blinded by seagull crap?" asks the cabin boy. "No," replies the pirate. "But Y'see, it was me first day with me new hook!"

* He was a particularly stupid pirate. He wore a patch over both eyes.

# PLAGIARISM

* "If you steal from one author, it's plagiarism. If you steal from many, it's research." *Wilson Mizner*

# PLANES AND FLYING

✳ An airline passenger approaches a flight attendant and asks why his flight is being delayed. "It's all right," replies the flight attendant. "It's just that the pilot didn't like the sound one of the engines was making—it's taken us a while to find another pilot."

✳ "If God had intended us to fly, He'd have sent us tickets." *Mel Brooks*

✳ A man pays to go for a spin in a two-seater plane at an air show. The pilot does a corkscrew, loops the loop, then free-falls toward the crowds below. "Half the people down there think we're going to have an accident!" jokes the pilot. The man replies, "Half the people up here have had an accident."

✳ A photographer wants to take some aerial shots of his neighborhood and arranges a flight at his local airport. The photographer is directed to the runway and told that his plane is waiting for him. The photographer sees a light aircraft with its engine running and gets in. "Let's go," he tells the pilot, and the plane taxis down the runway and takes off. "Okay," says the photographer. "If you do a low pass over the bridge, I'll take some pictures." "Why do you want to do that?" asks the pilot. "It's what I do," says the photographer. "I'm a photographer, I take pictures." The pilot replies, "Y'mean—you're not the flight instructor?"

✳ A plane carrying an Englishman, a Frenchman, a Mexican, and a Texan is about to crash. The pilot shouts back at them, "We have to lose weight! If three of you jump, the fourth might be saved!" The Englishman stands up, shouts "God Save the Queen!" and jumps. The Frenchman stands up, shouts "Vive la France!" and jumps. The Texan stands up, and shouts "Remember the Alamo!"—and throws out the Mexican.

✳ I used to be an airline pilot, but they sacked me when I left the handbrake off a 747. Before I knew it the whole thing had slipped straight back up in the air.

✳ I wouldn't say he was reckless pilot, but he never checked the train schedule before he flew through the tunnels.

✳ A plane is about to crash into the sea. A little old lady grabs a flight attendant and asks, "Are there any sharks in the ocean below?" "Yes, I'm afraid there are some," replies the flight attendant. "But not to worry, we have a gel designed especially for emergencies like this. Just rub the gel on to your arms and legs." "And if I do that the sharks won't eat me?" asks the old lady. "Oh, they'll still eat you," replies the flight attendant. "They just won't enjoy it as much."

✳ A plane carrying Mike Tyson, Bill Gates, the Dalai Lama, and a hippie is about to crash into the sea, and there are only three parachutes. Tyson stands up and says, "I am the world's greatest boxer and I deserve a parachute!" With these words he grabs a parachute and jumps out of the plane. Bill Gates then stands up and says, "Gentlemen, I am the world's smartest man and I should have a parachute also." So saying, he grabs one and jumps. The Dalai Lama and the hippie look at one another. The Dalai Lama says, "My son. I have lived a satisfying life and have known the bliss of true enlightenment. You have your whole life ahead of you. You take the parachute, and I will go down with the plane." The hippie smiles and says, "Don't sweat it, dude. The world's smartest man just jumped out wearing my backpack."

✳ A rich businessman is forced to charter a light aircraft to get to an appointment but is horrified at the cost of the flight. He gets on board with his wife and moans nonstop to the pilot about the price of the charter. Eventually the pilot says, "Tell you what. If you can make it through the rest of the trip without opening your mouth, I'll give you the flight for free; but if you can't, you have to pay double." The businessman agrees, but the pilot decides to have some fun and starts looping the loop, going into spins, and indulging in all sorts of aerobatics. Despite this activity, the businessman keeps his mouth shut until the plane lands. The pilot congratulates him. "You beat me," he says. "I never thought you'd stay quiet through all of that." "Well, it wasn't easy," says the businessman. "Especially when my wife fell out."

✳ An aircraft landing is simply a controlled midair collision with a planet.

✳ An airplane flies into turbulent weather and starts bucking around like a boat in a storm. To try and keep the passengers' minds off the disturbance, a flight attendant wheels out the drink cart. "Would you like a drink?" says the flight attendant to one of the passengers. "Yes, please," says the passenger. "I'll have whatever the pilot's having."

✳ Definition of the jet age: breakfast in Rome, lunch in Paris, dinner in London, bags in Singapore.

✳ How do you know if there's a pilot at your party? He'll tell you.

✳ If flying is so safe, why do they call the airport the terminal?

✳ One of the airlines recently introduced a special half-fare rate for wives accompanying their husbands on business trips. Anticipating some valuable testimonials, the airline sent out letters to all the wives of businessmen who used the special rates, asking how they enjoyed their trip. Responses are still pouring in, asking "What trip...?"

✳ I got strip-searched at the airport. Why those customs officers had to take their clothes off I've no idea.

✳ Passenger to flight attendant: "How often do these types of plane crash?" Flight attendant: "Once."

✳ Strange isn't it? You stand in the middle of a library and go "Aaaaaagghhhh!!" and everyone stares at you. Do it on an airplane and everyone joins in.

✳ What's the purpose of an aircraft propeller? To keep the pilot cool. (If you don't think so, just watch him sweat when it stops.)

✳ The pilot of a jumbo jet is getting ready to take off. He announces all the usual stuff over the intercom but forgets to turn it off. The copilot asks him how he's feeling. "I could really use some hot sex and a cup of coffee," replies the pilot. A flight attendant hears this and runs to the cockpit to tell them the intercom is on. As she passes, one of the passengers shouts, "Don't forget the coffee!"

✳ The plane is about to crash. "Does anyone on board believe in the power of prayer?" the captain asks the passengers. A priest puts his hand up. "That's great," says the captain. "We're one parachute short."

✳ The plane is going down. There's a priest on board so the captain says to him, "Father, in view of the terrible situation we're in, could you do something religious?" So the priest takes a collection.

✳ What I want to know is, how do you get off a nonstop flight?

✳ When two airplanes almost collide, why do they call it a near miss? It sounds like a near hit to me!

✳ How do you know when you're halfway through a date with a pilot? When he says, "That's enough about flying. Let's talk about me."

✳ Passenger to flight attendant: "Can you telephone from a plane?" Flight attendant: "If I couldn't do that I'd need my eyes tested."

✳ While sitting in business class of a Cathay Pacific 747, passengers heard the following announcement over the cabin PA system: "Ladies and gentlemen, we are overbooked and are offering anyone $1,000 plus a seat on the next flight in exchange for their seat on this flight." After a short pause, the offer was loudly accepted by someone in the cockpit.

✳ You know you're flying in a crappy airplane when you have a bird strike—from behind.

✳ A small timid man gets on board a plane and is seated by a window next to a big Texan. The plane takes off and the Texan falls asleep. Unfortunately the little man starts to get air-sick but is afraid to wake up the Texan so he can get to the lavatory. While he's plucking up the courage to wake the huge man, he suddenly throws up in the Texan's lap. The awful smell wakes the Texan, and he opens his eyes to find himself covered in vomit. The little man pats him on the shoulder and says, "Are you feeling better now?"

✳ We flew on a very old airplane. It had an outside toilet.

# PLUMBERS

✳ A Texan is admiring Niagara Falls when a local approaches him and says, "Bet you've got nothing like that where you come from." "No," admits the Texan. "But we've got plumbers who could fix it."

✳ A plumber calls at a house to do some emergency work. The door is answered by a woman wrapped in a towel who's obviously had her bathtime interrupted. "I'm afraid you've caught me in a terrible dilemma," says the lady. "That's all right," says the plumber. "The last lady I caught was in a dirty kimono."

✳ A pipe burst in a doctor's house so he calls a plumber. The plumber arrives, unpacks his tools, fixes the leak, then hands the doctor a bill for $400. The doctor exclaims, "This is ridiculous! I don't even make that much as a doctor!" The plumber replies, "Neither did I when I was a doctor."

✳ A plumber is called to a house to repair a leaking pipe. When he arrives he is pleased to discover that the lady of the house is both beautiful and very friendly. One thing leads to another, and the two end up in the bedroom. Suddenly the phone rings and the woman answers it. "That was my husband," she says when she puts down the receiver. "He's on his way home, but he's taking a flight out of town at eight. If you come back then, we can take up where we left off." The plumber looks at the woman in disbelief. "What?" he says. "On my own time?"

✳ A woman calls in a plumber when her washing machine breaks down. The plumber arrives, studies the machine, then produces a hammer and gives it a hefty whack. The washing machine starts working again, and the plumber presents a bill for $200. "Two hundred dollars?" says the woman. "All you did was hit it with the hammer." So the plumber gives her an itemized bill: "Hitting washing machine with a hammer—$5. Knowing where to hit it—$195."

✳ A doctor calls a plumber in the middle of the night. "Why are you calling me at this hour?" says the plumber. "Look, it's an emergency," says the doctor. "If it was the other way around you'd expect me to come out, wouldn't you?" "Okay," says the plumber. "What's the problem?" "The toilet's broken," says the doctor. The plumber says, "Give it two aspirin and call me again if it's not better in the morning."

# POLITICS

✳ A politician is in bed asleep with his wife when there's a massive storm and a bolt of lightning lights up the entire bedroom. The politician leaps up and shouts, "I'll buy the negatives! I'll buy the negatives!"

✳ Apologies for the mess. We've got the Republicans in.

✳ Capitalism is the exploitation of one man by another. Communism is the opposite.

✳ For every action, there is an equal and opposite government program.

✳ He's the finest politician money can buy.

✳ If voting really could change anything it would be illegal.

✳ An Englishman, a Swede, and a Russian are looking at a painting of Adam and Eve in the Garden of Eden. "Look at that beautiful garden," muses the Englishman. "Only an Englishman could grow a garden as beautiful as that." "Nonsense," says the Swede. "They're naked and unashamed. They must be Scandinavian." "Rubbish," says the Russian. "No clothes, no house, one apple between them, and they're told it's paradise— definitely Russian."

✳ In the days of the Cold War, three men are sitting in a Bulgarian café. One man looks at a newspaper, shakes his head and sighs. The second man looks at his newspaper shakes his head and sighs. The third man reaches for his hat and coat and says, "If you two are going to discuss politics, I'm off."

✳ No matter who you vote for, the government always seems to get in.

✳ Politicians and babies' diapers have one thing in common. They should both be changed regularly, and for the same reason.

✳ The President has left the country on a tour of friendly countries. He's expected home tomorrow.

✳ There are three kinds of lies: a small lie, a big lie, and politics.

✳ To succeed in politics, it is often necessary to rise above your principles.

✳ George Bush is skating on a frozen pond when the ice cracks and he falls in. Luckily three little boys are on hand to pull him out. "You've saved my life," says Bush. "How can I repay you?" "I'd like a toy car," says one boy. "I'd like a toy plane," says another boy. "I'd like a motorized wheelchair," says the third boy. "Why do you want a wheelchair?" asks Bush. "You look very healthy to me." "I am," says the little boy. "But I'm going to need one when my dad discovers I saved George Bush."

✳ What do Japanese men do when they have elections? Vote.

✳ Why do we use the word "politics" to describe the process of Government? "Poli" in Latin meaning "many" and "tics" meaning "bloodsucking creatures."

✳ "Too bad all the people who know how to run this country are busy driving taxis and cutting hair." *George Burns*

✳ Crime means you have to take the money and run. In politics you run, then you take the money.

✳ Politicians are wonderful people as long as they stay away from things they don't understand—such as working for a living.

✳ What's the difference between the government and the Mafia? One of them is organized.

✳ Two political opponents are having an argument. "There are many ways of making money," says the first. "But there is only one honest way." "And what's that?" asks the second. The first replies, "I had a feeling you wouldn't know."

✳ The four stages of Socialism: utopian, scientific, real, and curfew.

✳ Dick took a seat at the House of Representatives the other day. But they made him put it back.

✳ A man goes up to a politician at a party and says, "I've heard a lot about you." The politician replies, "But you can't prove any of it."

✳ Two city council members are attending a meeting at the Town Hall. One says, "Have you heard of George Pringle?" "No," says the other. "Well," says the first, "if you'd bothered to attend a few more council meetings, you'd know that he's now in charge of the county sewage works." "Oh," says the second member. "And have you heard of Thomas Harris?" "No," says the first man. "Who's he?" "Well," says the second, "if you'd attended fewer council meetings, you'd know he's the man who's been sleeping with your wife."

# PRAISE

✳ "He has not a single redeeming defect." *Benjamin Disraeli*

✳ "It's more than magnificent—it's mediocre." *Samuel Goldwyn*

# PRESIDENTS

✳ "If Lincoln were living today, he'd turn over in his grave." *Gerald Ford*

✳ "You can always tell when Richard Nixon is lying. His lips move." *John F. Kennedy*

✳ A Republican, a Democrat, and Bill Clinton are traveling in a car when a tornado suddenly comes along and whirls them into the air. When they eventually come down, they realize they're in the land of Oz. They decide to go to see the Wizard. "I'm going to ask the Wizard for a brain," says the Democrat. "I'm going to ask the Wizard for a heart," says the Republican. Clinton says, "Where's Dorothy?"

✳ A year ago Gerald Ford was unknown throughout America, now he's unknown throughout the world.

✳ President Calvin Coolidge once invited friends from his home town to dine at the White House. Worried about their table manners, the guests decided to do everything that Coolidge did. This strategy succeeded, until coffee was served. The president poured his coffee into the saucer. The guests did the same. Coolidge added sugar and cream. His guests did, too. Then Coolidge bent over and put his saucer on the floor for the cat...

✳ Sign in a public restroom: If you voted for Bush in the last election, you can't take a dump here. Your asshole is in Washington.

✳ President Clinton and Hillary are in the front row at Yankee Stadium. The row behind them is taken up with Secret Service agents. One of them leans over and whispers in the President's ear. Clinton nods, then grabs Hillary by the scruff of the neck and throws her over the railing. The Secret Service agent leans over again and says, "Mr. President, I said 'It's time to throw out the first pitch.'"

✳ The George W. Bush Presidential Library has just been destroyed by fire. Tragically both books were lost, and he hadn't even finished coloring in the second one.

✳ Bill Clinton looks out over the White House lawn one winter's day and sees the words "Clinton must die!" written in the snow. The CIA investigate and make their report. "It seems the message was written in urine," says the CIA agent. "As to its origins, we have bad news and really bad news." "So what's the bad news?" asks Bill. "We tested the urine and found it belonged to your Vice President, Al Gore," says the agent. "Oh no," says Bill. "But what's the really bad news?" The agent replies, "It was in Hillary's handwriting."

✳ What was the name of Ronald Reagan's last movie? Partial Recall.

✳ Bill Clinton liked Monica's dress from the moment he spotted it.

✳ Bill Clinton, Al Gore, and Bill Gates all die in a plane crash and go to meet their maker. God looks on Al and asks him what he thinks is the most important thing in life. Al tells him that protecting the earth's ecology is the most important thing. God says, "I like the way you think, come and sit at my left hand." God then asks Bill Clinton the same question. Bill says that he feels people and their personal choices are most important thing. God says, "I like the way you think, come and sit at my right hand." God then turns to Bill Gates, who is staring at him indignantly. "What's your problem Bill?" asks God. Bill replies, "You're sitting in my damn chair!"

✳ What did President Clinton say to Hillary when he felt like making love? "I'll be back in an hour!"

✳ What does Monica Lewinsky have on her resumé? "Sat on the presidential staff."

# PRIMATES

✳ A man walks into a bar with a pet monkey. While he's drinking, the monkey runs around looking for something to eat. It jumps up on a pool table, grabs the cue ball, and swallows it whole. The man apologizes for the monkey's behavior, pays for the ball, and leaves. Two weeks later the man and the monkey return, and the man orders another drink while the monkey runs about looking for something to eat. The bartender watches as the monkey finds a cocktail cherry, examines it carefully, then pushes it in and out of its bottom before swallowing it whole. The bartender asks the man why the monkey would do such a thing. "Well," says the man. "Ever since that damn cue ball, he makes sure it comes out as easy as it went in."

✳ What's light, white, and sweet and hangs from trees? A meringue-utan.

✳ Why did the monkey fall out of the tree? It was dead. Why did the second monkey fall out of the tree? It was tied to the first monkey. Why did the third monkey fall out of the tree? Peer pressure. Why did the warthog fall out of the tree? It was doing a monkey impression.

✳ Why do gorillas have big nostrils? Because they have big fingers.

✳ How do you catch a gorilla? Hide in a tree and make a noise like a banana.

# PRINCIPLES

✳ "Those are my principles. If you don't like them I have others." *Groucho Marx*

# PROBLEMS IN LIFE

✳ "The toughest time in anyone's life is when you have to kill a loved one just because they're the devil." *Emo Phillips*

✳ All your problems are caused by invisible people. To eliminate your problems, all you need to do is find them and kill them.

✳ Don't tell your friends your problems. Tell your enemies your problems. They're far more interested in hearing about them.

✳ Whoever said nothing is impossible never tried slamming a revolving door.

✳ A problem shared is a problem halved, so is your problem really yours or just half of someone else's?

# PROXIMITY

✳ "If I held you any closer, I'd be on the other side of you." *Groucho Marx*

# PUNCTUALITY

✳ The trouble with being punctual is people think you have nothing better to do.

✳ The trouble with getting anywhere on time is that there's never anyone else there to appreciate it.

# PUNS

✳ A boat carrying red paint and a boat carrying blue paint crashed into each other. Apparently the crews were marooned.

✳ A brown paper bag goes to his doctor feeling unwell. The doctor takes all sorts of samples and asks the bag to come back next week. The next week the bag returns, and the doctor says, "I'm afraid I have bad news. We discovered from your blood tests that you have hemophilia." "Hemophilia?" says the bag. "How can that be? I'm a brown paper bag." "Yes," replies the doctor, "but it seems your mother was a carrier."

✳ A frog walks into a bank, goes up to the teller, Ms. Patty Black, and says, "I'd like a loan." Patty Black replies, "Do you have any collateral?" The frog says, "Yes, I have a pink ceramic elephant." Patty Black goes to the manager's office and says, "Sir, there's a frog out there who wants a loan. He has a pink ceramic elephant for collateral. What should I do?" The manager says, "It's a knick-knack, Patty Black, but give the frog a loan."

✳ A ghost loses the tail of his sheet in a revolving door and goes to a liquor store to get a new one. "Sorry," says the man behind the counter. "We don't sell tails and we don't serve ghosts." "That's not true," says the ghost. "The sign in the window says you retail spirits."

✳ A good pun is its own reword.

✳ A man always buys his wife anemones on her birthday, but one day he goes to the florist and finds they've run out. There's no time to go anywhere else, so the man buys the only plant they've got left, a large fern. As luck would have it, his wife is delighted by the novel gift. "With fronds like these," she says. "Who needs anemones?"

✳ A tourist couple are visiting Moscow with their Russian guide, Rudolph. One day the couple decide they want to visit Gorky Park, but Rudolph looks at the sky and tells them they can't, as it will rain soon. Sure enough, a couple of hours later, it starts to rain. The next day the couple want to go to Red Square, but again Rudolph looks at the sky and predicts rain. Sure enough, a few hours later, it starts to pour down. The next day the couple decide they want to go to the Moscow woods, but Rudolph looks at the sky and tells them it will rain. "It can't rain," complains the husband. "Look at the sky. There's not a cloud to be seen." His wife pipes up, "I think we'd better skip the woods today. By now we know that Rudolph the Red knows rain, dear."

✳ A priest offers Harry $500 to paint his church. Harry buys some paint and starts working, but discovers he's using more paint than he expected. Harry adds some thinner to the paint to make it last, but finds he's still using too much, so he adds yet more thinner. The paint is now too thin to use properly, but Harry carries on regardless. Suddenly there's a crack of thunder and a voice booms out from the clouds, "Harry! Repaint and thin no more!"

✳ A Viking called Leif comes home after a long voyage to find that his name has been removed from the town register. He complains to the council. "I'm sorry," says the official. "I must have taken Leif off my census."

✳ A vulture boards an airplane, carrying two dead racoons. The stewardess looks at him and says, "I'm sorry, sir. Only one carrion allowed per passenger."

✳ A woman has twins and gives them up for adoption. One of them goes to a family in Egypt and is named Ahmal. The other goes to a family in Spain, and they name him Juan. Years later Juan sends a picture of himself to his natural mother. When she gets the picture, she tells her husband she wishes she had a picture of Ahmal too. Her husband says, "They're twins! If you've seen Juan, you've seen Ahmal."

✳ Did you hear about the Buddhist who refused Novocaine during the root canal treatment? He wanted to transcend dental medication.

✳ Did you hear about the painter who was fired for dropping things on people? He couldn't hold his lacquer.

✳ Fork, to spoon: "Who was that ladle I saw you with last night?" Spoon: "That was no ladle. That was my knife."

✳ Four men are in a boat. They decide to have a smoke, but discover no one has any matches. One of the men comes up with a solution and throws a cigarette into the sea—thus making the boat a cigarette lighter.

✳ Harry is tried for bigamy after marrying Kate and Edith. In court, the prosecutor declares that Harry wanted to have his Kate and Edith too.

✳ Harry sent ten different puns to a friend in the hope that at least one of the puns would make him laugh. Unfortunately, no pun in ten did.

✳ How do you catch a bra? Set a boobie trap.

✳ How do you catch a one-of-a-kind rabbit? Unique up on him.

✳ How do you make a hormone? Don't pay her.

✳ How many ears did Davy Crockett have? Three—his left ear, his right ear, and his wild front ear.

✳ Mahatma Gandhi walked barefoot everywhere and developed callouses over his feet. He also ate very little, which made him rather frail, while his odd diet gave him bad breath—he was indeed a super-calloused fragile mystic plagued with halitosis.

✳ The ashes of a famous general are due to be flown home for burial, but it's discovered that all the airlines are fully booked. Eventually a helicopter is found to take the urn home. The next day the newspaper headline reads "The Whirly Bird Gets the Urn."

✳ Three animals, a hawk, a lion, and a skunk, are arguing about which is the most fearsome. The hawk says it's the most fearsome as it's the fastest. The lion says it's the most fearsome because it's the strongest. The skunk says it's the most fearsome as it's the worst smelling. Just then a bear came along and swallowed them all: hawk, lion, and stinker.

✳ Three men are stranded in a small boat. After bobbing around for a week, they see a huge hand slowly rise out of the water. As they watch, the hand slowly dips to the right, then slowly to the left. It then submerges beneath the waves. "Whoa!" says one of the men. "Did you see the size of that wave?"

✳ Tom comes across a man in the street wearing a parka. The hood on the parka keeps jumping around and people are throwing money into it. Tom says to the man, "D'you earn a lot doing that?" "Yes," says the man. "It's my livelihood."

✳ What are the people who come to your house to demonstrate vacuum cleaners called? Je-hoover's witnesses.

✳ What did the zookeeper say when he was charged by a baby aardvark? "A little aardvark never hurt anybody."

✳ A man goes into a bar with a newt sitting on his shoulder. "I'll have a pint of beer and a glass of orange juice for Tiny here." "Why is he called Tiny?" asks the bartender. The man replies, "Because he's my newt."

✳ The manager of an old people's home decides to hire an animal act to entertain everyone at the home's annual tea party. He calls a theatrical agent and asks what sort of acts he has to offer. "I've got a tiger," says the agent. "It does a highwire act and juggles plates. "Too dangerous," replies the manager. "It might fall on someone or bite them." "How about a performing seal?" says the agent. "It can play musical instruments." "Too noisy," replies the manager. "The old folks won't like it. What we need is something unusual but nice and sedate, so it won't upset them." "I know," says the agent. "How about Morris the gibbon. He's very quiet. All he does is card tricks." "Sounds good," replies the manager. "Let's try a mellow gibbon round the old folk's tea…"

✳ Two weevils grew up in South Carolina. One went to Hollywood and became a famous actor. The other stayed behind in the cotton fields and never amounted to much. The second one, naturally, became known as the lesser of the two weevils.

✳ An old man goes to his doctor complaining that he keeps hearing music every time he puts on his hat. The doctor takes the hat into a back room then brings it out a few moments later and puts it on the old man's head. "That's incredible," says the old man. "I can't hear music anymore. What did you do to my hat?" "It was easy," replies the doctor. "I just removed the band."

✳ I bought a bureau the other day. I opened it up and fourteen people fell out. It seems it was a missing persons' bureau.

# RABBITS

\* Thirty rabbits get in a row and all start hopping backward—what do you have? A receding hare line.

\* A man accidentally runs over a rabbit in his car. He gets out to see if he can help, but the rabbit is dead. However, his wife has an idea. She gets a spray can out of her handbag and sprays the rabbit. The rabbit suddenly jumps up, waves its paw at the two of them, and hops off down the road. Ten feet away the rabbit stops, turns around, and waves again. It keeps doing this till it's out of sight. The husband is astonished, "What on earth is in that can?" His wife reads from the can's label, "Hair spray—Restores life. Adds permanent wave."

\* A rabbit walks into a tobacco shop and says to the clerk, "Hey, man. You got any carrots?" The clerk replies, "No, this is a tobacco shop. Try a grocery store." The rabbit leaves but comes back the next day, "Hey. You got any carrots?" says the rabbit. "No," says the clerk, "It's a tobacco shop. Now buzz off!" The rabbit goes, but the next day he's back. "Hey, man," says the rabbit, "you sure you haven't got any carrots?" "No, I haven't," shouts the furious clerk, "and if I see you again, I'm going to get a knife, skin you, chop you up in a cooking pot, and make a stew out of you!" The rabbit goes off but comes back the next day. "Hey, man," says the rabbit, "you got a knife?" "No!" shouts the clerk. "You got a cooking pot?" asks the rabbit. "No!" yells the clerk. "So," says the rabbit, "you got any carrots?"

\* Naamah, Noah's wife, is counting the animals on to the ark: "...two giraffes, two tigers, two shrews, two moles, twenty-six rabbits..." "What do you mean, twenty-six rabbits?" says Noah. "I told you to take in two of every animal." Naamah replies, "That was yesterday."

\* A man finds his dog with a dead rabbit in its mouth. He realizes that the rabbit is a pet of his next-door neighbor. In a panic he cleans the rabbit up and sneaks it into its cage, hoping his neighbor will think their pet died of natural causes. The next day he spots his neighbor digging a hole in the flower beds and goes over to investigate. "What are you doing?" asks the man. "Burying my rabbit again," replies the neighbor. "There sure are some sick people about. The rabbit dropped dead on Monday, I buried it on Tuesday, and on Wednesday some bastard dug it up, gave it a wash, and stuck it back in its cage."

\* What's invisible and smells like rabbits? Rabbit farts.

# RECYCLING

* Marrying a man who's been married before is ecologically responsible. There are more women than men in the world, so it's good sense to recycle.

* One woman says to another, "Do you recycle?" "Of course," says her friend. "After we divorced, I slept with my ex."

# REINDEER

* Why do reindeers wear bells? Because their horns don't work.

# RELIGION

* A boy is wandering through a hotel when he hears amorous sounds coming from a room. Curious, he opens the door to an unlit room. "Wow," he says. "It's dark in here!" A man shouts out, "Buzz off and leave us alone!" Startled, the boy shuts the door and runs away. Later that evening the boy passes the hotel laundry room and, again, hears amorous sounds coming from inside. He opens the door and says, "Wow. It's dark in here!" Again, a man shouts, "Go away and leave us alone!" And the boy shuts the door and runs away. The next day the boy's mother takes him to his first confession. The boy enters the confessional box and says, "Wow. It's dark in here." The priest says, "Are you following me around, you little bastard?"

* Religion is man's quest for assurance that he won't be dead when he will be.

* A mother is preparing pancakes for her sons, Kevin, five, and Ryan, three. The boys begin to argue over who gets the first pancake, and their mother sees the opportunity for a moral lesson. "If Jesus were sitting here," she says. "He would say, 'Let my brother have the first pancake. I can wait.'" Kevin turns to his brother and says, "Okay, Ryan. You be Jesus."

* A Sunday school teacher reads a Bible passage to her class. "And the Lord appointed a great fish to swallow up Jonah; and Jonah was in the belly of the fish three days and three nights. Then Jonah prayed to the Lord his God from the belly of the fish, saying, 'I called to the Lord of my distress and He answered me.' … and the Lord spoke to the fish,

and it vomited out Jonah upon the dry land." When she's finished reading, the teacher says, "Now, children. What does this story teach us?" Little Johnny raises his hand and says, "You can't keep a good man down?"

✳ At a church gathering, the priest stacks a pile of apples at one end of a table with a sign saying "Take only one apple please—God is watching." On the other end of the table is a pile of cookies Little Johnny places a sign by it saying, "Take all the cookies you want—God's watching the fruit."

✳ Little Johnny comes home from school and says, "Dad. Today we found out what God's name is. He's called Harold." "Harold?" replies his father. "What gave you that idea?" "It said so in the poem," replies Johnny. "Our Lord who art in heaven. Harold be the name."

✳ My husband and I divorced over religious differences. He thought he was God. I didn't.

✳ Remember there are seven deadly sins. One a day. So have a good week.

✳ Teacher: "Johnny, please list the Ten Commandments in any order." Johnny: "Okay: 3, 6, 1, 8, 4, 5, 9, 2, 10, 7."

✳ There's a horrible car crash. The driver of the car lies dying by the side of the road. A passerby suggests he say a prayer. "I don't know any," says the stricken man. "Haven't you had any contact with religion?" asks the passerby. "Well, as a boy we used to live next to a Catholic church!" "Try to remember," says the passerby. "Just repeat what you heard in the church!" "Uh, okay," says the dying man. "B15...Under the B–15... I22... Under the I–22...Bingo!"

✳ They had a bingo evening at the local church hall. The priest called out all the numbers in Latin so the atheists wouldn't win.

✳ What do Winnie the Pooh and John the Baptist have in common? Their middle name.

✳ What did the Virgin Mary say when she saw the wise men? "Typical. You wait ages, then three come at once."

✳ A married man goes to confession and says to the priest, "I almost had an affair with a woman." The priest asks, "What do you mean 'almost'?" The man replies, "Well, we got undressed and rubbed together, but then I stopped." The priest replies, "You sinful man! Rubbing together is exactly the same as putting it in. You must say five Hail Marys and put $100 in the collection box." The man walks over to the collection box, pauses for a moment, then heads for the door. "Wait a minute!" says the priest, "I saw that. You didn't put any money in the box." "No," says the man. "But I rubbed some money against it, and you said that was the same as putting it in."

✴ Televangelists—the Pro Wrestlers of religion.

✴ And when God, who created the entire universe with all of its glories, decides to deliver a message to humanity, He will not use a person on cable TV in a bad suit, with a bad hairstyle, as His messenger.

✴ People who want to share their religious views with you almost never want you to share yours with them.

✴ I recently took up meditation. It beats sitting around doing nothing.

✴ Man to priest: "Father, how can I be sure of getting to Heaven?" Priest: "You must live a godly life on the day you die." Man: "And how do I know what day I'll die?" Priest: "You don't."

# RELIGION: ATHEISTS AND AGNOSTICS

✴ An atheist is taking a hike through the woods when a huge bear starts chasing after him. The bear corners the atheist in a cave, and he falls on his knees, shouting "Lord, save me!" God calls down, saying "You hypocrite. All these years you've denied me and now you want my help." The atheist replies, "You're right. It is hypocritical to proclaim myself a Christian after all these years, but could you meet me halfway and make the bear a Christian." "I suppose so," says God and gives the bear religion. The atheist breathes a huge breath and walks past the startled bear. The bear turns and bites the atheist in the neck, killing him. The bear then puts its paws together and says, "Lord, for this bounty…"

✴ I swear to God, I'm an atheist!

✴ Did you hear about the "Dial-A-Prayer" telephone service for agnostics? You dial the number and no one answers.

✴ What's an atheist's favorite Christmas movie? Coincidence on 34th Street.

✴ Atheism is a non-prophet organization.

✴ What's the biggest problem for an atheist? No one to talk to during orgasm.

# RELIGION: BUDDHISM

* A Buddhist goes to a hamburger joint and says "Make me one with everything."

* A Buddhist monk opens a hot dog stand. His first customer pays with a $20 bill and is handed a hot dog. After a few moments, he asks, "So where's my change?" The monk replies, "Change must come from within."

# RELIGION: CHURCH

* Little Johnny is in church when he suddenly falls ill. "Run outside," says his mother, "and throw up in the bushes." A minute later Johnny is back, looking relieved. "Did you get to the bushes in time?" asks his mother. "I didn't have to," replies Johnny. "I got to the door and found a box labeled 'For the Sick.'"

* Going to church doesn't make you a Christian any more than standing in a garage makes you a car.

# RELIGION: DIVISIONS

* "I was walking across a bridge one day when I saw a man standing on the edge, about to jump off. So I ran over and said, 'Stop! Don't do it!' 'Why shouldn't I?' he said. I said, 'Well, there's so much to live for!' He said, 'Like what?' I said, 'Well, are you religious or atheist?' He said, 'Religious.' I said, 'Me too! Are you Christian or Buddhist?' He said, 'Christian.' I said, 'Me too! Are you Catholic or Protestant?' He said, 'Protestant.' I said, 'Me too! Are you Episcopalian or Baptist?' He said, 'Baptist!' I said, 'Wow! Me too! Are you Baptist Church of God or Baptist Church of the Lord?' He said, 'Baptist Church of God!' I said, 'Me too! Are you Original Baptist Church of God, or are you Reformed Baptist Church of God?' He said, 'Reformed Baptist Church of God!' I said, 'Me too! Are you Reformed Baptist Church of God, Reformation of 1879, or Reformed Baptist Church of God, Reformation of 1915?' He said, 'Reformed Baptist Church of God, Reformation of 1915!' I said, 'Die, heretic scum!' and pushed him off." *Emo Phillips*

✳ A young Irish boy falls in love with a girl and takes her home to meet his family. The boy, his lady-friend, and his family gather around the dining room table, and his mother asks the girlfriend what she does. The girl hesitates, then says, "I'm a prostitute." The mother screams, faints, and has to have water splashed in her face to bring her around. "Forgive me, my dear. But I don't think I heard you correctly. Did you say you were a prostitute?" "Yes," says the girl. The mother laughs and says, "Thank goodness. For a moment I thought you said you were a Protestant."

# RELIGION: FAITH

✳ A pastor tries to survive a flood by climbing onto the roof of his house. A man in a boat rows past and offers to take him with him. "No, thanks," shouts the pastor. "God will help me." The waters rise further and a man in a motorboat comes by to rescue the pastor. Again, the pastor declines. "No, thank you. God will help me." The waters get still higher and a helicopter arrives to winch the pastor to safety. "No, thanks!" shouts the pastor. "God will surely help me!" Finally the waters sweep over the top of the house and wash the pastor into the torrent. "God! Why has thou forsaken me?" glugs the drowning pastor. "What d'you mean, 'forsaken' you?" shouts back God. "First I send a rowboat, then I send a powerboat, then I send a helicopter…"

✳ A religious man lives next door to an atheist. The religious man prays day in, day out, and is constantly on his knees in communion with the Lord, while the atheist never looks twice at a church. However, the atheist's life is good, he has a well-paying job and a beautiful wife, and his children are healthy and good-natured, whereas the pious man's job is strenuous, and his wages are low, his wife is getting fatter every day, and his kids are vile. One day the religious man raises his eyes toward Heaven and says, "Oh God, I honor you every day and confess to you my every sin. Yet my neighbor, who doesn't believe in you, seems blessed with every happiness, while I'm poor and suffer many an indignity. Why, Lord? Why me?" And a voice bellows down from above, "Because you're a damn pest!"

✳ One morning a man hobbles into a church on crutches. He stops in front of the holy water, splashes some on both legs, then throws his crutches away. An altar boy witnesses the scene and runs into the rectory to tell the priest. "Son," says the priest. "You've just witnessed a miracle. Tell me, where is this man now?" The boy replies, "Lying on his back by the font."

✳ Notice on a church board: "Don't keep the faith—spread it around!"

# RELIGION: GOD

* "God don't make mistakes. That's how He got to be God." *All in the Family*

* "I played the part of God, in Gideon. It was method acting, so two weeks beforehand, I started to live the part offstage, Y'know. I really came on God, there, I was really fabulous, I put on a blue suit, I took taxi cabs all over New York. I tipped big, 'cuz He would have. I got into a fight with a guy, and I forgave him. It's true. Some guy hit my fender and I said unto him, 'Be fruitful and multiply,' but not in those words." *Woody Allen*

* "If triangles had a God, He'd have three sides." *Yiddish proverb*

* "Not only is there no God, but try getting a plumber on weekends." *Woody Allen*

* God did not create the world in seven days; he messed around for six days, then pulled an all-nighter.

* God is not dead but alive and working on a much less ambitious project.

* God is sitting in Heaven when a scientist flies up in a rocket and says, "God, we don't need you any more. Science has figured out a way to create life out of nothing. We can now do what you did in the beginning." "Really?" replies God. "What exactly do you mean?" "Well," replies the scientist. "We can take dirt and form it into your likeness and make it live." "That's something I'd like to see," says God. "Why don't you show me?" So the scientist bends down and starts to mold the dirt into the shape of a man. God grabs his arm and pulls him back. "Hey. Not so fast," he says. "Go and get your own dirt."

* I know God won't give me more than I can handle. I just wish He didn't trust me so much.

* If there is no God, who pops up the next Kleenex in the box?

* Yes, I believe God will provide. But if only He would till He does.

* "If only God would give me some clear sign! Like making a large deposit in my name at a Swiss bank." *Woody Allen*

* If God had wanted us to go metric He'd have appointed ten apostles.

* The more you complain, the longer God makes you live.

# RELIGION: JESUS

* Jesus walks into a bar and approaches three sad-looking men. "What's troubling you, my son?" says Jesus to the first man. "My eyes are bad," says the man. "Every year I see less and less." Jesus touches the man's head and his vision is immediately restored. Jesus goes to the second man and asks the same question. The man replies, "I'm lame in my right leg." Jesus touches the man's leg and he leaps to his feet. Jesus approaches the third man, who immediately picks up a barstool and fends Jesus off. "Get the hell away from me!" he shouts, "I'm on disability!"

# RELIGION: MORMONS

* I've got nothing against Mormons, but I wouldn't want my sisters to marry one.

* Two Mormons are going door to door. They knock on the door of one woman who tells them, in no uncertain terms, that she does not want to hear their message. She slams the door in their faces but to her surprise, it bounces back open. She tries slamming the door again, and again, and again, but it won't shut. "Get your damned foot out of my door," shouts the woman. "My foot isn't in the door," says one of the Mormons. "But you might want to move your cat."

* Why don't Mormons make love standing up? They worry it could lead to dancing.

# RELIGION: NUNS

* A man is enjoying a drink outside a bar when a nun comes along and starts lecturing him on the evils of booze. The man argues back, and it turns out that the nun has never had a drink in her life. "Tell you what," says the man. "I'll buy you some alcohol, you drink it, and tell me what you think." "Out of the question," replies the nun. "I could never be seen to be drinking in public. But I suppose if you put the liquid in a coffee cup, I might have a sip." The man agrees, goes inside, and orders a double brandy in a coffee cup. "Oh no," replies the bartender. "It's not that damn nun again is it?"

✳ A man rushes into a bar and orders a brandy. While the bartender is pouring, the man says, "How tall does a penguin grow?" "About two feet," replies the bartender. "Dammit!" says the man, knocking back his drink. "I've just run over a nun."

✳ Two nuns are driving through Transylvania when Count Dracula suddenly jumps on their car. "Quick, show him your cross!" says one of the nuns. The other nun shouts, "Hey, Dracula! Get off the Goddamn car!"

✳ A nun says to Mother Superior, "There's a case of syphilis in the convent!" Mother Superior says, "Thank goodness. I was getting tired of the Chablis."

✳ Some nuns are renovating a church and getting very hot and sweaty. The Mother Superior suggests they take off their clothes and work naked. The nuns agree but bolt the church door as a precaution. They've all stripped down when there's a knock at the door. "Who is it?" says the Mother Superior. A voice replies, "It's the blind man!" The Mother Superior opens the door and the man says, "Hey, nice tits, Sister. Where do you want these blinds?"

✳ Three nuns are talking. The first nun says, "I was cleaning the Father's room the other day and do you know what I found? A bunch of pornographic magazines! I threw them straight in the trash can." The second nun says, "Well, I can top that. I was in Father's room putting away the laundry and I found a pack of condoms!" "Oh, my!" gasps the first nun. "So what did you do?" "I poked holes in them," replies the second nun. "Oh, shit!" says the third nun.

✳ The Mother Superior is giving her novice nuns a talk before sending them out into the world. "Beware the temptations of the flesh," warns the Revered Mother. "An hour's pleasure could lead to an eternity of damnation. Now, are there any questions?" A novice sticks her hand up and says, "Yes, Reverend Mother. How do you make it last an hour?"

✳ Two old nuns are discussing their vacations. Sister Mary was hard of hearing, so Sister Jane was communicating with hand gestures. "I think I'll go to Florida, where the oranges are that big and the bananas are that long," says Sister Jane. "Huh?" replies Sister Mary. Sister Jane repeats herself, "I think I'll go to FLORIDA, where the oranges are that BIG and the bananas are that LONG." "What?" replies Sister Mary. Sister Jane tries again, "I THINK I'LL GO TO FLORIDA, WHERE THE ORANGES ARE THAT BIG AND THE BANANAS ARE THAT LONG." Sister Mary replies, "Father who?"

# RELIGION: PRAYER

✳ A couple invite some friends to dinner. At the table, a guest turns to the host's six-year-old daughter and says, "Would you like to say grace?" "I wouldn't know how to do it," replies the girl. "Just say what you've heard your daddy say," says the guest. The daughter bows her head and says, "Dear Lord. Why the hell did my wife invite all these people?"

✳ A young man visits his hillbilly uncle in the country and, due to lack of space, is required to share a bed with his young nephew. When the young man comes to bed, he sees the little boy kneeling at the side of the bed with his head bowed. The young man decides to follow his example and kneels down on the other side of the bed. The boy looks up and says, "Whatcha doin'?" "Why, the same thing you're doing," replies the young man. "Boy, Ma's gonna be mighty mad," says the boy. "The bucket's on this side."

✳ As long as there are exams, there will be prayer in school.

✳ A starving man is crawling through the desert. He comes across a church, goes in, kneels at the alter, and prays, "Oh Lord, give me some food!" As if by magic, a lump of meat drops at his feet. Overjoyed, he wolfs it down—then looks up and sees a leper painting the ceiling.

✳ When I was a kid I used to pray every night for a new bike. Then I realized that the Lord doesn't work that way—so I stole one and asked him to forgive me.

# RELIGION: THE BIBLE

✳ "Years ago, my mother gave me a bullet, and I put it in my breast pocket. Two years after that, I was walking down the street, when a berserk evangelist heaved a Bible out of a hotel room window, hitting me in the chest. The Bible would have gone through my heart if it wasn't for the bullet." *Woody Allen*

✳ 668: The neighbor of the Beast.

✳ Adam and his son Abel are walking past the Garden of Eden. "Who owns that place?" asks Abel. "That's where we used to live," replies Adam. "Before your mother ate us out of house and home."

✳ Moses is praying to God to release his people from bondage when the voice of God booms from the clouds. "Moses, I have good news and bad news!" "What's the good news?" asks Moses. God says, "If Pharaoh will not let my people go, I will send down a rain of frogs, a plague of locusts, and a plague of flies, and I will turn the Nile to blood." "Wow!" says Moses. "And if Pharaoh's army pursues you in your flight," continues God, "I shall open a path for you in the Red Sea only to close it again and drown his army." "That's incredible," says Moses. "But what's the bad news?" God replies, "Before I can do all this, you must write an environmental impact statement."

✳ A priest stays the night in a city hotel and manages to seduce the maid. The maid objects at first but the priest gets around her. "It's all right, my dear," he says. "It's written in the Bible." After a night of passion, the maid wakes up and wonders where in the Bible it says it's all right for a priest to sleep with hotel staff. To answer her question, the priest picks up the Bible on the bedside table and shows her the inside cover. Written in pencil are the words "The maid is easy!"

✳ God approaches Adam and says, "I've got some good news and some bad news. The good news is that I've got two new organs for you. One is called a brain. It will allow you to be very intelligent, create new things, and have intelligent conversations with Eve. The other organ is called a penis. It will allow you to populate this planet and make you and Eve very happy." Adam is very excited, "Wow, that's great," he says. "But what was the bad news?" God replies, "You're only getting enough blood to work one at a time."

# RELIGION: THE CLERGY

✳ A young woman slips on the pavement and is helped up by passing priest. "This is the first time I've rescued a fallen woman," says the priest. The woman replies, "And this is the first time I've been picked up by a clergyman."

✳ A priest is walking down the street when he notices a small boy trying to press the doorbell of a house. Unfortunately, the boy is very small, and the doorbell is too high to reach. After watching the boy's efforts, the priest walks up behind the little fellow and gives the doorbell a solid ring. Crouching down to the child's level, the priest smiles and asks, "And now what, my little man?" The boy replies, "Now we run like hell!"

✳ A priest is reading a sermon on the Ten Commandments. He notices that, at one point, one of his congregation, Ted, becomes very agitated then breathes a sigh of relief. After the service, the priest asks Ted what had been on his mind. "Ah well," says Ted. "My umbrella's gone missing, and when you mentioned the commandment 'Thou shalt not steal' it made me think someone has stolen it. But when you got to 'Thou shalt not commit adultery,' I remembered where I'd left it."

✳ Three priests are talking about their problems with cockroaches. The first says, "I've put down poison, but nothing seems to get rid of them." The second says, "I called in the exterminator, but he couldn't eliminate them." The third says, "I got rid of all mine. I just baptized them all and I haven't seen them since."

✳ A young priest goes to town one day. A girl approaches him and says, "Feel like a quickie, Father? Only five bucks!" The priest isn't sure what a "quickie" is, so he declines the offer. In the next street, another girl approaches him—"Feel like a quickie, Father? Only five bucks!" "No thank you," stammers the priest. Yet another girl approaches him saying, "Hi, Father. Only five bucks for a quickie." The priest has had enough and hurries back to the church. On the way back, he meets an old nun. "Excuse me, Sister," he says. "But what is a quickie?" The nun replies, "Five bucks. Same as in town."

✳ Father O'Hara asks Father Smith to tea. Father Smith notices that his host's housekeeper is a young attractive woman and worries that they might be having an affair. To test this theory he slips a silver cake knife into his pocket. The next week Father O'Hara notices the cake knife is missing. "Father Smith must have taken it," says Father O'Hara to his housekeeper. "There's no other explanation." "Don't accuse him of anything," says his housekeeper. "Send him a letter and write that you're not saying he did take it, and you're not saying he didn't take it, but just point out it's been missing since he was here." A couple of days later the couple get a letter from Father Smith. It reads: "Father O'Hara, I'm not saying you are sleeping with your housekeeper, and I'm not saying you're not, but I'd like to point out that if you'd been sleeping in your own bed, you'd have found that damn cake knife by now."

✳ A girl is speaking to her mother. "Mom, are you going to leave me to entertain the new priest all by myself?" "That's not the priest," says mother. "That's the new doctor. I asked him to give you a check-up." "Oh," says the girl. "I thought he was a bit familiar for a priest."

✳ A priest is leaving his parish after thirty years. "We're sorry to see you go, Father," says one woman. "Before you came to this parish we didn't know what sin was."

✳ Our priest is very liberal. He likes to show he's as imperfect as the rest of us. Halfway through confession, he often pulls back the screen so we can see him puffing on his crack pipe.

✳ Three trainee priests line up for a celibacy test. The first trainee goes into a room, strips down, and has a bell tied to his penis. A nude pole dancer then does her act for him and the inevitable happens: he gets excited and the bell goes "ting-a-ling-a-ling." "I'm sorry," says the head priest. "You don't have the strength of character to be a priest. Now go and have a shower." The second candidate enters the room, strips down, and has a bell tied on. But, again, when the pole dancer goes into her act, the bell goes "ting-a-ling-a-ling." "I'm sorry," says the head priest. "You're not up to the job. Go and have a shower." The third candidate enters the room, strips down, and has the bell put on him. When the pole dancer appears, he watches her with no reaction, no matter how hard she tries to arouse him. Eventually she gives up, and the head Priest walks over to congratulate the trainee: "Well done, my son! You showed remarkable forbearance. You're just what the church is looking for. Now go and join the other boys in the shower"..."ting-a-ling-a-ling."

✳ What do a Christmas tree and a priest have in common? Their balls are just for decoration.

# RELIGION: THE POPE

✳ The Pope is visiting a town and all the residents are lining the street hoping for a blessing. The Mayor is sure the Pope will stop and talk to him, but is surprised when the Pope ignores him completely and whispers a few words to a filthy old bum standing on the other side of the road. "Of course!" thinks the Mayor. "The Pope cares more for the poor and homeless, not the rich like me!" With this he dashes over to the bum, buys his clothes, gets into them, then runs to the end of the street and lines up again. Sure enough the Pope sees the Mayor and walks over to talk to him. "Hey, stinky," whispers the Pope. "I thought I told you to get lost."

✳ The Pope calls a meeting of cardinals and says, "I have some really good news and some very bad news." The cardinals want to hear the good news first, so the Pope says, "Jesus Christ has returned to the world." After the uproar has died down, the Pope says, "The bad news is he was calling from Salt Lake City."

✳ What happened to the Pope when he went to Mount Olive? Popeye beat him up.

# RESTAURANTS

✳ "At the all-you-can-eat barbecue near my house, you have to pay the regular dinner price if you eat less than you can." *Steven Wright*

✳ "Waiter! This water is very cloudy." "No, Sir, you just have a very dirty glass."

✳ A man goes into a restaurant and the waitress comes to take his order. "I want a quickie," says the man, and the waitress slaps his face. Another waitress passes, and the man says, "Please, can I have a quickie?" Again the waitress slaps his face. A third waitress passes. The man says, "All I want is a quickie." Again the man gets his face slapped. A diner on the next table leans over and says, "It's pronounced 'keesh.'"

✳ Harry took his date to an upscale restaurant and ordered the entire meal in French. Even the waiters were impressed—especially since it was a Chinese restaurant.

✳ It's a very authentic Mexican restaurant. They bring you a glass of water then warn you not to drink it.

✳ Mr. Smith and his wife enter an expensive restaurant. "I'm sorry," apologizes the maître d', "but there are no tables available." Mr. Smith replies, "I bet if the President came in and asked for a table, there'd be one available. "Yes," admits the maître d', I suppose there would." "Then I'll take that one," says Mr. Smith. "The President isn't coming."

✳ There are two things you should avoid approaching from the rear – horses and restaurants.

✳ Two ladies go for their regular restaurant appointment and order a meal. "And make sure I have a clean glass," says one of the ladies. "The one I had last week was filthy." A few minutes later the waiter returns, sets out the food, and says, "And which one of you ordered the clean glass?"

✳ We were eating in an open-air café when it started raining really heavily. It took us an hour and a half to finish our soup.

✳ A man in a restaurant knocks his spoon off the table. A waiter immediately comes along and takes a fresh spoon out of his pocket. "That's very efficient," says the man. "Thank you, sir," says the waiter. "All the staff carry a spare spoon in case of emergencies." The man then notices a string hanging out of the waiter's fly. "Do you know you have a piece of string hanging out of your pants?" he asks. "Why, yes, sir," replies the waiter. "It's attached to my penis. If I have to answer a call of nature, I can go to the bathroom and pull my penis out with the string. We find this much faster and more hygienic than the normal method." "I'm extremely impressed," says the man. "But tell me, how do you get your penis back inside your pants without touching it?" The waiter replies, "Well, I usually poke mine back with a spoon."

✳ It used to be a successful restaurant, but it became so crowded people stopped going there.

✳ Waiter to customer: "And how would you like your eggs cooked, sir?" Customer: "Does it make a difference in the price?" Waiter: "No, sir." Customer: "In that case I'll have them cooked with beans, potatoes, and three sausages."

✳ I found a café that serves chicken dinners for fifty cents. You sit down and they bring you a plate of bird seed.

# RESTAURANTS: WAITER

✳ "Waiter! Do you have frogs' legs?" "Oui, monsieur." "Then hop over the counter and get me some cigarettes."

✳ "Waiter! There's a fly in my soup!" "That's not a fly, that's a vitamin Bee."

✳ "Waiter! This food isn't fit for a pig." "In that case I shall take it away and bring you some that is."

✳ "Waiter! This plate is wet." "No, that's your soup."

* "Waiter! This soup tastes funny." "Then why aren't you laughing?"

* "Waiter! What's this fly doing in my soup?" "It looks like the backstroke."

* "Waiter! Why is there a dead cockroach in my soup?" "Surely you don't expect a live one at these prices?"

* "Waiter! There's a fly in my soup!" "Don't worry, sir, it's not hot enough to burn him."

* "Waiter! Why does this chicken only have one leg?" "It was in a fight, sir." "Well, take it away and bring me the winner."

* "Waiter! This egg is bad!" "Don't blame me. I only laid the table."

* "Waiter! There's a fly in my soup!" "No, that's the chef. The last customer was a witch doctor."

* "Waiter! There's a fly in my chicken soup!" "No, that's the chicken."

# RIDDLES

* If two's company, and three's a crowd, what are four and five? Nine!

* If you have a green ball in your left hand and a green ball in your right hand, what do you have? Kermit's undivided attention.

* Say "coast" fives times quickly then answer this question—what do you put in a toaster? (No, you put bread in a toaster.)

* Say "silk" fives times quickly then answer this question—what do cows drink? (No, they drink water.)

* What cheese is made backward? Edam.

* What did the man say when he saw a dinosaur coming down the path wearing sunglasses? Nothing! He didn't recognize him.

* What do you call a boomerang that doesn't come back? A stick.

* What do you call a camel with a flat back? Humphrey.

* What do you call a dead tractor collector? An ex-tractor fan.

* What do you call a deaf monster? Whatever you like—he can't hear you!

✳ What do you call a deer with no eyes? No idea. What do you call a deer with no eyes and no legs? Still no idea.

✳ What do you call a donkey with three legs? A wonkey.

✳ What do you call a film about mallards? A duckumentary!

✳ What do you call a fish on a motorcycle? A motor pike!

✳ What do you call a fish with no eyes? A fsh.

✳ What do you call a sheep with no legs? A cloud.

✳ What do you call a sleepwalking nun? A roamin' Catholic.

✳ What do you think Abraham Lincoln would be doing if he were alive today? A) Writing his memoirs, B) Advising the President, C) Desperately clawing at the inside of his coffin.

✳ What do you call cheese that doesn't belong to you? Nacho cheese.

✳ What do you call something that runs around your garden all day and never stops? The fence!

✳ What do you call the costume of a one-legged ballerina? A one-one.

✳ What do you call the place where parrots make films? Pollywood!

✳ What do you do if you come across a tiger in the jungle? Wipe him off, apologize, and run!

✳ What d'you call an unemployed jester? Nobody's fool.

✳ What goes Moooooooz? A jet flying backward!

✳ What happened to the two bedbugs who fell in love? They got married in the spring.

✳ What happens when you throw a green stone in the Red Sea? It gets wet!

✳ What has forty feet and sings? A choir!

✳ What has wheels and flies? A garbage truck.

✳ What is Cole's Law? Mostly it's thinly sliced cabbage.

✳ What is half of infinity? Nity.

✳ What is red and dangerous? Strawberry and tarantula jelly!

✳ What lies on its back a hundred feet in the air? A centipede.

✴ What runs but never walks? Water!

✴ What word is always pronounced incorrectly? Incorrectly.

✴ What's smelly, round, and laughs? A tickled onion.

✴ What's brown and sounds like a bell? Dung.

✴ What's brown and sticky? A stick.

✴ What's green and looks like a bucket? A green bucket.

✴ What's green and says, "Blub blub"? A green Blub Blub. What's blue and says, "Blub blub"? Nothing, there are no blue Blub Blubs.

✴ What's green and would kill you if it fell out of a tree? A pool table.

✴ What's pink and fluffy? Pink fluff.

✴ What's red and bad for your teeth? A brick.

✴ What's red and white? Pink!

✴ What's round, hard, and sticks so far out of his pajamas a man can stick his hat on it? His head.

✴ What's the quickest way to make anti-freeze? Hide her nightie.

✴ What's twelve feet long, has big teeth, and eats people while going up and down? A shark in an elevator.

✴ When is a door not a door? When it's ajar.

✴ Where do you find the most fish? Between the head and tail.

✴ Where does success come before work? In the dictionary!

✴ Which two words in the English language have the most letters? Post Office!

✴ Why are there so many Smiths in the phone book? They all have phones.

✴ Why did the chicken run on to the soccer field? Because the ref blew for a foul.

✴ Why did the Marxist only drink fake tea? Because all proper tea is theft.

✴ Why did the raisin go out with the prune? Because she couldn't find a date.

✴ Why do white sheep eat more than black ones? Because there's more of them.

✳ Why is duct tape like "The Force"? It has a light side and a dark side, and it holds the universe together.

✳ Why is getting up at five in the morning like a pig's tail? It's twirly.

✳ Why was six unhappy? Because seven eight nine.

✳ What do you get if you divide the circumference of a pumpkin by its diameter? Pumpkin pi.

✳ What do you get if you put a canary in a food blender? Shredded tweet.

✳ What did the grape say when it was stepped on? Nothing. It just let out a little wine.

✳ What do you call a disguise worn by an elk? A false moosetache.

✳ What do you call a judge with no thumbs? Just his fingers.

✳ What do you call people who ride on double-decker buses? Passengers.

✳ What gets smaller the more you put in it? A hole in the ground.

✳ What has two humps and is found at the North Pole? A lost camel.

✳ What's the difference between a genealogist and a gynecologist? The genealogist looks up trees, the gynecologist looks up bushes.

✳ What was Dick van Dyke's real name? Penis van Lesbian.

✳ What was the name of the Scottish dentist? Phil McCavity.

✳ What's green and smells? Hulk's fart.

✳ What's green and walks through walls? Casper the friendly cabbage.

✳ What's twelve feet long and smells of lavender and stale pee? A line dance at an old people's home.

✳ Which bus crossed the ocean? Columbus.

✳ Why do policemen have bigger balls than firemen? They sell more tickets.

✳ Why was the Old Testament prostitute arrested? She was trying to make a Prophet.

✳ What's black, white, and red all over? Half a cat.

✳ What's brown and lives in a bell tower? The lunch bag of Notre Dame.

✳ What goes "Mark!"? A dog with a hare lip.

❋ What's the difference between a hill and a pill? One is hard to get up, the other is hard to get down.

❋ What's big, green, and can't fly? A field.

❋ What can you put in a wooden box that will actually make it lighter? Holes.

# RIDDLES: BACKWARD

❋ Answer: Melancholy. Question: What kind of salad can you make with a cantaloupe and Lassie?

❋ Answer: Put your left leg in and shake it all about. Question: What's the worst known way to clean your toilet?

❋ Answer: Spam and the Unabomber. Question: Name two things that will be in the can for the next eighteen years.

❋ Answer: Hey diddle diddle. Question: How do you greet your diddle diddle early in the morning?

# RIDDLES: BRAIN TEASERS

❋ A child is born in Boston, Massachusetts, to parents who were both born in Boston, Massachusetts. The child is not a United States citizen. How is this possible? The child was born before 1776.

❋ A rooster sits on a barn roof. If it lays an egg, on which side will it roll off? Neither, roosters don't lay eggs.

❋ Before Mount Everest was discovered, what was the highest mountain on Earth? Mount Everest—it just hadn't been discovered!

❋ How many times can you subtract the number five from twenty-five? Only once, then you are subtracting it from twenty.

❋ If there are three apples and you take away two, how many do you have? You have two, you took them, remember?

❋ How many birthdays does the average man have? Just one!

✳ In Okmulgee, Oklahoma, you cannot take a picture of a man with a wooden leg. Why not? You have to take a picture of a man with a camera.

✳ Some months have thirty-one days—how many have twenty-eight? All of them!

✳ The maker doesn't want it, the buyer doesn't use it, and the user doesn't see it. What is it? A coffin.

✳ Which is correct to say—"The yolk of the egg are white," or "The yolk of the egg is white"? Neither, the yolk of the egg is yellow.

✳ You have an oil lamp, a stove, and a fireplace, which do you light first? A match!

✳ Is it legal for a man in California to marry his widow's sister? No—he's dead!

# RIDDLES: CROSSING THE ROAD

✳ Why did the chewing gum cross the road? It was stuck to the chicken's foot.

✳ Why did the dinosaur cross the road? Because chickens hadn't been invented yet.

✳ Why did the one-handed man cross the road? To get to the second-hand shop.

✳ Why did the horse cross the road? Because the chicken needed a day off.

✳ Why did the salmon cross the road? Just for the halibut!

# RIDDLES: WHAT DO YOU GET IF YOU CROSS...

✳ What do you get if you cross a black hat with a rocket? A fast bowler.

✳ What do you get if you cross a chicken with a zebra? A four-legged dinner with it's own barcode.

✳ What do you get if you cross a hundred pigs and a hundred deer? Two hundred sows and bucks.

✳ What do you get if you cross a philosopher with a Mafia hitman? Someone who'll make you an offer you can't understand.

✳ What do you get if you cross a snowflake with a man-eating shark? Frostbite.

✳ What do you get if you cross a star with a silver cup? A constellation prize.

✳ What do you get if you cross an alligator with a gorilla, a lion, and a parrot? I don't know, but when it talks, you listen.

✳ What do you get if you cross an elephant with a fish? Swimming trunks.

✳ What do you get if you cross Cameron Diaz with Santa Claus? A thank you from Santa!

✳ What do you get if you cross the moon with a nun? A nocturnal habit.

✳ What do you get if you cross a rooster with an owl? A cock that stays up all night.

✳ What do you get if you cross an elephant with a prostitute? A two-ton pick-up.

✳ What do you get if you cross Bambi with a ghost? Bamboo.

# SCIENCE

✳ "If I melt dry ice, can I swim without getting wet?" *Steven Wright*

✳ "If you were in a vehicle and you were traveling at the speed of light, and then you turned your lights on, would they do anything?" *Steven Wright*

✳ "It's a good thing we have gravity, or else when birds died they'd just stay right up there." *Steven Wright*

✳ How many balls of string would it take to reach the moon? Just one—if it's long enough!

✳ A day without radiation is a day without sunshine.

✳ A man is playing Trivial Pursuit. He rolls the dice and lands on Science & Nature. The question is "If you are in a vacuum and someone calls your name, can you hear it?" The man thinks for a moment before asking, "Is the vacuum on or off?"

✳ A neutron walks into a bar. "I'd like a beer," he says. The bartender promptly serves up a beer. "How much will that be?" asks the neutron. "For you?" replies the bartender. "No charge."

✳ A mathematician, a physicist, and an engineer were all given a red rubber ball and told to find the volume. The mathematician carefully measured the diameter and evaluated a triple integral. The physicist filled a beaker with water, put the ball in the water, and measured the total displacement. The engineer looked up the model and serial numbers in his red-rubber-ball table.

✳ A physics professor is giving a lecture on lighting. "The moon is more useful than the sun because the moon shines at night when you want the light, whereas the sun shines during the day when you don't need it."

✳ A research scientist drops a piece of buttered toast on the floor and is astonished to find that it lands butter-side up. He takes the toast to a colleague and asks him how on earth the toast landed butter-side up when, according to experience, it always lands butter-side down. The colleague thinks for a moment then comes up with the answer. "It's easy," he says. "You must have buttered the wrong side."

✳ I went live on the internet myself the other day—I was plugging in my modem and got my finger stuck in the socket.

✳ Statistics are like a lamppost to a drunken man—more for leaning on than for illumination.

✳ "I put tape on the mirrors in my house so I don't accidentally walk through into another dimension." *Steven Wright*

✳ "If it weren't for electricity we'd all be watching television by candlelight." *George Gobel*

✳ Astronomers, go outside during the night of the next spring equinox and face south. Bend over to an angle of 45 degrees, slightly relax your knees, and lower your head so you can look back between your legs. Now hold a small mirror in your left hand and adjust the angle so it's parallel with your face. With luck you should now see Uranus.

✳ An astronomer, a physicist, and a mathematician are vacationing in Scotland. Glancing from a train window, they observe a black sheep in the middle of a field. "How interesting," observes the astronomer. "All Scottish sheep are black." The physicist responds, "No, no! Only some Scottish sheep are black!" The mathematician tells them, "In Scotland there exists at least one field, containing at least one sheep, at least one side of which is black."

✳ A seminar on Time Travel will be held two weeks ago.

✳ Did you know that Hannibal was the first man to experiment with genetics? He crossed a mountain with an elephant.

✳ Does the name Pavlov ring a bell?

✳ The thing I really like about the Oxford Dictionary of Differential Calculus is that it doesn't try to glamorize the subject in any way.

✳ Two hydrogen atoms are talking. One says, "I think I've lost an electron." The other asks, "Are you sure?" The first replies, "Yes, I'm positive."

✳ What's a quark? The noise made by a well-bred duck.

✳ A mathematician, a biologist, and a physicist are sitting in a street cafe watching people going in and coming out of the house on the other side of the street. First they see two people going into the house. Time passes. After a while they notice three people coming out of the house. The physicist says, "The measurement wasn't accurate." The biologist says, "They have reproduced." The mathematician says, "If now exactly one person enters the house, it will be empty again."

✳ A scientist is surprised to see a horseshoe hanging over the desk of a colleague. He asks what it's doing there and is told it brings him luck in his experiments. "I'm amazed you believe in superstitious rubbish like that," says the scientist. "Oh, I don't believe in it," says his colleague. "But apparently it works whether you believe in it or not."

✳ I think the surest sign that intelligent life exists somewhere else in the universe is that none of it has bothered to contact us.

✳ What do the starship *Enterprise* and toilet paper have in common? They both circle Uranus looking for black holes and hope to wipe out the Klingons.

✳ When NASA first started sending up astronauts, they quickly discovered that ballpoint pens would not work in zero gravity. To combat the problem, NASA scientists spent a decade and $12 billion to develop a pen that writes in zero gravity, upside down, underwater, on almost any surface, including glass, and at temperatures ranging from below freezing to 300°C. The Russians used a pencil.

# SEA LIFE

✳ A humble crab falls in love with a lobster princess. They enjoy an idyllic relationship until, one day, the princess tells the crab that her father the King will not let her see him any more. "But why?" asks the crab. "Daddy says that crabs are common," sobs the princess. "You're a lower class of crustacean, and you walk sideways." The crab is shattered and scuttles away to drown his sorrows. That night is the occasion of the Great Lobster Ball, lobsters coming from far and wide to feast and dance. The lobster princess, however, sits by her father's side, inconsolable. Suddenly, the doors crash open and in walks the crab. He painstakingly makes his way to the throne, walking dead straight, one claw after another. All the lobsters' eyes are on the crab as, step by painful step, he approaches the throne. He reaches the feet of the King and looks him in the eye. There's a deadly hush. Finally the crab says, "Oh, man, I'm wasted!"

✳ How does seaweed find work? It looks at the kelp-wanted ads.

✳ Why are dolphins smarter than humans? Within three hours they can train a man to stand at the side of a pool and feed them fish!

✳ "I have the world's largest seashell collection. I keep it scattered on beaches all over the world. Maybe you've seen it?" *Steven Wright*

# SEMI-TRADITIONAL SAYINGS

✳ Don't worry about a thing—I reckon I've got an ace up my hole.

✳ Gentlemen, the ball is now squarely on our shoulders.

✳ I don't need a compass to tell me which way the wind shines!

✳ I don't want to put all my monkeys in one barrel.

✳ I learned my lessons at the school of Fort Knox.

✳ I tell you, if we can't lead them with a stick, we're going to have to beat them with a carrot.

✳ I tell you, we're going to come out of this smelling like geniuses!

✳ I tell you, you're cutting your throat to spite your face.

✳ I want quality, not quantity; but lots of it.

✳ I wouldn't trust that feller with a nine-foot pole.

✳ I'll tell you one thing, you're never going to fail unless you try.

✳ Is everyone else in the world a moron, or is it just me?

✳ It's like the blind talking to the blind here!

* It's no skin off my teeth!

* Steady now. You're opening a whole can of Pandora's worms.

* The ball is in his camp now.

* The service is available 24-7, five days a week.

* This is quite simply an exercise in fertility.

* This should find out what separates the wheat from the sheep.

* We need to find a solution here, even if it isn't the right one.

* Why, this is just like six of one and two dozen of the other.

* Yes, sir, I gave him a real good mouthful.

* You don't want me here breathing down your throat.

* You're a minefield of information.

* You're still a bit green under the collar.

* He's just a flash in the pants.

* I think I can finally see the carrot at the end of the tunnel.

* My darling, you are the wind beneath my cheeks.

* This sounds like sour milk, and I don't like the smell of it.

* Don't look for a gift in the horse's mouth.

* Eventually the penny will come home to roost.

* I didn't have two dimes to pee on.

* I'd like to be a fish on the wall at that meeting.

* In the last year, you've turned around 150 percent.

* It was a huge incontinence for me.

* I think you might have hit the nail on the button.

# SEX

✳ "I'd like to meet the man who invented sex and see what he's working on now." *George Carlin*

✳ "She's the original good time that was had by all." *Bette Davis*

✳ "When my old man wanted sex, my mother would show him a picture of me." *Rodney Dangerfield*

✳ "Women need a reason to have sex. Men just need a place." *Billy Crystal*

✳ A circus owner advertises for a lion tamer. Two people show up—one is a young man and the other is a gorgeous girl. The circus owner says, "I'm not going to lie to you. This is a ferocious lion. He ate my last tamer, so you guys better be good. Here's your equipment; a chair, whip, and a gun. Who wants to try out first?" The girl volunteers. She walks past the whip and the gun, steps into the lion's cage, and sits in the chair. The lion charges, but the girl throws open her coat revealing that she's naked underneath. The lion stops dead in his tracks, licks her legs, then rests its head in her lap. The circus owner is astonished, "I've never seen anything like that in my life." He turns to the young man and says, "Can you top that?" The young man replies, "Sure I can—as soon as you get that damn lion out of the way."

✳ A little boy is always biting his nails. In the end his mom gets angry and says, "If you continue biting your nails, you'll get bigger and bigger and bigger until you blow up like a balloon!" A few days later the little boy is on the bus when a very pregnant woman sits opposite him. After a few minutes, she realizes the boy is staring at her. "Do you know me?" she asks. "No," says the boy. "But I know what you've been doing."

✳ A man picks up a gorgeous woman at a bar, and they go back to her place. The man is surprised to see how many teddy bears and stuffed toys the woman has at her apartment—every surface is piled high with them. After a night of passion, the man rolls over and says, "So. How was I?" The woman replies. "Take any prize from the bottom shelf."

✳ A new monk arrives at the monastery and starts to help copying old texts by hand. However, the monk notices that there are errors in the text and that the monks are copying copies, not the original books. The new monk goes to the abbot of the monastery and points out that if there was an error in the first copy, that error would be continued. The abbot agrees and decides to go and check the original books in the cellar. Hours later the abbot still hasn't returned, so one of the monks goes to look for him. The monk hears sobbing coming from the back of the cellar and finds the abbot leaning over one of the books crying. "What's wrong?" asks the monk. The abbot looks at him and says, "The word is 'celebrate.'"

✳ A newlywed couple didn't know the difference between putty and Vaseline. A week after the marriage, all their windows fell out. Which was the least of their worries.

✳ At the retreat, Jill and John are each told to write a sentence using the words "sex" and "love." Jill writes, "When two mature people are both passionately and deeply in love with one another to a high degree and they respect each other very much, just like John and me, it is spiritually and morally acceptable for them to engage in the act of physical sex with one another." John writes, "I love sex."

✳ "I wouldn't mind being the last man on Earth—just to see if all of those girls were telling me the truth." *Ronnie Shakes*

✳ Did you hear about the transvestite who wanted a night on the town? He wanted to eat, drink, and be Mary.

✳ Harry is very quick with the ladies—before they can tell him they're not that sort of girl, it's usually too late.

✳ I think you'll find that any of my lady companions will tell you I'm a "five times a night man." I really shouldn't drink so much tea before I go to bed.

✳ I wish my girlfriend had warned me about the ceiling mirror in her bedroom. I lay down ready for her, then ran out screaming—I'd looked up and thought I was being attacked by a naked skydiver.

✳ Man, to woman: "Am I the first man you ever made love to?" Woman: "You might be. Now you come to mention it, your face does look familiar."

✳ Man, to woman: "Do you want sex?" Woman: "Your place or mine?" Man: "Well, if you're going to argue. Forget it."

✳ Patrick and Michael go to a bar for a drink and see a sign reading, "Buy a double whiskey and get a chance of free sex." They both buy a double then ask the bartender how to get the sex. "It's simple," he says. "I think of a number between one and ten, and if you can guess what it is, you get laid." "Okay," says Patrick. "I'll guess, three." "Sorry," says the bartender. "You're out of luck." The next day, the pair return and, again, Patrick tries his luck at the free sex quiz, he guesses four. "Sorry," says the bartender. "Better luck next time." The next day, the pair come back and Patrick guesses two. "Sorry," says the bartender. "Wrong again." Patrick turns to Michael and says, "Y'know I'm beginning to think this contest is rigged." "Oh no," says Michael. "My wife tried it last week and she won three times."

✳ The priest never entertained lewd thoughts—they always entertained him.

✳ Two men are having a drink together. One says, "I had sex with my wife before we were married. What about you?" "I don't know," says the other. "What was her maiden name?"

✳ There is nothing wrong with sex on TV—as long as you don't fall off.

✳ Two teenage boys go to confession. In the booth, the first boy admits having sex with a girl but refuses to name her. The priest asks, "It wasn't Mary Jones, was it?" The boy says, "No, Father, it wasn't." The priest asks, "Was it Angela Brown?" The boy replies, "No, Father, it wasn't." The priest asks, "It wasn't Jane Carter, by any chance?" The boy says, "No, Father it wasn't." The priest gives up and says, "Well, for your penance say fifty Hail Marys and leave half your pocket money in the poor box." When the boy leaves his friend asks him how it went. The boy replies, "Not bad, a $5 fine and three great leads."

✳ What's a man's definition of safe sex? Meeting his mistress at least thirty miles from his house.

✳ When I was young, my sister used to play with dolls and I played with soldiers—now we do it the other way around.

✳ Why is it called sex? Because it's easier to spell than Uhhhhh.. oooohh… Ahhhhhh… AllEEEEEEE!

✳ "During sex, my girlfriend always wants to talk to me. Just the other night she called me from a hotel." *Rodney Dangerfield*

✳ "If it weren't for pickpockets, I'd have no sex life at all." *Rodney Dangerfield*

✳ "My classmates would copulate with anything that moved. But I never saw any reason to limit myself." *Emo Philips*

✳ A couple and their ten-year-old son live in an apartment in the city. The couple decide that the only way they can have a Sunday afternoon quickie with their son in the apartment is to send him out on the balcony and get him to report on all the neighborhood activities. The couple go to bed, and the boy begins his commentary: "There's a car being towed from the parking lot," he says. "An ambulance just drove by." A few moments pass. "Looks like the Andersons have company," he calls out. After a minute he says, "Hey, Matt's riding a new bike and the Coopers are having sex." Mom and Dad shoot up in bed. "How do you know the Coopers are having sex?" says Dad. The boy replies, "Because their kid is standing out on the balcony too."

✳ A couple have just had sex. The woman says, "If I got pregnant, what would we call the baby?" The man takes off his condom, ties a knot in it, and flushes it down the toilet. "Well," he says. "If he can get out of that, we'll call him Houdini."

✳ A father catches his young son coming out of the woods with the neighbor's daughter. The father asks the boy what they've been getting up to, and the son confesses that they've been indulging in hanky-panky. Father tells him not to do it again but gives the boy a cookie as a reward for telling the truth. The next day, the father catches his son doing exactly the same thing. Again he questions him, gets an answer, and again gives the boy a cookie for telling the truth. The next day, the same happens again and, again, the son is told off but given a reward for speaking the truth. The next day the son and the neighbor's daughter are caught yet again. This time, father goes into the kitchen and starts frying eggs. "Eggs?" says mother. "What happened to the cookies?" Father replies, "He can't keep that up living on cookies."

✳ A honeymoon couple go into a hotel and ask for a suite. "Bridal?" asks the desk clerk. "No thanks," replies the bride, "I'll just hang onto his shoulders."

✳ A little girl asks her mother about her origin. "How did I get here, Mommy?" she says. Her mother replies, "Why, God sent you, Honey." "And did God send you too, Mommy?" she continues. "Yes, sweetheart, He did." "And Daddy, and Grandma and Grandpa, and their moms and dads, too?" "Yes, Honey, all of them, too." The child shakes her head, "So you're telling me there's been no sex in this family for about 200 years? Heck, no wonder everyone's so grouchy!"

✳ A man and a woman get into an argument about who enjoys sex more. The man says, "Men obviously enjoy sex more than women. Why do you think we're so obsessed with it?" "That doesn't prove anything," says the woman. "Think about this—when your ear itches and you put your finger in it and wiggle it around, what feels better, your ear or the finger?"

✳ A man goes to the doctor with a broken leg. "How did this happen?" asks the doctor. "Twenty years ago I went on vacation to a farm," says the man. "The farmer had a beautiful young daughter, and on the first night I was there, she came to my room in her nightie and asked if there was anything I'd like to give her. I told her I couldn't think of anything. On the second night, she came back and asked if I was sure there wasn't anything I could give her. I said I still couldn't think of anything. Then on the third night, she came back and asked if I was positive there wasn't anything I could give her. I said no, I still couldn't think of anything." "So what's that got to do with breaking your leg?" asks the doctor. "Well," replies the man. "This morning I was up a ladder when I suddenly realized what I could have given her."

✳ A woman goes into a noisy laundromat and asks the owner to do a double wash. "What?!" shouts the owner. "Come again?!" "No!" shouts back the woman. "This time it's mustard!"

✳ A woman is standing in her front garden talking to her friend when she notices her husband coming home, carrying a bunch of flowers. Her friend says, "Isn't that nice. He's bringing you a bouquet!" The woman replies, "Yeah, great. That means another weekend flat on my back with my feet up in the air!" The friend says, "What's the matter? Don't you have a vase?"

✳ A young couple get between the sheets for the first time. In a flash it's over. The boy says, "If I'd known you were a virgin I'd have taken more time." His girlfriend replies, "If I'd known you were going to take more time, I'd have taken off my tights."

✳ A young honeymoon couple rent a cottage from an old lady. The cottage is in beautiful countryside just by a fishing lake, but the couple spend all their time indoors. Finally the old lady knocks on the door to see if they're okay. "We're fine," says the young man. "We're living on the fruits of love." "I guessed as much," says the old lady. "But would you mind not throwing the peels out of the window—they're choking my ducks."

✳ An elderly Italian man goes to confession. "Father," he says. "I'd like to ask you a moral question." "Certainly, my son," says the priest. "During the war a beautiful Jewish woman knocked on my door," says the old man. "And she asked me to hide her in return for sexual favors." "That was wrong of you," replies the priest. "You shouldn't have taken advantage of the woman. But you did a good deed in saving her life. Say fifty Hail Marys." "No, father," says the old man. "That wasn't the question." "Then what is your question?" asks the Priest. The old man says, "Do I have to tell her the war is over?"

✳ How can you make your wife scream for an hour after sex? Wipe your dick on the curtains.

✳ How do you know if your wife wears tights in bed? Her toes curl up when you screw her.

✳ How do you know when your cat's finished cleaning himself? He's smoking a cigarette.

✳ I'm not cheap, but I am on special this week.

✳ Kids in the back seat cause accidents; accidents in the back seat cause kids.

✳ Little Johnny goes to stay on his uncle's farm. One morning his aunt tells him to feed the animals, but little Johnny is in a bad mood and he kicks at the chickens when he scatters their corn. He kicks the cow when he gives it its hay. And he kicks the pig when he fills its trough. "I saw what you did," says his aunt when he comes inside. "For kicking that chicken, you'll get no eggs this morning. For kicking the cow, you'll get no milk and, for kicking the pig, you'll get no bacon." At that moment, Uncle comes in and kicks the cat away from his chair. Little Johnny looks at his aunt and says, "Are you going to tell him or shall I?"

✳ Man to woman: "Tell me, after having sex do you ever smoke?" Woman: "I've never looked."

✳ Mary and Jane are talking. Mary declares that she's finally got pregnant after years of trying. "How did you manage it?" asks Jane. "I went to that hypnotherapist on Main Street," replies Mary. "I got pregnant within two months." "Oh, my husband and I tried seeing him years ago," says Jane. "It didn't work for us." "Of course it wouldn't," replies Mary. "You have to go alone."

❋ Mary to Jill: "My last boyfriend said he fantasized about having two girls at once. Jill: "Most men do. What did you tell him?" Mary: "I said, "If you can't satisfy one woman, why would you want to piss off another one?"'

❋ Mary to Jill: "I told my husband he didn't arouse me anymore!" Jill: "That's pretty forthright! What did he say?" Mary: "He said, 'Maybe you have a dry well.' So I said 'Maybe you need a new drill.'"

❋ One night a policeman shines his flashlight on a man and his girlfriend making out in a parked car. "We aren't doing anything, officer," says the man. "Really?" says the policeman. "Well, in that case I'll get in the car, and you can take the flashlight."

❋ Randy Rachel has got a speech impediment—she can't say no.

❋ Sex isn't the answer. Sex is the question. Yes is the answer.

❋ She was hungry for love and didn't know where her next male was coming from.

❋ She's like train tracks—she's been laid across the country.

❋ Small boy to friend: "What would you do if a girl kissed you?" Friend: "I'd kiss her back. What would you do?" Small boy: "I'd kiss her front."

❋ Tom is driving around town in a Rolls Royce when he sees his friend Harry. He pulls over to say hello. "How did you get the car?" asks Harry. "Well," says Tom. "I was walking down the street when a gorgeous woman pulled up in this car and offered me a ride. I got in, and she asked me to kiss her, so I did. Then she parked up in a lane and took off all her clothes except her silk panties. Then she lay back in her seat and said, 'Take anything you want from me...'" "Wow," says Harry. "What did you do then?" "Well," says Tom. "I could see her underwear would never fit me, so I took the car."

❋ Two policemen are walking the beat when one says, "When I get home, I'm going straight upstairs and tearing off the wife's underwear." "Feeling frisky?" asks the other. "No," says the first. "The elastic is killing me."

❋ What are the small bumps around women's nipples? It's Braille for "suck here."

❋ What did the Irish spinster keep saying in her prayers? "Good Lord, please have Murphy on me..."

❋ What do you call kinky sex with chocolate? S&M&M.

✳ What happened when the chef got his hand caught in the dishwasher? They both got fired.

✳ What two things in the air can make a woman pregnant? Her feet.

✳ What's the difference between "Oooh!" and "Aaah!"? About three inches.

✳ What's the difference between erotic and kinky? Erotic is using a feather. Kinky is using the whole chicken.

✳ Why can't gypsies have babies? Because their husbands have crystal balls.

✳ Why do men like having sex with the lights on? It makes it easier to put a name to the face.

✳ "He had ambitions at one time to become a sex maniac, but he failed his practical." *Les Dawson*

✳ "I believe that sex between two people is a beautiful experience. Between five it's fantastic!" *Woody Allen*

✳ Why do women fake orgasms? Because they think men care.

✳ Why is it that when a man talks nasty to a women, it's sexual harassment, but when a women talks nasty to a man, it's $3.99 a minute?

✳ Woman to doctor: "Doctor, every time I sneeze I have an orgasm." Doctor: "And what are you taking for it?" Woman: "Pepper."

✳ "Of course I believe in safe sex. I've got a handrail around the bed." *Ken Dodd*

✳ "Programming is like sex. One mistake and you have to support it for the rest of your life." *Michael Sinz*

✳ "There are a number of mechanical devices which increase sexual arousal, particularly in women. Chief among these is the Mercedes-Benz 380SL convertible." *Steve Martin*

✳ "If sex is such a natural phenomenon, how come there are so many books on how to do it?" *Bette Midler*

✳ "I'm too shy to express my sexual needs except over the phone to people I don't know." *Garry Shandling*

✳ "If God had meant us to have group sex, he'd have given us more organs." *Malcolm Bradbury*

✳ It isn't premarital sex if you have no intention of getting married.

✴ "After making love, I said to my girl, 'Was it good for you too?' And she said, 'I don't think this was good for anybody.'" *Garry Shandling*

✴ "Bisexuality immediately doubles your chances for a date on Saturday night." *Rodney Dangerfield*

✴ Man to priest: "Do you approve of sex before marriage?" Priest: "Not if it delays the service."

✴ "I believe that sex is one of the most beautiful, natural, wholesome things that money can buy." *Steve Martin*

✴ "Most of us spend the first six days of each week sowing wild oats, then we go to church on Sunday and pray for a crop failure." *Fred Allen*

# SEX: APHRODISIACS AND MARITAL AIDS

✴ I tried some of that aphrodisiac rhino horn and it really worked. I'm really beginning to like those rhinos now.

✴ I tried some of that aphrodisiac rhino horn. Now I've got an overwhelming desire to charge at Land Rovers.

✴ On the beach, how can you recognize a guy who uses an inflatable sex doll? He doesn't stare at the bikinis, he stares at the beach balls.

# SEX: BISEXUAL ANIMALS

✴ Did you hear about the bisexual donkey? It had a hee in the morning and a haw at night.

# SEX: CONDOMS AND CONTRACEPTION

✴ "I was involved in an extremely good example of oral contraception two weeks ago. I asked a girl to go to bed with me, and she said 'No.'" *Woody Allen*

✳ "One year they wanted to make me poster boy—for birth control." *Rodney Dangerfield*

✳ A father and son go to a grocery store and see a display of condoms. The son asks his father why there are so many different boxes. The father replies, "Well, you see that three-pack? That's for when you're in high school. You have two for Friday night and one for Saturday night." " What's the six-pack for?" asks the son. The father replies, "That's for when you're in college. You have two for Friday night, two for Saturday night, and two for Sunday morning." "So what's the twelve-pack for," asks the son. The father replies, "That's for when you're married. You have one for January, one for February…"

✳ A guy walks into a drug store and asks for a pack of condoms. The pharmacist says, "That'll be $5.00 with the tax." "Tacks?" the guy exclaims. "I thought you rolled them on!"

✳ A man is being shown around a rubber factory. In one room, he's shown a machine that goes, "Bang, hiss, bang, hiss, bang, hiss…" "This is the machine that makes teats for babies' bottles," says the factory owner. "The 'bang' sound is the noise made when the teat is formed, and the 'hiss' sound is caused when we puncture a hole in the end of it." In the next room, the man is shown a machine that goes, "Bang, bang, bang, bang, hiss, bang bang…" "This is our condom-making machine," explains the factory owner. "But why does it go 'hiss'?" asks the man. The owner replies, "It's to make sure there are enough babies for our teats."

✳ A woman walks into a pharmacy and asks if they sell extra-large condoms. "Yes, we do," says the sales clerk. "Would you like to buy some?" "No thanks," replies the woman. "But if you don't mind, I'll wait here for someone who does."

✳ A man is out shopping when he discovers a new brand of Olympic condoms. He buys a pack and shows his wife. "They're in three colors," he tells her, "Gold, silver, and bronze." "So what color are you going to wear tonight?" she asks. "Gold of course," replies the man. "Why don't you wear silver?" replies his wife. "It would be nice if you came second for a change!"

✳ A man with a nervous tic applies for a job in a store. Unfortunately his tic makes it look as if he's winking all the time and it starts to put customers off. The store manager calls him over and explains the situation. "It's not a problem," says the man. "I forgot to take my aspirin. All I need is a couple of pills, and the winking will stop for the day." So saying, he reaches into his pockets to find some aspirin and starts dragging out handfuls of condoms. "Why all the condoms?" asks the manager. "You're not some sort of sex maniac are you?" "No," replies the man, "But they're what you get if you walk into a pharmacy winking and ask for a pack of aspirin."

✳ A man's wife has gone away on a trip, so he takes the opportunity to take his secretary home and seduce her. The pair are on the bed getting steamed up when the man suddenly realizes he doesn't have any condoms. "I know," he says. "You can use my wife's diaphragm. She keeps it in the dresser." The man looks but can't find it. Eventually he ends up turning out all the drawers but still can't find it. "Damn the woman!" he shouts. "I always knew she didn't trust me."

✳ A woman is smoking a cigarette at a bus stop when it starts to rain. A man is doing the same and, when he feels the first drop of rain, he takes a condom out of his pocket, tears the end off, and slips it over his cigarette to keep it dry. "What a great idea," thinks the woman and hurries over to a pharmacy. "Can I have a pack of condoms," she says to the sales clerk. "Certainly, madam," he says. "What size?" The woman replies, "One that will fit a Camel."

✳ An old lady goes to her doctor and asks for contraceptive pills, claiming they help her sleep at night. "Why would contraceptive pills make you sleep any better than normal?" asks the doctor. The old lady replies, "Because I put them in my granddaughter's coffee."

✳ Condoms are not completely safe. A friend of mine was wearing one and he got hit by a bus.

✳ Did you hear about the idiot who put ice in his condom? He wanted to keep the swelling down.

✳ Did you hear about the new contraceptive pill for men? You put it in your shoe and it makes you limp.

✳ Did you hear about the new "morning after" pill for men? It changes their blood type.

✳ Men, don't buy expensive "ribbed" condoms; buy an ordinary one and slip in a handful of frozen peas.

✳ Murphy the bus driver is sitting in his cab when his supervisor comes along. "Hello, Murphy," he says. "What time did you pull out this morning?" "I didn't," replies Murphy. "And I've been worrying about it all day."

✳ One Monday morning a customer walks into a pharmacy with a complaint. "Last Friday you sold me a value pack of a hundred condoms," he says. "But when I counted them up, there were only ninety-seven." "I'm so sorry," says the pharmacist, bagging up the missing three condoms. "Hope I didn't spoil your weekend."

✳ She's got her very own method of birth control. She takes her makeup off.

✳ The colonel of a regiment goes into a pharmacy and places a tattered old condom on the counter. "How much to repair that?" asks the colonel. "Oh dear," replies the pharmacist. "It's in a bad state. I can sew it up there, and glue it here and here, but it'll need tape down the edges and a very thorough wash. To be honest, it might be better to buy a new one." The colonel promises to think about it. The next day he returns and says, "I'll take one of your condoms, please. I had a word with the men, and they think a new one would be a good investment."

# SEX: FEMININE HYGIENE

✳ Three prisoners are locked in a cell. One takes out a harmonica and says, "At least I can play a little music and pass the time." The second prisoner pulls out a pack of cards and says, "We can play games too." The third man pulls out a pack of tampons. "Those aren't much use," says the first prisoner. "Yes they are," says the third prisoner. "On the pack, it says we can use them to swim, play tennis, and ski."

# SEX: FOR SALE

✳ "A hooker once told me she had a headache." *Rodney Dangerfield*

✳ A beautiful woman sits next to a drunk in a bar. He turns to her and says, "Hey, Honey. How about you and me getting it on? I've got a couple of dollars, and it looks like you could use the money." The woman turns to him and says, "What makes you think I charge by the inch?"

✳ A husband and wife are walking down the street when a beautiful young woman blows the husband a kiss. "I met her last week," explains the husband. "Professionally of course." The wife replies, "Which profession? Yours or hers?"

✳ A man is sitting in a bar when an exceptionally gorgeous young woman enters. She's so striking, the man can't take his eyes off her. The woman notices his attentive stare and walks over. "I can see you're interested," says the woman. "So tell you what, I'll do anything you want me to do for $100. But there's one condition." "What's that?" stammers the man. The woman replies, "You have to tell me what you want me to do in just three words." "And you'll do absolutely anything I want?" says the man. "Anything," replies the woman. The man thinks for a moment, then takes $100 out of his wallet. He gives her the money, looks into her eyes, and says, "Paint my house."

✳ A sex researcher calls one of the participants in a survey to check on a discrepancy. He asks the man, "In response to the question on frequency of intercourse, you answered 'twice weekly.' Your wife, on the other hand, answered 'several times a night.'" "That's right," replies the man, "And that's how it's going to be until the mortgage is paid off."

✳ A tourist in Sweden is drinking in a bar when an attractive woman sits next to him. "Hello," he says. "Do you speak English?" "Oh I speaking not much English," replies the woman. "How much?" asks the man. The woman replies, "200 Kroner."

✳ An old lady walks into a psychiatrist's office and says, "Doctor, I think I might be a nymphomaniac." "I might be able to help you," replies the psychiatrist. "But I should warn you that I charge $100 an hour." "That's reasonable," replies the old lady. "But how much for the whole night?"

✳ Two men visit a prostitute. The first man goes into the bedroom. He comes out ten minutes later and says, "Heck. My wife is better than that." The second man goes in. He comes out ten minutes later and says, "You know? Your wife IS better."

✳ One Monday evening a tourist visits a brothel in Paris and, on leaving, is very surprised to be handed €5,000. The next evening he goes back and the same thing happens. He goes back on the third night, but doesn't get any money this time. Upset, he complains to the concierge. The concierge says, "Why should we pay you? We don't film on Wednesdays."

✳ Paul is on the beach when he sees a beautiful busty girl in a bikini. He goes up to her and says, "I want to feel your breasts." "Get lost!" shouts the girl. Paul then offers her $20 to feel her breasts. "$20?!" she shouts. "Are you nuts!? Get away from me!" "Okay," says Paul. "I'll make it $100." "No way," says the girl. "Final offer," says Paul. "I'll give you $500." The girl thinks and says, "$500 and all you want to do is feel my breasts?" "That's all," says Paul. "Well, okay," says the girl. "For $500 you can help yourself." So she undoes her bikini top and Paul starts massaging her huge bust. "Oh my God," mutters Paul under his breath. "Oh my God. Oh my God. Oh my God. Oh my God. Where am I going to get $500…?"

✳ The big difference between sex for money and sex for free is that sex for money usually costs a lot less.

✳ Man to woman: "Have you ever had sex?" Woman: "That's my business!" Man: "Ahh, a professional."

# SEX: GENITAL MISFORTUNE

✳ "Its been a rough day. I put on a shirt and a button fell off. I picked up my briefcase and the handle came off. I'm afraid to go to the bathroom." *Rodney Dangerfield*

✳ I haven't been the same since my testicles dropped. Mind you, I was hanging from a tree by them at the time.

✳ A man picks up an nasty infection in his penis and goes to a doctor. "I'm sorry," says the doctor. "I can't cure it. We're going to have to amputate." The man is horrified and goes to get a second opinion. "I'm sorry," says the second doctor. "But your penis has got to come off." The man can't accept this and seeks a third opinion. "There's good news and bad news," says the third doctor. "The good news is that we don't have to cut off your penis." "And what's the bad news?" asks the man. The doctor replies, "It just came off in my hand."

✳ A surgeon is operating on a man when he slips up and accidentally cuts off the man's testicles. To hide his mistake, the surgeon slips an onion into the man's scrotum and sews it up. A month later the man comes back for a check-up. "So, have you noticed any differences since your operation?" asks the surgeon nervously. "A few," replies the man. "I cry when I pee, my wife gets heartburn if she gives me a blow-job, and I get an erection every time I go near a hot-dog stand."

✳ Three hunters are sitting around a campfire exchanging their worst experiences. The first guy says he was once up scaffolding washing windows when the scaffolding collapsed and he broke every bone in his body. The second guy says he was hitchhiking once when a Greyhound bus ran over him, breaking his back. The third guy says, "Well, I'll tell you the second worst experience I ever had. One time I was out hunting and I had to take a crap, so I stepped behind a tree, dropped my pants, and crouched. Then wham! A bear trap snapped shut on my testicles." "Wow!" says the first guy. "If that was the second worst, what was the worst?" The third man replies, "That would be when I reached the end of the chain…"

# SEX: HEALTH

✳ Life is a sexually transmitted disease.

✳ Well, you know what they say: Unlucky in love, get the clap.

✳ What do nostalgic gynecologists do? Look up old friends.

# SEX: IN OLD AGE

✳ "Sex for an old guy is a bit like shooting pool with a rope." *George Burns*

✳ A ninety-year-old man and his eighteen-year-old bride return home from their honeymoon. "We made love nearly every night," he tells a friend. "We nearly made love on Monday. We nearly made love on Tuesday. We nearly made love on Wednesday…"

✳ An eighty-year-old man is having his annual physical. After listening to the old man's chest, the doctor says, "You have a serious heart murmur. Do you smoke?" "No," replies the old man. "Do you drink to excess?" asks the doctor. "No," replies the man. "Do you have a sex life?" asks the doctor. "Yes, I do!" says the old man. "Well," says the doctor. "I'm afraid you'll have to cut your activity by half." "Which half?" asks the old man. "The looking or the thinking?"

✳ An old man goes to a church, and makes a confession. "Father, I'm seventy-five years old. I've been married for fifty years. All these years I had been faithful to my wife, but yesterday I was intimate with an eighteen-year-old model." The priest replies, "I see, my son. And when was your last confession?" The old man says, "Never. I'm Jewish." "So why are you telling me?" asks the priest. "I'm not just telling you," says the old man. "I'm telling everybody!"

✳ Two old men hobble into the pub. One says, "I've heard Guinness puts lead in your pencil. Shall we try some?" "All right," says the other. "But, to be honest, I've got nobody to write to."

✳ Harry announces his plan to marry a nineteen-year-old stripper on his seventy-fifth birthday. His doctor says to him, "I think you should reconsider. Prolonged sex with a girl that young could be fatal." Harry shrugs and says, "If she dies, she dies."

✳ Two old soldiers, Fred and Harry, are sitting in their club. Harry turns to Fred and says, "When was the last time you made love to a woman?" Fred thinks for a moment then says, "1947." "Good heavens," says Harry. "That's a very long time ago." "Not really," says Fred. "It's only five past eight now."

✳ A middle-aged couple are discussing their plans. "When I'm eighty," says the man, "I plan on finding myself a pretty twenty-year-old, and I'll have myself a real good time." The wife replies. "Well, when I'm eighty, I'm going to find myself a handsome twenty-year-old. And as you know, twenty goes into eighty a lot easier than eighty goes into twenty!"

✳ A ninety-year-old man is boasting to a friend that he's just got his eighteen-year-old wife pregnant. The friend says, "Let me tell you a story. This hunter I knew went out to shoot a bear but picked up his umbrella instead of his gun. Now, when he found that bear he pointed his umbrella at it and shot it through the head. What d'you think of that?" "But that's impossible," replies the old man. "If it's true, someone else must've shot that bear." "My point exactly," says the friend.

✳ A very old man and his young bride are in their honeymoon bed. The old man turns to his wife and says, "Darling, I hope your mother explained the facts of life to you." "No," replies the girl, "she didn't." "Oh dear," replies her elderly husband. "It's just that I seem to have forgotten them."

✳ An old couple decide to get married after years of courting. They sit down to discuss the marriage arrangements and the prospective bridegroom brings up the subject of sex. "Oh dear," says his aging fiancée. "As far as sex goes, I'd have to say, infrequently." "Pardon?" replies the bridegroom. "Was that one word or two?"

✳ An eighty-five-year-old man marries a lovely twenty-five-year-old woman. Because her new husband is so old, the woman decides that they should have separate honeymoon suites to prevent the old man from overexerting himself. On the night, there's a knock on the door, and her groom comes in ready for action. After they've finished, he leaves her, and she prepares to get some sleep. A few minutes pass and there's another knock on the door. The bride opens the door to find her husband ready for more action. They go back to bed, have sex, and the old man leaves again. Once more the bride gets ready for sleep, but after a few minutes there's another knock on the door, and the elderly groom presents himself for another romp. Again they have sex. Afterward, the young bride compliments her husband on his stamina. "Three times in one night," she says. "There's not many men who could manage that." The old man looks confused and says, "Manage what?"

✳ An elderly couple go to a pharmacy to buy a pack of condoms. "Do you mind my asking how old you are?" asks the shop assistant. "I'm seventy-five," replies the old man. "And my wife is seventy-three." "Well in that case you don't need condoms," says the assistant. "It's very unlikely that you will conceive at that age." "Oh we don't want them for that," replies the old man. "It's for the wife. She loves the smell of burning rubber."

✳ An elderly couple go to a doctor complaining about the quality of their sex life. They ask if he'll watch them having sex to see if anything is wrong. The doctor agrees and, after their romantic session, the doctor assures them that everything is fine. A week later they come back and ask to do it again. Again the doctor agrees, watches them at it, and tells them they're fine. However, a week later they're back again with the same request. The doctor is annoyed, "This is the third time you've been in here. There's nothing wrong with the way you make love!" he says. "What's really going on?" "Well," the elderly man replies. "We're both married, but not to each other. So I can't go to her place, and she can't go to mine. The local hotel charges $45 for a room, but you charge $35 for an office visit, plus we can write off 30 percent to Medicare."

✳ An elderly man is having trouble getting his young wife pregnant, so he goes to a clinic to have a sperm count. The doctor gives him a specimen cup and tells him to go home and fill it. The next day the old man shuffles into the doctor's office with an empty cup. "I'm sorry, doctor," he says. "I tried, but couldn't manage it. Then my wife tried for me and she couldn't manage it either. I even got my friend Jake over so he could have a go. Then he called his son over and he couldn't do it either. Didn't matter what we tried—couldn't get the lid off this damn cup."

✳ An old gentleman goes to his doctor to complain about a problem with his sex drive. "I don't seem to have as much pep as I used to," says the old man. "I see," says the doctor. "And how old are you and your wife?" "I'm eighty-two," says the old man. "And my wife is seventy-eight." "And when did you first notice the problem?" asks the doctor. The old man replies, "Twice last night and once again this morning."

✳ How did the octogenarian car mechanic make love? He attached leads to his nipples and got a jump start from a younger man.

✳ An old lady is at her husband's funeral. She tells her granddaughter that, throughout their married life, they had enjoyed physical relations each and every Sunday morning in time to the church bells. "Maybe he was getting a little old for that sort of thing," says the daughter. "Nonsense," replies the old lady. "If it hadn't been for that ice cream van, he'd be alive today."

✳ An old man goes to his doctor and says, "Can you give me something to lower my sex drive?" The doctor replies, "I would have thought at your age it's all in the mind," "It is," agrees the old man. "That's why I want it lower."

✳ An old man makes it shakily through the door of a Nevada brothel and is accosted by the doorman. "You gotta be in the wrong place," says the doorman. "What the hell you looking for, old timer?" The old man replies, "Is this where all the gals are ready for hire? I'm hankering for a good time." "Just how old are you, Pops?" asks the doorman. "Ninety-two," replies the old man. "Ninety-two!" exclaims the doorman "Boy, you've had it, Gramps." A moment of confusion crosses the old man's face, "Really?" he says, fumbling in his wallet. "How much do I owe you?"

✳ An old man wakes up in the middle of the night and finds that his pecker is as hard as a rock for the first time in years. He wakes his wife and shows her his erection. "Look at that!" he exclaims happily. "What do you think we should do with it?" His wife replies, "Well, seeing as you've got all the wrinkles out, now might be a good time to wash it."

✳ Two old ladies are discussing their dead husbands. "Tell me," says one. "Did you have mutual orgasms?" "No," says the other. "I think we were with Prudential."

# SEX: LACK OF IT

✳ "I recently sold the rights of my love life to Parker brothers, they're going to turn it into a game." *Woody Allen*

✳ My sex life is terrible—when I called one of those phone sex lines, the voice said, "Not tonight. I have an earache."

✳ My sex life isn't dead, but the buzzards are circling.

✳ Sex is like air—it's not important until you're not getting any.

✳ "My wife is a sex object. Every time I ask for sex, she objects." *Les Dawson*

✳ "The last time I was inside a woman was when I visited the Statue of Liberty." *Woody Allen*

✳ "You know that look women get when they want sex? Me neither." *Drew Carey*

✳ An old woman dies a virgin and requests the following inscription on her headstone, "Born a virgin, lived a virgin, died a virgin." However, the undertaker economizes—he inscribes "Returned unopened."

# SEX: LESBIANS

✳ An old cowboy goes to a bar and orders a drink. As he sits sipping his whiskey, a young lady sits down next to him. "Are you a real cowboy?" she asks. He replies, "Well, I've spent my whole life on the ranch, herding horses, mending fences, and branding cattle, so I guess I am." The woman says, "Well I'm a lesbian. I spend my whole day thinking about women. As soon as I get up in the morning, I think about women. When I shower, watch TV or eat, I think of women. In fact everything seems to make me think of women." The woman leaves and a little while later a man sits down next to the old cowboy. "Are you a real cowboy?" asks the man. The cowboy replies, "Well, I always thought I was, but I just found out I'm a lesbian."

✳ Dick notices a woman sitting at the other end of the bar and tells the bartender he's going to try his luck. "You'll get nothing there," says the bartender. "She's a lesbian." Dick isn't put off. He goes over and says, "So, which part of Lesbia are you from?"

# SEX: MASTURBATION

✳ Harry is better at sex than anyone he knows. Now all he needs is a partner.

✳ How did Pinocchio find out he was made of wood? When his hand caught fire.

✳ Man to friend: "I read a survey that said half the men in the US masturbate in the shower, and the other half sing. Do you know what they sing?" Friend: "No I don't." Man: "I thought you wouldn't."

✳ Mothers have Mother's Day and fathers have Father's Day. What do single guys have? Palm Sunday.

* Pinnochio gets a girlfriend, but she complains of getting splinters when they make love. Pinnochio goes to his doctor for advice and is told to use a sheet of sandpaper. The next week the doctor sees Pinnochio in the street. "How's it going with the girlfriend?" asks the doctor. "Girlfriend?" says Pinocchio. "Who needs a girlfriend?"

* What's the definition of a Yankee? Same thing as a "quickie," but you do it yourself.

* Why is sex like a game of bridge? You don't need a partner if you've got a good hand.

# SEX: ORAL

* How do women get rid of unwanted pubic hair? They spit it out.

* Smile. It's the second best thing you can do with your lips.

* Why don't you sit on my face and let me eat my way to your heart?

# SEX: PENISES (LARGE)

* A college lecturer asks Susie to stand up and tell the class what part of the human body enlarges to seven times its original size when stimulated. Susie stands up and says, "Well, I think I know, but I'm too embarrassed to tell you." The lecturer says, "Sit down, Susie. John, tell us what part of the human body enlarges to seven times its size when stimulated." John says, "The pupil of the eye enlarges to seven times its original size when stimulated by light." The lecturer says, "That's right." He then turns to Susie and says, "Two things: first, you have a dirty mind, and second, as far as men are concerned, you're in for a big disappointment."

* A fireman says to his wife, "You know, we have a great new system at the fire station. Bell one rings, and we all put on our jackets. Bell two rings, and we all slide down the pole. And when bell three rings, we're on the fire truck ready to go. From now on when I say "bell one," I want you to strip naked. When I say "bell two," I want you to jump in bed. And when I say "bell three," we are going to make love all night." The next night he comes home and yells, "bell one!" His wife promptly takes her clothes off. Then he yells, "bell two!", and his wife jumps into bed. Then he yells "bell three!", and they begin making love, but after a few moments the wife yells, "bell four!" "What the hell is bell four?" asks the husband. "Roll out more hose," she yells. "You're nowhere near the fire!"

* A little boy goes to the zoo with Mommy. "Mommy," he says. "What's that thing hanging down from the elephant." "That's his trunk," says mommy. "No," said the little

boy. "Further back." "That's his tail," replies mommy. "No," says the little boy. "The thing hanging down between his trunk and his tail." "Oh," says mommy. "Er, that's nothing." Back home the little boy asks his dad the same question. "What's that thing that hangs down from an elephant?" "That's his trunk," says Dad. "No," says the little boy. "Further back." "That's his tail," replies Dad. "No," says the little boy. "Between his trunk and his tail. I saw one at the zoo today with Mommy, and Mommy said it was nothing." "Ah, well," says Dad. "Your mommy's been spoiled."

✳ A man goes to his doctor to see if there's anything that can be done about his lisp. After an examination, the doctor tells the man that his huge penis is pulling his lips off-center. The only way to cure the lisp is to cut off the huge organ. Reluctantly the man agrees and has the operation. However, a month later the man is back, "I want my penis back," says the man. "I was a fool to have that operation. I can live with the stupid lisp, but I can't do without my giant penis." "Oh yeah," says the doctor. "Well thcrew you."

✳ A man is shipwrecked on a desert island and survives for thirty years. One day a beautiful woman is washed ashore. She asks him how he's managed to survive so long on a barren island. "I pick berries and dig for clams," replies the man. "And what do you do for love?" asks the women. "Love?" replies the man. "It's been so long, I've forgotten how to do it." "Then let me show you," responds the woman, which she then does— three times in a row. "So what did you think of that?" asks the woman when they'd finished. "That was great," replies the man. "But look what you did to my clam-digger!"

✳ A woman is divorcing her husband on the grounds of cruelty. His organ is so large, it hurts her to have sex. After she has explained her problem to a lawyer, he tells her that he'll file her petition. "Forget that!" says the woman. "Why can't you go around and sandpaper his down a bit."

✳ What did Adam say to Eve? "Stand back! I don't know how big this thing gets!"

✳ What did the elephant say to the nude man? "It's cute, but can it pick up peanuts?"

✳ A Texan goes into a New York department store to buy a new suit. "Can I ask your chest size?" asks the sales assistant. "Fifty-four inches," replies the Texan. "We grow them big in Texas." "And your outside leg?" asks the assistant. "Forty-four inches," replies the Texan. "We grow them big in Texas." "And if, sir, won't mind my asking about his…?" says the assistant. "Way ahead of you," says the Texan. "It's four inches." "Four inches?" replies the assistant. "I'm bigger than that and I'm from California." "Hold on, sonny," replies the Texan. "That's four inches from the ground."

✳ Men are like vacations—they never seem to be long enough.

✳ Harry and Pete are on the beach, and Harry can't understand why Pete is getting so much female attention. "It's simple," says Pete. "Just stick a potato down your swim trunks and walk around for a while." Harry takes this advice, sticks a potato down his trunks, and parades up and down the shoreline. However, after many hours, he fails to arouse any female interest at all. Discouraged, he goes back to Pete, who immediately identifies the problem, "You're supposed to put the potato down the front of your trunks…"

✴ Mr. Jones goes to his doctor and tells him that he can't get an erection when he's in bed with his wife. "Bring her back with you tomorrow," says the doctor. "We'll see what I can do." The next day Mr. Jones returns with his wife. "Take off your clothes, Mrs. Jones," says the doctor. "Now turn around. Lie down please. Uh-huh, I see. Okay, you may put your clothes back on." The doctor takes Mr. Jones aside. "You're in perfect health," he says. "Your wife didn't give me an erection, either."

✴ Game show host: "In the Garden of Eden, what were the first words Eve said to Adam?" Contestant: "Gosh, that's a hard one!" Game show host: "Excellent. Two points."

✴ The kings of Spain, France, and England are standing on stage ready to show the world who of the three has the largest penis. The king of Spain takes his out and, as its impressive proportions are seen, all the Spanish people shout *"Viva España!"* The king of France is next. He drops his pants, and his is even larger. All the French scream "Vive la France!" Next comes the king of England. He drops his pants and, after a stunned silence, everyone exclaims "God save the Queen!"

# SEX: POOR PERFORMANCE

✴ "I'm a bad lover. Once I caught a peeping Tom booing me." *Rodney Dangerfield*

✴ "My wife only has sex with me for a purpose. Last night she used me to time an egg." *Rodney Dangerfield*

✴ My girlfriend always laughs during sex—no matter what she's reading.

✴ Why don't women blink during foreplay? They don't have time.

✴ The famous sex therapist was on the radio taking questions when a caller asked, "Doctor, why do men always want to marry a virgin?" To which the doctor responded, "To avoid criticism."

✴ It's the morning after the honeymoon. The wife says, "You know, you're a really lousy lover." The husband replies, "How can you possibly tell that after only thirty seconds?"

✴ The four words most hated by men during sex? "Is it in yet?"

✴ The three words most hated by men during sex: "Are you done?" The three words most hated by women during sex: "Honey, I'm home!"

# SEX: PROBLEMS

* "Doctor, I suffer from premature ejaculation. Can you help me?!" "No, but I can introduce you to a woman with a short attention span!"

* Apparently, he's trying to become a father again, even though he's now eighty-seven. And you have to admit that is an exceptionally low sperm count.

* How can you tell if your girlfriend's frigid? When you open her legs, the lights go on.

* In bed, my girlfriend used to mentally dress me.

* My doctor examined my testicles for me and found two small lumps. Luckily it turned out they were my testicles.

* My girlfriend used to fake foreplay.

# SEX: VIAGRA

* A man falls asleep on a beach and gets severe sunburn. He's rushed to the hospital by his wife where the doctor rubs lotion over him and prescribes Viagra. "Viagra?" exclaims the wife. "What good is Viagra in his condition?" The doctor replies, "It'll help keep the sheets off him."

* "The marketers of Viagra have a new slogan, 'Let the Dance Begin.' This is better than the original, 'Brace Yourself, Grandma!'" *Jay Leno*

* A teenage boy overdosed on ten bottles of Viagra. Not only is he lucky to be alive, he's lucky not to have taken his eye out.

* A lady walks into a pharmacy and says, "Do you have Viagra?" "Yes," replies the pharmacist. "Does it work?" asks the lady. "Certainly," says the pharmacist. "Can you get it over the counter?" asks the lady. "Only if I take six," says the pharmacist.

* Father hears banging from the basement and wanders downstairs to see what's happening. He finds his son, Timmy, pounding a nail into the wall. "Why are you banging that nail?" asks father. Timmy replies, "It's not a nail, it's a worm. I mixed some chemicals from my chemistry set, put it on it the worm, and it became as hard as a rock." "Tell you

what, son," says Father. "Give me your formula, and I'll buy you a new Volkswagen." Timmy agrees and the next day he and Father go into the garage to look at the new car. However, all Timmy can see is a brand new Mercedes. "Where's my Volkswagen?" asks Timmy. "Behind the Mercedes," says Father. "By the way, the Merc's from your mother."

✳ Following the approval of Viagra by the FDA, the first shipment arrived yesterday at JFK airport; however, it was hijacked on the way to the warehouse. The FBI have warned the public to be on the lookout for a gang of hardened criminals.

✳ Last night I tried a Viagra for the first time. When I swallowed it, it got stuck in my throat. This morning I woke up with a stiff neck!

✳ Mix Viagra and Prozac and you have a guy who is ready to go, but doesn't really care where.

✳ Scientists have just released Viagra in the form of eye drops. Apparently it does nothing for your sex life, but it makes you look really hard.

✳ What do Viagra and Disney World have in common? You have to wait an hour for a two-minute ride.

✳ They've started giving Viagra to old men in nursing homes. It keeps them from rolling out of bed!

✳ What's the difference between Niagara and Viagra? Niagara Falls.

✳ A man goes to his doctor and asks for three Viagra pills. "I have a girl coming around Friday," explains the man, "and another on Saturday, and a third on Sunday." The doctor gives him the pills and tells him to come back for a check-up on Monday. The next week the man comes back with his arm in a sling. "What happened to you?" asks the doctor. "Not much," replies the man. "They all canceled."

✳ A truck loaded with Viagra crashed into the Willamette River in Oregon. Now none of the bridges will come down.

✳ Did you hear about the fifteen-year-old boy who took a bottle of Viagra? He was rushed to the hospital with third degree friction burns.

✳ Have you heard about the Viagra computer virus? It turns your 3-1/2 inch floppy into a hard disk.

✳ Since the release of Viagra, exotic dancers now claim they're receiving a lot more standing ovations.

# SEX: WITH ANIMALS

✳ A farmer goes to market to buy a cow but discovers the only thing he can afford is a zebra being sold off by a local zoo. Thinking he might find some use for it, he buys the zebra and takes it home. The zebra wants to be useful but is unsure of what she can do, so she asks some of the other farm animals how they keep busy. "I peck corn all day," says the chicken. "I can't do that," says the zebra. "I lie in the mud all day," says the pig. "I can't do that either," says the zebra. Eventually she comes across the bull and asks him what he does. "It's difficult to explain," replies the bull. "But if you take off your pajamas, I'd be delighted to show you."

# SEX: WITH MYTHOLOGICAL BEINGS

✳ Thor, the Norse god of Thunder, gets bored of Valhalla and descends to Earth to get some action. He meets a girl in a bar and she takes him back to her place. Thor, having the stamina of a god, then has constant sex with her for fourteen hours. Later Thor is boasting to his fellow gods about his prowess, but Odin tells him off. "You can't submit human women to so much divine sex," he says. "They don't have the strength. You might have injured her. Go back to Earth, find this woman, and apologize." So Thor goes back to the girl's apartment and knocks on the door. The girl shuffles to the door and opens it. "Look," says Thor. "Sorry about last night and everything. I should explain. You see, I'm Thor…" "Oh. You're thor are you?" complains the girl. "Poor you. I can't even pith."

# SHARING

✳ Harry and Tom are walking down the road. Harry turns to Tom and says, "If you had two Rolls-Royce convertibles would you give one to me?" Tom replies, "We've been friends for years—of course I'd give you one." Harry then says, "And if you had two speedboats, would you give me one of them as well?" Tom replies, "After all we've been through together, I surely would give you a speedboat." Harry says, "So what if you had two chickens. Could I have one of those?" "No," says Tom. "I'd keep both of them." Harry says, "Why? You'd give me a car and a boat but you wouldn't give me a chicken? What's the difference?" Tom replies, "The difference is, you know damn well that I've got two chickens."

# SHE WAS ONLY...

✳ A lawyer's daughter, but she kept a tight hold on her briefs.

✳ A patrolman's daughter, but she wouldn't let the Chief Inspector.

✳ A fisherman's daughter, but when she saw my rod, she reeled.

✳ An architect's daughter, but she knew all the angles.

✳ An artist's daughter, but she knew where to draw the line.

✳ An electrician's daughter, but she had all the right connections.

✳ A plumber's daughter, but she sure gave my heart a wrench.

✳ The stableman's daughter, but all the horse manure.

# SHEEP

✳ Two sheep are talking in a field. "Baaaaaa," says the first. "Damn," says the second. "I was going to say that."

✳ Where do you get virgin wool from? Ugly sheep.

# SHOES

✳ He's so stupid he ended up with his shoes on the wrong feet—he'd put them on while he had his legs crossed.

✳ If the shoe fits—buy it in every color.

✳ "I get into an amazing amount of physical encounters for someone my size. About thirteen weeks ago, I had my shoes shined against my will. Tremendous shoeshine boy said to me, 'I'm shining your shoes.' 'Yes you are,' I said. He did give me an excellent shine though, I might add. But they were suede shoes." *Woody Allen*

✳ A little boy puts his shoes on by himself, but his mother notices he's got them mixed up. "Sweetie," she says. "You've put your shoes on the wrong feet." The little boy looks at her and says, "But these are the only feet I've got!"

# SHOPS AND SHOPPING

✳ "I bought some used paint the other day. It was in the shape of a house." *Steven Wright*

✳ A man goes into a bookstore. He approaches a woman behind the counter and says, "Do you keep stationery here?" "No," replies the woman. "Sometimes I wriggle around a bit."

✳ A man goes into a grocery store to buy a bar of soap when he realizes he's being followed around by a little old lady. The old lady shadows him as he goes up and down the aisles and then follows him to the register. The old lady comes up to him and says, "I'm sorry if I made you uncomfortable with my staring, but you look just like my dead son. Listen, I hate to ask, but it would make me so happy if you could say goodbye to me. My son was taken suddenly and never had the chance." The man is touched by this request and waves goodbye to her as she leaves the store pulling her bag of groceries with her. "Goodbye, Mother," he cries. "Goodbye!" He then turns to the cashier and pays for his soap. "That's $112.90," says the cashier. "What?" replies the man. "I only bought soap." "Yes," replies the cashier. "But your mother said you'd be paying for her groceries too."

✳ A man is a person who will pay two dollars for a one-dollar item that he wants. A woman will pay one dollar for a two-dollar item that she doesn't want.

✳ A woman picks up a sweater in a clothes store. "This is a little overpriced, isn't it?" she says to the clerk. "Not really, madam," the clerk replies. "The wool comes from a rare breed of albino sheep only found in the highest mountains of Tibet. It's a beautiful yarn." "Yes," replies the woman. "And you tell it so well."

✳ A man goes to buy a high-tech coffee maker with all the latest gadgets. The salesman explains how everything works: how to plug it in, fill it up, and set the timer so that hell awake to a fresh cup of coffee. A few weeks later he's back in the store. The salesman asks him how he likes the coffee maker. "It's wonderful!" he says. "But there's one thing I don't understand. Why do I have to go to bed every time I want a cup of coffee?"

✳ A woman is shopping in an exclusive shoe shop when she sees a beautiful pair of stilettos. The store owner comes over and says, "They're very expensive, but if you go to bed with me, I'll let you have them for nothing." "Well, okay," says the woman. "But don't expect me to enjoy it." The owner gives her the shoes and takes her home. In the bedroom, they get down to business. The owner drops his pants, takes off the woman's underwear, pushes her back over the bed, and hoists her legs over his shoulders. As he thrusts away, the woman says, "Oh God, yes! Yes. Fantastic! Absolutely fantastic…"

"Oh really?" says the owner. "And I thought you said you wouldn't enjoy sex with me?" "I don't," replies the woman. "I'm admiring my new shoes."

✳ The service at our local shop is so slow you can line up to get Christmas cards and end up buying Easter eggs.

✳ My wife and I always hold hands. If I let go, she goes shopping.

✳ Two lions are walking down the aisle of a supermarket, one turns to the other and says, "Quiet in here today, isn't it?"

✳ An attractive girl walks into a fabric shop. "I want to buy this material for a dress," she says. "How much does it cost?" "Only one kiss per yard," replies the male clerk. "Fine," replies the girl. "In that case, I'll take ten yards." The clerk gives her the fabric and the girl points to a little old man standing next to her. "Thanks," she says. "Grandpa's paying the bill."

✳ An elderly gentleman goes into a fur shop with his young lady and buys her a mink coat costing $15,000. "Will a check be okay?" asks the man. "Certainly, sir," says the sales assistant. "But we'll have to wait a few days for it to clear. Can you come back on Monday to take delivery?" "Certainly," replies the old man, and he and his girlfriend walk out arm in arm. The next Monday the man returns. The sales assistant is furious— "You've got some nerve coming back here. It turns out there's hardly a penny in your bank account; your check was worthless." "Yes, sorry about that," replies the man. "I just came in to apologize—and thank you for the greatest weekend of my life."

✳ Customer, to salesman: "When I bought this rug you said it was used but in perfect condition. I get it home and find it's got a hole in the middle!" Salesman: "That's correct, sir. But if you'll recall, I did say it was in mint condition."

✳ "Today I was arrested for scalping low numbers at the deli. I sold a number three for fifty dollars." *Steven Wright*

✳ Ever wondered about those people who pay a fortune for those little bottles of Evian water? Try spelling Evian backward…

✳ For a few months I worked in one of those sweat shops—but after a while people just seemed to stop buying sweat.

✳ How do you identify people who can't count to ten? Simple. They're the ones in front of you in the supermarket express lane.

✳ I had a good talk with my wife about cutting down on her extravagant shopping bills. As a result, there's definitely going to be some changes—I'm giving up smoking.

✳ I went to a bookstore and said to the saleswoman, "Where's the self-help section?" She said, "If I told you, it would defeat the purpose."

✳ I went to the 24-hour grocery store. When I got there, the guy was locking the front door. I said, "Hey, the sign says you're open twenty-four hours." He said, "Yes. But not all at once."

✳ I went to the mall yesterday and treated myself to a toilet brush. It's no good though. I'm going to have to go back to paper.

✳ The Episcopal Church is opening its own string of supermarkets. They're going to be called Jesus Christ Superstores.

✳ They have a good deal going on at the local store. If you buy something then see the same product in another store for a lower price, tell them—then they'll go around and smash the other store's windows.

✳ A man goes into a DIY store and asks for some bolts. "How long do you want them?" asks the clerk. "To tell you the truth," says the man. "I was really hoping to keep them."

✳ A woman walks into an office supply store and asks the manager if he has any notebooks. "Sorry," says the manager. "We're all out." The woman says, "Well, do you have any pencils?" "Nope, don't have those either," replies the manager. The woman says, "Do you have erasers?" The manager shakes his head, "No. Sorry." "How about ring-binders?" asks the woman. "Nope. Don't have them," replies the manager. "My God!" shouts the woman, "If you don't have anything, you should lock up the damn store!" The manager shrugs and says, "Don't have the key."

✳ An old man is riding in an elevator with two glamorous women. One woman takes a perfume bottle out of her bag and sprays her neck. She turns to the other woman and says, "Romance by Ralph Lauren. $150 an ounce." The other woman takes a perfume bottle out of her bag, sprays herself, and says, "Chanel No. 5. $200 an ounce." The elevator stops and the doors open. The old man steps out and lets off a huge rumbling fart. As the doors close, he looks back and says, "Broccoli. Forty-nine cents a pound."

✳ I bought some kitchen cleaner and it was really strong. I must have knocked the bottle over on my way out. When I got home the whole house was gone.

✳ My wife has a black belt in shopping.

✳ Man to grocer: "I asked for six apples. You only gave me five." Grocer: "I know, but one was rotten, so I saved you the trouble of throwing it away."

✳ I went window-shopping today. I bought four windows.

✳ When you've seen one shopping center, you've seen a mall.

✳ Man to shopkeeper: "Have you got any four-watt, two-volt bulbs?" Shopkeeper: "For what?" Man: "Actually, no, two." Shopkeeper: "Two what?" Man: "Yes." Shopkeeper: "No."

# SHORTNESS

✳ He's so short, he thinks it's unlucky to walk under a black cat.

✳ He's so short, he was offered a job standing around in a bar. They thought he made the drinks look bigger.

✳ He's very short. In fact, he's the one who poses for trophies.

✳ What's E.T. short for? Because he has little legs.

✳ Yo momma's so short, you can see her feet on her driver's license picture.

✳ You're so short, when it rains you're always the last one to know.

✳ He's so short, he's a lumberjack for bonsai trees.

✳ You're so short, your hair smells like feet.

# SHOW BUSINESS

✳ "Knock, knock." "Who's there?" "Kylie." "Kylie who?" "That's showbiz."

✳ A man walks into a grocery store and says, "I want to buy every rotten egg you have." "Who wants rotten eggs?" says the clerk. "No one wants rotten eggs, unless you're going to see that lousy comedian at the club on the corner." The man replies, "I know. I am the lousy comedian at the club on the corner."

✳ "The audience were with me all the way, but I managed to shake them off at the station." *Harry Secombe*

✳ A man takes a dog and a cat to audition for a TV talent show. While the man conducts, the dog plays the piano and the cat sings. "That's incredible," says the TV producer. "The dog plays wonderfully, and the cat's singing is superb." The man replies, "Look, I don't want to put you off but I've got a confession to make; the cat can't sing a note—the dog's a ventriloquist."

✳ A man walks into the office of a theatrical agent and announces he does bird imitations. "Bird imitators are ten a penny," says the agent. "It's not worth putting you on my books." "Oh well," says the imitator. "I'll leave you my card just in case you change your mind." Then he drops his pants, lays an egg, and flies out of the window.

✳ An agent is telling a nightclub owner about a new striptease act he's got. "You should see the size of her," says the agent. "She's got a 96-26-36 figure." "And what sort of dance does she do?" asks the owner. "Well, it's not a dance as such," says the agent. "She crawls on-stage and tries to stand up."

✳ His animal impressions are particularly good. He not only does the sounds, he does the smells as well.

✳ Tom's circus is so unsuccessful, even his elephants have forgotten when they had their last booking.

✳ Why did the bad comedian tell the same jokes three nights running? His audience could have caught him if he'd been standing still.

✳ Two sailors are on shore leave. They have a few drinks and decide to go to a variety show. At the intermission one of them needs to pee and asks directions from the usher. "Go through the exit, turn left along the corridor, turn first right, then left, then right again," he says. The sailor follows the directions with some difficulty, relieves himself, and eventually finds his way back to his seat. "You missed the best act," says his friend. "While you were gone, a sailor came on stage and pissed into the orchestra pit."

✳ A man goes to the doctor's because his arm is covered in sores. "What do you do for a living?" asks the doctor. "I work in the circus," says the man. "It's my job to give the elephants enemas. I have to shove my arm right up their backsides and clean them out." "My goodness," says the doctor. "No wonder your arm's in such a state. Don't you think you should look for another job?" "What?" says the man. "And give up show business?"

✳ There's one great advantage in being a failure in show business: You never have to worry about making a comeback.

✳ "The important thing in acting is to be able to laugh and cry. If I have to cry, I think of my sex life. If I have to laugh, I think of my sex life." *Glenda Jackson*

✳ People laughed at me when I told them I intended to become a comedian. Well, they're not laughing now.

✳ Do you know why the summer camp fired the hypnotist? He got thirty people on the stage, put them in a trance, then tripped on a stool and said, "Crap!" It took them a whole day to clean up.

# SIGNS

✴ At the electric company: "We'd be delighted if you send in your bill. However, if you don't, you will be."

✴ In a funeral home: "Drive carefully—we can wait."

✴ In a music library: "Bach in a minuet."

✴ In a vet's waiting room: "Back in five minutes. Sit! Stay!"

✴ On a maternity room door: "Push, Push, Push."

✴ In a podiatrist's window: "Time wounds all heels."

✴ In a baker's window: "Try our homemade pies—they're a real threat."

✴ On the side of an electrician's truck: "Let us remove your shorts."

✴ Outside a radiator repair shop: "Best place in town to take a leak."

✴ In a taxidermist's window: "We really know our stuff."

✴ In a butcher's window: "Let me meat your needs."

✴ On a house fence: "Salesmen welcome. Dog food is expensive."

✴ In a dry cleaner's window: "Drop your pants here."

✴ In a restaurant window: "Don't stand there and be hungry, come in and get fed up."

✴ On the back of a T-shirt worn by a member of the LAPD Bomb Squad: "If you see me running, try to keep up."

# SKIING

✴ Two men are arguing about the best way to ski down a particular hill. They ask a man pulling a sled for his opinion. "Sorry," says the man. "There's no use asking me. I'm a tobogganist." "Oh," says one of the men. "In that case, could I have a pack of Marlboro Lights?"

＊ Two men, Jack and John, go on a skiing trip and get caught in a blizzard. They pull into a farm and ask the lady of the house, a good-looking widow, if they can sleep on her couch. She agrees and they turn in for the night. The next morning they go on their way and enjoy a weekend of skiing. A few months later, Jack gets a letter from the widow's lawyer. He says to John, "You remember that good-looking widow we met on our skiing vacation?" "Yes," says John. "In the middle of the night, did you go up to her room and have sex with her?" asks Jack. "Yes," admits John, a little embarrassed. "I see," says Jack. "And when you had sex, did you happen to use my name instead of yours?" John's face turns red. "Yeah, sorry," he says. "I'm afraid I did." "Well," says Jack. "You must have been damn good. She's just died and left everything to me."

＊ If God had wanted Texans to ski, he would have made bullshit white.

# SKIING: WATERSKIING

＊ "I was on waterskis, stripped to the waist, skiing fast across the top of the surf, my hair back. My wife was in the boat ahead of me, rowing frantically." *Woody Allen*

＊ My next-door neighbor is selling his waterskis. He says he couldn't find a lake on a hill.

# SKYDIVING

＊ Bob is taking his first skydiving lesson. The instructor tells him to jump out of the plane and pull his ripcord. After he's done so, the instructor jumps out of the plane after him. The instructor pulls his ripcord, but his parachute doesn't open. As he struggles to pull the emergency cord, he shoots downward past Bob. Bob undoes the straps on his own parachute and yells, "So you wanna race, huh?"

＊ For Sale: Parachute. Only used once, never opened, small stain.

＊ He's invented a new type of parachute. It opens on impact.

＊ What's the difference between a bad golfer and a skydiver? One goes "Whack! Awwwwghk!" The other goes, "Awwwghk! Whack!"

＊ If at first you don't succeed, skydiving is not for you.

＊ Skydivers: good to the last drop.

✴ What do you call it when your parachute doesn't open? Jumping to a conclusion.

✴ Why do female skydivers wear jock straps? So they don't whistle on the way down.

✴ Harry goes skydiving, but nothing happens when he pulls his ripcord. He pulls the cord on his secondary chute, but this too is broken. Suddenly Harry sees a man in blue overalls shooting up toward him, "Hey!" shouts Harry. "Know anything about parachutes?!" "No!" shouts the man. "Know anything about gas boilers?!"

✴ Words to live by: Do not argue with a spouse who packs your parachute.

✴ No one has ever complained of a parachute not opening.

# SLEEP

✴ "I hate it when my foot falls asleep during the day – it means it's going to be up all night." *Steven Wright*

✴ "I was once arrested for walking in someone else's sleep." *Steven Wright*

✴ "I went to the doctor because I'd swallowed a bottle of sleeping pills. My doctor told me to have a few drinks and get some rest." *Rodney Dangerfield*

✴ "When I woke up this morning, my girlfriend asked if I'd slept well. I said, 'No, I made a few mistakes.'" *Steven Wright*

✴ A woman wakes up one morning and says to her husband, "I dreamed you gave me a pearl necklace for Valentine's day. What do you think it means?" "You'll know tonight, darling," he says. That evening the husband comes home with a small package and gives it to his wife. Delighted, she opens it—and finds a book entitled *The Meaning of Dreams*.

✴ A woman went to the doctor to get some more sleeping pills for her husband. He'd woken up.

✴ Drive your partner crazy. Don't talk in your sleep, just grin.

# SLOWNESS

✴ "I have bad reflexes. I was once run over by a car with a flat tire being pushed by two guys." *Woody Allen*

✴ He was slower than a herd of turtles stampeding through peanut butter.

* He who laughs last, thinks slowest.

* Martin is a slow worker. He gets a job at the local zoo and the keeper, aware of his reputation, tells him to take care of the tortoises. Later the keeper drops by to see how Martin is getting on and finds him standing by an empty enclosure. "Where are the tortoises?" asks the keeper. Martin shrugs, "I just opened the door and…Whooooosh!"

* Why is the time of day with the slowest traffic called the "rush hour"?

* You're so slow, you have to speed up to stop.

* Why do those signs that say "Slow Children" always have a picture of a running child?

# SMALL TOWNS

* I come from a town so small, we closed the zoo when the chicken died.

* I spent a year in that town one night.

* My home town is so small, the street map is actual size.

* My home town is so small, when I plug in my electric razor, the street lamps dim.

* The town is so small and dull, they print the local paper three weeks in advance.

* Our town is so small and boring, anyone who stays up to watch the eleven o'clock news counts as a playboy.

# SMOKING

* "I met the Surgeon General. He offered me a cigarette." *Rodney Dangerfield*

* After going through dozens of articles on the dangers of smoking, Harry decided to give up—not smoking, reading.

* I quit smoking. I feel better. I smell better. And it's safer to drink out of the old beer cans laying around the house.

* I recently stopped my wife from smoking in bed. I hid her pipe.

✳ I've managed to stop smoking thanks to these special patches you can buy. I stuck one over each of my eyes. Now I can't find my cigs.

✳ Not only is smoking bad for you, apparently it's one of the leading causes of statistics.

✳ What should you do if your boyfriend starts smoking? Slow down.

✳ What's the best way to get a guy to stop smoking after sex? Fill his waterbed with gasoline.

✳ I tried to give up smoking using those nicotine patches, but it was useless. They burned my arm every time I tried to light them.

✳ Three little boys are sitting on the porch. One says, "My daddy smokes, and he can blow smoke rings." The second pipes up, "Well, my dad smokes, and he can blow smoke out of his ears." Not to be outdone, the third says, "My dad can blow smoke out of his ass." "Have you actually seen him do that?" ask his friends. "No," he says. "But I've seen the tobacco stains on his undies."

✳ "I've taken up smoking. My doctor says I'm not getting enough tar in my diet." *Steve Martin*

✳ "Having a smoking section in a restaurant is like having a peeing section in a swimming pool." *George Carlin*

✳ Pupil to teacher: "Can you give me a cigarette?" Teacher: "No, of course I'm not going to give you a cigarette. Do you want to get me into trouble?" Pupil: "Well, okay. But I'd rather have a cigarette."

# SOCCER

✳ A soccer player is walking down the street when he sees a fire in a block of apartments. He runs over to help and hears a woman calling from the top of the building. "Will someone save my baby!" she yells. "The stairwell is blocked! There's no way down! If I throw down my baby, can somebody catch him?" The player shouts back, "Fear not. I'm a professional goalkeeper! Throw down your baby, and I promise I won't drop him!" So the mother throws down the baby, and the goalkeeper makes a perfect catch—before bouncing it twice and kicking it 30 yards down the road.

✳ A junior soccer team is playing a match one Sunday. Just before the kick-off, the team coach approaches one of his young players. "Do you understand that you mustn't swear at the ref if he gives you a card and you mustn't attack an opponent if he fouls you?" "Yes," replies the boy. "Good," says the coach. "Now go and explain that to your mother."

✳ A man arrives at a soccer match midway through the second half. "What's the score?" he asks. "Nil nil," is the reply. "Oh," says the man. "And what was the score at halftime?"

✳ Two flies are having a game of soccer in a saucer. "Our game had better improve soon," says one. "Next week we're playing in the cup!"

✳ Why was the centipede dropped from the insect soccer team? He took too long to put his boots on!

✳ Harry has tickets for the World Cup final. As he sits in the stadium, a man comes over and asks if anyone is sitting in the seat next to him. "No," says Harry. "That seat is empty." "That's incredible!" says the man. "Who in their right mind would have a seat like this for the World Cup final and not use it?" Harry replies, "Well, actually, I've got the tickets for both these seats. My wife was supposed to be here with me, but she passed away." "I'm sorry to hear that," says the man. "But couldn't you find a friend or relative to take the seat?" Harry shakes his head, "No, they're all at the funeral."

# SPEECH IMPEDIMENTS

✳ "My wife has a slight impediment in her speech. Every now and then she stops to breathe." *Jimmy Durante*

✳ A man spots an old schoolfriend getting out of a new Rolls-Royce. "How did you do so well?" asks the man. "Oh," says his stuttering friend. "J-j-j-j-j-j-j-just by selling c-c-c-c-c-c-c-copies of the B-b-b-b-b-b-bible d-d-d-d-d-door to d-d-d-d-d-door." "That's amazing," says the man. "How do you manage to sell so many?" "W-w-well," says his friend. "I j-j-just kno-o-ock on p-p-p-p-p-p-p-people's d-d-d-d-doors, show them a co-o-o-py of the B-b-b-b-b-bible and ask them if they w-w-w-w-w-w-would rather b-b-b-b-b-buy it or h-h-h-have me r-r-r-ead it to them."

✳ Teacher to Jenny: "Jenny. What is a thimble?" Jenny: "Is it a thort of thign?"

✳ A tourist in New York goes up to a young man and says, "Can you tell me where I can find the 42nd Street ferry? The young man replies, "Thpeaking."

# SPEECHES AND SPEECHMAKING

✳ "I'm going to make a long speech because I've not had time to prepare a short one." *Winston Churchill*

✳ "Speaking in front of a crowd is considered the number one fear of the average person. I found that amazing. Number two was death! That means, to the average person, if you have to be at a funeral, you would rather be in the casket than doing the eulogy." *Jerry Seinfeld*

✳ "Tonight I feel like Zsa Zsa Gabor's fifth husband. I know what to do. But how do I make it interesting?" *David Niven*

✳ As Henry VIII said to each of his wives, "I shan't keep you long."

✳ Harry is in the middle of a speech when someone at the back calls out, "I can't hear you." Someone at the front calls back, "Could we swap places?"

✳ A guest speaker is trying to make himself heard over the racket of a boisterous group of diners. He complains to the president sitting next to him, "It's so noisy I can't hear myself speak." "I wouldn't worry about it," replies the president. "You're not missing anything."

✳ Advice to public speakers—if you don't strike oil within two minutes, stop boring.

✳ After that speech, I feel refreshed and inspired. It's amazing what a short nap can do.

✳ I'd like to praise the committee here. In other clubs, half the committee does all the work, and the other half is completely hopeless. But here it's quite the reverse.

✳ The secret of a good sermon is to have a good beginning and a good ending—and have the two as close together as possible.

✳ They asked me to talk about something off the top of my head. So here's a short talk about dandruff.

✳ A politician has been making a speech for over an hour. A man joins his friend outside. "Is he still speaking?" asks the friend. "Yes," replies the man. "What's he talking about?" asks the friend. The man replies, "He didn't say."

✳ Making a speech is like having a baby. Fun to conceive but hell to deliver.

✳ There's only one thing wrong with this show: the seats all face the front.

✳ After such a tremendous welcome, I can hardly wait to hear what I've got to say.

✳ I won't say our next speaker is popular, but when he passes away, I predict that hundreds, if not thousands, of people will attend his funeral—just to make sure he really is dead.

✳ Three rules for a successful public speaker: stand up, speak up, shut up.

✳ After addressing a meeting, the guest speaker meets a member of his audience and asks how he found it. "Fantastic," replies the man. "Very refreshing. I felt like a new man when I woke up."

✳ A politician makes the mistake of criticizing the style one of his speechwriters. That night he's addressing a large meeting when he turns a page of his script and finds the words "Let's see you do better by yourself" scrawled across a blank page.

✳ If all the people who slept through after-dinner speeches were laid end-to-end, they would be far more comfortable.

✳ A toastmaster is the man who stands up to tell you that the best part of the dinner is over.

✳ Tom and Dick go to hear a politician speak. Tom nods off, and when he wakes up, he finds the politician is still talking. "Hasn't he finished?" he says to Dick. "He finished about half an hour ago," replies Dick. "But he hasn't stopped yet."

# SPEECHES AND SPEECHMAKING: LOQUACIOUSNESS

✳ "I like to do all the talking myself. It saves time and prevents arguments." *Oscar Wilde*

✳ After all is said and done, he usually says a little more.

✳ He regards free speech as not so much a right, more as a continuous obligation.

✳ I could listen to you forever. And I think I just did.

✳ I enjoyed that speech. Although I was sorry to miss my children growing up.

✳ I spent an hour talking to him for a few minutes.

✳ I wouldn't say she was chatty, but advertisers have tried to book billboard space on her tongue.

✳ I'm not crazy about making speeches, but I've been married for thirty-five years, and this is the one chance I get to see if my mouth still works.

✳ That speech was like a fine pot of coffee. Rich, full bodied, and it kept us up half the night.

✳ He wasted no words in his speech. He used every single one of them.

# SPIDERS

✳ What would happen if tarantulas were as big as horses? If one bit you, you could ride it to the hospital!

# SPORTS

✳ "Hockey is a sport for white men. Basketball is a sport for black men. Golf is a sport for white men dressed like black pimps." *Tiger Woods*

✳ "I asked my old man if I could go ice-skating on the lake. He told me, 'Wait till it gets warmer.'" *Rodney Dangerfield*

✳ "I was watching the Indy 500. I was thinking that, if they left earlier, they wouldn't have to go so fast." *Steven Wright*

✳ A boxer goes to a doctor complaining of insomnia. "Have you tried counting sheep?" asks the doctor. "It doesn't work," replies the boxer. "Every time I get to nine, I stand up."

✳ A man and wife are at a volleyball game when they notice a very affectionate couple who are running their hands over each other passionately. "I don't know whether to watch them or the game," says the man. "Watch them!" says his wife. "You already know how to play volleyball."

✳ Why did the captain lose the yacht race? He found himself in a no-wind situation.

✳ He used to be an all-around athlete. Now he's just all round.

✳ My dad is really annoyed—I had the TV on and he accidentally saw the entire football game—he'd just wanted to watch the results on the news.

✳ The hardest thing about prizefighting is picking up your teeth wearing a boxing glove.

✳ There was a tragic end to the water polo championships—all the horses drowned.

✳ They presented him with a cup when he was a boxer. It was to keep his teeth in.

✳ Two women are talking. "You know," says one. "Eighty percent of men think the best way to end an argument is to make love." "Well," says the other. "That will certainly revolutionize the game of hockey!"

✳ While giving a physical, a doctor notices that his patient's shins are covered in dark, savage bruises. "Tell me," says the doctor. "Do you play hockey or soccer?" "No," said the man. "But my wife and I play bridge."

✳ A cowardly matador used to go into the arena with a white sheet instead of a red cape. If things got rough, he surrendered.

✳ There was a terrible tragedy concerning the local ice hockey team. They drowned during spring training.

✳ I've got nothing against watching a darts match. I just wish my IQ were low enough to enjoy it.

✳ Two men get talking on a train. "I'm originally from Minnesota," says one. "I'm sure glad I left. The only people you'll find in Minnesota are whores and hockey players." "I'll have you know that my wife is from Minnesota," says the second man. "Really?" replies the first. "Which team did she play for?"

# STAMPS

✳ "I don't know much about philately, but I know what I lick." *Philip French*

# STATISTICS

✳ "People can come up with statistics to prove anything. Fourteen percent of people know that." *Homer Simpson*

✳ A statistician is walking down the corridor when he feels a twinge in his chest. Immediately he runs to the stairwell and hurls himself down. His friend visits him in the hospital and asks why he did it. The actuary replies, "The chances of having a heart attack while falling down the stairs are much lower than the chances of just having a heart attack."

✳ Half the people you know are below average.

# STRESS

* I don't suffer from stress. I'm a carrier.

* I read this article that said the typical symptoms of stress are eating too much, smoking too much, impulse buying, and driving too fast. That's my idea of a perfect day.

* If it weren't for stress I'd have no energy at all.

# STUPIDITY

* A husband is talking to his wife—"I'm feeling very depressed. Sometimes I think I'm nothing but a half-wit moron." His wife replies, "Don't worry, darling. Lots of people feel like that. In fact, most of the people we know think you're a half-wit moron."

* Harry left a note on his office door saying "Back in an hour." When he got back from lunch he saw the sign—so he sat down and waited.

* Artificial Intelligence is no match for Natural Stupidity.

* Dick and Tom find three hand grenades in a field and decide to take them to the police station. "But what if one of them blows up?" says Dick. "Well, in that case, we'll just tell them we found two," says Tom.

* Don't be fooled by the fact that he looks stupid. That doesn't necessarily mean he isn't.

* Emily-Sue gets sick and Billy-Bob calls for an ambulance. The operator asks Billy-Bob where he lives. "1132 Eucalyptus Drive," replies Billy-Bob. "Can you spell that for me?" asks the operator. There's a long pause. Finally Billy-Bob says, "How 'bout if I drag her over to Oak Street?"

* Even if he had two guesses, he couldn't tell which way an elevator was going.

* Germs attack people where they are weakest. This explains the number of head colds.

* God must love stupid people; He made so many of them.

* Ignorance can be cured. Stupid is forever.

✳ John is showing Tom his newborn triplets. "What d'you think, then?" asks John. Tom says, "Well, if it were up to me, I'd keep the middle one."

✳ Harry gets a job painting white dotted lines down the middle of roads. On his first day he does very well and paints six miles of road. On the second day he does four miles, but by the third day he's down to two. "I don't understand it," says his foreman. "You were doing so well. What happened?" "Well, it's obvious," says Harry. "Every day I'm getting further and further away from the can of paint."

✳ Harry to Dick: "Add this up for me. A ton of sawdust, a ton of old newspaper, and a ton of fat. Now, have you got all that in your head?" Dick: "Yes." Harry: "Yeah, I thought so."

✳ Johnny has two brains; one is lost, and the other is out looking for it.

✳ Tom says he's not stupid. He knows a lot but just can't think of it at the moment.

✳ How do you confuse an idiot? Forty-two.

✳ I always give people the benefit of the doubt. I never attribute to malice what can adequately be explained by crass stupidity.

✳ Last night we discovered we'd been living with a perfect stranger for the last eight years, I thought the little old lady at our house was her mother, and she thought she was mine.

✳ My uncle isn't very bright, he painted his sundial with fluorescent paint so he could tell the time at night.

✳ Next time I want to send an idiot on some errand, I'll go myself.

✳ Nothing is foolproof to a sufficiently talented fool.

✳ One way to compensate for a tiny brain is to pretend to be dead.

✳ The gates are down, the lights are flashing, but the train isn't coming.

✳ What's a gross ignoramus? One hundred forty-four times worse than an ordinary ignoramus.

✳ Simon goes to the carnival and takes his girlfriend through the Tunnel of Love. At the tunnel's exit, a staff member sees Simon and his young lady wading through the water. "Did your boat sink?" he asks. Simon replies, "You mean there's a boat?"

✳ "He may look like an idiot and talk like an idiot but don't let that fool you—he really is an idiot." *Groucho Marx*

✳ Dick walks into his house holding a dog turd in his hand. He shows it to his wife. "The streets in this neighborhood are filthy," says Dick. "Look what I almost stepped in!"

✳ He's so stupid that if he got amnesia, he'd get smarter.

✳ Nature has a way of compensating for weaknesses, which is why stupid people have big mouths.

✳ Paddy dies in a fire, but since he is very badly burned, the police need help to double-check the identity of the body. Paddy's two best friends, Michael and Sean, are sent for. Paddy's face has been burned away, so Michael and Sean asks the mortician to turn the body over. "No, that's not him," says Michael when he sees the corpse's rear end. "He's right. It definitely could not be Paddy," says Sean. "Are you certain?" says the mortician. "We have good reason to believe this is Paddy." "It can't be," says Michael. "Paddy had two assholes." "How do you know that?" asks the mortician. "Because," says Sean. "Whenever me, Paddy, and Michael went into town everyone would say, 'Hey look, there's Paddy with the two assholes.'"

✳ They say light travels faster than sound. Is that why some people appear bright until you hear them speak?

✳ Two Irishmen are walking through town when they see a little old lady walking toward them. "Hey," says one. "I reckon that old lady's Mother Theresa." "Isn't she dead?" says the other. "I thought so," says the first. "But she looks exactly like her. I'm going to ask if it is her." So saying, the man goes up to the old lady and says, "Excuse me, but aren't you Mother Theresa?" The old lady looks at him and says, "Ah, why don't you fuck off you big idjeet." She then kicks him in the shin and ducks up an alley. The second Irishman watches her go, "Ah dear," he says. "Now we'll never know."

✳ People have the right to be stupid, but some abuse that privilege.

# STUPIDITY: DUMB INSTRUCTIONS

✳ On a bag of Fritos: "You could be a winner! No purchase necessary. Details inside."

✳ On a Dial bath bar: "Directions—Use like regular soap."

✳ On a bottle of NyQuil (a sleeping aid): "Warning—May cause drowsiness."

✳ On a child's Superman costume: "Wearing of this garment does not enable you to fly."

✳ On a hotel-provided shower cap box: "Fits one head."

✳ On a Japanese food processor: "Not to be used for the other use."

✳ On a Korean kitchen knife: "Warning—Keep out of children."

✳ On a package of Sunmaid raisins: "Why not try tossing over your favorite breakfast cereal?"

✳ On a string of Chinese-made Christmas lights: "For indoor or outdoor use only."

✳ On a Swedish chainsaw: "Do not attempt to stop chain with your hands."

✳ On Robitussin children's cough medicine: "Do not drive car or operate machinery after taking this medication."

✳ On curling iron instructions: "Do not put into eyes."

✳ On instructions for a hairdryer: "Do not use while sleeping."

✳ On packaging from a clothing iron: "Do not iron clothes on body."

✳ On Planter's peanuts: "Warning—contains nuts."

✳ On a frozen dinner package: "Serving suggestion—defrost."

✳ On an American Airlines package of nuts: "Instructions—open package, eat nuts."

✳ On tirimisu dessert: "Do not turn upside down." (Printed on the bottom of the box)

# STUPIDITY: YO MOMMA...

✳ Yo momma's so stupid, she called the 7-11 to see when they closed.

✳ Yo momma's so stupid, she died before the police arrived because she couldn't find the "11" button in "9-1-1."

✳ Yo momma's so stupid, she got fired from the M&M factory for throwing away all the Ws.

✳ Yo momma's so stupid, she ordered her sushi well done.

✳ Yo momma's so stupid, she put lipstick on her forehead, because she wanted to make up her mind.

✳ Yo momma's so stupid, she thinks Johnny Cash is a pay toilet.

✳ Yo momma's so stupid, she took a ruler to bed to see how long she slept.

✳ Yo momma's so stupid, she took a spoon to the Super Bowl.

✳ Yo momma's so stupid, she went to a mind reader and was only charged half price.

✳ Yo momma's so stupid, when I told her it was chilly outside, she ran and got a bowl.

✳ Yo momma's so stupid, she cooks with Old Spice.

✳ Yo momma's so stupid, when she went to a movie and it said "Under 17 not admitted," she went home to find sixteen relatives.

# SUCCESS AND FAILURE

✳ "Behind every successful man is a woman—behind her is his wife." *Groucho Marx*

✳ "If at first you don't succeed—you're fired." *Lord Grade*

✳ "I've worked myself up from nothing to a state of extreme poverty." *Groucho Marx*

✳ "No one is completely unhappy at the failure of their best friend." *Groucho Marx*

✳ "There is no sweeter sound than the crumbling of your fellow man." *Groucho Marx*

✳ "You tried your best and you failed miserably. The lesson is never try." *Homer Simpson*

✳ If at first you don't succeed, destroy all evidence that you tried.

✳ If at first you don't succeed, redefine success.

✳ If at first you don't succeed, try management.

✳ Just when you thought he'd hit absolute rock bottom, he crashed right through and found a new bottom you didn't even know was there.

✳ Nothing recedes like success.

✳ If at first you don't succeed, blame someone else and seek counseling.

✳ There are two rules for success in life. One: never tell everything you know.

## SUNTAN

✳ "I'm red-headed and fair-skinned, and when I go to the beach, I don't tan, I stroke." *Woody Allen*

# SUPERNATURAL

✳ A woman comes home from psychic fair with a crystal ball she's just bought. "How much was that?" asks her husband. "Fifty dollars," answers the woman. "Fifty!" says the husband. "They must have seen you coming."

✳ All those who believe in psychokinesis raise my hand.

✳ How would you rate that psychic you saw last week? Medium.

✳ Never moon a werewolf.

✳ Tonight's meeting of the clairvoyants' society has been canceled due to unforeseen circumstances.

✳ Notice on a psychic's door: "To avoid confusion, please use bell."

✳ Rodney walks into a bar and says, "Bartender, give me two beers. One for me and one for my best buddy here." So saying, he pulls a three-inch man from his pocket. "Wow!" says the bartender. "You mean to say that little guy can drink a whole beer?" "Sure," says Rodney, so the bartender pours a beer, and the little guy drinks it all up. "What else can he do?" says the bartender. "Can he walk?" "Sure," says Rodney, and flicks a coin to the end of the bar. The little guy runs to the end of the bar, picks up the coin, and runs back again. "That's amazing," says the bartender. "What else can he do? Does he talk?" "Sure," says Rodney, turning to the little guy. "Hey, Dad, tell him about the time you were in Africa and you pissed off that witch doctor."

✳ Telepath wanted. You know where to apply.

✳ The really weird thing about *The X-Files* is, after I've taped it, I can never find it again.

✳ The Wolf Man comes home after a long day at the office. "How was work, dear?" his wife asks. "I don't want to talk about work!" he shouts. "Okay," she says. "So would you like to sit down and have dinner?" "I'm not hungry!" he yells. "I don't wanna eat! Can't I come home from work and do my own thing without your forcing food down my throat?" His wife sighs and says, "Well, I guess it's that time of the month…"

✳ Tom takes a short cut through a graveyard at midnight and is disturbed to hear a regular tapping sound. The noise gets louder, and Tom stumbles across a man in a suit tapping away at a headstone. Tom looks over the man's shoulder and sees he's adding an "e" to the end of the name carved in the stone. "A little late for work like that isn't it?" says Tom. "Yes," says the man. "But it couldn't wait. They spelled my name wrong."

✳ Why did the tiny ghost join the football team? He heard they needed a little team spirit.

✳ Why don't skeletons like parties? They have no body to dance with.

✳ Secretary to boss: "Excuse me, sir, but the Invisible Man is waiting outside." Boss: "Tell him I can't see him."

✳ Why don't witches like to ride their brooms when they're angry? They're afraid of flying off the handle!

✳ What do you call a haunted chicken? A poultry-geist.

✳ What do ghosts serve for dessert? Ice scream.

# SWEARING

✳ If a person who is deaf swears, does his mother wash his hands with soap?

✳ Little Johnny is caught swearing by his teacher. "Johnny, you shouldn't use that kind of language," says the teacher. "Where on earth did you hear such talk?" "My daddy said it," replies Johnny. "Well, that doesn't matter," explains the teacher. "You don't even know what it means." "I do, too!" replies Johnny. "It means the car won't start."

# SWIMMING

✳ A woman came in last in the 100-meter breaststroke at the local swim meet. She later complained, "The other girls were using their hands!"

✳ Tom to Harry: "Where did you learn to swim?" Harry: "In the water."

✳ I called my local swimming pool and said, "Is this the local swimming pool?" They said, "Well, that depends on where you're calling from."

✳ My father taught me to swim the hard way—he threw me out into the middle of a lake! Learning to swim that way wasn't easy, but the really hard part was getting out of the sack!

✳ The manager of a health spa is worried by the increasingly murky water in his swimming pool. Eventually he sends a sample off for analysis. A week later he receives a report saying, "This horse is seriously ill and should be put down immediately."

✳ Little Johnny is approached by the lifeguard at the public swimming pool. "You're not allowed to pee in the pool," says the lifeguard. "I'm going to report you." "But everyone pees in the pool," said little Johnny. "Maybe," says the lifeguard. "But not from the diving board!"

✳ Little boy to mother: "Mommy, can I go swimming?" Mother: "Certainly not. The sea's too rough, there's a terrible rip tide and a dangerous offshore current, and I've heard this coast is infested with jellyfish and sharks." Little boy: "But Daddy went swimming!" Mother: "I know, but he has excellent life insurance."

# T-SHIRT SLOGANS AND BUMPER STICKERS

✳ A conclusion is the place where you got tired of thinking.

✳ Boycott shampoo! Demand the real poo!

✳ Change is inevitable, except from a vending machine.

✳ Anybody going slower than you is an idiot. And anyone going faster is a maniac.

✳ Chaos. Panic. Disorder. My work is done here.

✳ Coffee. Chocolate. Men. Some things are better rich.

✳ Constant change is here to stay.

✳ Corduroy pillows: they're making headlines!

✳ Depression is merely anger without enthusiasm.

✳ Don't bother me. I'm living happily ever after.

✳ Down with categorical imperatives!

✳ Eat one live toad first thing in the morning. Nothing worse will happen to you for the rest of the day.

✳ Friends may come and go, but enemies accumulate.

✳ Give me ambiguity, or give me something else.

✳ Home is where you hang your @

✳ Honk if you love peace and quiet.

✳ I didn't use to finish sentences, but now I

✳ I intend to live forever—so far, so good.

✳ I love my wife—for $20 you can too.

✳ I used to be indecisive, but now I'm not so sure.

✳ I want patience… AND I WANT IT NOW!

✳ I'd give my right arm to be ambidextrous.

✳ If you can read this—I've lost my caravan.

✳ If you're looking for me, I just left.

✳ Illiterate? Write today for free advice.

✳ I'm out of bed and dressed. What more do you want?

✳ It's lonely at the top, but you eat better.

✳ It's not just the ups and downs that make life difficult. It's the jerks.

✳ Kentucky: five million people, fifteen last names.

✳ Laughing stock: cattle with a sense of humor.

✳ My kid beat up your honor student.

✳ Pardon my driving, I'm reloading.

✳ Preserve nature—pickle a squirrel.

✳ Procrastinate…Now!

✳ Puritanism: the haunting fear that someone, somewhere may be happy.

✳ Seen it all. Done it all. Can't remember most of it.

✳ Some days you are the pigeon. Some days you are the statue.

✳ Sometimes I wake up grumpy. Other times I let him sleep.

✳ Support your right to bare arms—wear short sleeves.

✳ The only substitute for good manners is fast reflexes.

✳ There are three kinds of people—those who can count and those who can't.

✳ Too many freaks. Not enough circuses.

✳ What am I? Flypaper for freaks?

✳ When everything's coming your way, you're in the wrong lane.

✳ When you're finally holding all the cards, why does everyone else decide to play chess?

✳ Who are these kids and why are they calling me Mom?

✳ You're just jealous because the voices are talking to me.

✳ Cleverly disguised as a responsible adult.

✳ Due to budget cuts, the light at the end of the tunnel has been turned off.

✳ I have plenty of talent and vision—I just don't care.

✳ I'd kill for a Nobel Peace prize.

✳ Just hand over the chocolate and no one will get hurt.

✳ Pride is what we have. Vanity is what others have.

✳ Souport publik edekashun.

✳ When I'm not in my right mind, my left mind gets pretty crowded.

# TALKING TO STRANGERS

✳ I was walking down the street when a man stuck his hand in my pocket. "What do you want?" I said. "A match," says the man. "Why didn't you ask me?" I said. He said, "I don't talk to strangers."

# TATTOOS

✳ "I want to get a tattoo over my entire body of myself, but taller." *Steven Wright*

✳ As an obstetrician, I sometimes see unusual tattoos. One patient had some type of fish tattooed on her abdomen. "That sure is an unusual-looking whale," I commented. With a sad smile she replied, "It used to be a dolphin."

✳ A woman is frustrated with her love life because her husband has a massive crush on Brigitte Bardot and ignores her completely. To win back his attention, she goes to a tattoo shop to have the letters "BB" tattooed on her breasts. The tattoo artist warns her that age and gravity will probably make this unattractive later in life, and suggests she have the tattoo on her ass instead. She agrees, and bends over to receive a "B" on each buttock. When her husband gets home from work that night, she greets him by turning around, bending over and lifting her dress to expose the artwork. "What do you think?" says the wife. "Who the hell's Bob?" asks her husband.

# TEENAGERS

✳ Advice for teenagers: leave home now while you still know everything.

✳ I'm finally eighteen, and now legally able to do everything I've been doing since I was fifteen.

✳ Two teenagers are found smoking a joint in the middle of a park. They're both arrested and taken to the town jail. The sergeant advises them they're entitled to one phone call. A while later a man enters the station. The sergeant says, "I assume you're the kids' lawyer." "Heck, no," replies the man. "I'm here to deliver a pizza."

✳ Why do teenagers say they're not like anyone else and then all dress exactly alike?

✳ Teenager to father: "How can you expect me to be independent, self-reliant, and stand on my own two feet on the tiny allowance you give me."

# TELEPATHY

* He almost had a telepathic girlfriend. But she left him before they met.

# TELEVISION

* "I must say, I find television very educational. The minute somebody turns it on, I go to the library and read a book." *Groucho Marx*

* "Television has raised writing to a new low." *Sam Goldwyn*

* "The other day a woman came up to me and said, 'Didn't I see you on television?' I said, 'I don't know. You can't see out the other way.'" *Emo Phillips*

* It was totally embarrassing the other day. I was watching TV with my mom and dad when suddenly there was a no-holds-barred completely explicit sex scene. I didn't know what to do. I just carried on watching the news and tried to ignore them.

* A New York TV station calls the British ambassador and asks him what he'd like for Christmas. "I couldn't possibly accept gifts in my position," says the ambassador. The TV station insists and says he can have anything he wants no matter how big or small. "Well," says the ambassador. "If you insist, I suppose I could accept a small box of chocolates." A month later the ambassador is watching TV when the newscaster says, "A while back we asked a number of ambassadors what they'd like for Christmas. The French ambassador said he'd like universal peace. The German ambassador said he'd like prosperity for the world's poor. And the British ambassador said he'd like a small box of candy."

* He's so stupid, his lips move when he watches TV.

* I love that TV show with all the different video clips of things going disastrously wrong all the time. What's it called? Oh yes, the news.

* Imitation is the sincerest form of television.

* Television is a device that lets people with nothing to do spend their time watching people who can't do anything.

* Why do you press harder on a remote control when you know the battery is dead?

✳ "There's so much comedy on television. Does that cause comedy in the streets?"
*Dick Cavett*

✳ Late-night TV is very educational. It teaches you that you should have gone to bed earlier.

✳ Why are some people willing to get off their asses to search the entire room for the TV remote but refuse to walk to the TV to change the channel manually?

# TEMPTATION

✳ Don't worry about avoiding temptations as you get older—they'll start avoiding you.

✳ Lead me not into temptation—I can find the way myself.

# THEATER

✳ A theater usher notices a man stretched across three seats. He walks over and whispers, "Sorry, sir, but you're allowed only one seat." The man moans but doesn't budge. "Sir, if you don't move, I'll have to call the manager," says the usher. Again the man moans but stays put. The usher returns with the manager, who also asks him to move without success. Finally they call a cop. "All right, buddy," says the cop. "What's your name?" "Joe," mumbles the man. "Where you from, Joe?" asks the cop. The man whispers, "The balcony."

✳ A retiree goes to the theater and asks about the seat prices. The ticket clerk reads off the list, "Balcony seats are $40. Circle seats are $30. And seats in the stalls are $25. Programs are $2." "All right," says the retireee. "I'll buy a program and sit on that."

✳ An out-of-work actor applies for a job in a zoo and is given a gorilla suit. "Our gorilla died," says the zoo manager. "You have to fill in for him until we find a replacement." The actor agrees and has a great time pretending he's a gorilla. He does all sorts of tricks, and the crowd loves him. However, as time goes on, the crowds tire of his antics and start paying attention to the new lion that's installed in the next cage. To win back his audience, the actor starts teasing the lion, pulling its tail through the bars, and throwing banana peels at it. One day the actor decides to do something really daring and steals the keys to the lion's cage. He waits till the lion is asleep then creeps in its cage with a bucket of water. The zoo visitors can't wait to see the gorilla soak the lion, and a huge crowd gathers. Unfortunately the lion wakes up before the actor can get near him and starts chasing him around the cage. Fearing for his life the actor starts screaming for help. The lion jumps on him, puts a paw on his mouth, and whispers, "Shut up, you moron, d'you want to get us fired?"

✳ Actor to fellow thespian: "At the end of my last recitation, it took the audience forty-five minutes to leave the theater." Thespian: "Goodness, was it very well attended?" Actor: "No, he was on crutches."

✳ An actor is onstage doing a terrible version of Hamlet. He's so bad, the audience start booing. Finally the actor stops, looks at the audience and says, "Don't blame me! I didn't write this garbage!"

✳ His mother egged him on to be an actor, but his first audience egged him off.

✳ Harry and Tom go to the theater, but Harry gets up to leave after the curtain closes for the first intermission. "Where are you going?" asks Tom. "It's not worth the wait," says Harry. "Look in the program. Act two—one month later."

✳ Little Johnny is performing in the school play when he falls through a large crack in the floor. Johnny's father turns to his mother and says, "Don't worry. It's just a stage he's going through."

✳ My uncle was thrown out of a mime show for having a seizure—they thought he was heckling.

✳ Thank you for that applause. You know, applause like that is better than sex. And in my case it lasts longer.

✳ The doctor had treated so many actors, he became known as "The Butcher"—all he did was cure hams.

✳ The show had a happy ending. The audience was delighted it was over.

✳ "The secret of acting is sincerity. If you can fake that, you've got it made." *George Burns*

✳ An aspiring young actor asks his girlfriend's father if he can have her hand in marriage. The father says, "I would never let my daughter marry an actor." The actor replies, "Sir, I think you may change your mind if you see me perform. Won't you at least come and see the play?" So the father goes to see the play and calls the actor the next day, "You were right. I did change my mind. Go ahead and marry my daughter. You're certainly no actor."

✳ The play was so bad, I asked the woman in front of me to put her hat on.

✳ "Washington is no place for a good actor. The competition from bad actors is too great." *Fred Allen*

# THEORY

＊ In theory, there is no difference between theory and practice. But, in practice, there is.

# THREATS

＊ "Why, I'd horse-whip you if I had a horse." *Groucho Marx*

# TIME AND TIMEKEEPING

＊ "Men love watches that have multiple functions. My husband has one that is a combination address book, telescope, and piano." *Rita Rudner*

＊ "Why should I care about posterity—what has posterity ever done for me?" *Groucho Marx*

＊ Time is what keeps everything from happening at once.

＊ A tourist walking through Cairo asks the time from an old man standing next to a camel. The old man grabs the camel's balls lifts them up and says, "It is now noon." The tourist is very impressed. He goes back to his hotel and tells a fellow guest that he's met an old man who can tell the time by the weight of his camel's balls. The next day both of them go to the man and ask him the time. The old man lifts the camel's balls and says, "It is half past nine." This is correct, and the two tourists go back to the hotel and tell a third guest of their discovery. The next day all three go to the old man to ask the time and, again, the old man obliges by feeling the camel's balls. "Say," says the first tourist. "That's such a great trick. Can you teach me how to do it?" "Certainly," says the old man. "First you must grasp the testicles of the camel…" The tourist does so. "Then you must raise them to the belly of the camel…" the tourist does so. "Then you must part the two testicles with your thumbs…" The tourist does so. "And in this way, we have clear view of the big clock in the tobacco shop's window…"

＊ Always try to do things in chronological order—it's less confusing that way.

＊ When a clock is hungry, it goes back four seconds.

＊ The person who takes their time is usually taking yours as well.

# TOILETS AND SEWAGE

✳ "Knock, knock." "Who's there?" "I Dunnop." "I Dunnop who?"

✳ "Men who consistently leave the toilet seat up secretly want women to get up to go to the bathroom in the middle of the night and fall in." *Rita Rudner*

✳ A man is in a public restroom, but soon discovers there's no toilet paper. He calls into the next stall, "Do you have any tissue paper in there?" "No," comes the reply. "Do you have any newspaper?" asks the man. "Sorry!" is the reply. "Okay," says the man. "So could you give me two fives for a ten?"

✳ If you're American when you enter the bathroom, and you're American when you leave the bathroom, what are you while you're in the bathroom? European.

✳ Life is a bit like being a pubic hair on the side of a toilet bowl. Eventually you will get pissed off.

✳ Why buy a product that it takes 2,000 flushes to get rid of?

# TORTOISES

✳ Some tortoises are playing cards when they run out of beer. They pick one of their number, Billy, to go to the liquor store. Billy goes off, but after waiting two days, the others start getting impatient. "Billy is really getting slow," says one. "He's not what he used to be," says another. A voice shouts from behind the door, "Hey! If you're going to talk about me behind my back, I'm not going."

✳ Where do you find a tortoise with no legs? Exactly where you left it.

# TOYS

✳ "I could tell that my parents hated me. My bath toys were a toaster and a radio." *Rodney Dangerfield*

✳ An unbreakable toy is useful for breaking other toys.

✳ He who dies with the most toys is, nonetheless, dead.

✳ A little old man is in a toy shop when he spots a fantastic train set with a red locomotive that whistles and blows real steam. "I'll have one of those," he says to the sales assistant. "Excellent choice," replies the assistant. "They're very popular with the grandchildren." "You're right," says the old man. "Billy would love one. In that case I'd better have two."

# TRANSPORTATION, TRAVEL, AND TOURISM

✳ "I like Milwaukee. I go there every year for a sensory deprivation experiment." *Emo Phillips*

✳ A tourist visiting New York City stops a passerby. "Excuse me," he says. "Can you tell me where the Empire State Building is, or should I go fuck myself again?"

✳ "I have just returned from Boston. It is the only thing to do if you find yourself there." *Fred Allen*

✳ "A travel agent told me I could spend seven nights in Hawaii. No days, just nights." *Rodney Dangerfield*

✳ A guide is showing a group of tourists around a ruined castle. "Not a stone in this building has been touched in the last four hundred years," exclaims the guide. "Really?" says one of the visitors. "We must have the same landlord."

✳ A hillbilly visits his cousin in the valley and is fascinated by the railroad he finds there. He's never seen a train, so he doesn't know to get out of the way when one comes whistling and steaming down the tracks toward him. Luckily the train has a cowcatcher on the front, and the hillbilly is swept off the tracks without being killed. The injured hillbilly is carried back to his cousin's shack to recuperate. The cousin puts a kettle on the stove to make some tea then goes out to get some wood. He returns to find the hillbilly beating the hell out of his kettle with a hammer. "What y'all doing to ma good kettle?" cries the cousin. "These things is dangerous," replies the hillbilly. "I'm a-killin' it before it gets a chance to grow up!"

✳ A husband and wife rent an old country cottage for a vacation. The wife goes to take a bath and only emerges three hours later. "It doesn't usually take you so long to get ready," says the husband. "No," replies the wife. "But there's no curtains. I had to get out of the tub every five minutes and breathe on the windows."

✳ A man goes to a travel agent to book his summer vacation. "Last year you sold me a vacation to Bermuda and my wife got pregnant," says the man. "The year before it was Monte Carlo and my wife got pregnant again. And the year before that it was Hong Kong and my wife got pregnant then as well." "I see," says the travel clerk. "And what did you have in mind this year?" "Somewhere cheaper," replies the man. "So she can come with me for a change."

✳ A man is having breakfast at a greasy spoon when three bikers come in looking for trouble. The first biker spits in the man's food. The second pours coffee over the man's head, and the third pulls away his chair so he falls over. Without a word the man gets up and walks out. "Not much of a man," says one of the bikers to the waitress. "Nope," replies the waitress. "And he's not much of a driver either, he just drove his truck over three bikes."

✳ A river pilot is guiding a ship up an estuary. Suddenly the ship grounds itself. The captain is furious. He yells at the pilot, "You said you knew every sandbank in this river!" "I do," says the pilot. "And that was one of them."

✳ "If you look like your passport photograph, in all probability you need the vacation."
*Earl Wilson*

✳ A passenger cruise ship passes a small desert island. Everyone watches as a ratty-looking bearded man runs out on the beach and starts shouting and waving his hands. "Who's that?" asks one of the passengers. "I've no idea," replies the captain. "But every year we sail past and he goes nuts."

✳ A train steward calls the police after coming across a young couple having sex in a car. The young man is arrested for having a first-class ride with a second-class ticket.

✳ A woman calls the lost-and-found office of the railroad company and asks them if they've found a stray octopus—they ask her what color it is.

✳ A young man asks his father, a preacher, if he can borrow the family car. "Only if you get your hair cut," says his father. "Why?" asks the son, "Moses had long hair, and so did Samson, and Jesus." "They did," replies Dad. "And they also walked everywhere."

✳ Barry and Michael are driving their truck down a country lane when they come to a bridge with a sign saying "Warning. Eleven-foot clearance." "Dammit," says Barry. "And our truck is twelve feet high." Michael looks out of the window and checks for onlookers. "I say we go for it," he says. "There's no one out here to report us."

✳ Fifty men are crammed into a train car when one shouts, "The next car is completely empty!" So they all get into that one.

✳ Harry is being interviewed for a job as a railroad signalman. "What would you do if two trains were approaching each other on the same line?" asks the interviewer. "I'd switch the points in the signal box," replies Harry. "And what if the signal switch was broken?" asks the interviewer. "I'd use the manual lever," replies Harry. "And what if that didn't work?" asks the interviewer. "I'd use the emergency phone to call the next signal box," says Harry. "And what if there was no answer?" asks the interviewer. "I'd call my uncle and tell him to come over," replies Harry. "What good would that do?" asks the interviewer. "None," replies Harry. "But he's never seen a train crash."

✳ Harry went to Chicago on a sleeper train but didn't get a wink of sleep. There was a worried little person in the top bunk who spent all night pacing up and down.

✳ If ignorance is bliss, then tourists are in a constant state of euphoria.

✳ The best time to visit Paris is between eighteen and thirty-four.

✳ Three passengers are on a train discussing why the train company is losing money. "Bad management," says one. "Too many staff," says another. "Not enough investment," says the third. Then they hear the ticket inspector coming and all run to hide in the toilets.

✳ A couple are listening to their friends' vacation experiences in the Southern California. "My," says one. "We knew you were planning to drive around Los Angeles, but we hadn't realized you were going to take in San Diego and Santa Barbara too." "We hadn't planned to," replies the woman. "But Ted refuses to ask for directions."

✳ What happened to the man who locked himself in his truck? His friends had to use a coat hanger to get him out.

✳ What's the best cure for seasickness? Sit under a tree.

✳ A man phones a taxi company because his cab hasn't shown up. "I'm supposed to be at the airport for nine o'clock," says the man. "Don't worry," says the girl. "The taxi will get you there before your plane leaves." "I know it will," says the man. "I'm the pilot."

✳ Cruise passenger to purser: "I wish to complain. I just went into my cabin and I found a common seaman using my shower!" Purser: "Who did you expect in second class? The captain?"

✳ Instructor, to trainee park ranger: "You see an enraged grizzly bear approaching a group of tourists. What steps do you take?" Park ranger: "Large ones—in the opposite direction."

✳ Two country bumpkins are riding a train for the first time. They've brought along a bag of apples for lunch and, just as one bites into his apple, the train enters a long tunnel. "Have you taken a bite out of your apple yet?" asks one. "No." says the other. "Well, don't," replies the first. "I just did and I went blind."

✳ A boulevard and an avenue walk into a bar. The avenue turns white with fear and starts shaking. "What's wrong?" asks the boulevard. "Look at the crazy guy in the corner," replies the avenue. "How d'you know he's crazy?" says the boulevard. "It's obvious," replies the avenue. "He's a cycle path!"

✳ I cheated the railway company the other day. I bought a return ticket and didn't go back.

✳ I had a terrible vacation. It only rained twice; once for three days and once for four.

✳ A husband and wife are on vacation. "Oh my God!" exclaims the wife. "I just remembered I left the oven on." "Don't worry about it," replies her husband. "The house won't burn down. I just remembered I left the bath running."

# TWINS

✳ I used to be twins. My mother has a picture of me when I was two.

✳ Man, to friend: "My wife is one of a pair of twins." Friend: "Really? How do you tell them apart?" Man: "Her brother has a beard."

✳ Why did the American conjoined twins emigrate to the U.K.? So the other one had a chance to drive.

# UGLINESS

✳ "I knew a girl so ugly, I took her to the top of the Empire State Building and planes started to attack her." *Rodney Dangerfield*

✳ "I knew a girl so ugly, she had a face like a saint—a Saint Bernard!" *Rodney Dangerfield*

✳ "I knew a girl so ugly, the last time I saw a mouth like hers it had a hook on the end of it." *Rodney Dangerfield*

✳ "I knew a girl so ugly, they use her in prisons to cure sex offenders." *Rodney Dangerfield*

✳ "I was so ugly, when I was born, the doctor slapped my mother." *Henny Youngman*

✳ "I'm so ugly. My father carries around the picture of the kid who came with his wallet." *Rodney Dangerfield*

✳ "Yes, darling, let me cover your face with kisses—on second thought, just let me cover your face." *Groucho Marx*

✷ He has the sort of face only a mother could love, and apparently his mother hates it.

✷ A doctor examines a woman and takes her husband aside. "I don't want to alarm you," he says, "but I don't like the way your wife looks." "Me neither, doctor," said the husband. "But she's a great cook and real good with the kids."

✷ A girl walks into a supermarket and buys a bar of soap, a toothbrush, a tube of toothpaste, a pint of milk, and a single frozen dinner. The checkout guy looks at her and says, "Single, huh?" The girl replies, "Yes. How'd you guess?" He says, "Because you're ugly."

✷ A woman is sitting in the park with her baby when a man comes over and says, "I'm sorry, lady, but that's the ugliest baby I've ever seen!" The woman bursts into tears. Another man sees this and comes over to comfort her. He hands her a tissue and says, "Miss, I don't know what that guy said, but it's not worth crying over." She smiles back at him as he reaches into his pocket. "You cheer up now. Look. I've even got some peanuts for your monkey!"

✷ Don't you need a license to be that ugly?

✷ He was an ugly baby. His mother only started to get morning sickness after he was born.

✷ He was so ugly, when he was a baby his mother left him on the steps of a police station—then went and turned herself in.

✷ How do you know if you're really ugly? Dogs hump your leg with their eyes closed.

✷ I dream of being be rich, powerful, and well respected. And while I'm dreaming, I wish you weren't so damn ugly.

✷ If someone tells you you're big boned and not conventionally good-looking, don't take it the wrong way. What they mean is you're fat and ugly.

✷ "I knew a girl so ugly that she was known as a two-bagger. That's when you put a bag over your head in case the bag over her head falls off." *Rodney Dangerfield*

✷ I went to see my doctor. "Doctor, every morning when I get up and look in the mirror I feel like throwing up. What's wrong with me?" He replied, "I don't know, but your eyesight is perfect."

✷ I wouldn't say my wife is ugly, but every time she sunbathes on the lawn a pair of vultures starts circling the garden.

✷ If I were as ugly as you are, I wouldn't say hello, I'd say boo!

＊ If you were cast as Lady Godiva the horse would steal the show.

＊ I'm not saying he's ugly—he just looks as if his hobby is stepping on rakes.

＊ Moonlight becomes you, but total darkness suits you even better.

＊ Oh my God! Look at you—anyone else hurt in the accident?

＊ Polly wasn't a very attractive girl; all the boys used to chase her, but they gave her a five-mile head start.

＊ The camera always caught her worst side—her outside.

＊ They broke the mold when they made him. In fact, I think they might have broken the mold before they made him.

＊ Tom to Dick: "Hey, have you ever gone to bed with an ugly woman?" Dick: "No, but I've woken up with plenty."

＊ What are you going to do for a face when the baboon wants his ass back?

＊ Wife to husband: "I just got back from the beauty shop." Husband: "What happened? Was it closed?"

＊ You have a face designed in a wind tunnel.

＊ You should have been born in the Dark Ages—you look terrible in the light.

＊ You were born ugly and built to last.

＊ "I was such an ugly kid—when I played in the sandbox, the cat kept covering me up." *Rodney Dangerfield*

＊ You're so ugly, robbers give you their masks to wear.

＊ You've got that faraway look. The farther you get, the better you look.

＊ "How do you make an ugly kid?" "I don't know. Ask your parents."

＊ "I'm so ugly. I worked in a pet shop, and people kept asking how big I'd get." *Rodney Dangerfield*

＊ An extremely ugly man walks into a psychiatrist's office. "Doctor," he says, "I'm so depressed and lonely. I don't have any friends, no one will come near me, and everybody laughs at me. Can you help me accept my ugliness?" "Certainly," says the psychiatrist. "Just go over there and lie face down on the couch."

✳ I'm so ugly. When I walk out of a pet store, the alarm goes off!

✳ To be honest, he's not conventionally good-looking. On the other hand, he is conventionally ugly.

✳ You're so ugly you can even make blind kids cry.

# UGLINESS: YO MOMMA...

✳ Yo momma's so ugly, her dentist treats her by mail order.

✳ Yo momma's so ugly, her shadow quit.

✳ Yo momma's so ugly, if she were a scarecrow, the corn would run away.

✳ Yo momma's so ugly, she can look up a camel's butt and scare its hump off.

✳ Yo momma's so ugly, she makes onions cry.

✳ Yo momma's so ugly, she practices birth control by leaving the lights on.

✳ Yo momma's so ugly, she pretends she's someone else when she's having sex.

✳ Yo momma's so ugly, the Elephant Man would have paid to see her.

✳ Yo momma's so ugly, the last time she heard a whistle, she got hit by a train.

✳ Yo momma's so ugly, when she looks in the mirror, her reflection ducks.

✳ Yo momma's so ugly, when she passes by a bathroom, the toilet flushes.

✳ Yo momma's so ugly, when she takes her bra off, she looks like she has four big toes.

✳ Yo momma's so ugly, when she walks in the kitchen, the rats jump on the table and start screaming.

✳ Yo momma's so ugly, when she was lying on the beach, the cat tried to bury her.

✳ Yo momma's so ugly, when your dad wants to have sex in the car, he tells her to get out.

✳ Yo momma's so ugly, her mom had to tie a steak around her neck to get the dog to play with her.

✳ Yo momma's so ugly, her pillows cry at night.

* Yo momma's so ugly, if you look up "ugly" in the dictionary, there's a picture of her.

* Yo momma's so ugly, people make jokes about her.

* Yo momma's so ugly, she got arrested for mooning when she looked out of a window.

* Yo momma's so ugly, the army doesn't use guns any more—they use her picture.

* Yo momma's so ugly, the government moved Halloween to her birthday.

* Yo momma's so ugly, they put her face on boxes of laxatives and sold it empty.

* Yo momma's so ugly, when she joined an ugly contest, they said "Sorry, no professionals."

* Yo momma's so ugly, when they took her to the beautician it took twelve—for a quote!

* Yo momma's so ugly, she got a sex change, and the surgeon had to flip a coin.

* Yo momma's so ugly, they use her face as a cure for constipation.

* Yo momma's so ugly, yo daddy takes her to work just so he doesn't have to kiss her goodbye.

* Yo momma's so ugly, she has to get her vibrator drunk first.

# ULTIMATUMS

* I want answers now, or I want them eventually!

# UNDERSTANDING

* "Honey, just because I don't care doesn't mean I don't understand!" *Homer Simpson*

* "Why, a child of four could understand this report. Run outside and get me a child of four. I can't make head or tail of it." *Groucho Marx*

* If you're not confused then you don't really understand what's going on.

# UNIONS

✳ A union leader goes to Las Vegas and checks out the brothels. In the first one, he asks if the girls belong to a union. "No," replies the madam. "And what cut do the girls get?" asks the leader. "They take 20 percent," replies the madam. Offended by this unfairness, the union leader goes to a second brothel and asks the same questions. Here he finds that the girls do belong to a union and get to keep 80 percent of their takings. "That's better," says the union leader. "I'd like to have the redhead in the corner." "Sure you would," says the madam, beckoning to an old fat blonde. "But Ethel here has seniority."

✳ The shop steward announces the results of negotiations with the employers. "From now on," he tells his members, "all wages are going to be doubled, vacations will be six months a year, and we are only going to have to work on Fridays." "What!" comes a cry from the back of the hall. "Every damn Friday?"

✳ A union boss is telling his son a bedtime story, "Once upon a time and a half…"

# UNIQUENESS

✳ Always remember you're unique—just like everyone else.

✳ So what if you're one in a million. That means there are more than 6,000 of you.

# UNIVERSAL TRUTHS

✳ All that glitters—has a high refractive index.

✳ Did you ever notice that when you blow in a dog's face, he gets mad at you, but when you take him on a car ride, he sticks his head out of the window?

✳ Every man has, at some stage while taking a pee, pulled the handle halfway through then raced against the flush.

✳ Everyone had an uncle who tried to steal their nose.

✳ Good news rarely comes in a brown envelope.

✳ No one knows the origins of their metal coat hangers.

✳ One of the most awkward things that can happen in a bar is when your beer-to-toilet cycle gets synchronized with a complete stranger.

✳ Rummaging in an overgrown garden will always turn up a bouncy ball.

✳ The most embarrassing thing you can do as schoolchild is to call your teacher mom or dad.

✳ Triangular sandwiches taste better than square ones.

✳ You know you've turned into your dad the day you put aside a thin piece of wood specifically to stir paint with.

✳ You never know where to look when eating a banana.

✳ Despite constant warnings, you have never met anybody who's had their arm broken by a swan.

✳ Nobody ever dares make cup-a-soup in a bowl.

✳ You never ever run out of salt.

# VASECTOMY

✳ A man goes to his doctor to get a vasectomy, but is horrified to find out how much they cost. "I could do you a cheap one," says the doctor. "But it's painful." "I can take it," says the man, so the doctor hands him a large firecracker. "Take this home," he says. "Light it and hold it in your hand while counting to ten." "How's that going to give me a vasectomy?" asks the man. "You'll find out," says the doctor. The man takes the firecracker home, lights it, and holds it in his right hand while he counts to ten. When he gets to five he tucks the firecracker between his legs and holds up his left hand, "...six, seven, eight..."

✳ A vasectomy is never having to say you're sorry.

✳ What's the definition of macho? Jogging home after a vasectomy.

✳ A newly married couple are arguing about how many children to have. The bride says she wants three children, while the husband says two will be enough. The argument gets extremely heated and eventually the husband says, "After our second child, I'll just have a vasectomy." His wife replies, "Well then, I hope you'll love the third one as if it were one your own."

# VEGETARIANISM

* Eating vegetables is much crueler than eating animals. At least the animals have a chance to run away.

* Helpful advice if you have vegetarians coming to dinner: Just serve them a nice bit of steak or veal. Since they're always going on about how tofu and tempeh taste like the real thing, they shouldn't notice the difference.

* If we aren't supposed to eat animals, why are they made of meat?

* To attract a vegetarian, make a noise like a wounded vegetable.

* Invited by vegetarians for dinner? Tell them about your special dietary requirements and ask for a nice steak.

# VETS

* A lady discovers her dog is not moving. She calls a vet who, after a brief examination, announces the dog is dead. "Are you sure?" the woman asks. "Isn't there the slightest chance you can revive him?" The vet thinks for a second then leaves the room and comes back with a cat. The cat walks over to the dog, sniffs it from head to foot, looks at the vet, and shakes its head. "I'm sorry," says the vet. "Your dog is definitely dead." Satisfied that the vet had done everything possible, the lady asks for his bill. "That will be $1,430," the vet replies. The lady is astonished. "I don't believe it," she says. "What did you do that cost $1,430?" "Well," replies the vet. "It's $30 for a call-out fee, $100 for a consultation, and $1,300 for a CAT scan."

* Late one night a little old lady calls her vet and asks the best way to separate two mating dogs. "Try prying them apart with a stick," says the vet. A few minutes later the old lady calls back. The stick hasn't worked, can he suggest something else. "Oh, I dunno," says the vet. "Throw some water over them." A few minutes later the old lady calls again. The water hasn't done anything. What else can she try? The irritated vet says, "Go and tell one of the dogs that it's wanted on the phone." "Will that work?" asks the old lady. The vet replies, "Well, it's already worked three times with me!"

* Mrs. Evans takes her cat to the vet. The vet examines the animal and says, "I can tell your cat is seriously ill just by looking at its stools. "Is it because they're a funny color?" asks Mrs. Evans. "No," replies the vet. "It's because they're coming out of its eye."

# VICES

* "He hasn't a single redeeming vice." *Oscar Wilde*

# WAITING

* If I'm not back in five minutes—just wait longer.

# WAR AND MILITARY

* "I was classified '4P' by the draft board. In the event of war, I'm a hostage." *Woody Allen*

* "Military justice is to justice what military music is to music." *Groucho Marx*

* "Men are brave enough to go to war, but they are not brave enough to get a bikini wax." *Rita Rudner*

* A group of soldiers take a first-aid course. After they've finished they're given a test by their instructor. The instructor points to one of the solders and says, "The sergeant sustains a head injury during a cross-country march. What do you do about it?" The soldier replies, "I wrap a tourniquet around his neck and tighten it until the bleeding stops."

* A group of marines are stranded on a Pacific island after the war. After a few months the sergeant decides he has to do something to boost morale. "Good news, men," he says. "We're going to have a change of underwear." It's not much, but the marines are cheered up. The sergeant continues, "Johnson you change with Kropowlski. Kropowlski you change with Peterson..."

* A knight and his men return to their castle after a hard day of fighting. "How are we faring?" asks the king. "Sire," replies the knight. "I have been robbing and pillaging on your behalf all day, burning the towns of your enemies in the west." "What?" shrieks the king. "I don't have.

* "Remember, men, we're fighting for this woman's honor—which is probably more than she ever did." *Groucho Marx*

✳ A Navy psychiatrist is interviewing a potential recruit. The psychiatrist says, "What would you do if you looked out of that window and saw a battleship coming down the street?" The recruit replies, "I'd grab a torpedo and sink it." "Really? And where would you get a torpedo?" asks the psychiatrist. The recruit replies, "The same place you got your battleship!"

✳ A sniper takes a pot-shot at a general visiting the front line. "We know exactly where he is, sir," says one of soldiers. "He's been up there for weeks." "Then why don't you bump him off?" asks the general. The soldier replies, "Because if we got rid of him they might replace him with someone who can actually shoot straight."

✳ An army platoon is on maneuvers in the Florida swamps. The men are running low on water, so the sergeant tells a private to go down to the creek and fill up their canteens. "But, Sarge," says the private. "I saw an alligator in the creek." "Don't be such a coward," replies the sergeant. "That alligator is four times as frightened of you as you are of it." "He might be," replies the private. "But even if he's only twice as frightened as I, that water still won't be fit to drink."

✳ An admiral is standing on the deck of his battleship when the enemy is spotted on the horizon. "Fetch my red shirt," says the admiral to a nearby petty officer. "If I'm wounded fighting this enemy ship, I don't want the men to see that I'm bleeding." "Excuse me, sir," says the petty officer. "But it's not one ship, there are fifteen." "In that case," replies the admiral, "forget the shirt and pick up my brown trousers."

✳ An Israeli soldier asks his commanding officer for a three-day pass. The officer says, "Are you crazy? You have to do something spectacular to get a pass like that!" So the soldier goes off and comes back a day later in an Arab tank. The officer is impressed. "How did you do it?" he asks. "Well," says the soldier. "I jumped in a tank, went to the border, and drove along it till I saw an Arab tank. Then I shouted to the driver, "Hey! Do you want to get a three-day pass?" And we exchanged tanks."

✳ Three military men are introduced to each other. One steps forward and says, "John Collingworth. General. Married. Two sons, both doctors." The second one steps forward and says, "Marcus Hil. General. Married. Two sons, both lawyers." The third man steps forward and says, "Bill Marsh. Lance corporal. Not married. Two sons, both generals."

✳ To avoid getting drafted, a young man slips into a nunnery to hide from some draft board agents who are after him. Desperate, he approaches a nun and asks her to hide him. "Get under my robes," says the nun. "No one will look for you there." The nun lifts up her robes and the man says, "Hey, that's a fine pair of legs you've got there, sister." "Yeah, well if you look any higher you'll see a fine set of balls," replies the nun. "I didn't want to get drafted either."

✳ Why did so many black GIs get killed in Vietnam? Because every time the sergeant shouted, "Get down!" they stood up and started dancing.

✳ "The Vietnam War finally ended in an agreement neither side intended to honor. It was like one of Zsa Zsa Gabor's weddings." *Bob Hope*

✳ A sergeant and two men from his platoon go to a bar. The sergeant asks an attractive waitress to join him in a game of pool, but she tells him she'd rather play with his privates.

✳ During World War II a group of German soldiers capture a French village. "Hand over all your food," says the German officer to the Mayor. "But all we have left is a few scraps of bread," protests the Mayor. "War is war," replies the officer. "Hand it over." After the Germans have eaten, the officer says, "Now give us your wine." "We have nothing but a single bottle," says the Mayor. "Tough," says the officer. "Hand it over. War is war." Once the Germans have drunk the wine, their officer says, "Now we want women. Hand over every girl in the village." "But we have none," replies the Mayor. "They have all fled. The only woman left is Madame Blanc, and she is over 90 years old." "We don't care," says the officer. "War is war. Hand her over." So the Mayor brings out Madame Blanc, who slowly starts taking off her clothes. The German officer gulps as he watches the old woman undress, "Uh, look, on second thought, we won't bother..." he says. "Not so fast, Fritz," replies Madame Blanc, dropping her underwear, "War is war."

✳ "Countries are making nuclear weapons like there's no tomorrow." *Emo Phillips*

✳ "War is God's way of teaching us geography." *Paul Rodriguez*

# WEATHER

✳ A motorist is making his way down a flooded road after a night of torrential rain. Suddenly he sees a man's head sticking out of a large puddle. He stops his car and asks the man if he needs a lift. "No thanks," says the man. "I'm on my bike."

✳ A hobo sees an old hillbilly standing in a field holding a short length of rope. "What's the rope for?" asks the hobo. "It's an old country way of telling the weather," says the hillbilly. "And how does it work?" asks the hobo. "Well," replies the hillbilly. "When it swings around, it's windy. And when it's wet, it's raining."

✳ A ship's captain radios a lighthouse keeper, "Radio reception is very bad. Please spell out your weather report." The keeper replies, "W-E-T-H-O-R R-E-P-O-R-T." The captain says, "My God, that's the worst spell of weather I've had in a long time."

✳ Harry gets a job as a weatherman in the Far East; however, try as he might, he can never get a forecast right. Eventually he's fired and has to fly home. A friend asks why he's back so soon. Harry replies, "The climate didn't agree with me."

✳ Harry had a fantastic country house with two wings, sadly it flew off the last time they had a big storm.

✳ It was so cold, the politicians had their hands in their own pockets.

✳ Harry to Tom: "How did you find the weather while you were away?" Tom: "It was just outside the front door."

✳ Little Johnny walks into his classroom wearing a single glove. His teacher asks him what he's doing. "Well ma'am," says Johnny. "I was watching the weather report on TV, and it said it was going to be sunny, but on the other hand it could get quite cold."

✳ Tom arrives at a hotel in a Scottish village on a cold, grey, drizzly day. The weather remains the same for two weeks. Exasperated, Tom stops a little boy in the street. "Does the weather here ever change?" he asks. "I don't know," replies the boy. "I'm only six."

✳ A famous scientist visits an observatory and is shown the latest radio telescope. The scientist looks at the picture on the computer screen and says, "It's going to rain." That's incredible!" says one the astronomers. "D'you mean that, merely by looking at the stars on that screen, you can predict when it will rain here on earth?" "No," says the scientist. "I mean my corns hurt."

✳ Thirty people are sheltering under an umbrella. How many of them get wet? None— who said it was raining?

✳ A small boy is woken by a huge crash of thunder. He runs into his parents' room, where his father comforts him. "Don't be afraid of the thunder," he says. "It's just a noise that God makes when someone tells a lie." "But why is it thundering now?" asks the boy. "It's the middle of the night and everyone is asleep." I know," replies father. "But it's around this time that they start to print the newspapers."

✳ The weather was terrible on my vacation. Mind you, I did come home brown—with rust.

✳ "Everybody talks about the weather, but nobody does anything about it." *Charles Dudley Warner*

# WISDOM

✳ "By the time you're eighty years old, you've learned everything. You only have to remember it." *George Burns*

✳ A word to the wise isn't necessary—it's the stupid ones who need the advice.

✳ By the time a man is wise enough to watch his step, he's too old to go anywhere.

✳ By the time you can make ends meet, they move the ends.

✳ It's so simple to be wise. Just think of something stupid to say and then don't say it.

✳ Knowledge is knowing a tomato is a fruit; wisdom is not putting it in a fruit salad.

✳ Wisdom is the comb that life gives you after you lose your hair.

✳ Experience is that marvelous thing that enables you recognize a mistake when you make it again.

✳ Age doesn't always bring wisdom; sometimes it arrives alone.

# WITHOUT ONE ANOTHER

✳ How can I miss you if you won't go away?

✳ If you can't live without me—why aren't you dead already?

✳ I'm so miserable without you, it's almost like having you around.

# WORDS OF WISDOM

✳ "If you can't beat them, arrange to have them beaten." *George Carlin*

✳ "The bigger they are, the worse they smell." *George Carlin*

✳ "The day after tomorrow is the third day of the rest of your life." *George Carlin*

✳ A friend is someone you can call to help you move. A best friend is someone you can call to help you move a body.

✳ A spoken contract isn't worth the paper it's written on.

✳ A thing not worth doing isn't worth doing well.

✳ All generalizations are false.

✳ All things are possible, except skiing through a revolving door.

✳ Always keep your words soft and sweet—just in case you have to eat them.

✳ As you journey through life, take a moment every now and then to think about others—as they could well be plotting something.

✳ Better to be occasionally cheated than perpetually suspicious.

✳ Do not meddle in the affairs of dragons—because you are crunchy and taste good with ketchup.

✳ Don't become superstitious—it's bad luck.

✳ Don't hate yourself in the morning—sleep till noon.

✳ Don't kick a man when he's down unless you're absolutely certain he won't get up.

✳ Don't take life too seriously; after all, no one gets out alive.

✳ Drive carefully—it's not only cars that can be recalled by their maker.

✳ Everybody lies, but it doesn't matter since nobody listens.

✳ Everyone seems normal, until you get to know them.

✳ Everywhere is walking distance if you have the time.

✳ For every action, there is an equal and opposite criticism.

✳ Good judgment comes from bad experience, and a lot of that comes from bad judgment.

✳ Good news is just life's way of keeping you off balance.

✳ If a band of motorcyclists, all wearing black leather vests and covered with tattoos, cuts you off on the highway, just think the obscenities quietly to yourself.

✳ If a thing's worth doing, it would have been done already.

✳ If flattery gets you nowhere, try bribery.

✳ If life gives you lemons, squeeze the juice into a water gun and shoot other people in the eyes.

✳ If you can smile when things go wrong, you have someone in mind to blame.

✳ If you can tell the difference between good advice and bad advice—you don't really need advice.

✳ If you live in a glass house, you should change clothes in the basement.

✳ Intelligence has much less practical application than you'd think.

✳ "If you can't be a good example, then you'll just have to be a horrible warning." *Catherine Aird*

✳ "To do is to be." *Descartes;* "To be is to do." *Voltaire*; "Do be do be do." *Frank Sinatra*

✳ If you lend someone $20 and never see that person again, it was probably worth it.

✳ It is easier to get forgiveness than permission.

✳ It's a small world. So you gotta use your elbows a lot.

✳ Needing someone is like needing a parachute. If they aren't there the first time you need them, chances are you won't be needing them again.

✳ It's better to have someone inside the tent peeing out, than outside peeing in.

✳ It's easier to suffer in silence if you're sure someone is watching.

✳ Most of us know a good thing as soon as someone else sees it.

✳ Never entrust your life to a surgeon with more than three Band Aids on his fingers.

✳ Never get in line at the bank behind someone wearing a ski mask.

✳ Never go to a plastic surgeon whose favorite artist is Picasso.

✳ Never hit a man with glasses—use your fist.

✳ Never try to teach a pig to sing. It wastes your time and annoys the pig.

✳ Never underestimate the power of stupid people in large groups.

✳ No man is really successful until his mother-in-law admits it.

✳ Not one shred of evidence supports the notion that life is serious.

✳ One good turn usually gets most of the blanket.

✳ Opportunities always look bigger going than coming.

✳ Quitters never win, winners never quit. But those who never win and never quit are idiots.

✳ Show me a man who has both feet on the ground, and I'll show you a man who can't put on his pants.

✳ Support bacteria. It's the only culture some people have.

✳ Talk is cheap because supply exceeds demand.

✳ The 50-50-90 rule: any time you have a 50-50 chance of getting something right, there's a 90 percent probability you'll get it wrong.

✳ The grass is always greener on TV.

✳ The great thing about teamwork is that you never have to take all the blame yourself.

✳ The lion shall lie down with the lamb. But the lamb probably won't get much sleep.

✳ The meek shall inherit the Earth, but not till the rest of us are done with it.

✳ The severity of the itch is inversely proportional to the ability to reach it.

✳ The sooner you fall behind, the more time you have to catch up.

✳ There is no substitute for genuine lack of preparation.

✳ Those who can't laugh at themselves leave the job to others.

✳ Too many people find fault as if there's a reward for it.

✳ We cannot change the direction of the wind—but we can adjust our sails.

✳ Whatever hits the fan will not be evenly distributed.

✳ When it's you against the world, I'd bet on the world.

✳ You can fool some of the people some of the time, and that is sufficient.

✳ You're never quite as stupid as when you think you know everything.

✳ "Don't go around saying the world owes you a living. The world owes you nothing. It was here first." *Mark Twain*

✳ "You can't have everything. Where would you put it?" *Steven Wright*

✳ Always try to be modest. And be damn proud of it!

✳ If you can keep your head when all around you are losing theirs, then you probably haven't understood the seriousness of the situation.

✳ Don't sweat the petty things and don't pet the sweaty things.

✳ Exaggeration is a billion times worse than understatement.

✳ If it were truly the thought that counted, more women would be pregnant.

✳ If you tell the truth, you don't have to remember anything.

✳ It's hard to make a comeback when you haven't been anywhere.

✳ Never test the depth of the water with both feet.

✳ No one is listening until you fart.

✳ People are like teabags. You don't know how strong they'll be until you put them in hot water.

✳ The bigger they are the harder they hit.

✳ The things that come to those that wait may be the things left by those who got there first.

✳ When you're arguing with an idiot, try to make sure he isn't doing the same thing.

✳ One day the lion and the lamb will lie down together—when the lamb hasn't got anything the lion wants.

✳ If you can't see the bright side of life, polish the dull side.

✳ It is more impressive when others discover your good qualities without your help.

✳ Always speak well of your enemies—after all, you made them.

✳ People will believe anything if you whisper it.

✳ Never confuse your career with your life.

✳ Where there's a will there are 500 relatives.

✳ Variety is the spice of life, but monotony buys the groceries.

✳ If you want to forget all your troubles, buy a pair of tight shoes.

✳ No matter what happens, somebody will find a way to take it too seriously.

✳ It is better to have loved and lost than to listen to "Lost In Love" by Air Supply.

# WORK AND BUSINESS

* A man goes to his bank manager for advice: "How do I set up a small business?" he asks. "Easy," replies the bank manager. "Buy a big one and wait."

* A businessman gets on an elevator in his office building. A woman already inside greets him saying, "T-G-I-F." He smiles at her and replies, "S-H-I-T." The woman looked at him, puzzled, and again says, "T-G-I-F." Again the man answers her with, "S-H-I-T." The woman says, "Do you know what I'm saying? T-G-I-F means, 'Thank God it's Friday.'" "I know," replies the man. "But S-H-I-T means, 'Sorry, honey, it's Thursday.'"

* "We're overpaying him, but he's worth it." *Samuel Goldwyn*

* A man asks a judge to let him off jury duty. Judge: "But surely your firm can manage without you for a few weeks." The man replies, "Certainly. They can manage without me altogether—and I don't want them to find out."

* A man takes the ferry to work every day, but one morning he oversleeps. He hurries to the docks and sees the ferry ten feet from the shoreline. Determined not to miss it, he takes a running jump and, by the skin of his teeth, just manages to grab hold of the ferry's passenger rail. One of the crew helps pull him up over the side. "Y'know," he says. "If you'd waited another second or two, we'd have docked."

* Business is looking up. It's flat on its back.

* A new employee is called into the personnel manager's office. "What's the meaning of this?" asks the manager. "When you applied for your job, you told us you had five years' experience. Now we discover this is the first job you've ever had." "Yes," replies the young man. "But your ad also said you wanted somebody with imagination."

* A small child asks a businessman, "What do two and two make?" The businessman replies, "Are you buying or selling?"

* According to the latest statistics, there are twelve million Americans who aren't working. And there are plenty more if you count the ones with jobs.

* After ten years working for the same firm, he was finally given the key to the executive bathrooms. Then after he'd given them a good clean, he had to give it back.

* Any suggestions on how to rescue the company, please put them in the suggestion box down the hall. And don't forget to flush it.

* An art collector is walking down the road when he notices a mangy cat in a shop doorway lapping milk from a saucer. He realizes that the saucer is extremely old and

valuable, so walks into the store and offers to buy the cat for two dollars. The store owner replies, "I'm sorry, but the cat isn't for sale. The collector says, "Please, I need a cat around the house to catch mice. I'll pay you twenty dollars for it." The owner says "Okay. Sold." And hands over the cat. The collector continues, "Hey, for the twenty dollars, I wonder if you could throw in that old saucer. The cat's used to it and it'll save me from having to buy a dish." The store owner says, "Sorry, chum. That's my lucky saucer. So far this week I've sold sixty-eight cats."

✳ Applebottoms's Apple Pie and Associated Apple Pastry Products factory has announced very disappointing results. They've had 500 men and women working nonstop all year and only managed to produced a single triangular apple pastry. The manager admitted this represented a very small turnover.

✳ At work we now have one day a week where we just leave the phones ringing and don't answer them. Which is good because it really can get quite stressful at the Samaritans.

✳ God is speaking to the archangel Gabriel. "Y'know I just created a twenty-four-hour period of alternating light and darkness." "Wow," replies Gabriel. "What are you going to do now?" "I think I'll call it a day," replies God.

✳ Chairman, to his directors: "Gentlemen. Last month we were teetering on the edge of a precipice. Today we are going to take a great step forward."

✳ Harry operates a one-day dry-cleaning service. People give him clothes on the understanding that one day, they might get them back again.

✳ He made his fortune walking the streets selling batteries—every Christmas morning, just after the kids opened their presents.

✳ I work for a really good firm. They let me work from home and they gave me a company car. Of course, because I work from home, they gave me a car that doesn't work.

✳ Helium was up, feathers were down. Paper was stationary. Fluorescent tubing was dimmed in light trading. Knives were up sharply. Pencils lost a few points. Elevators rose, while escalators continued their slow decline. Mining equipment hit rock bottom. Diapers remain unchanged. Balloon prices were inflated. Scott tissue touched a new bottom.

✳ How do you get twenty vice-presidents in a minivan? Promote one and watch the other nineteen crawl up his backside.

✳ I get home so seldom, that if I'm seen around the house, the neighbors gossip.

✳ I'd quit my job but I need the sleep.

✳ If lawyers are disbarred and clergymen defrocked, doesn't it follow that electricians can be delighted, musicians denoted, cowboys deranged, models deposed, tree surgeons debarked, and dry cleaners depressed?

✳ If work were so good, the rich would keep more of it for themselves.

✳ It was always my dream to work at home and now it's come true in a way—my wife's thrown me out, so I have to sleep at the office.

✳ It's terrible, the hours I have to do in my job. I'm only at home with my family six weeks in the entire year. But it's all right. The six weeks soon pass.

✳ No one could ever call me a quitter. Do you know why? I always get fired.

✳ My office has sick building syndrome. I got to work yesterday, and the building wasn't there. It phoned in later saying it had a sore throat.

✳ One day the manager of a brokers' firm walks past a new employee counting put and call slips. The guy does it faster than anyone he has ever seen. "That's amazing," says the manager. "Where did you learn to count like that?" "Yale," answers the employee. "Yale? I don't believe it. I went to Yale too. What's your name?" "Yimmy Yohnson," says the employee.

✳ Things are very bad at the shop—a man bought something with a $50 bill, and we had to make him a partner before we could give him his change.

✳ "If you really want something in this life, you have to work for it. Now, quiet. They're about to announce the lottery numbers!" *Homer Simpson*

✳ Two business owners are comparing working practices. One says to the other, "I make sure each of my employees takes a week off every two months." "Why on earth would you do that?" asks the other. The first replies, "It's the best way of finding out which ones I can do without."

✳ Sure I multi-task. I read in the bathroom.

✳ This isn't an office; it's Hell with fluorescent lighting.

✳ Tom is driving along in his car when his boss calls him on his cell. "I'm promoting you to Sales Manager," he says. Tom is so surprised, he almost loses control of the car. A few seconds later the phone rings. It's the boss again: "Henderson has resigned, I'm promoting you to take his place as Sales Director." Again Tom is so surprised, the car swerves all over the place. Seconds later the phone rings a third time. Again it's the boss.

"Harris has had a heart attack," he says. "You're the new Managing Director." Tom is so astonished, he loses control completely and crashes the car into the embankment. Later a policeman asks him what caused the accident. Tom says, "I careered off the road."

✳ Two businessmen are fishing in a row boat when a storm blows up and capsizes them. One of the men can swim but the other can't. "Can you float alone?" shouts the swimmer to his sinking partner. The partner shouts back, "This is no time to talk shop!"

✳ Wanted: Man to test for gas leaks with a lit match. Must be willing to travel.

✳ A firm advertises for a "Problem Solver" with a salary of $100,000. Tom goes for an interview and is offered the job on the spot. "That's great," says Tom. "But tell me, how can you afford to pay me such a high salary?" "That," says his employer, "is your first problem."

✳ Two teams from American and Japanese corporations have a boat race. On the big day, the Japanese win by a mile, and the discouraged Americans hire a consulting firm to investigate the problem. The findings are that the Japanese team had eight people rowing and one person steering, while the American team had one person rowing and eight people steering. Based on these results, the American team is completely reorganized to include four steering managers, three area steering managers, and a new performance review system for the person rowing the boat to provide work incentive. The following year the Japanese win again, so the Americans lay off the rower for poor performance and give the managers a bonus for discovering the problem.

✳ "I think Mr. Smithers picked me for my motivational skills. Everyone always says they have to work twice as hard when I'm around!" *Homer Simpson*

✳ A man is flying in a hot air balloon and realizes he's lost. He reduces height and shouts to a farmer in a field, "Excuse me! Can you tell me where I am?!" The farmer says, "Yes! You're in a hot air balloon, hovering 30 feet above this field!" "You should work in Information Technology!" shouts the balloonist. "Everything you've told me is technically correct, but it's no use to anyone!" The farmer answers, "You must work in business! You don't know where you are, or where you're going, but you expect me to be able to help! You're in the same position you were before we met, but now it's my fault!"

✳ An astronaut in orbit is being interviewed by a reporter. "Do you feel safe up there?" asks the reporter. "Not really," replies the astronaut. "I'm stuck on top of 20,000 parts, each one supplied by the lowest engineering bidder."

✳ I know an immigrant who came to this country ten years ago with nothing in his pocket. Through sheer hard work and determination, that man today owes $978,000.

✳ Elevator operator: "Sorry, did I brake too suddenly?" Passenger: "No, I always stand with my pants around my ankles."

✳ What's the difference between your job and your wife? After twenty years your job still sucks.

✳ Anyone can do any amount of work provided it isn't the work he/she is supposed to be doing.

✳ A successful businessman has a meeting with his new son-in-law. "To welcome you into the family," says the father-in-law, "I'm making you a 50-50 partner in my business. All you have to do is go to the factory and learn the ropes." The son-in-law interrupts, "Sorry, I hate factories. I can't stand the noise." "I see," replies the father-in-law. "Well, then you'll work in the office and take charge of some of the operations." "No, I hate office work," says the son-in-law. "I can't stand being stuck behind a desk." "Wait a minute," says the father-in-law. "I just make you half-owner of a money-making organization, but you don't like factories and won't work in a office. What am I going to do with you?" "Easy," replies the young man. "Buy me out."

✳ Harry to Tom: "How long have you worked for your company?" Tom: "Ever since they threatened to fire me."

✳ "Treat employees like partners and they act like partners." *Fred Allen*

✳ Work is the greatest thing in the world, so make sure you save some for tomorrow.

✳ Tom, Dick, and Harry put in bids for work at the town hall. Tom goes to the town clerk and puts in a bid of $3,000: $1,000 for him, $1,000 for his staff, and $1,000 for materials. Dick puts in an offer of $6,000: $2,000 for him, $2,000 for his staff, and $2,000 for materials. Harry comes in and puts in a bid for $9,000. "$9,000!" says the Town Clerk. "I've had offers as low as $3,000. How can you justify so much money?" "Easy," says Harry. "$3,000 for me, $3,000 for you, and $3,000 for Tom for doing all the work."

✳ When you see an office worker with their desk piled high with paper, ask yourself the question, "Are they busy or just confused?"

# WORK AND BUSINESS: ABSENTEES

✳ A boss accosts his employee coming through the door at ten in the morning. "You should have been here at nine," he says. "Why?" asks the employee. "What happened?"

✳ A boss asks an employee if he believes in life after death. "Why do you want to know?" asks the employee. The boss replies, "Because while you were at your grandmother's funeral, she popped in to see you."

✳ A boss is chastising one of his employees for persistent lateness. "Do you know when we start work in this office?" he asks. "No," replies the employee. "They're usually hard at it by the time I get here."

✳ A man's boss asks him why he went for a haircut when he should have been at work. "Why shouldn't I get it cut during office hours?" says the man. "It grows while I'm at work." "It doesn't all grow while you're at work," says the boss. "Yes," replies the man. "And I don't have it all cut."

✳ Two guys are working in a city park. One digs a hole, and the other comes in behind him and fills it in. All day the two men work furiously. One digging, the other filling. A passerby watches this activity and eventually comes over to ask what they're doing. The hole digger explains. "I guess it must look funny," he says. "But the guy who plants the trees is sick today."

✳ I used up all my sick days, so I'm calling in dead.

✳ Tom found it hard to get to sleep, so he overslept in the morning and arrived late for work. Eventually his boss threatened to fire him if he didn't do something about it, so Tom went to his doctor. The doctor gave Tom a pill and told him to take it before he went to bed. Tom took the pill and slept very well. He woke up on time, had a leisurely breakfast, and drove to work. "That pill the doctor gave me really worked!" says Tom to his boss. "Well that's great," replies the boss. "But where the hell were you yesterday?"

# WORK AND BUSINESS: INTERVIEWS AND APPLICATIONS

✳ A young man goes for a job interview and is asked what sort of employment package he expects. "What I expect is a $30,000-a-year starting salary. Six weeks vacation a year and a Jaguar for a company car." "Okay," says the interviewer. "How about this? We pay you $40,000 a year, rising to $60,000 after two years. You get eight weeks annual leave. You get your own executive assistant, and we promote you to board level after four years?" "Wow!" says the young man. "You've got to be joking!" "I am," replies the interviewer. "But you started it."

✳ An applicant is being interviewed for admission to a prominent medical school. "Tell me," inquires the interviewer. "Where do you expect to be ten years from now?" "Well, let's see," replies the student. "It's Wednesday afternoon. So I guess I'll be on the golf course."

✳ An applicant is filling out a job application. When he comes to the question "Have you ever been arrested?" he answers "No." The next question, intended for people who have answered in the affirmative, is "Why?" The applicant writes "Never got caught."

✳ "Whenever I fill out a job application, for the part that says 'In Case Of Emergency Notify,' I put 'Doctor.' What's my mother going to do? 'Okay, I'm here. Open him up.'"
*Steven Wright*

✳ Employer to job applicant: "In this job we need someone who's responsible." Applicant: "I'm the one you want. On my last job, every time something went wrong, they said I was responsible."

✳ Four job applicants are told that they have to answer a single question, and the one who gives the best answer will get the job. The question is "What's the fastest thing in the world?" The first applicant comes in and gives his answer "Thought is the fastest thing," he says. "It's instantaneous." The second applicant comes in and says, "A blink is the fastest thing. It's a reflex that you don't even have to think about." The third applicant comes in and says, "It must be electricity. You can throw a switch, and twenty miles away, a light will come on." Finally the fourth applicant shuffles in looking very ill. "I guess the fastest thing in the world must be diarrhea," he says. "Last night in bed I had terrible cramps in my guts and before I could think, blink, or turn on the light…"

✳ Employer to job applicant: "Do you think you can handle a variety of work?" Applicant: "I should, I've had ten different jobs in four months."

✳ Harry goes for a job interview. Sitting next to him is a well-spoken applicant wearing a Harvard University tie. After a moment the applicant notices Harry's apparel. "I say," says the well-spoken man. "I see you're wearing a Harvard tie as well." "Yup," replies Harry. "I hope you don't mind my saying," observes the applicant. "But you don't look like the sort of man who'd have gone to Harvard." "Nope," says Harry. "Tell me," asks the applicant, "when you were at Harvard, what did you do there?" "I bought a tie," says Harry.

✳ An executive is interviewing a nervous young man for a position in his company. "If you could have a conversation with someone, living or dead, who would it be?" asks the executive. The man responds, "The living one."

✳ Interviewer to job applicant: "You start at $100 a week, and after six months it goes up to $130." Applicant: "All right then, I'll come back in six months."

✳ Tom to Dick: "Are you able to do anything that other people can't?" Dick: "Well, I can read my handwriting."

# WORK AND BUSINESS: JOBS

✳ "I used to be a narrator for bad mimes." *Steven Wright*

✳ Boss, to worker: "I'm going to mix business with pleasure. You're fired."

✳ I became a professional fisherman—then discovered I couldn't live on my net income.

✳ I became a writer, but I couldn't stand the paperwork.

✳ I found being an electrician interesting, but the work was shocking, and I was discharged.

✳ I got a job with a pool maintenance company, but it was just too draining.

✳ I used to work for a paper company, but they folded.

✳ I wish my brother would learn a trade, so I would know what kind of work he's out of.

✳ My brother was a lifeguard in a car wash.

✳ The only thing worse than being unemployed is having a job.

✳ I got a job as a historian, but I realized there was no future in it.

✳ Tom gave up work shortly after he was given his job.

✳ Two men go to sign on for unemployment benefits after being laid off at a factory. The first man goes for an interview and tells the employment clerk that he was a panty stitcher. He's given $150 a week in benefits, and leaves. The second man goes in and tells the clerk he was a diesel fitter. He's given $200 a week, and leaves. Later the two men are in the bar, and the panty stitcher finds that the diesel fitter is getting $50 more than he is. Outraged, he goes to the unemployment office to complain. "Why should a diesel fitter get more than a panty stitcher?!" he shouts. The clerk replies, "It's a new grant given to skilled workers. Engineers like diesel fitters are eligible." "He wasn't an engineer!" says the panty stitcher. "He was in quality control. After I'd stitched a pair of panties I'd give them to him. If he could pull them over his ass he'd say, 'Yeah, diesel fitter.'"

✳ Harry decided to go into the cement business. He'd always been a good mixer.

✳ Why did Harry want to go to Jeopardy? He heard there were thousands of jobs there.

# WORK AND BUSINESS: MANAGEMENT

✳ Tell your boss what you really think of him, for the truth shall surely set you free.

✳ A man turns to his coworkers and says, "I feel like punching the boss in the face again." "What d'you mean 'again'?" asks the coworker. "I felt like punching him yesterday," says the man.

✳ A new manager is saying goodbye to the man he's replacing. The departing manager says, "I've left three numbered envelopes in the desk drawer. Open an envelope if you encounter a crisis you can't solve." Three months later there's an emergency, and the manager finds he can't cope. He opens the first envelope. The message inside says "Blame your predecessor!" Six months later there's another crisis, and the manager opens the second envelope. The message inside reads "Blame your staff!" Three months later yet another disaster strikes the company, and the manager opens the third envelope. The message says "Prepare three envelopes."

✳ A pheasant is standing in a field talking to a bull. "I would love to be able to get to the top of that tree," sighs the pheasant. "But I don't have the energy." "Why don't you nibble on my droppings?" suggests the bull. "They're packed with nutrients." So the pheasant pecks at the dung and finds he has the strength to fly to the first branch of the tree. The next day he eats some more dung and reaches the second branch, and so on. A week later he's eaten so much dung that he can perch on the very top of the tree, at which point a farmer shoots him dead. The moral of the story: bullshit might get you to the top, but it won't keep you there.

✳ An organization is like a tree full of monkeys, all on different limbs at different levels. Some monkeys are climbing up, some down. The monkeys on top look down and see a tree full of smiling faces. The monkeys on the bottom look up and see nothing but asses.

✳ Boss, to employees: "This is just a suggestion. No one needs to follow it unless they want to keep their jobs."

✳ I admired the candor of the department manager. I asked how many staff worked in his area, and he said, "About half of them."

✳ I went to my boss's house and mistook his bidet for a drinking fountain—it wouldn't have been so bad, but he was using it at the time.

✳ "I don't want any yes-men around me; I want everybody to tell me the truth, even if it costs them their jobs." *Sam Goldwyn*

✳ In the office restroom, the boss placed a sign above the sink. It had a single word on it— "Think!" The next day he found another sign above the dispenser; this one said "Thoap!"

✳ What do your boss and a slinky have in common? They're both fun to watch tumble down the stairs.

✳ When blue-collar workers go out together at the weekend, they talk about football. When middle management are together, they talk about tennis, whereas top management discuss golf. Conclusion: the higher up you are, the smaller your balls.

✳ Why is Christmas like a day at work? You do all the work, and a fat guy in a suit gets all the credit.

✳ An orphaned blind bunny and an orphaned blind snake bump into each other in the forest. They get talking and discover that neither can see, and neither is exactly sure what sort of creature they are. "Tell you what," says the snake. "We'll feel each other all over and tell each other what we think we are." The bunny agrees, so the snake slithers all over the bunny and says, "Well, you're covered with soft fur, you have long ears, and a cottony tail. I'd say you must be a rabbit." "Oh, thank you!" cries the bunny. "Now it's my turn." So saying, the bunny feels the snake all over and says, "Well, you're smooth and slippery. You have a forked tongue, and no balls. I'd say you must be a team leader or possibly someone in senior management."

✳ The management board have their own version of musical chairs. It differs from the usual version in one respect. Every time the music stops, they add a chair.

✳ There's always room at the top—the people who get there before you tend to fall asleep and roll off the side.

✳ A man goes up to his boss and says, "Here! My paycheck was zero last week." "I know," says the boss. "But I pay people what they're worth, and in your case it turned out they don't make money in small enough denominations."

✳ I can't help admiring my boss. If I don't, he'll fire me.

✳ "You've all heard my arguments," says the CEO to his board. "Now let's vote on it. Anyone who doesn't agree with me, raise your right hand and say, 'I resign.'"

# WORK AND BUSINESS: OFFICE MOTTOS

✳ "If it ain't broke, break it." *George Carlin*

✳ A clean desk is a sign of a cluttered desk drawer.

✳ According to my calculations the problem doesn't exist.

✳ Avoid employing unlucky people—throw half the resumes in the trash without reading them.

✳ Doing a job right the first time gets the job done. Doing the job wrong fourteen times gives you job security.

✳ Don't be irreplaceable. If you can't be replaced, you can't be promoted.

✳ Go ahead and take risks. Just be sure that everything will turn out okay.

✳ How do I set a laser printer to stun?

✳ I can only please one person per day. Today is not your day. Tomorrow is not looking good either.

✳ I don't work here. I'm a consultant.

✳ I love deadlines. I especially like the "whooshing" sound as they go flying by.

✳ I must be a proctologist—I work with assholes!

✳ I thought at one point I could see the light at the end of the tunnel—turned out to be some bastard with a flashlight bringing me more work.

✳ I thought I wanted a career. It turns out I just wanted a paycheck.

✳ If everything's going much better than expected, it can only mean one thing—you've overlooked something.

✳ If it wasn't for the last minute, nothing would ever get done.

✳ If you've got to work for an idiot, you may as well work for yourself.

✳ In an office the authority of a person is inversely proportional to the number of pens they are carrying.

✳ Monday is an awful way to spend 1/7th of your life.

✳ Never put off until tomorrow what you can avoid altogether.

✳ Never be afraid to try something new. Remember, amateurs built the Ark. Professionals built the Titanic.

✳ Never do today that which will become someone else's responsibility tomorrow.

✳ Of course I don't look busy. I did it right the first time.

* Process and procedure are the last hiding place of people without the wit and wisdom to do their job properly.

* Sarcasm is just one more service we offer.

* Success always occurs in private, and failure, in full view.

* Talk is cheap—supply exceeds demand.

* Teamwork means never having to take all the blame.

* Tell me what you need, and I'll tell you how to get along without it.

* The screw-up fairy has visited us again.

* The world is full of willing people. Half willing to work, the other half willing to let them.

* There is always one more imbecile than you counted on.

* Too much ambition results in promotion to a job you can't do.

* Warning: dates in calendar are closer than they appear.

* Who is General Failure, and why is he reading my hard disk?

* Work harder. People on welfare depend on you.

* You have to get 100 percent behind your boss. It really is the only way to stab him in the back.

* You should give 100 percent at work: 12 percent Monday; 23 percent Tuesday; 40 percent Wednesday; 20 percent Thursday; 5 percent Friday.

* You will always get the greatest recognition for the job you least like.

* A person who smiles in the face of adversity…probably has a scapegoat.

* Excuses are like asses: everyone's got them, and they all stink.

* Failure is not an option! It comes bundled with the software.

* I pretend to work. They pretend to pay me.

* Make it idiot-proof, and someone will make a better idiot.

* Plagiarism saves time.

* The longer the title, the less important the job.

✳ When everything's coming your way, it can only mean one thing. You're driving on the wrong side of the road.

✳ Working here is a little like being a mushroom. You're kept in the dark and have shit thrown over you from a great height.

✳ If you ain't makin' waves, you ain't kickin' hard enough!

✳ The eleventh commandment: thou shalt not whine!

✳ If no one ever disagrees with you, you're either very clever or you're the boss.

# WORK AND BUSINESS: REPAIRS

✳ My printer's type began to grow faint, so I called a local repair shop. A friendly man informed me that the printer probably needed to be cleaned. Because the store charged $50 for this service, the man told me I might be better off trying the job myself. Pleasantly surprised by his candor, I asked, "Does your boss know that you discourage business?" "Actually it's my boss's idea," replied the employee. "We usually make more money on repairs if we let people try to fix things themselves first."

✳ If you can smile when everything around you is going wrong, you're probably in the repair business.

# WORK AND BUSINESS: SALES

✳ A hunter rents a cabin and a hunting dog for the season and catches lots of game. The next year he comes back and asks for the same cabin and the same dog. "Was that the dog called 'Salesman'?" ask the cabin owner. "Sure was," replies the hunter. "He's the best dog I ever worked with." "Not anymore," says the owner. "Some jerk came by and started calling him 'Sales Manager.' Now all he does is sit on his ass and bark all day."

✳ A software manager, a hardware manager, and a sales manager are driving to a meeting when a tire blows. They get out of the car and look at the problem. The software manager says, "I can't do anything about this—it's a hardware problem." The hardware manager says, "Maybe if we turned the car off and on again, it would fix itself." The sales manager says, "Hey, 75 percent of it is working—let's ship it!"

✳ Used car salesmen aren't in it for the money. They just like lying to strangers.

＊ A salesman out touring his territory has a heart attack in his motel room and dies. The motel owner calls the salesman's company and relates the tragedy to the sales manager. The sales manager says, "Return his samples by freight and search his pants for orders."

＊ He was such a great salesman, he could sell underarm deodorant to the Venus de Milo.

＊ Dick gets a job selling toothbrushes but doesn't do very well, whereas Harry, the top salesman, is selling thousands of toothbrushes a week. Dick gets desperate and asks Harry for the secret of his success. After much pleading, Harry agrees to divulge his method and gets out a large pot of brown sludge and a plate of crackers. "What I do," says Harry, "is take this pot to the airport with a big sign saying 'Free crackers and dip,' then I tell passengers to help themselves." "How does that help you sell toothbrushes?" asks Dick. "Try it yourself," says Harry. Dick takes a cracker and uses it to scoop some dip in his mouth. He spits it out straight away. "Oh my God!" Dick shouts, "It tastes like dog shit!" "I know!" says Harry. "Want to buy a toothbrush?"

# WORK AND BUSINESS: TECHNOLOGY

＊ Dick has just started his own firm and leased a new office. On his first day he sees a man come into the outer office and, wishing to look like a hotshot, picks up the phone and pretends he's in the middle of a huge business deal. After a few minutes of animated conversation, Dick concludes his business, puts down the receiver, and turns to the man. "Can I help you?" asks Dick. "Yeah," replies the man, "I'm here to connect your phone."

＊ I photocopied my butt on the office copier. Not for a joke—I wanted to improve my tan.

＊ An executive assistant is going on her lunch break when she notices her clueless boss standing in front of a shredder. The assistant walks up and asks if he needs help. "Yes, please!" says the boss. "This is very important." "Glad to help," says the assistant as she turns on the shredder and inserts the paper. "Gee, thanks," says the boss. "I only need the one copy."

# WORK AND BUSINESS: UNEMPLOYMENT

＊ It was Tony's last day at work on Friday. It was a shame, really, because the only card we could find said "Good Luck In Your New Job," which was almost right—we just had to cross out "In Your New Job."

* My father came home and told us he'd been fired. His company had replaced him with a machine that was able to do everything he could, but do it much, much better. The tragic thing was my mother went out and bought one too.

* A boss is forced to cut back on staff and decides it has to be one of two employees, Jack or Jill. The boss decides on a plan. He watches Jack closely for one day and sees how he comes in early, works hard, skips lunch, and leaves late. The next day the boss watches Jill. She comes in late, pops out to buy some aspirin, has an extra long coffee break, takes some aspirin, leaves early for lunch, stays out till three, then comes back with more aspirin. The boss is not impressed. He calls Jill into his office and says, "Jill, I am afraid I have to either lay you or Jack off." To which Jill replies, "Well, you're going to have to jack off, because I have a headache."

# WORMS

* How can you tell which end of a worm is which? Tickle it in the middle and see which end laughs.

* Why don't worms have balls? They can't dance.

* What were the worms doing in the graveyard? Screwing in Ernest.

# WRONGS AND RIGHTS

* Two wrongs are only the beginning.

* Two wrongs don't make a right, but three lefts do.

# YOU KNOW IT'S GOING TO BE A BAD DAY WHEN...

* ...you put your bra on backward and it fits better.

* ...you start to pick up the clothes you wore home from the party last night—and can't find any.

✳ …you turn on the news and they are showing escape routes out of the city.

✳ …the bird singing outside your window is a vulture.

✳ …you call the Samaritans and they put you on hold.

✳ …you discover that your child's idea of humor is putting super glue in your hemorrhoid lotion.

✳ …you wake up, discover your waterbed has sprung a leak… and then remember you don't have a waterbed.

✳ …your horn sticks on the freeway behind thirty-two Hell's Angels.

✳ …the gypsy fortuneteller offers you a refund.

# ZEBRAS

✳ What did the idiot call his pet zebra? Spot!

# ZOOS

✳ A zookeeper sees a visitor throwing five dollar bills into the monkey cage. "What are you doing that for?" asks the keeper. "The sign says it is okay," replies the visitor. "No, it doesn't," says the keeper. "Yes, it does," replies the visitor. "It says, 'Do not feed. $5 fine.'"

✳ The Crist family worked at a zoo. At the same time each year they predicted the general luck and overall mood of the forthcoming year by watching the gnu. If the gnu's ears were forward, it meant a successful, joyous year was almost certain to happen. But if his ears were laid back flat against his head, it meant that an unlucky or very unhappy year was sure to come. One year it was young Mary's turn to "survey" the animal and come up with the prediction, and it was her first time solo. In her excitement, she forgot to take the key to the cage and was late in coming to check on the gnu. Well, she saw the wrong ear position and predicted a bad year, when in fact it was quite good. To explain the error, the local newspaper ran the following headline a year later: MARY CRIST MISSES A HAPPY GNU'S EAR

✳ Harry hears that a zoo has managed to train a lion to live in the same cage as a lamb. He pays a visit and finds that the two animals are indeed sitting next to each other in a cage. Harry approaches the keeper in charge. "It's incredible," says Harry. "How did you manage it?" "Well, it hasn't been easy," says the keeper. "And most mornings we do have to buy a new lamb."

✳ A man is at the zoo and asks the keeper, "Have you got any talking parrots?" "No," says the keeper, "but we've got a woodpecker that knows Morse code."

✳ A father and his small son are standing in front of the tiger's cage at the zoo. Father is explaining how ferocious and strong tigers are, and the boy is taking it all in very seriously. In the end, the little boy asks, "Dad, just one thing. If the tiger gets out of his cage and eats you up…" "Yes, son?" says the father. "Which bus do I take home?" asks his son.

✳ A leopard kept trying to escape from the zoo, but it was no good. He was always spotted.

✳ Why don't you see many reindeer in zoos? They can't afford the admission.

# ZZZEEE LAST JOKES

✳ "Go and never darken my towels again!" *Groucho Marx*

✳ "In summing up, I wish I had some kind of affirmative message to leave you with, I don't. Would you take two negative messages? My mother used to say to me when I was younger, 'If a strange man comes up to you, and offers you candy, and wants you to get into the back of his car with him…GO!'" *Woody Allen*

✳ And now in response to a number of requests I've received…Goodnight.

✳ "I'm going now. Don't bother showing me to the door." "Oh it's no bother. In fact, it's a pleasure."

✳ "I'm going to go now…because I can." *Jack Dee (concluding a performance before inmates at a prison)*